MW01109713

Youth Double Wing II
The Gun!

Coach Jack Gregory
www.gregorydoublewing.com

Edited by Coach Michael R. Moreno, PhD

Wordclay
1663 Liberty Drive, Suite 200
Bloomington, IN 47403
www.wordclay.com

First published by Wordclay on 9/20/2010.
ISBN: 978-1-6048-1804-8 (sc)

Library of Congress Control Number: 2010939304

Printed in the United States of America.

This book is printed on acid-free paper.

Dedication

To my two sons Kaden and Blake, who will grow up knowing that Dad loves God, our family, our country, and this wonderful game!

To my wife, whom I love and admire for all that she does.

To Coach Don Markham for his crazy invention.

To every one of my dear friends on the Double Wing Forum whom I respect, admire, and call family.

Acknowledgement

This is the third book I have written and there are plenty of people in my life that I feel have given me the courage and ability to do so. First and foremost, there is nothing we accomplish in life without the blessings of God. Although I don't consider myself a very religious person, I do consider myself a Christian and strive live by those values as best I can. As a coach to kids, I feel that among the many responsibilities of a coach, one of the most important is to be a good example and mentor to those that allow us to be in their lives. Frankly, every kid has a choice to be on a team or to leave; I consider it an enormous compliment that I have had the opportunity to coach so many kids for multiple seasons and see them grow into young men. It is a very rewarding aspect of coaching. I would strongly encourage any new youth coach to consider the tremendous impact one has on a kid's life, as not only a challenge, but a great responsibility as well. Secondly, I don't think I would have ever started writing or even thought about publishing a book of any sort, were it not for my beautiful wife, who gave me the courage to do so. I have never really considered myself a writer and frankly, it never crossed my mind; but thanks to her encouragement and to a lot of fellow coaches that kept saying "you should really write a book on this stuff", I did it and here I am on my third book. Finally, I really want to take a moment to thank Derek Wade, Dave Potter, JJ Lawson, and Kenny Mead as they have had a big impact on my coaching philosophy and the way I perceive the game of football. I know I am a far better coach and human being because of these guys; they have been mentors, friends, and family to me.

Special thanks to all of the great coaches on the Single Wing Forum with whom I have had the opportunity to communicate over the course of ten years. Although I don't consider myself a 'single wing' coach, I have acquired a wealth of knowledge about the single wing philosophy of football, football history, and coaching from them, and that has made me a better coach.

Editor's Note

Like many serious youth coaches I have another job that pays the bills. As an academic researcher, I have always looked to books and other publications to expand my knowledge base. I have an extensive library of over 70 football coaching and strategy books, including many collectible antiquarian items. Enthusiasts of football coaching literature will recognize classic works by Walter Camp, Amos Alonso Stagg, Parke H. Davis, Glenn Scobey "Pop" Warner, Knute Rockne, Vince Lombardi, etc. The seminal work, providing the first published description of what has evolved into the modern Double Wing (DW), is The Toss by Jerry Valloton. When I first became interested in running the DW, this essential book was out-of-print and hard to find. Living in the "Information Age", we as coaches are now inundated with opportunities to learn via clinics, videos, websites, books, and other publications. Committed to installing the DW with my Pop Warner team – the Bryan Buccaneers – I began acquiring materials from many notable DW sources, including Jack Gregory. I found that many of these sources had something meaningful and worthwhile to offer and I included these elements in my offense - but Jack's first DW book, Youth Double Wing: A Winning Youth Football Offense became the book that I literally wore out with use. As I began my initial install of this offense, I just found it to be more descriptive and more insightful in many ways.

Coach Jack Gregory's books comprehensively describe a DW system that in my opinion provides an unprecedented combination of sophistication and simplicity. The coverage is among the most thorough that I have seen, yet retains a unique clarity that renders it accessible to the coach that is new to the DW. While I have a great appreciation for other notable Double Wing architects (Don Markham, Jerry Valloton, Hugh Wyatt, Tim Murphy, Steve Calande, etc.), in my opinion, with this second offering, the collective work of Coach Gregory is the most substantial contribution to the DW literature since The Toss.

After installing my base DW offense, I began to look at some complimentary schemes. I eventually added some ideas from Ken Keuffel's Winning Single Wing Football, because I wanted the tactic of shifting into a direct snap unbalanced set (Jack alludes to this in his first book, e.g. SHIFT OVER, but did not provide details – until now). I also added elements of Bruce Eien's Shotgun Jet Sweep, because I wanted to take my QB out from under center in a more conventional manner while retaining some of my base DW core concepts (e.g. blocking schemes, pre-flow, misdirection, etc.). Our team went undefeated in the first season of running this system. Soon afterward, I began corresponding with Jack and learned of his plans for a second book focusing on shotgun and direct snap formations. I became very intrigued and couldn't wait to see it – fortunately, I wouldn't have to wait long.

As I survey the published works (print, web, symposiums, etc.) that Coach Gregory has offered over the years, it becomes quite evident that he is the consummate student of the game – always learning, always researching, always collegial in his sharing of knowledge – a true Professor of the Double Wing. It has been an honor to work with him in expressing his current ideas in Youth Double Wing II: The Gun! Here we see an elegant expansion of ideas previously set forth, as well as the cultivation of new ideas, and complimentary schemes - all thoroughly presented in a book designed to be read cover-to-cover or as a broad reference source. Chapters 1-7 describe fundamental and advanced concepts (I particularly like the chapters on reading and manipulating the defense to optimize play calling) relevant to all play series, while Chapters 8-16 can be approached as independent frameworks that do not need to be read in sequence. There is some redundancy in these latter chapters that is deliberate, and intended to allow the reader to view these chapters in any order.

We've also included an expansive Appendix that is essentially a book within the book, rounding out a very informative body of work that any football coach will appreciate. In contributing to this effort I have learned a great deal from a master coach that has left no stone unturned in his efforts to better understand and teach what is necessary to build and sustain a successful football program. The appendices are substantive and reveal much about Jack's personal coaching philosophy as it relates to the responsibilities he assumes for the kids he trains; they offer a unique insight into his perspective on developing a team of young athletes -

> "Success is not always derived by having a winning season, but on how well your players develop into a team of warriors committed to a common cause."
>
> *- Jack Gregory*

I love this comment, because in the end, some of my fondest memories as an athlete and a coach are of games that I did not win - games that revealed the character of my teammates, players, and/or coaches. Games played with extreme passion, uncommon determination, and undying spirit, in unity, to the very end. The memories of those games are in many ways more vivid and enduring than games in which I was among the victors. Victory is sweet, but I savor those moments just before the outcome is known, when warriors approach the line of battle, full of adrenalin, in anticipation of the challenge before them, and full of faith in themselves and each other. Cultivating that sense of unity, "a team of warriors committed to a common cause", is both an art and a science. When a team attains that collective warrior spirit, wherein the whole exceeds the sum of the parts, and the commitment to the common cause is evident in the sacrifice of the individual – leaving it all on the field - it is truly a masterpiece that transcends the outcome.

Sincerely,

Coach Michael R. Moreno, PhD
Bryan Buccaneers - Brazos Valley Pop Warner
Bryan, TX

Coach Moreno works as a Research Professor in the Department of Biomedical Engineering at Texas A&M University. His research is focused on cardiovascular and orthopedic biomechanics. Dr. Moreno has numerous publications in scholarly journals and textbooks; as well as several medical device patents. In addition, he has sporadically coached youth sports in recreation leagues and at the high school level, for over 20 years. He would like to thank his fellow coaches in the Bryan Buccaneers organization for their help and support with his most recent coaching efforts – Edwin Mosley, Steve De La Rosa, Josh DeAtley, Felix Conde, Paul Blanton, Mark Taplette, and Kevin Reaves. And most importantly, he would like to thank his family – Cindy, Erica, and Matthew for their love and support while working on this project.

Table of Contents

Legend of Abbreviations and Terms

BB	Blocking Back (also known as a full back)
BCR	Bootleg, Counter, Reverse; a defensive key on the backside of power, power sweep, or play action pass.
BSG	Back Side Guard
BST	Back Side Tackle
BSWB	Backside Wing Back
DEMLOS	Defensive End Man on the Line Of Scrimmage
DLM	Defensive Lineman (Linemen)
Down block	An inside angle block that walls off the defender from the alley
EMLOS	End Man on the Line Of Scrimmage
Fan block	An outside angle block that walls off the defender from the alley
HHM	Hinge-Hinge-Mirror; used on the backside in sprint pass protection
KKM	Kick-Kick-Mirror; used on the backside in deuce/joker pass protection
LEG	Three step blocking progression; LOAD, EXPLODE, GO
LEG & TURN	Blocking progression on the third step (GO) the blocker explodes his butt towards the ball and walls off the defender by pinning him inside
LEM	Load Explode Mirror; used when the blocker is covered in pass protection
LOF	Line Of Force; a line that is pointed at the LOS and goes through at least two running backs
MDM	Most Dangerous Man (used in the uncovered concept to tell the blocking receiver which defender has the most chance of breaking up our uncovered pass to the open receiver and he is the man that needs to be blocked)
MOFO	Middle Of the Field Open (cover 0, 2, 4). Key to throwing the ball in the middle of the field
MOFC	Middle of the Field Closed (cover 1, 3, Robber, Tampa 2). Key to not throwing the ball in the middle of the field
OEMLOS	Offensive End Man on the Line Of Scrimmage
PG	Pull Guard
PIN	An aggressive reach block that uses a vertical step instead of a bucket step - uses the LEG & TURN concept on the three step progression
PSG	Play Side Guard

PST	Play Side tackle
PSTE	Play Side Tight End
PSWB	Play Side Wingback
PT	Pull Tackle
PTE	Pull Tight End
QB	Quarterback
SAB	Severe Angle Blocking
SSM	Slide-Slide-Mirror; used when the blocker is uncovered in pass protection
TB	Tailback
TKO	Track and Kick Out
Trap	A kick out block from the inside out by either a backside line men
Tunnel	Space created between the wall and the kick out blocks
Wall	The angle blocking wall made up of the play side linemen
WB	Wingback
WG	Wall Guard
Wham	A kick out block from the outside in by a back or slot
WT	Wall Tackle
WTE	Wall Tight End

Introduction

Jack Gregory. A name that is synonymous with excellence and innovation.

I first met Jack back in 2003, at the initial Double Wing Symposium that he set up in Dallas, Texas. Although I already had an idea as to the type of person and coach that Jack is, it was meeting him in person that was the confirmation: He's someone who demands the best of himself. His symposium was (and still is) the finest football clinic anyone has yet assembled. His five-disc DVD series on the Double Wing is thorough and comprehensive, yet easy to understand. His "Triple B" playbook is the gold standard of playbook design, organization, detail and ease of use. And his books have helped youth football coaches around the world.

Jack is a leader and innovator: an outside the box thinker. His products are leading edge. This latest work is proof of that. There simply aren't any Youth Gun Double Wing books out there. Like his other projects, he proves time and again to be far ahead of his contemporaries in new ideas, execution, and quality.

For years now, Jack has educated kids and coaches. With this book, he continues to help coaches educate kids. Jack Gregory is a man I respect.

This is Jack Gregory's third book. Like the first two ("Youth Double Wing: A Winning Youth Football Offense" and "63 Defense: A Winning Youth Defense"), "Youth Double Wing II: The Gun!" is clear, concise and detailed. The most experienced Double Wing coach will no doubt find a treasure trove of new ideas. The novice coach will learn from a master innovator.

Dave Potter
Head Football Coach
Durham War Eagles

Offensive Coordinator
Kestrel Heights High School
"Hawks Football"

Chapter 1
Youth Double Wing Basics

Following the release and huge success of my first book, I went to work testing some theories I had developed. I had experimented and played around with these concepts and schemes for a long time, but never really explored all of the variations and many possibilities they offered. This past season I got a chance to really test them, stress them, and push them to their respective limits; to see if they were sound, and more importantly, functional within the Youth Double Wing system. It was very important to me that the concepts in this book be functional and easily adapted into the system with minimal time and effort. I have found that, as youth coaches, we have very little time to install extra components. Therefore, we need to maximize our efforts toward developing a philosophy and system wherein everything we do integrates easily otherwise our ability to execute the offense at a high level will be compromised.

This book is designed to be used in conjunction with my first book <u>Youth Double Wing: A Winning Youth Offense</u> but the concepts can be easily adapted into any offense with a series based philosophy. Obviously the main focus of the book is the use of direct snap components that have made the single wing straight series so successful throughout football history. In fact, because of their fundamental soundness, there has been a recent reemergence of these concepts at the Division I and NFL levels.

Key Points to the System:

1)   We are a power off tackle running team first and foremost. We want to run the ball using power and deception. We do this with a set of core plays (power series) and we have the ability to use various formations to adjust the offense to better attack specific defenses and improve our lines of force. We must execute the core plays to perfection as this allows the team to gain confidence in our philosophy and offensive system.

2)   We will use misdirection, play action passing and a perimeter passing game to attack defenses that over-pursue or over-defend our power offense (WB Power, WB Power Sweep, and BB Wedge).

3)   We must keep our system simple and try to paint a mental picture for our players to follow as we teach each blocking scheme, play, edge adjustment and backfield adjustment. The success of our system is the result of its simplicity and efficiency.

4)   We are a four down offense the vast majority of the time. We will use all four downs to make a first down whenever possible. This places an enormous amount of pressure on the defense to execute for four plays (not three), to stop the first down and the continuation of the offensive series.

5)   We use Angle Blocking Concepts (ABC's) versus the classic double team systems of GOA, GOD, or GOL, as well as, the Markham/Vallotton systems. We stress the angle block first and the double teams second; while the vast majority of

Double Wing teams stress the double team first and the angle block second. We have the ability to double at the point of attack (POA) as an adjustment and we teach it to our kids, but the emphasis is on washing defenders away from the hole, while denying penetration on the line of scrimmage (LOS). We do this mainly with the Track and Kick Out angle blocking scheme (TKO).

The Base Offense:

1)   To tailor our offense for young players we base it on a set of core plays from which we derive our complete offensive playbook. In the power series, these plays are the WB seal, BB wedge, WB monster sweep, along with BB kick and WB kick. We also have the Buck Wedge series, Rocket Wedge series, and Fenton series that compliment the Power series.

2)   At the youth level, it is very important that you have a play that you can always go to, that will sustain the drive, and get you first downs. I believe this is the wedge (in various forms) early on, because it is a true team work play that puts a tremendous amount of stress on a defense. In addition, it transfers easily from one series to the next. This is especially true at the younger age levels, but as you deal with a more mature team I believe the WB Seal must become your base play, as it forms the nucleus of everything else you do in this offense.

3)   The WB Seal play is the foundation of our power running game and a very important part of our power series. Whereas the wedge is power in the middle, the WB Seal is our power play at the edge (the classic off-tackle hole). We have several ways to adapt this play to the defense and therefore may run our base offense, even as the defense adjusts to stop it.

4)   The WB and BB counter plays are the primary misdirection plays against the defense as they begin to overreact to the WB Seal play. We have other misdirection plays, but these plays are the core of our misdirection. They allow us to attack a defense that is looking to stop our power plays with over pursuit from the back-side.

5)   The Double Wing uses all of the aforementioned approaches to good effect resulting in an offense that couples power, misdirection and a good play-action passing game, into one system that creates as much confusion in the defensive backfield as possible. The play-action pass must be based off of actions the defense will see a lot, and that you are successful at executing. This means that our pass protection will look very similar to our base run schemes. The entire initial action looks like 'run' and thereby forces the defense to respond accordingly.

6)   The key to this offense is identifying what the defense is doing, i.e. the defensive tendencies, and then attacking with the understanding of what will work against the defensive scheme. One of the keys to deciphering the defensive scheme is reading the "perimeter triangle" and calling plays based on the triangle's numbers (see Chapter 3 for a detailed discussion on this important topic). Understanding the function of the perimeter triangle and developing an ability to read it, is perhaps the coach's most important 'game time' skill as it optimizes the

play calling process, enabling play calling decisions that have the highest probability of success.

7)   The ability to run the WB Seal play at will, i.e. whenever you desire, is an important objective of this system. I feel this is one of the plays that your team should be most comfortable executing at any time (the Wedge play would be the other) during a game. One of the points you will see emphasized repeatedly in this book, is the importance of establishing the power play; the offense is most lethal when you establish the ability to run power over and over again, using various edge and backfield adjustments to confuse the defense and manipulate defenders.

8)   Edge adjustments play a major role in what we do because they allow us to put defenders into conflict, remove them, or isolate them from our power play. The ability to manipulate defenders in this way is indispensible as we run an angle blocking scheme that uses very few blocking adjustments, and we don't rely on double teams at the point of attack. We have to utilize edge adjustments that allow us to do this to the perimeter defense (OLB, DE, and CB). With these edge adjustments, and constant drilling against loaded fronts and overloaded numbers on the play-side, the offense becomes conditioned to be mentally tough and well-prepared to handle these types of situations during a game. This, in turn, instills confidence and contributes to the team developing of an attitude that a given play can be run at will.

What You Are Going to Find in This Book

First and foremost, this is a book that takes the Youth Double Wing concepts presented in my first book and demonstrates how to use them in conjunction with a direct snap, singlewing, or shotgun variation. There are four backfield or formation variations that are discussed in this book. Second, there is a much more comprehensive look at the perimeter triangle and edge adjustments, and how they are utilized to manipulate the defense, i.e. to move defenders away from the point of attack or isolate specific defenders so that you can maximize your base. Third, there are enhancements that I've developed for the angle blocking schemes which are designed to make them much more adaptive and easier to use. There is also an improved explanation of how the blocking schemes work and how to employ them. Fourth, there is a detailed breakdown of several play adjustments that change what a few players do in the power play to give a different 'look' with very little alteration to the play. Finally, there is a detailed breakdown of our "Bird of Prey" formation series and the adjustments that we use with it.

I had two primary goals when I wrote this book. I wanted to demonstrate how the power series can be made more robust and sustainable by using formation variations, 'edge adjustments' and 'play adjustments'. Ideally, we want to overwhelm the defense with our power series as it is run over and over again. To accomplish this objective we must be able to vary the look, show a variety of lines of force, and manipulate the defense. The aforementioned adjustments allow us to do all of these things. I also wanted to present some improvements to the angle blocking schemes that are used in the Youth Double Wing. I started using the "Bird of Prey" series a few years ago, after doing some research on the zone read and other spread concepts that I thought I could blend into the YDW. The main purpose of the offense is obviously to score and keep scoring; but the ability to adapt to anything you face while remaining true to your overall philosophy is just as important. As coaches, we always want as many tools in the tool box as possible, as we never know when we will need a different look or variation to remain successful.

Advantages of the Direct Snap and the Gun Approach

1.   We can use time-tested simple single wing concepts.

2.   We can employ an established Single Wing Straight Series (SW Power Series).

3.   We can alter our base formation into a direct snap formation that complements our base plays while staying true to our blocking scheme, play scheme, edge tags, and base formation.

4.   We can keep formation changes simple and make sure they blend into our overall offensive philosophy.

Pros to Using the Gun Approach

1.   It alleviates potential center/QB exchange issues.

2.   It gives our interior linemen more space in which to operate, e.g. for pulling, folding, zone blocking, and pass blocking.

3.   It increases the amount of time the backfield has to carry out fakes and make pass reads.

4.   It speeds up the play by 0.2 to 0.5 seconds. I have timed it!

5.   It puts the ball into our best player's hands and creates immediate misdirection with split flow.

6.   It gives us the ability to adapt to the loss of a QB (injury/grades/travel/sickness).

7.   It gives our opponents a different look while running our base offense, i.e. it gives the appearance of being multiple when we are actually running the same plays over and over again.

8.   It gives us more options, to adapt the play with tags and adjustments, than we have from under center - especially on the backside, which creates further stress on the perimeter and the secondary.

Cons to Using the Gun Approach

1. The snap must be consistent or the play will not be consistent. Inconsistent snaps can result in turnovers; which is why we use a straight snap.

2. It can be sub-optimal in poor weather (rain, snow, ice, hard wind).

3. The back receiving the snap must have good hands and secure the ball quickly, often while on the move. The backs must be good at taking the snap.

4. Direct snaps allow defensive ends and other perimeter defenders to attack the landing point, i.e. where the ball will be. You have to use misdirection (split flow) to keep the perimeter defenders pre-occupied with defending the edge.

Chapter 2
Play Calling

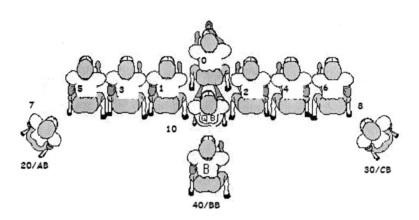

Figure 2A. The TIGHT Formation – The TIGHT Formation is our base formation in the Youth Double Wing (YDW). This formation is characterized by very tight line splits, double tight ends, the angled WB stance and the BB within an arm's reach of the QB.

In this chapter we will discuss the play calling systems we use. Again, I suggest stressing simplicity over complexity when introducing kids to this system. The idea is for the players to be comfortable learning this material, while optimizing practice time rather than waste it trying to teach complex play calling structures or blocking schemes.

Our base formation is the "Tight" formation (Figure 2A). If no formation is called before the play, this will be the base formation (TIGHT). Linemen are foot to foot and as far off the ball as legally permitted. Example: each lineman's head, excluding the center, should be even with the center's belt. Wings shall align outside the TE with their toes lined up with the QB's heels. The QB is directly under center. The FB shall be lined up one arms length directly behind the QB.

Coaching Keys:
Linemen should have a balanced stance with even weight distribution.
This makes pulling easier for the guards and tackles.

Snap Count: The center calls "DOWN" and the QB calls "GO". All plays are executed on the command "GO" and nothing else. If motion is needed, the QB will signal the motion back by lifting his near heel twice very quickly or by calling "SET". I have found that both are very easy to install, so whichever makes your team most efficient is the best to use.

Non-Numbering System (Naming): I prefer this method with players 11 and younger as I have found that some kids will struggle with decoding the odd/even numbering system along with left and right system built into the numbering method. You want your team to be as successful as possible and eliminating confusion is one way to help ensure success.

QB = QB
BB = BB
LWB = AB
RWB = CB

Plays are called in this manner: Edge tag, formation or backfield tag, motion/direction, back getting the ball, blocking scheme, direction of the play and play adjustment tags (Figure 2B). Note that adjustment tags will be discussed in detail in Chapter 3.

> Examples: Rip AB Seal Right, Rip BB Wedge Left, or Rip CB Kick Left.

> The passing game is called without a back tag, unless a back other than the QB is passing the ball.

> Example: Tight Rip Power Pass Right; however, if the LWB passes the ball it is Tight Rip AB Power Pass right.

Although I prefer using this method of play calling there are advantages to using a numbering system in that it allows you to pinpoint land marks for the runner to hit. In addition, it reduces the overall length of the play being called.

Play Numbering: The tens digit identifies the running back getting the ball and the singles digit identifies the AT MAN that the play is targeting.

10 = QB
20 = LWB (AB)
30 = RWB (CB)
40 = BB

Plays are called in this manner: Tight Rip 26 Seal, Tight Rip 40 Wedge or Tight Rip 35 Kick (these are the same plays as above).

In the passing game we use the same structure as the non-numbering to further highlight to the offense that it is not a run but a pass.

> Example: Tight Rip Power Pass Right; however, if the LWB passes the ball it is Tight Rip AB Power Pass Right. This gives the entire offense an easy way to identify run or pass in our system when using the numbering method.

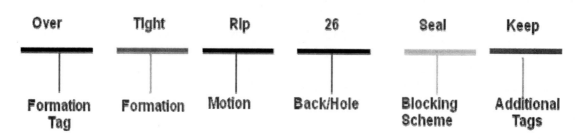

Figure 2B. Play Calling System – The play calling system follows the format and sequence illustrated above. Some plays will not require tags but the sequence remains the same. Tags will be discussed in detail in chapter 3.

Motion/Action:

Rip/Liz Motion – The WB executes this when given the motion signal. He takes a cross over step with his outside foot behind his inside foot, sliding inside as he does so, he steps forward with his inside foot aiming at the AT MAN'S outside hip. He should get the pitch just under the back-side C gap.

Note: Rip/Liz also indicates the direction of shift in the case of our direct snap/gun formations.   In this case it simply means the direction the backfield has shifted and it implies the direction of strength.

Rocket/Laser Motion – The WB executes this when given the motion signal. He takes a cross over step with his outside foot in front of his inside foot, so that he can rapidly turn his hips. His inside foot will step aiming at a point 4 to 5 yards deep behind the BB. He should sprint full speed so that on the snap of the ball he gets the pitch behind the play-side C gap.

Final Notes on Play Calling:

The important thing to remember, when play calling at the youth level, is that it doesn't really matter how you call the play as long as the kids understand what you want them to do and how they should do it. So, if you just call DUMBO and they know that means TIGHT RIP 26 SEAL, and it works, then it is effective. Don't get caught up in trying to emulate your high school, some college, or some NFL team, or even this manual. It is far more important to get your point across on the field and maximize execution. Don't try to be fancy just be simple and effective.

FOCUS FIRST AND FOREMOST ON THE WB SEAL - THAT IS THE MAIN PLAY THAT YOU WANT TO RUN - SO YOUR EFFORT SHOULD ALWAYS BE ON RUNNING THAT ONE PLAY - TO PERFECTION - FOR MAXIMUM EFFECT.

Yes, there are times when you will probably run another play more than the WB SEAL play or with more success, but the reason will be that the defense is intent on stopping your WB SEAL play. If they are that focused on stopping it, then you should be that focused on trying to get back to running it. Put another way, the WB Seal is the power play that sets up everything else in the offense. As the defense converges on the edge to shut it down, they become vulnerable in other areas. The misdirection, perimeter, and play-action passing game open up. In taking advantage of these vulnerabilities we are in essence setting up the ability to return to the WB Seal – we are "trying to get back to running it" while eating up huge chunks of yardage. The defense soon realizes there is a price to pay for vacating the back-side, secondary, and/or perimeter in order to protect the edge. They are forced to try and shut down an enormous amount power without exposing themselves elsewhere. There is nothing more back breaking to a defense, than running the very play they are desperately and futilely attempting to stop - over and over again with success. This entire book is focused on that one objective, so keep that in mind as you read through this book.

Chapter 3
Reading the Perimeter Triangle to Optimize Play Calling

Introducing the Perimeter Triangle

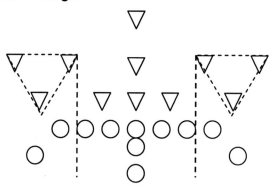

Figure 3A. The Perimeter Triangle – The defensive end, cornerback, and outside linebacker typically comprise an entity that I define as the Perimeter Triangle.

The "perimeter triangle" is a term I started using to describe the three most common players defending the perimeter - typically in contain, force and alley schemes (Figure 3A). Every defense must have these three assignments covered or risk the possibility of having the exposed perimeter exploited by the offense. The perimeter triangle is typically manned by the defensive end (DE), cornerback (CB) and the outside linebacker (OLB). I wanted a simple method of determining what these defenders were doing on the perimeter as this would determine how I would attack the defense. It is very important that the offensive coordinator be able to quickly adapt to the defense, to attack and counterattack. Often as youth coaches we need to be able to do it from the sideline as we are not likely to have scouting assistance from an elevated position. This is specifically why I developed the concept of the perimeter triangle. In developing an understanding of the perimeter triangle, one can effectively read the defense and make informed play calling decisions that have the highest likelihood of success. This cannot be overstated. The perimeter triangle concept has been a key component in training my coaching staffs and players the philosophy and strategy behind the YDW offense. Thus, in this chapter we will (1) develop an understanding of the function of the perimeter triangle in the defense, (2) develop an ability to read the perimeter triangle as a means of deciphering the defensive scheme, (3) develop an ability to optimize play calling based on the perimeter triangle read, and (4) develop an ability to use formations, motions, and play-calling to manipulate the perimeter triangle and expose vulnerabilities in the defense.

Elements of the Perimeter Triangle

Contain – This is the defender who has the job of keeping the ball inside and/or behind the line of scrimmage. He must keep the ball on his inside shoulder and not allow it to get past him at any time. Contain responsibility is often assumed by the defensive end, but this can be the corner back or even an outside linebacker, depending on the defensive scheme and variations in calls. More often than not the defensive end will be the contain defender and he is often the defender we key and target because he is the most susceptible to vacating the perimeter responsibilities.

Force – The force defender's job is to turn the ball back inside (squeeze) or deep outside and towards the line of scrimmage (spill). More than likely, if you are facing a spill defense, the force defender will be inside of the contain defender, and will more than likely be the defensive end or outside linebacker. The spill technique is a pressure technique so the force defender is closer to the ball and more aggressive as compared to the contain defender who is outside of him, providing a safety net on the perimeter, which is essential due to the aggressive nature of the technique. If you are facing a squeeze defense, the contain defender will be on the inside of the force defender. In this case he is the last line of defense on the perimeter. His job is to turn the ball back inside in the event it gets by the contain defender. Because the contain defender is on the inside of the force defender, the technique is often not as aggressive.

Alley – This responsibility may be assumed by an interior linebacker, or possibly a safety playing near the LOS and the perimeter; but it is more than likely the responsibility of an outside linebacker. The alley defender's main role on the perimeter is to maintain a mirrored relationship with the ball. Now there are variations in the alley approach, e.g. some defenses will play with a tight outside leverage approach while others play with a tight inside leverage approach. Typically, in squeezing defenses you will see an outside leverage approach; whereas with spilling defenses you will see an inside leverage approach. The key function of the alley defender is to prevent the ball from crossing the line of scrimmage; to apply downhill pressure on the ball from the opposite side of the force as a means of keeping the ball behind the line of scrimmage.

Understanding the Perimeter Triangle

 Regardless of the defensive alignment, every legitimate defense has a 'contain', 'force', and 'alley' defender on each side of the ball. The arrangement of those defenders often determines how the defense will play the perimeter, edge and pass. More often than not, the 'force' defender is the corner back, the 'contain' defender is the defensive end, and the 'alley' defender is the outside linebacker or strong safety. In a typical defense the reason the defensive end is the contain man is because his job is to make sure the ball stays inside of him; he is typically the first defender on the perimeter and nearest the ball. Most defenses try to keep the ball as far inside as possible (often called squeezing him inside), and in turn, use the 'force' defender, who is often the cornerback, as a safety valve. In this case, as the cornerback comes off of pass and into run, the responsibility is to force the ball to stay inside so the pursuit can run the ball down from the inside out. Thus, the corner is forcing the ball; the force can be applied either back inside or outside/behind the LOS (squeeze and spill).

Now, I should further elaborate on this concept as the location of the 'contain' compared to the 'force' will determine what type of perimeter scheme the defense is playing. There are two specific types of perimeter schemes with the most common being a squeeze technique (Figure 3B). This is characterized by the contain defender being on the inside of the force defender (DE is contain and the CB is the force). The DE will contain (squeeze) the ball on the inside, while the CB will force the ball back inside if it does happen to get outside of the DE. If the DE is the 'force' and the CB is 'contain', then more than likely the technique employed will be a spill technique (Figure 3C).

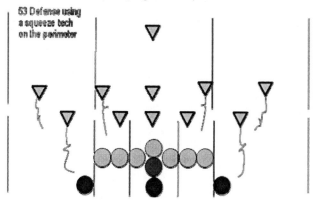

Figure 3B. Squeeze Technique – Characterized by the DE playing contain while the CB plays force.

The spill technique is characterized by the DE forcing the ball to spill deep outside. The DE accomplishes this by taking an aggressive track inside towards the runner. The CB then contains the ball behind the LOS requiring the runner to remain flat while moving toward the sideline, or to stop and redirect to the alley defender. In either case, the alley defender's job is to attack the ball from the inside–out, while the force defender's job is to attack the ball from the outside-in. The contain defender's job is to ensure the ball stays in the area that is most assessable to the pursuit defenders.

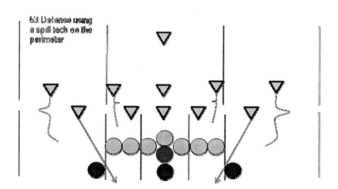

Figure 3C. Spill Technique – Characterized by the DE playing force while the CB plays contain.

There are occasions when defenses will swap these players around such that the defensive end is the force player and the corner is the contain player; or alternatively, the outside linebacker will swap with the defensive end, etc. Regardless of the scheme, these three elements are always in place – contain, force and alley.

When we read the perimeter triangle, we do so from the *outside hip of the offensive tackle* (inside offensive tackle when in OVER). This is important to understand because as you will see below I define the perimeter from the *outside hip of the tight end*. The reason the read of the perimeter triangle occurs at the outside hip is because we want to read all the defenders past the offensive tackle as those defenders can immediately defend the perimeter. Any defender inside of the tackle must defend the edge.

Understanding the Points of Attack

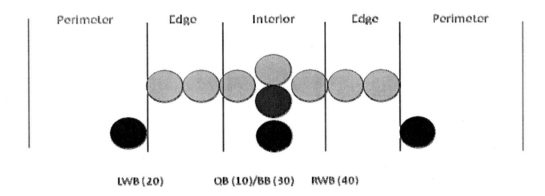

LWB (20)   QB (10)/BB (30)   RWB (40)

Figure 3D. Points of Attack in the Running Game – Though we can specify gaps or holes as specific points of attack, our blocking schemes typically create situations wherein it is generally unnecessary to define the point of attack with such specificity. Moreover, it is useful to think in more general terms when developing a game plan.

Let's define a few terms so that we understand each other as we discuss the perimeter triangle and how we read it to attack the defense. First and foremost, what is the perimeter? Simply put the perimeter extends from the outside hip of the tight end (or EMLOS) to the sideline. Any play that we use that aims for the outside hip of the tight end (EMLOS) will be a 'perimeter' play. The 'edge', which is the primary point of attack for this offense, extends from the outside hip of the guard to the outside hip of the tight end. Anything within the inside hip of the guard is considered an 'interior' play (Figure 3D). That is really all you need to know about how we target the attack of the defense on each side, as far as the *running game* goes. The *passing game* however, requires further elaboration (Figure 3E). In this case our most common point of attack is the perimeter (also called the flat) followed by the vertical outs (from the outside hip of the tight end to the boundary) and then the vertical middle (from the inside of the tight end's outside hip on each side).

One of the nice things about using angle blocking concepts is that it starts to eliminate the need to use gaps (A, B, C, D) to define the point of attack because the TKO WALL often opens the B and C gaps. Thus, it is feasible to attack the B gap one play and the C gap the next depending on how the defense is adjusting and attacking a given play. In reality we have three main points of attack on each side of the center (as described above) - the interior (A gap), the edge (B and C gap), and the perimeter (D gap). We really don't need to get any more specific than that when pinpointing plays because of the method of blocking we use (wedge and angle blocking) for the vast majority of our plays. While we have several perimeter schemes, including a monster scheme, wide scheme, and pin scheme; however, we are essentially a power off tackle football team, so the main thing we do is run at the edge. That said, the potency of the offense is sustained by varying the attack. In attacking the three basic locations defined above (on each side of the ball), we can achieve sufficient variation to produce a successful ground based attack focused on maintaining a power advantage at the edge.

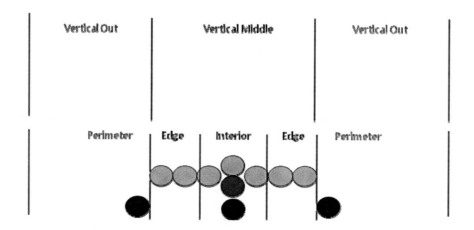

Figure 3E. Points of Attack in the Passing Game – Our most common point of attack in the passing game is the perimeter, followed by the vertical out, then the vertical middle.

Reading the Perimeter Triangle

The concept of the perimeter triangle provides a foundation wherein we can read each side of the defense and resolve play calling decisions based on how many players are in the respective perimeter triangles. The elegant aspect of this approach is that you really don't need to know specifically who is playing what technique. All you really need to do is simply count the defenders that are in the perimeter pre-snap and eventually post-snap.

Initially the perimeter triangle read will be a simple pre-snap read. As your coaching staff develops proficiency reading the defense's reaction to your schemes, this will evolve to become an initial pre-snap read in conjunction with a post-snap read, i.e. the perimeter read will include an additional read conducted following the snap. For example, you may begin reading the defensive end's post-snap reaction, particularly as they tend to slide down the line of scrimmage or crash into the backfield. When this happens, they are compromising their perimeter responsibility, evidence of a weaker two man perimeter triangle (and a force tech by the DE). The outside backer blitzing into the B gap is another two man perimeter triangle indicator you will see a lot. The blitzing linebacker is vacating his perimeter responsibility, thereby weakening the perimeter defense. And there are times when the corner back will fill the tunnel hard putting him in or near the B gap. This would also be indicative of a two man perimeter triangle as his ability to defend the perimeter is compromised by the predisposition to shut down the edge or interior threat. It is not uncommon to see two or even all three of these reactions by an overzealous perimeter triangle hell bent on stopping the power play. Now if you have defenses that are exhibiting two or even three of these behaviors, then the perimeter triangle is vulnerable to not only sweeps but the pass as well. It should now be evident that with an understanding of how the defense must protect the perimeter, this simple perimeter triangle read provides a relatively full proof method of deciphering schemes on both sides of the defense; thereby enabling informed play calls to either side of the field, based on the offense's capabilities and what you desire to do that particular defense.

The Overloaded Perimeter Triangle

One defensive scheme you will likely encounter, especially with compressed formations like the classic double tight double wing formation (and various other double tight formations), is an overloaded perimeter triangle (four defenders on the perimeter). This is characterized by a defense that moves a safety or interior defender (often an inside linebacker as the backers have shifted over) to the perimeter triangle as a means of increasing manpower and overloading a particular side (Figure 3F). It really doesn't matter what type of technique the additional defender is playing, all you need to know is that there are four defenders in that particular perimeter triangle. This immediately tells you that the perimeter on that side is over-manned and therefore it would be unwise to run to that particular perimeter as the likelihood of a successful pass or off-tackle play is not as great as the other side – assuming the other side is not also overloaded, which would leave the interior extremely vulnerable.

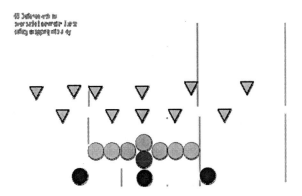

Figure 3F. An Overloaded Perimeter Triangle – Note the extra perimeter defender on the left side of the offense. This is characteristic of a four man perimeter triangle.

Now I will say that if you can quickly determine whether the extra defender is a contain defender or force defender, you can determine if the defensive scheme is simply a loaded perimeter triangle or a loaded pressure perimeter triangle. If it is the latter, then running off-tackle is not recommended as the defense is attempting to overload the tunnel while maintaining an extra contain defender to prevent outside threats from doing damage. Note that you can still run inside of the two contain defenders by simply kicking out the inside contain defender thereby isolating two defenders for the price of one. This approach is pretty common in 7-2 and 7-3 fronts, where the defense rolls the corners up on the LOS with the defensive ends both playing contain, as opposed to force. I see this approach frequently, and believe it is typically out of desperation by the defense.

The Reduced Perimeter Triangle

When we see a reduced perimeter triangle (two or less in the perimeter) we are in essence seeing the removal of one of the perimeter responsibilities. The important point to consider is that with a reduced perimeter triangle there is an increased likelihood of success for plays targeting the perimeter due to the fact that the perimeter defense is under-manned. What I often see is the alley or contain defender vacating their responsibilities. When that is the case, and the force defender is the corner back, the application of play action pass, perimeter pass, and power sweeps becomes viable on that perimeter, along with perimeter misdirection schemes.

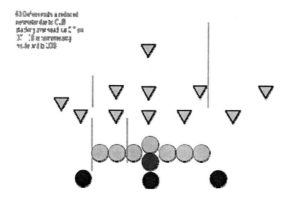

Figure 3G. Reduced Perimeter Triangle – Note the weakened perimeter defense on the left side of the offense. The OLB is playing stacked over the tackle compromising his ability to contribute to the perimeter defense. This is characteristic of a two man perimeter triangle.

Using the Perimeter Triangle Read to Optimize Play Calling

It has been my experience that the ability to read the perimeter at pre-snap is the simplest method of deciphering the defensive game plan; particularly if we have not had the opportunity to scout our opponent. As we get to know the defense and how they are adapting to our offense, specifically our play calling, we can begin to rely more on post-snap reads. For example, we can use perimeter triangle post-snap reads to determine how the secondary is responding to our running game, and subsequently get a good feel for when the time is right to open up the passing game. Of course, if we have had the chance to scout a defense, then we can make some educated guesses about how their perimeter and secondary are going to respond to our offense. In this case, we may determine that it is worthwhile to employ the play-action pass at the onset of the game in order to take advantage of a big play opportunity. Otherwise, we're going establish our power game and read the perimeter to get a feel for the defensive game plan. We'll use formations, motion and play calls to probe the defensive scheme, observing the perimeter response to our action. Then we'll formulate our attack and counterattack accordingly.

Tables 3A and 3B illustrate the pre-snap and post-snap reads for the power series, respectively. Table 3C also provides post-snap reads but is expanded to include plays from the complimentary wedge series (Buck, Rocket, and Fenton). The key to post-snap reads is observing the defenders closely to determine their tendencies as the ball is snapped and the backfield moves. For example, it is not uncommon to see the OLB collapse inside to the B gap and/or the DE move down the line of scrimmage hoping to get to the WB behind the line. In either case, they are vacating the perimeter and isolating the other perimeter defenders. These cues are evidence that the perimeter is vulnerable.

To fully appreciate how this system really works, it is important to understand a few fundamental concepts. First and foremost, we want to establish and maintain an effective WB SEAL play. Second, we always want a four man TKO wall or greater on the play side when we run to the edge. Third, we must always react and adjust to the number of defenders on each perimeter. If there are two or less we must overwhelm the edge, get outside, and force the defense back to neutral (3 defenders) so we can go back to running the WB SEAL. Whether running to the edge or around it to the perimeter, we must understand how our blocking scheme will handle the perimeter triangle defenders. To illustrate this point we'll consider a typical three man perimeter triangle. When running to the edge the most important block is the kick out on the DE. We also want to kick the CB, while sealing the OLB inside the run (Figure 3H). When running to the perimeter, the most important block still remains on the DE but now we want to seal him inside the run. We also want to seal OLB, but we'll kick out or wall off the CB (Figure 3I).

Number	Where to Run	Play to Run
Two Defenders or less (reduced)	Run to the Perimeter	28/47 Monster Sweep 28/47 Wide 28/47 Reverse
Three Defenders (neutral)	Run to the Edge	26/45 Seal 16/15 Seal 26/45 Kick 33/34 Kick
Four Defenders (overloaded)	Run to the Interior	10 Wedge (Sink) 30 Wedge (Sink)

Table 3A. Pre-Snap Read for the Basic Power Series – The number of defenders in the perimeter gives evidence of the strengths and weaknesses in the defense. This table illustrates the plays with the highest probability of success against the given perimeter defense prior to the snap. A complete description of the plays listed here is beyond the scope of this text as they correspond with the power series described in detail in my first book. It is worth mentioning that the Kick and Reverse are misdirection plays.

Number	Where to Run	Play to Run
Two Defenders or less (reduced)	Run to the Perimeter	28/47 Monster Sweep 28/47 Wide 28/47 Reverse Bounce Tag (back side) Razzle Tag (back side) Tiger Tag (back side) Fly Tag (vertical pass)
Three Defenders (neutral)	Run to the Edge	16/15 Seal 26/45 Seal 26/45 Kick 33/34 Kick
Four Defenders (overloaded)	Run to the Interior	10 Wedge (Sink) 30 Wedge (Sink) Jump Tag

Table 3B. Post-Snap Read for the Basic Power Series – The well-coached defense may show one look pre-snap and another post-snap. Therefore, it is ultimately essential that you develop proficiency with the post-snap read as well. This table illustrates the plays with the highest probability of success against the given perimeter defense as determined by the action following the snap, e.g. a defender in the perimeter pre-snap may vacate immediately post-snap. The additional plays here are designed to exploit tendencies exhibited post-snap. A complete description of the plays listed here is beyond the scope of this text as they correspond with the power series described in detail in my first book. It is worth mentioning that the Kick and Reverse are misdirection plays. Similarly, the Tag plays are deception plays designed to complement the power game.

Number	Where to Run	Play to Run
Two Defenders or less (reduced)	Run to the Perimeter	28/47 Monster Sweep 28/47 Wide 28/47 Reverse Boot Tag (back side) Razzle Tag (back side) Tiger Tag (back side) Fly Tag (vertical pass) 28/47 Rocket Wedge 28/47 Buck Wedge 18/17 Buck Wedge 18/17 Fenton Wedge 28/47 Fenton Wedge
Three Defenders (neutral)	Run to the Edge	26/45 Seal (QB Seal) 26/45 Kick 33/34 Kick 14/15 Rocket Wedge
Four Defenders (overloaded)	Run to the Interior	10 Wedge (Sink) 30 Wedge (Sink) 30 Buck Wedge (Sink) 30 Rocket Wedge (Sink) 20/40 Fenton Wedge (Sink)

Table 3C. Post-Snap Youth Double Wing Chart – This expanded chart includes complimentary series to the basic power series, the Rocket Wedge, Buck Wedge, and Fenton Wedge. A complete description of the plays listed here is beyond the scope of this text as they are described in detail in my first book, It is worth mentioning that the Kick and Reverse are misdirection plays. Similarly, the Tag plays are deception plays designed to complement the power game.

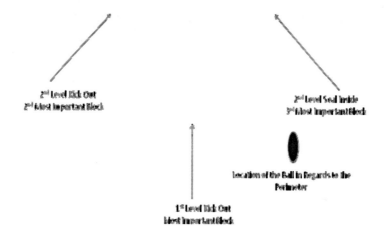

Figure 3H. Blue Print for Attacking the Edge – Assuming a typical three man perimeter triangle, our most important block when attacking the edge the Kick Out on the DE. As we penetrate the second level of the defense we want to kick out the CB and seal the OLB inside.

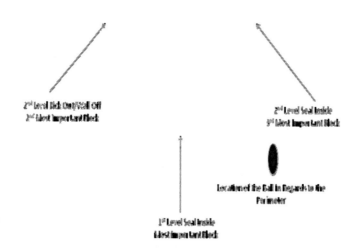

Figure 3I. Blue Print for Attacking the Perimeter - Assuming a typical three man perimeter triangle, our most important block when attacking the perimeter is the Seal on the DE. As we penetrate the second level of the defense we want to kick out or wall off the CB and seal the OLB inside.

When the objective is to establish a play action passing threat, it is imperative that you watch not only the CB but the Safety as well. If the CB is playing run and not respecting the pass threat, this is a clue that you should check what the safety is doing. If he is sitting in the middle of the field and simply flowing to run or coming up fast to play run, then POWER PASS is open as you can flood the play side and pin the safety in the middle of the field. Don't be surprised if you see him overload a specific perimeter triangle; particularly if they are deciphering your formation, motion, backfield alignment, and wall/pull sides of the line. This is especially true if you are blocking their alley defender, as the safety is the only defender left that can assume his alley responsibility. This would be an example of circumstances under which you want to have that all important sideline audible that gives the ability to immediately attack the other side, i.e. the side that no longer has safety support and/or is compromised by a weakened perimeter triangle.

Reading the Perimeter and Coverage to Determine Interior Defenders

Once you determine the number of defenders in the perimeter triangle you can then determine the number of defenders in the interior by simply counting the safeties. Given that there are eleven defenders total, we can determine the number of interior defenders by simply subtracting the number of safeties and the number of perimeter defenders, the remaining defenders are on the interior (Table 3D). Normally, you only have to check this a few times during the game since most youth teams maintain the same secondary coverage. I typically check it at the beginning of the game, during short yardage situations, and at the beginning of the 2nd half. Most of the time spotting a change in coverage is pretty easy as most youth teams play in either cover 0, cover 1, or cover 2. It is not usually difficult to pick up a change in coverage because it is pretty dramatic. Knowing how many defenders are setting in the interior after you have figured out the perimeter numbers is the key to determining if the defense is biased toward defending the sweep, seal, wedge, or pass. Once you figure that out, you can adjust or adapt your attack to take advantage of weaknesses resulting from this bias.

Perimeter	Coverage	Interior Defenders
2	0	7 (loaded front)
	1	6 (loaded front)
	2	5
	3	4
3	0	5
	1	4
	2	3
	3	2
4	0	3
	1	2
	2	Not likely
	3	Not likely

Table 3D. Determining the Number of Interior Defenders Based on Reading the Perimeter and Coverage – Given that there are eleven defenders total, we can determine the number of interior defenders by simply subtracting the number of safeties and the number of perimeter defenders, the remaining defenders are on the interior.

When using the perimeter triangle, first focus on the simple perimeter rules. Let me reiterate, when you first start using the perimeter triangle use the simple perimeter rules.

As you acquire proficiency reading the perimeter, you should progress to incorporate the more advanced keys for misdirection and play-action passing. Note that the simple rules will still apply; we simply add the more advanced keys to our arsenal.

Simple Perimeter Rules:

1)   Run WB SEAL if there are three defenders beyond the perimeter line (attack the edge).
2)   Run the WB MONSTER SWEEP/WB WIDE if there are two defenders or less beyond the perimeter line (attack the perimeter).
3)   Run QB or BB WEDGE to the interior if there are four defenders beyond the perimeter line.
4)   Play action pass if there are three defenders or more near the LOS and beyond the perimeter line.

Misdirection Perimeter Rules:

1)   Run WB KICK if there are three pre-snap and two post-snap defenders on the backside perimeter line but containing the perimeter.
2)   Run BB KICK if there are three pre-snap and two to four post-snap defenders on the backside perimeter line containing the perimeter.
3)   Run WB REVERSE if there are three pre-snap and two post-snap defenders collapsing into edge.
4)   Run BB WEDGE or QB WEDGE if the interior is playing to the perimeter edges and there are three or more defenders on the perimeters.
5)   Run RAZZLE AUDIBLE/AUTOMATIC if there are two or less pre-snap defenders on the back side collapsing to edge. (TIGHT/NASTY/OVER)
6)   Run BOUNCE AUDIBLE/AUTOMATIC if there are two or less pre-snap defenders on the back side and the corner is playing run.
7)   Run TIGER AUDIBLE/AUTOMATIC if there are two or less pre-snap defenders on the back side not accounting for the QB in coverage.

Play Action Perimeter Rules:

1)   If the play side perimeter triangle is compressing down on the edge and/or perimeter, then power pass. (Play action pass to perimeter/deep out)
2)   If the backside perimeter triangle is compressing down on edge and/or perimeter, then BOUNCE AUDIBLE/AUTOMATIC (BOOTLEG)
3)   If in LOOSE or TRIPS/BUNCH and we have '2 on 1' or '3 on 2' within 10 yards of the receivers, call LOOK/ROOK (SE QUICK PASS) or BROKEN/BLENDER (SLOT QUICK PASS).

Applying Stress to the Perimeter Triangle

The ability to manipulate the perimeter triangle via edge tags, formation tags, and play calling is one of the key advantages of the YDW. We can apply stress by isolating the perimeter triangle from the interior defenders or by expanding the perimeter triangle so that we isolate the defenders inside of the perimeter triangle from each other - often we can do both. The ability to manipulate the perimeter triangle allows us to attack the interior, edge, and perimeter; as well as utilize the passing game to get behind and outside of the defense.

It is important to realize that human beings are creatures of adaption, and athletes are among the best examples of creatures of *instantaneous* adaption. So whether by design or intuition, the defense will eventually adapt to what the offense doing. With this understanding, we realize that it is important to develop the ability to simultaneously (1) inhibit the ability of the defense to adapt and (2) exploit the tendency of the defense to adapt to what we're doing on offense. We want to add sophistication to the offense at minimal expense. The accomplished offense incorporates multiple formations, motion, and deception to stifle attempts by the defense to adapt and predict what the offense is doing.

We use a variety of 'tags' to make it more difficult for the defense to recognize and adapt to our schemes; and to manipulate the defense into doing what we want them to do – to impose our will on the defense. Tags that alter the formation provide pre-snap advantages, while those that prescribe motion or movement offer post-snap advantages. "Edge" tags are a very simple way of changing the appearance of a formation, particularly at the perimeter, without disrupting the base play structure. "Formation" tags alter the appearance of the backfield such that the formation is no longer symmetrical (tight). This offers LOF (line of force) advantage(s) to the offense. Edge and Formation tags are discussed in chapter 4. "Play" tags (such as Jet and Tornado) identify motion or movement that places stress on a perimeter. In addition to Edge, Formation, and Play tags, the use of 'sideline audibles', or 'influence audibles' as I call them, provides another great means of immediately attacking and weakening a perimeter triangle.

The key is to develop proficiency with the pre- and post-snap perimeter triangle read; while using edge, formation, and play tags to create additional confusion and pressure. Keep in mind that the whole point of the perimeter triangle concept is to develop a simple read on how the defense is defending the perimeter by determining if the three basic perimeter defenders are playing their responsibilities. Once you establish whether you have a reduced perimeter (2 or less) or an overloaded perimeter (4 or more) or a neutral perimeter (3); you essentially know not only how and when to attack that perimeter, but how to effectively attack the defense as a whole. The information you garner on each side can tell you a lot about the interior and the secondary as the game develops. In deciphering the defense's perimeter triangle patterns, you can easily discern what you can do to the entire defense. Moreover, the use of tags provides the means to manipulate the perimeter triangle into a configuration that is most conducive to the success of a play you want to run. This is precisely what I do during every game I call.

Chapter 4
Manipulating the Defense with Edge and Formation Tags

Edge Tags and Manipulating the Perimeter Triangle

Purist Double Wingers will tell you that you can sit in the tight formation and overwhelm your opponent with perfect execution, play calling, and blocking adjustments. Obviously, my opinion differs on this, as I believe we are adaptable creatures and that given enough time against a specific tactic, we as individuals, and as a group, will begin to adapt to the situation. I don't believe it is wise nor in my team's best interest to simply sit back in the tight formation and run the same plays over and over again with the notion that the opponent is not creative or smart enough to adapt to what I am doing against him. To me that is simply not a sound strategy over the course of an entire season or the span of a coaching career in the same league. Coaches and the players on the opposing defense should not be underestimated. When they see the same formation, the same cadence, and the same set of plays over and over again, at some point they will begin to learn the rhythm of the offense and even the play calling.

In my opinion it is far better to develop an offensive philosophy that is more robust. This can be accomplished relatively easily by incorporating adaptations into the offensive formations that not only give a different 'look' but also offer other specific advantages. Consider for example, the EDGE tags (Table 4A); the purposes of these tags are threefold. First, they allow us to manipulate the perimeter players into compromising positions and isolate defenders away from the point of attack (POA). Second, they give us the appearance of being multiple in formations when in reality we are simply manipulating three defenders on the perimeter to give us a leverage advantage. Third, and often the most important in youth football, is that they allow us to adapt to the variety of talent and type of players we have from year to year. Some years I have an abundance of linemen and big back type players which are fine, in that they allow us to sit in the tight formation and simply use OVER and NASTY all the time; while there are other years that I have an abundance of smaller or thin players that are not suited for playing in compressed formations. Consequently, loose, trips, and bunch give me not only leverage advantages, but the ability to adapt to the type of players I have on hand.

In my first book, I presented the edge adjustments as functional groupings, i.e. specific combinations, because that is how I used them when I first started running them. Unfortunately, this was ultimately limiting because it made the edge adjustments inflexible at times. So instead of exclusively using combinations such as 'ON-OVER-OFFSET' or 'LOOSE-OVER-OFFSET', now I simply use individual tags (Table 4A), and group them together as needed to get the best result for a given situation. More recently, LOOSE, OVER, and BUNCH have been the edge tags I have used the most, especially since they transfer easily with the backfield adjustments, as you will see later in the book.

TAG	How It Works	Why
ON	Tells the play-side wing to shift to the LOS on "DOWN" and he now becomes the AT MAN on the TKO WALL.	Increases the width of the TKO WALL by forcing a DE lined up over the TE to either widen (increasing the kick out distance) or get caught inside of the TKO WALL. We are adding width to our TKO wall and moving the EMLOS away from the ball carrier.
OVER	Tells the BST to line up on the play-side between the PST and PSTE.	Same as above except you still get the WB's seal block on the FBI (first backer inside) and it unbalances the line on the play-side. Again we are adding width to the TKO wall.
OFFSET	Tells the BB to align in a sniffer position under the PSG's outside hip.	Allows the BB to get to his kick out target faster reducing the effect of a crashing or squeezing DE.
LOOSE	The play side wing back and tight end (now a split end) split out. SE splits out 8 to 12 yards depending on play called. If it is WB SEAL should widen out to 12 yards. WB aligns as a slot 1 to 2 yards inside of SE and inside foot should be up for both and the slot's inside foot should be aligned with back foot of SE.	This allows you to widen the second level tunnel and isolate a corner away from the hole. It also kicks out the OLB with the QB vice sealing him inside with the WB who now gets the FBI (ILB).
NASTY	The play side wing back and tight end exchange locations. The tight end will fan block (outside down block) the DE if he aligns to the outside.	This forces the DE to either widen out with the TE leaving a wider gap on the inside or align inside of the tight end and be kicked out.
BUNCH	The split end will align eight to twelve yards wide with the near side wing back aligning on the outside of the SE and the far side wing back aligning on the inside. They will be foot to heel depth as LOOSE and one yard away from SE.	If the defense is plays cover 1 man free this will force the CB, OLB, and ILB to cover down on the trips leaving the PSDE isolated.
TRIPS	The split end will align as above with the near side wing back aligning on the inside of the SE 2 yard away and the far side wing back aligning 2 yards away.	If the defense is plays cover 1 man free this will force the CB, OLB, and ILB to cover down on the trips leaving the PSDE isolated.

Table 4A. Edge Tags and How They Work – Edge tags are an excellent means to manipulate the perimeter triangle, expose vulnerabilities in the defense, and create new lines of force for offense.

The Effect on the Perimeter Triangle – Stretching and Isolating the Triangle

Tight On

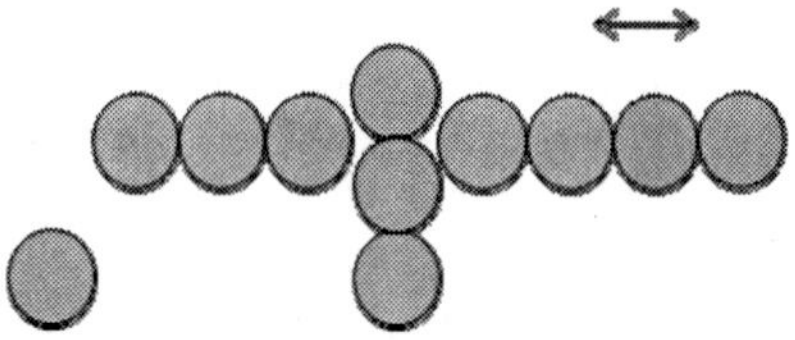

Tight Offset

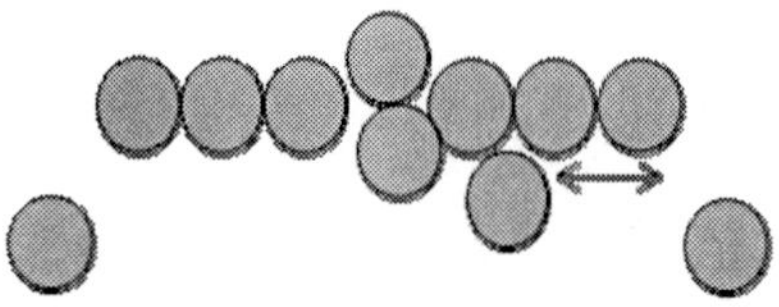

Tight On Over

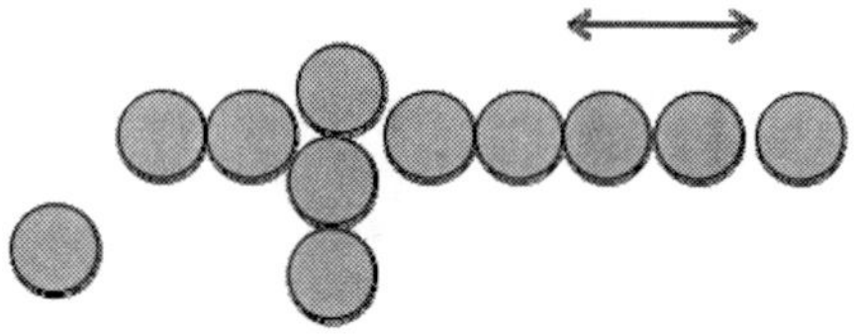

Tight On Over Offset

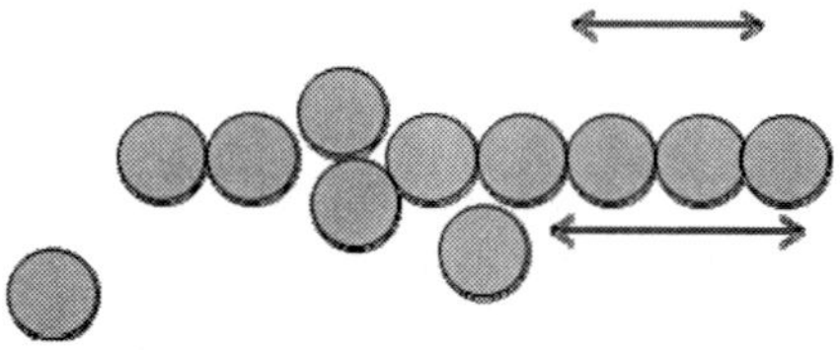

Tight

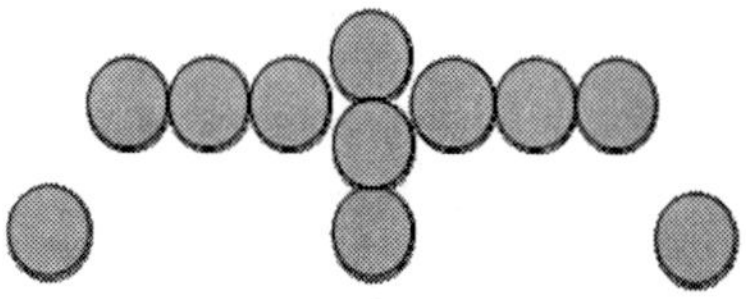

Loose

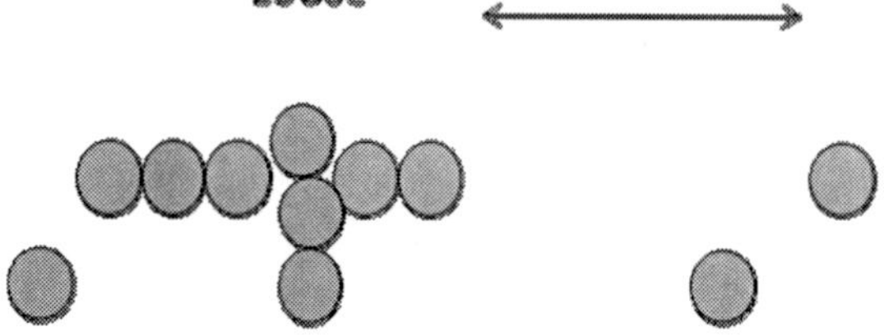

Over

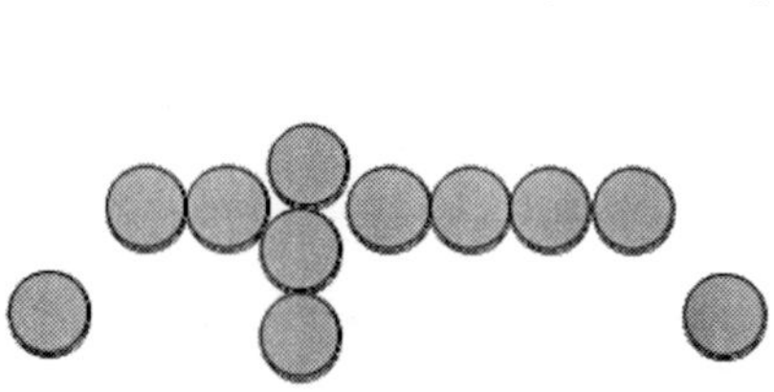

Loose Over

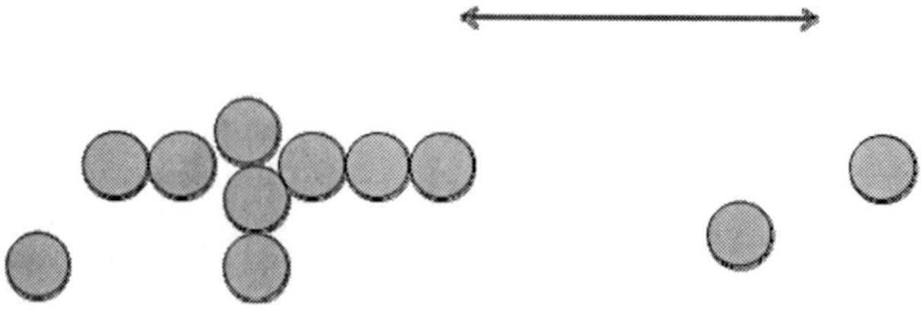

Nasty

Nasty Over

Bunch   Over Bunch

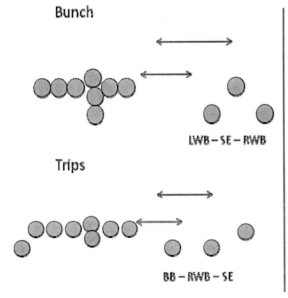

LWB – SE – RWB

LWB – SE - RWB

Trips   Trips Over

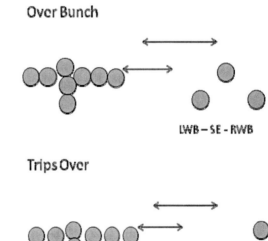

BB – RWB – SE

BB – RWB – SE

The Effect on the Perimeter Triangle – Manipulating Perimeter Defenders

Tight	Over
Loose	Loose Over
Nasty	Nasty Over
Bunch or Trips	Bunch Over or Trips Over

Using Tags to Manipulate the Perimeter Triangle to Optimize the Run

• First, we may isolate the perimeter triangle away from the interior defenders. The use of ON, OVER, and NASTY edge tags is a great way of accomplishing this pre-snap. By isolating the perimeter defenders away from the interior defenders you open a natural gap at the edge allowing you to attack the interior and edge.

• Second, we may expand the perimeter triangle so that we isolate the defenders within the perimeter triangle away from each other, thereby preventing them from providing support to each other. The use of LOOSE, TRIPS, and BUNCH edge tags is a great way of accomplishing this pre-snap. This in turn allows you to attack the edge, perimeter, and take advantage of the perimeter and vertical passing game.

• The use of OVER and LOOSE, TRIPS, and BUNCH provides a means to isolate the perimeter triangle from the interior, and further isolate specific perimeter triangle defenders away from each other. This is why I use OVER a lot when running power; it not only allows me to get an extra blocker on the play side, it also gives me a simple method of opening a huge gap in the defense pre-snap.

• Remember, the 1st level defender is always the primary defender that we must take into account in the running game, as we are a power off-tackle or a power edge running team. If we don't open the 1st level consistently the majority of our plays will not work!

Adjusting the POA for the Runner (numbering system)

If you are using the numbering system, the play call specifies the exact location the runner will target – the outside hip of the AT MAN, except for 0 (wedge – right behind the center). This allows us to adjust the path of the ball carrier by simply calling a number inside or outside to relocate the runner to a different AT MAN.

Example: We consider Rip 26 Seal to be our normal power at the edge play, RIP 24 Seal tells the LWB to aim at the 4 man's (OT) outside hip, which is one man tighter than the normal Rip 26 Seal. Hence, we can fine tune how we attack the edge with a given play. You can do this with any play except for 0 (wedge) plays.

As the use of OVER could potentially muddle this description, let me clarify that it is best to consider OVER as the widening of the gap, and not the addition of another blocker (Figure 3J). Bear in mind we are still aiming at the play-side tight end (PSTE) who is the 6 man (and the AT MAN). All we did is effectively widen the gap by one blocker.

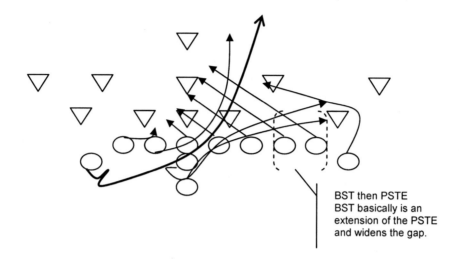

BST then PSTE
BST basically is an
extension of the PSTE
and widens the gap.

Figure 4A. OVER RIP 26 SEAL – Note that this play is called OVER RIP 26 SEAL because the PSTE is the 6th man, the last WALL blocker, and the AT MAN. The BST is not part of the numbering equation when he goes OVER.

The play diagrammed in Figure 4A is OVER RIP 26 SEAL because the PSTE is the 6th man, the last WALL blocker, and the AT MAN. The back-side tackle (BST) is not part of the numbering equation when he goes OVER. In the case of LOOSE, when the PSTE becomes a SPLIT END, the BST is now the 6 man. In the case of NASTY the PSTE is in a slot position with the WB inside, so the BST again becomes the 6th man. He is nothing more than an extension of the wall and specifically the PSTE on the inside. In summary, the BST is only considered part of the numbering system when the PSTE is positioned somewhere other than the normal tight location, e.g. in the slot or split.

Formation Tags

Formation tags are nothing more than formulated changes to the backfield designed to create positive leverage and numbers at the point of attack. The formation tags are applicable to any backfield set, in this book we'll discuss formation tags designed specifically for direct snap or "shot gun" backfields. The formations corresponding with the tags introduced herein each offer specific advantages and provide various means to attack the defense using the direct snap/gun concepts.

Here are some of the advantages that the formations in this book offer to the coach:

• These tags adjust our backfield into various alignments while using the core blocking schemes.

• These formations allow us to gain leverage and line of force advantages on the defense.

• "Gun" or direct snap formations simplify and speed up our power series.

Leverage:

1) The action of a lever.

2) The mechanical advantage of a lever.

3) Positional advantage; power to act effectively

Line of Force (LOF):

1. The perceived direction of the offense.

2. An imaginary line drawn through two or more backfield players towards the line of scrimmage that indicates a primary path for the ball to go.

3. The versatility of a given backfield alignment can described in terms of the lines of force it provides – the more lines of force, the more versatile.

4. The more running backs in a line of force, the more powerful the line of force.

5. A formation with multiple running backs in a given line of force, tends to lack versatility as the alignment cannot provide as many lines of force.

The Four Base "Gun" Formations:

Shift – This is our primary formation in the "Gun" (Figure 4B). It provides us with a clear line of force and a leverage advantage to one side. You have a three back LOF pointed at the strong side edge with the BB, QB, and backside WB. You also have a two back LOF pointed at the strong side perimeter with the backside WB and play side WB. You have one more two back LOF which extends from the strong side WB to the BB pointed at the backside perimeter. This gives you a total of three lines of force, with two pointed at the strong side and one pointed at the backside. This formation gives a clear leverage advantage to the strong side edge via the three back LOF.

Star – This is a secondary formation in the "Gun" (Figure 4B). This configuration allows us to transform the BB into a primary power play back. It offers a clear four back LOF to the perimeter but also has a two back LOF to the edge, as well as a two back LOF to the back side perimeter. The ability to overload the perimeter is a key element of this formation. The other benefit is the ability to get three receivers from the edge immediately into the route.

Comet – This is the classic beast or Yale formation (Figure 4B). This formation gives a clear leverage and LOF advantages to the edge and perimeter on the strong side. It gives you a three back LOF to the backside as well. I use the comet formation when I have a power quarterback type that can throw and run, as this presents a real problem to the defense.

Nova – This is based on the Hugh Wyatt Wildcat formation (Figure 4B). It is a variation, as I don't have the backs as close to the center as the traditional Wildcat and the wingbacks are a little wider to account for the motion and the pitch. Following the motion, the QB (back nearest the motion) will spin towards the motion to pitch, or fake pitch, to the motion back. This is a big difference between the Wyatt Wildcat and the Nova. Coach Wyatt does not run a classic power play out of the Wildcat as he opts to hand off and boot back-side. I want my power scheme, and more specifically the QB lead, to be part of every formation I use in my system. The LOFs are aimed at the EDGE and the PERIMETER with two backs on each side of the formation - making it a well balanced symmetrical attack formation.

Eagle Formation (Spread YDW)

Though it is not a *base* GUN formation, since it is technically a gun formation, I want to comment on the EAGLE (Figure 4C). It is simply a 2x2 spread formation with the RB determining the strong side. We call strong side by tagging EAGLE with BLUE or RED to place the RB on the LEFT (BLUE) or RIGHT (RIGHT) side. Obviously the LOF is to the perimeter on each side when you run a line from the SLOT to the RB and/or the QB. Our trap game (TANK SCHEME) is directed at the edge, due to the threat of the vertical and perimeter passing game, and the perimeter running game.

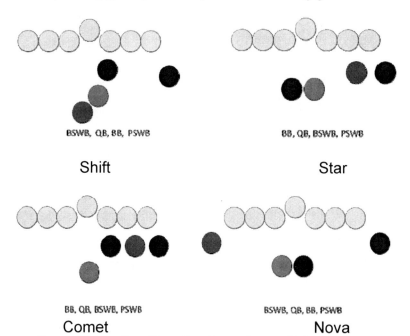

BSWB, QB, BB, PSWB   BB, QB, BSWB, PSWB

Shift   Star

BB, QB, BSWB, PSWB   BSWB, QB, BB, PSWB

Comet   Nova

Figure 4B. The Four Base Gun Formations – Shift is our primary gun formation. Star is a secondary gun formation that allows us to transform the BB into a primary power play back. Comet is the classic Beast or Yale formation. Nova is our variation of Hugh Wyatt's Wildcat formation – our backs are deeper and our wings are wider. Perhaps more importantly, our motion post-snap and play series differ.

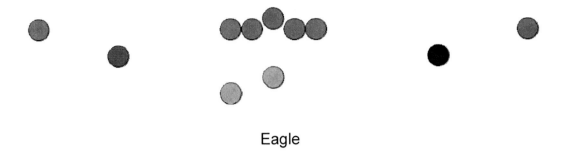

Eagle

Figure 4C. The Eagle Formation – Though not considered one of our base Gun formations, this spread formation offers unique lines of force coupled with vertical and perimeter passing threats. These qualities serve the TANK scheme (trap) well.

One may utilize all or just one of these formations in their Youth Double Wing system. Alternatively, one may install a GUN only system instead of using the GUN as an addition our compliment to some other base offense. The key is to use what will enhance your player's abilities, as well as your offensive philosophy. With younger teams (ages 5 to 8) I would only use one formation but with a 9 to 11 year old team I would probably use two or more formations - depending on the team's ability to handle the additional payload of information while remaining capable of execution at a high level. That is the real key - adding only what your team can execute and execute well.

Flipping Your Line in the YDW

Coach Lawson actually turned me on to the concept of "flipping the line" with the double wing. If you are short on four good pulling linemen or you have a set of really good wall blocking linemen and a set of really good pulling linemen then this is a very solid concept for you to consider. It is pretty simple; rather than have 'left' and 'right' linemen, you have 'WALL SIDE', and 'PULL SIDE' linemen. The center is considered a WALL SIDE lineman. All three players blocking on the pulling side of the center, i.e. the PULL SIDE linemen, will 'flip' on any pulling scheme plays to the backside. That is, the PULL SIDE linemen will always line up on the back-side of a play with a pulling scheme. This means on SEAL, KICK, WIDE, and MONSTER, the WALL SIDE will be the side near the play and the PULL SIDE will be the backside. On <u>WEDGE</u> (no pulling linemen) plays, the line will line up with the WALL side on the right and the PULL side on the left. I tried letting them flip to whatever side they wanted on interior plays but found that the wedge scheme can suffer as the execution level can drop on those plays. It is simply better to drill the line on forming the wedge from one side and keep it that way.

Now the big question the skeptical coach wants to ask is: "Can't the defense read "wall side" and basically use that as a key?" My answer to that question is a fearless "YES THEY CAN". You really want them reading that PRE-SNAP key along with your MOTION/BACKFIELD keys as it will allow you to employ INFLUENCE audibles such as RAZZLE, BOUNCE, and TIGER. When you consider the 'line flip' as just another pre-snap key that you can use to manipulate the defense, then you can set up a situation where timely audibles rack up huge chunks of yardage and points, as the defense over shifts and stems to get a perceived leverage advantage. It really comes down to making the defense pick their poison, so to speak.

So my thoughts on this are really three fold: 1) flipping the line gives the coaching staff the ability to put more physical blockers on the WALL SIDE (guys with size and slower foot speed and less agility) while placing more athletic blockers, who are often smaller, on the PULL SIDE (you also have a place to put a back up BB - at pulling guard - to allow him to work on kicking out). This means you only need two pullers instead of four. It also gives you more time to develop wall blockers into pullers. 2) It reduces teaching time and increases play productivity especially at the beginning of the season. 3) Although I know there are teams that run the DW without motion, I think the most significant benefit we have is the use of motion and backfield alignments that give the pre-flow key of us going in one direction - with power. When a defense sees motion they see power coming. Now when they see the wall side, motion towards that side, and in some cases, backfield alignments that indicate a clear line of force to that side, their immediate thought is going to be POWER going that way. This opens up your counter game and passing game. With the use of influence audibles and a perimeter/play action passing game, your offense becomes exponentially more potent and productive.

It is important that in practice all linemen get time working on TKO blocking, pulling, cut off blocking, and any other fundamentals and techniques associated with it. Ultimately we want all of our linemen to become, and remain, capable of executing every portion of the blocking scheme. The point is to put the best wall blockers on one side and the best pulling linemen on the other side. I don't see the line flipping key as a disadvantage, rather I see it as an enormous advantage. If I know the defense is going to read all these obvious keys and I know the outcome of those reads, then I know where the defense is going to be. All I need to do is have a plan for blocking the remaining defenders. It is the same theory I apply when not blocking a safety, yet making sure I block the LOS and LINE BACKER levels. If my power play is getting stopped by a safety at or near the LOS, then I know what I need to do to take advantage of that - PLAY ACTION PASS - throw the ball to the vacated spot.

In summary, I would rather know where the defense is going to be based on what they think they see, and approach my play calling in that manner. This is why I use the perimeter triangle concept in the first place. The influence audibles are just a simple extension of that and flipping the line now alleviates a lot of problems I have with locating spots for big kids and linemen in general, as well as giving more false keys to the defense - which I love to do.

For more details on flipping your line I would strongly recommend getting JJ Lawson's Coaching A Dominant Offensive Line you can download it a my website at www.gregorydoublewing.com on the article page. It is a fantastic resource on angle blocking, TKO, wedge blocking, and the LEG progression along with several solid theories on line play by Coach Lawson. Coach Lawson is one of the first coaches that I know of that blended the concept of flipping and the double wing together. My use of it is totally based on his work with it. Although the way he does it with his teams and the way I do it are a little different, I give him total credit for getting me to think along those lines. Coach Lawson also has a great youth football coaching website called www.footballhelpdesk.com.

Chapter 5
Advances and Changes in Angle Blocking Concepts (ABC) and Interior Blocking Schemes

Change is a fundamental part of life motivated by the need to adapt to a dynamic and evolving environment. As new challenges present themselves it is essential to incorporate new schemes and capabilities to cope with those challenges in order to remain at the top of the "food chain".   I have been using angle blocking concepts (ABC) with the double wing since 2001. The opportunity to work with these concepts on the field, to experiment with various permutations, and to exchange ideas with fellow coaches that utilize angle blocking concepts, has inspired me to fine tune my thinking as it relates ABC. As I discover variations that work, I incorporate them fully into my offense. It takes me a while to do this because I need to be able to incorporate these new ideas into the offense without negatively affecting any aspect of the basic scheme and philosophy.   When I wrote the first book, I deliberately constrained my discussion of ABC to the basic concepts and the power series, so that the book did not overwhelm the first time coach. My intention was to write a second book on advanced concepts that coaches could utilize once they mastered the concepts of the YDW. This book is essentially that second book, and although the focus is centered on direct snap concepts, it covers some advanced concepts that can be used with the YDW as well.

Due to the importance of the basic concepts of ABC, this chapter will appear to look exactly like Chapter 5 Angle Blocking Concepts in the YDW book. I want to be sure that coaches that did not purchase the YDW book have access to all the instructional and technical information on the ABC's (Angle Blocking Concepts). For those that have read the first book, I am going to list the new material so that you may easily distinguish the differences between this chapter and chapter 5 of the YDW book.

1) Tags are discussed herein as individual standalone concepts and not necessarily built into sets of three as with the YDW book, wherein I covered some of the more useful combinations in the relevant context. This allows for the use of single or multiple tags when needed. You will find that OVER is the most common one used in the system described herein, as it allows us to move from balanced to unbalanced quickly.
2) The addition of the WIDE scheme to SEAL and KICK.
3) The addition of the GRUNT/TANK scheme for the Eagle Read series and gap pressure defenses.
4) How to trap while using the angle blocking concepts.
5) Additional drills for improving line play.

Rationale for use of ABC's

"If a defense depends on movement like slanting, stunts and blitzes, or if they go into an even front, we will utilize our seven technique. The center makes the seven call, which basically has us abandoning our double teams and going into a down blocking mode on the onside...No matter what front we see, we can block it with seven". – *Jerry Valloton,* excerpt from The Toss.

The aforementioned comment is the main reason I decided to give SAB a try. Coach Vallotton basically stated, no matter what front he sees, if all else fails, he knows that his down scheme can block it. That understanding simplified my entire system and makes my limited practice time more effective. Therefore, I turned to SAB and eventually TKO as my primary scheme when running the power series.

The one problem I have found with complex rules is that it only takes one person to miss the rule or use the wrong part of the rule and you have a problem that costs you a play.

Example: Gap-On-Down (GOD) - When a coach tells you he uses GOD blocking schemes and they are very easy; what he is not telling you is that GOD is only one rule in a very large group of rules.

For instance, when blocking the basic power scheme, the center uses Man-on-Man Away (MOMA), the PSG and PST use GOD and the PSTE blocks Gap Down (GD), which by my calculation is at least three separate blocking rules for that one blocking scheme. Now include adjustment calls (new set of rules for a different set of circumstances) such as Domino or Dynamite (or whatever little name you use when the defense presents a loaded front that requires your offense to use some sort of down scheme), and things get even more complicated. Moreover, you have to count on that call actually being made, and every play-side blocker hearing it and adapting to the appropriate set of rules. This is a lot to ask kids (age 5 to 13) to process effectively in the span of 5 to 10 seconds, and expect to get a positive result 100% of the time.

To be clear, I am not suggesting this scheme doesn't work, because I have used the scheme for three seasons with a middle school team and managed to go to three championships with it. However, the potential for success with such a scheme depends greatly on the available practice time, and the maturity (and experience) of the players. I have not had the luxury of those types of players, nor the time to create a similar situation since then. While such a scheme can be very effective, don't let anyone fool you into believing it is simple - it isn't. In fact, as you can see from the above example, it can get pretty complex in the span of 5 to 10 seconds and we have yet to factor in defenders moving around because they aligned in the wrong spot, or shifting, or stemming, or stunting. Now imagine you are a ten year-old lineman in your first year of playing football, rushing to the LOS to assume a stance that feels uncomfortable, while attempting to decipher a rule as you look at the defenders in front of you who have just moved three times; then you hear DYNAMITE and suddenly, you hear GO, and the ball is snapped. Get my point? It can be unnecessarily overwhelming.

ABC describe the concepts we use in this offense to be successful. "Track and Kick Out" (TKO) is one of those concepts as are the other techniques and adjustments we use to enhance the TKO concept. Severe Angle Blocking (SAB) is an angle blocking concept as well, but in my opinion the TKO concept is superior to the SAB concept. The original intent of SAB was to track on a fixed 30 degree track all the way to the boundary. This can create gaps in the SAB wall as some blockers engage defenders while others do not. Linemen that do not encounter a defender move quickly down their track while the engaged linemen are slowed as they attempt to drive their defender to the boundary. With TKO, this problem is eliminated because each play-side blocker has a fixed landmark and a certain amount of steps he must achieve to open the TKO wall, i.e. they are not required to drive to the boundary. As with SAB, every blocker fires off at an angle. If a defender crosses a lineman's face, the linemen drives that defender to his landmark; if no defender crosses his face, he simply gets to his landmark. Either way, once to the lineman reaches their respective landmark, they set up and hold that position, and do not allow a defender to go through them. They don't chase defenders and they don't separate them from their landmark. Thus, the line establishes a solid wall that the defenders can't go through.

Simply put, the linemen assume a good stance with foot to foot splits, and then explode off the LOS, toward their landmark; the first defender to cross their face gets blocked to that landmark. As Darrin Fisher of the Abita Springs Warriors eloquently puts it, "I want my God given right to five yards!"

The ability to stress basic blocking fundamentals while eliminating complex blocking rules is an enormous benefit to youth football coaches with limited amounts of practice time. I am not saying we eliminate rules because TKO applies rules. However, the rules are intuitive and a part of the natural progression of blocking. There is no real thought process involved in the execution other than – GOOD STANCE, FIRE OFF, BLOCK THE FIRST MAN THAT CROSSES MY FACE AS I GET TO MY LANDMARK. That simple philosophy allows us to focus on the real keys to blocking at this level – stance, get off, blocking progression, and technique.

Excerpt from Coaching a Dominant Offensive Line White Paper on the Philosophy of TKO blocking by JJ Lawson

It all starts with the ability to block well and do it aggressively no matter what you face. You look at any successful offense that performs game in and game out throughout an entire season and it is because they could block any defense they faced and they did it with high intensity, flawless execution and proper technique. You MUST instill the belief in your team that blocking is all-important and it will be the base of your offense. Without it you rarely beat more talented teams. I believe that our blocking schemes must do certain things well if we are going to succeed.

BLOCKING SCHEME KEYS TO SUCCESS:
• Protect the inside gap and negate leakage across the entire front. Interior penetration kills production. Outside pressure is easier to run from.
• Give smaller linemen a technical and physical advantage. Many of our schemes actually work better with smaller quicker more aggressive linemen.
• Keep assignments simple to allow for aggressive play. The less our linemen have to think about, the easier it is to just fire off and whip somebody. And the time we save in practice, can be used to work on technique and aggression.

INSTILLING PRIDE IN OUR OFFENSIVE LINEMEN:
We constantly work to teach our linemen that they are the most important players on the team. There are many ways to express this to your linemen:

• Always be certain the HC spends more time with the linemen than the backs.
• Always have more linemen than backs as team captains on game day.
• Always show them special attention whenever possible.
• Always talk about what they will do or what they did do to help us win before discussing anything else during pre-game and post-game speeches.

CREATING BETTER, FASTER, STRONGER OFFENSIVE LINEMEN:

• Speed & Agility Drills for linemen are a MUST.
• Incorporate L.E.G. steps into EVERYTHING we do.
• Muscle memory drills like foot fire and L.E.G. progression that build core strength and increase flexibility and stamina.

What is TKO?

TKO is an aggressive angle/track blocking scheme that is designed to collapse interior defenders away from the hole while denying penetration via the line splits and angle of attack. When TKO is properly executed it can handle any alignment, stunting, stemming or blitzing the defense employs while creating a distinct lane (tunnel) for the running back. It allows the blockers to be more aggressive as they can focus on getting off the LOS and into the wall. They are not encumbered by concerns with which rule to follow nor are they burdened with waiting for a call change and readjusting. The TKO scheme creates unity within the line as they must work as a team at all times to ensure the success of the play.

The Five Components of the Track and Kick Out (TKO) Scheme

1) The BASE Blocker - The BASE blocker (center) is usually the farthest TKO blocker from the point of attack (AT MAN). He sets the landmark after tracking for two steps to the nearest defender and is now the base for the rest of the wall (SAB Blockers). After the base blocker takes his angle and sets his block, the next blocker must get to his landmark - this is the near shoulder of the base man. Each blocker on the play-side blocking TKO is going to drive to his landmark (the next man's near shoulder).

The center must only block for two steps so that any cut-off block being made towards the play-side from the back-side does not cause the center to run into the cut-off or cause an accidental CHOP BLOCK. The center must hold his ground if a defender advances or he must pin the blocker to the back-side if he becomes engaged. The objective of the BASE BLOCKER is to set the wall and create a stalemate at the base. His two steps are always the same and are aimed at the next gap back-side. This allows the line to learn that the wall will always form the same way, no matter what type of defense they must face.

2) TRACK Blocker – every blocker after the base blocker must get to their respective "landmark" which is the near shoulder of the blocker nearest the base. They must never allow any defender to cross their face as they track to their landmark. If a defender does cross their face, they must drive that defender to their landmark and hold their ground. When done properly the first TRACK blocker will be one yard up field from the base. Each TRACK blocker including the AT MAN will add about one yard to the wall. Each track will require approximately one extra step to reach the respective landmark (i.e. assuming the center takes two steps to reach his landmark, the PSG will take three, the PST will take four and the PSTE will take five steps, to reach their respective landmarks).

3) AT MAN – the AT MAN is the last TRACK blocker on the wall and is AT THE POA. The runner will always aim at the outside hip of the AT MAN. All rules for the TRACK BLOCKER apply to the AT MAN. If every blocker from the BASE to the AT MAN reaches their landmark they will have created a wall that is essentially diagonal up the field. The more TRACK blockers, the further the wall will extend up the field. If executed correctly, it will be nearly impossible for any defender to penetrate the wall; whether they attempt to do so via aggressive penetration, reading, stunting, stemming, or blitzing. Remember, to keep the play tight, the runner must read the outside hip of the AT MAN (usually the PSTE) and move such that his inside hip rubs the outside hip of the PSTE as he enters the tunnel. If using a numbering system or vice naming system, the one's digit will indicate the AT MAN (26 would be the TE but 24 would have the runner aim at the outside hip of the PST). This allows us to tell the runner to go inside or outside of the normal AT MAN based on what the defense is doing.

4) Man Outside the AT (MOAT) – any blocker outside of the AT MAN will not take the same track to the wall. Instead, he'll get clear of the LOS by jumping through to the second level to block the First Backer Inside (FBI). He drives him to the top of

the wall or to the outside shoulder of the AT MAN. If there is no backer between him and the AT MAN, he should work to get his inside hip to the outside hip of the AT MAN as fast as possible to seal the top of the wall off. Every blocker on the outside of the AT MAN executes this rule. Obviously, the LB can prevent the blocker from reaching the top of the wall, but the MOAT must always attempt to get to the top of the wall. The farther in this block is executed, the bigger the hole is for the runner. So the MOAT must get clean of the LOS quickly and get into his block on the backer. The MOAT can use an influence block on the EMLOS, to slow the EMLOS, thereby giving the KICK OUT block more time to develop. This is done by simply rubbing the near shoulder of the EMLOS as he releases. This turns the EMLOS's attention towards the MOAT thereby giving the KICK OUT blocker the time necessary to get to his block.

5) <u>KICK OUT</u> – to open the outside edge of the running play. In the SEAL scheme, the BB is the kick out blocker, whereas in the KICK scheme, the back-side guard is the kick out blocker. In both cases, the blocking rule is that he kicks out the first defender to cross his face and drives him outside as far as he can. He should aim for his near arm pit and then wheel his rear end into the hole to isolate the defender away from the tunnel and the runner.

What Makes the ABC's Click!

In my opinion it is not only the TKO concepts that make it easier for YDW coaches to execute this offense, it is also the simple approach we have to the basic rules of each blocking scheme. I have found that giving each blocker a basic rule that applies to any circumstance, is a far better approach than assigning specific defenders to particular blockers.

For example, in the SEAL scheme I never use PSWB (play side wing back) blocks the PSOLB (play side OLB). Instead, in the SEAL scheme we use PSWB blocks FBI (first backer inside); i.e. we teach the WB that if the OLB flies outside to let him go and take the next backer inside. If the OLB fills hard to the hole let him go and take the next backer inside.

The reason we teach this basic concept to the PSWB is because the rest of the rules in the SEAL scheme account for variations in the defense. For example, when that PSOLB fills hard in the tunnel our rules for the BB, QB, and BSG cover this fill, so our PSWB can let him go and not concern himself with chasing that OLB. For example, the BB's blocking rule for the SEAL scheme is that he kicks out the first defender to cross his face as he goes down the LOS. The QB's rule is that he kicks out the first defender to cross his face as he aims for the space above the BB's inside shoulder. The BSG's rule is he kicks out the first defender to cross his face as he aims for the space above the QB's inside shoulder. These rules basically establish who kicks on the first level and who climbs above the first level into the second level and how they execute their technique.

In the end, the simplicity of the rules and the way they mesh allow for execution against any defensive front.

FUNDAMENTALS OF TKO (S.A.T – Stance Alignment Technique)

- Good Stance
- Zero Line Splits
- Alignment
- Aiming Point/Landmarks
- Footwork – Load, Explode and GO.
- Hat, Shoulder, Hand Placement. (Blocking surface!)
- Stay Low! (Leverage!)
- Explode Off the LOS!

Good Stance

This is a very important part of the success of any play on offense. Everything the line does starts with a great stance. The linemen must get into a stance that must be comfortable and effective for them. They must be able to explode out of that stance and execute their techniques at a high level throughout the entire game.

The base stance we use for the line is called the Murphy 3-point stance. I feel this is the best stance for a Double Wing team because it offers great explosive movement in all directions.

As a substitute for kids that are unable to get out of a 3-point stance over the duration of an entire game (e.g. due to poor leg and core strength), we use a 2-point modified stance.

Both stances are time tested and work; it is up to the coach to decide which stance to use with his offensive line. I have used the 3-point stance on the entire line, though with a few linemen I have used the 2-point stance. In some cases I have had the entire line use the 2-point stance when we have the need for it. It all depends on the ability level of my offensive linemen and what is going to make them more effective.

Zero Line Splits

One of the biggest advantages I think our offensive linemen have is the ability to operate in confined spaces. It simplifies the offensive linemen's thinking process when facing defensive fronts and provides several key benefits that are essential for this offense to function optimally. This offense would be difficult execute at the highest level with extended splits in the interior line, as it is designed to work in a compressed space and widen the perimeter space thereby forcing the defense to keep three plus defenders on each side. This allows us to isolate to the outside as we run power and counter inside of the perimeter defenders, i.e. this allows us to attack the interior and edge with a numbers advantage in our power game while the defense has to defend the entire field. In summary, the benefits of the 'zero line splits' approach are:

- Reduces inside penetration and inside blitzing
- Simplifies defensive linemen alignments down to COVERED, SPLIT, and UNCOVERED
  - COVERED: defensive linemen (DLM) is directly over the blocker
  - SPLIT (COVERED): DLM is lined up directly over the feet of the two zero split blockers and the inside blocker is considered covered
  - UNCOVERED: there is no DLM over the blocker so he takes the first defender to show going towards play side
- This increases the size of the perimeter on both sides
- The holes or soft spots in the defense are essentially the uncovered blockers
- We force the defense to defend those soft spots while also defending the perimeter and the verticals (passing game)

The one hundred dollar question: can you really run inside with zero splits? The simple but honest answer is - Yes! Typically if your primary focus is the interior and edge you would use expanded splits (9" to 24" in most cases), which are common in the Wing-T, Fly, Zone-based, and Spread offenses. Zero splits can absolutely be effective for the inside running game when properly blocked. The caveat is that you must be able to threaten the edge and perimeters (as wells as the perimeter/vertical passing lanes) on both sides and force three defenders to stay disciplined, eliminating at least six players for the first four to five steps of your play. As your front compresses due to the zero splits the perimeters on both sides expand forcing the defense to compress on the interior while staying neutral (3 defenders on each side) on the perimeters so that they can maintain proper leverage on the outside (contain, force, and alley). This simple truth allows you to attack the interior and edge easily while utilizing zero splits. One other important point about zero splits, is that when you have an offense that is capable of misdirecting a defense away from the point of attack by threatening both perimeters, this often forces the defense to flow farther away from the point of attack. This is due to the compressed front, which forces the defense to take more false steps than they typically would need to take, if we were in a conventional alignment with typical splits. I like to tell my offense that when we compress and fake the XX action behind our interior and edge plays, we force the perimeter defenders on both sides to expand, thereby isolating the interior defenders we are attacking.

Alignment

Alignment is one of the first things a defense sees and it is often how a defensive coaching staff will judge if an offense is crisp and disciplined. If your alignment looks sharp and clean then there is a good chance the offense is sharp. If it looks sloppy and ill-formed the odds are the offense will execute poorly. Everything starts with a sharp stance and crisp alignment. Attention to detail and focusing on the little things is what makes an offense great.

J.J. Lawson said it well in his Coaching a Dominant Offensive Line (CDOL):

> *If a team lines up sloppy, they will have sloppy play execution. They will run, block, and tackle sloppy. They will play sloppy football. **WE ABSOLUTELY WILL NOT PLAY SLOPPY FOOTBALL!!!***

> *This disciplined approach to the game is the first thing that separates us from the 'sandlot football teams'. These teams are undisciplined and sloppy so they make a lot of mistakes and they tend to fall apart late when the game is on the line. This attention to detail also breeds confidence in our players, parents and program. Confidence is so important that anything we can do to increase it gets immediate priority.*

Line Splits

Foot-to-foot line splits are stressed to our linemen to keep the formation compressed thereby forcing the defense to play in small spaces. This also opens the edges as the defense tends to bunch up on the perimeters to stop the off-tackle power/misdirection running game leaving us a lot of grass on the perimeters.

Line Depth

Shoulders are aligned to the belt buckle of the center. This is about half the legal depth as normally the head must break the plane of the hip to be legal. We do this because we often pull our linemen, and have found that the added depth allows us to get them down the LOS (LOS) with little or no interference from the interior line. Moreover, when we pull the backside interior linemen, our TE will typically cut off their defenders; the depth of alignment enables the TE to freely move across and in front of the defenders he is cutting before they can penetrate or breach the LOS.

Aiming Points/Landmarks

BASE: The Center takes two steps with his aiming point being the Back-side gap at 45 degrees (or slightly less) with the key being that it is ALWAYS THE SAME for the base blocker. This assures that the landmark for the track blockers and the AT MAN are exactly the same. If no defender crosses his face, he sets the base and holds his ground letting no defender by. If a defender does cross his face (NT slanting back-side), he engages him and drives him to his landmark. Always aim the face mask to the far arm pit of the defender that crosses your face as you engage him.

TRACK/AT MAN: The near shoulder (outside shoulder) of the next TKO blocker inside. If no defender crosses his face he gets to his landmark and holds his ground not allowing any defender to cross his face. If a defender does cross his face he must drive him to his landmark. Like the BASE you should always aim the face mask to the far arm pit of the defender that crosses your face as you engage him.

MOAT: First backer inside is his landmark. He should drive him to the top of the TKO WALL (AT MAN) and seal him to inside. He should aim his face mask to the far arm pit so that the backer cannot take a direct path to the tunnel by crossing the MOAT's face.

KICK OUT: His path should be through the center's hip and he should kick out the very first defender that crosses his face. This ensures that if there is any leakage or free blitzing LB, he will be kicked out so that we may run inside of him. He should aim for the near pit and wheel his rear end into the hole to isolate the defender away from the tunnel and the runner.

Footwork

We use L.E.G as our teaching progression when coaching footwork and blocking technique. We stress this one component along with stance constantly to our line. They must LOAD – EXPLODE – GO every time they come off the LOS and are blocking.

LOAD – Load Step
EXPLODE – Explode Step
GO – Go Step
Run your feet!!!

L - We call the first step the **"LOAD STEP"**, as they must get that foot up and down quickly (literally, "stomp the ground") into their track, i.e. with a fast short step, while staying low (head up, chest on knee). The back should not rise up at all on this step. The step should be no longer than six inches - of course, if you tell them three inches, understand you will likely get six. The step should be taken with the foot near the track.

You must load your arms on this step quickly (thumbs behind the hips as you cock your arms back at 90 degrees). You must get out of your stance and into this step as fast as possible. Load your body and take a short stomp step.

E - The next step we call the **"EXPLODE STEP"**, as that is the back foot taking a short power step down the track to the base/landmark. Starting low, the back should rise as the feet, ankles, knees, hips, back, shoulders, elbows, inside forearm and the outside hand explode upward into the body of the defender (chest plate and ribs). It is important to get this second step down as quickly as possible - this is the step where first contact is made. The arms/hands should explode into the defender has the foot makes contact with the ground which creates an additional force production via Ground Force Reaction – SYNERGY.

Coaching Keys:

The arms should unload hard into the body so that the defender is literally being punched in the chest (forearm) and ribs (hand) with the outer portion of the heels of the hands. Aim for the middle of the breast plate, near the arm pit, and then drive the defender up on his heels as you uncoil your body through the ground.

The facemask does not make contact with the body. The facemask is a reference so that the eyes have a landmark for the body to follow.

G - The next step (and every step thereafter) is the **"GO STEP" (go to your landmark)**; the near foot again takes a short power step into the track that is quick and explosive. Maintaining a wide base is key, as you step and re-elevate. As you take the step you immediately drop your hips by coiling your ankles, knees, hips and lower back. Re-elevate as your foot makes contact (a mini-explode step) from the ground up, i.e. unloading from the feet, ankles, knees, hips, shoulders, arms and hands. You should stay under the defender and maintain contact as you elevate him. Literally elevating through him driving your hands inward and upward as you drive him down the track to your land mark.

Run Your Feet!!!

Whether you get to your land mark or get into a stalemate with a defender keep your feet moving using powerful, explosive, choppy steps. Never stop moving your feet until the sound of the whistle. Keep all seven cleats on the ground by taking short power steps unless you get the defender on his heels, then sprint through him for the pancake!

Blocking Surface

Every blocker, as they explode off the LOS, must initially aim for the near shoulder of the next blocker inside. Once on that track, if a defender crosses his face he must aim for the far arm pit of the defender, engage, and drive the defender to his landmark. We aim for the far arm pit to get the blocker's body to cross the defender's body in front of the gap. By doing this we eliminate leakage and put our blocker in the best possible situation to execute his blocks consistently. Remember one of our primary concerns is to eliminate leakage on the play-side; aiming for the far arm pit while exploding into the defender puts the head, near shoulder and near hip across the defender's body as contact is made. Since every blocker is attempting to get his near shoulder locked on the near shoulder of the next blocker, all blockers are able to see both their respective landmark and block their respective defender.

Stay Low

Linemen must be taught that they should never stand tall while playing the game of football. They must play with their hips and knees bent and they must keep their center of gravity low to the ground, to not only better control their body but also any defender they engage.

Explode off the LOS

Last but not least the linemen must learn to **GET OFF THE LOS** as fast as possible and into their track, engaging the first defender that crosses their face. They must realize that they have to be the **first to move on every play to win the battle at the LOS.**

Basic Schemes of TKO

In the first book SEAL and KICK were the basic edge schemes of our TKO blocking concept. SEAL is our POWER blocking scheme with the BB/QB kicking out first/second level, while the BSG and BST pull and seal inside as the BSTE cuts off/shoe shines. The KICK is our COUNTER blocking scheme which has the BSG kicking out and the BST sealing off the inside and the BB sealing off the outside. Since the first book, I have added a new scheme that I consider to be a basic element as well (Figure 5A). The WIDE scheme is a perimeter scheme that we employ when we see the OLB and DE of the perimeter triangle filling hard to stop the edge when they see the wall forming. Often the OLB will fill the tunnel fast trying to stop the edge play as the DE crashes inside trying to collapse the tunnel from underneath. The WIDE scheme allows us to counter this by (1) sealing the DE inside with the WB and (2) influencing the OLB to fill the tunnel, thereby allowing us to get the BB, QB, and BSG outside to lead for the running back. All three of these schemes, if executed properly, can handle a variety of defenses as they complement each other well, but we also have some simple adjustments that enable us to handle anything else we might face. Before we discuss those adjustments, one important modification I made to the SEAL scheme is that the BSG will always kick out the third defender rather than seal off the inside of the wall. Thus, the BST will always seal off the backside by staying tight to the wall in order to wall off any defender climbing the top of the wall. The BSG is the 'adjustment' blocker for the line in each scheme. In SEAL he kicks out the third defender to show, in KICK he kicks out the first defender to show, and in WIDE he kicks out the widest defender (force or CB).

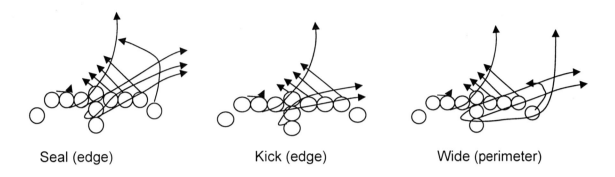

| Seal (edge) | Kick (edge) | Wide (perimeter) |

Figure 5A. Basic Schemes of TKO

In addition to these basic schemes, we have several variations that we can use as alternatives; or as in the case of the EAGLE series, as a base scheme (Figure 5B).

GRUNT – TKO from CENTER to PSTE with BSG kicking out first defender to show and BST and BSTE cutting off to play side. This is also an alternative scheme used in the EAGLE series.

TANK – TKO from BSG to PSTE with BST executing a kick out on first defender to cross his face. The BSG is the base of the TKO wall and the BSTE cuts off. In the case of the EAGLE series when we only have a five man front this allows us to use the four blockers play side as the TKO wall while the end line man on the backside kicks out the first defender to cross his face.

Both of these schemes are alternatives when facing pressure gap fronts as well (10-1, GAM, GAP 8, and STACK fronts that stunt), as it allows you still get a plus one advantage at the point of attack.

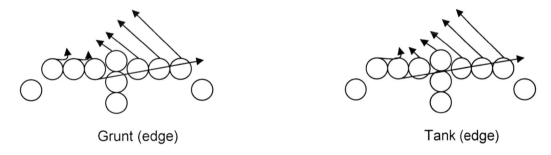

| Grunt (edge) | Tank (edge) |

Figure 5B. Variations to the Basic TKO Schemes

As discussed earlier these adjustments allow us to handle a "6 tech" DE who is aligning head up or slightly inside of the play-side TE and causing problems with the kick out block by wrong arming and squatting on the LOS or crashing down the LOS and stuffing the kick out. Often the technique used to stop a down blocking offense, has the defender crash down the line off the outside hip of the down blocker. We must have ways of handling this problem. I PROMISE YOU WILL SEE THIS TACTIC AND YOU MUST HAVE A SOLUTION IN PLACE; THE EASIEST WAY TO HANDLE IT IS TO EXPAND THE EDGE BY ADDING A BLOCKER TO THE WALL.

ON – Tells our WB to shift to the LOS on down, where he then becomes the AT MAN on the LOS. This forces the EMLOS to do one of two things: 1) stay put and get down blocked by the WB, or 2) widen and line up over the WB thereby granting the kick out block more time to be made. It is a simple adjustment and if you don't see an issue with the PSLB jumping the tunnel (and letting the QB, BSG and BST pick up the backer), then this is a great solution. It essentially widens the TKO wall by one man.

OVER – Tells our BST to move over in-between the PST and the PSTE. It does the same thing as the ON call by shifting over a back-side lineman establishing an unbalanced line with the BSG pulling, as the BST is already in place on the play-side and in the TKO wall.

OFFSET – Tells the BB to shift to a sniffer position under the PST (between the PST/PSG) to get him closer to the EMLOS and allow him to take on a problematic defender (crashing/squatting).
LOOSE – Tells the PSWB and PSTE to expand out to a SLOT and SE position to force the perimeter triangle to expand with them allowing us to isolate the DE while moving the OLB and CB out.

NASTY – Tells our PSWB and PSTE to exchange positions allowing us to expand the perimeter triangle if the DE widens with the PSTE. Often a DE who has a rule to play containment will expand and in doing so opens the edge and allows us to isolate him. Often used with OVER to get an unbalanced look that expands the edge while the LOOSE expands the perimeter triangle.

BUNCH/TRIPS – Allow us to expand and isolate the perimeter triangle by forcing the CB, OLB, and ILB to expand with the receiver unit allowing us to isolate the DE. Often used with OVER to get an unbalanced look that expands the edge while the BUNCH/TRIPS expands the perimeter triangle.

As stated earlier in the book we can use these calls in combinations as well. We will OVER-OFFSET as well as ON-OVER-OFFSET a lot to completely overload the defense. The most common call is OVER as it allows us to transition from a balanced to unbalanced front seamlessly - often the defense fails to catch on to this tactic.

Trapping in the YDW

If a defender is over or inside of the PST and is athletic and fast enough that he is getting across too quickly, then let him go and let the KICK OUT BLOCKER take him out; then the pullers and ball carrier may run inside of him (Figure 5C). The PST and PSTE will step up and over the defender instead of taking a LOAD step down. They simply take their load and explode step going forward and then redirect down on their go step. They will LOAD and EXPLODE vertically as they get skinny and then turn inside and get to their landmark. We basically bypass the trapped defender and re-seal the gap as he goes by, then we get to our respective landmarks. The runner must always stay tight to the wall, along with any second puller who is pulling vertical to seal. As long as they do this it doesn't matter who the kick out blocker blocks (FIRST DEFENDER TO CROSS HIS FACE).

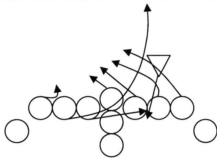

Figure 5C. Trap Concept against an attacking DT.

This trap concept can be used with SEAL, KICK, GRUNT, and TANK. Obviously the SEAL concept can be a little more difficult due to the location of the kick out blocker (BB). In SEAL scheme we will typically only attempt to "trap" a defender over or outside of the PST but in the KICK, GRUNT, and TANK schemes we can "trap" a defender that is over or outside shade of the PSG. The benefit of using this trapping concept is that even when you face a really tough interior defender you still have the ability to beat him by simply letting him get by the wall, then closing the wall off, and kicking him out while you run inside of him. The combination of down blocks, cut offs, wedge, and kick out blocks is often more than enough to slow down even the most aggressive defender. In the YDW we had the COMBO (double team method described below) to use against exceptional interior defenders and now that we have the TRAP and COMBO method it gives us the ability to place a tremendous amount of pressure on interior defenders while staying true to our angle blocking concepts.

Covered/Uncovered Concept Blocking

I feel this is an advanced concept but it is one I am starting to use more and more as I learn to appreciate the advantage that zero splits provides to our blockers. Due to the compression of the line it eliminates defenders ability to align in various shades and alignments. They can either be over a blocker or splitting two of our blockers and that is about it. Essentially it is base blocking or drive blocking made simple.

What are the benefits? Once your opponents know you are an angle blocking team, their mindset, as to how they will defend you, will change so they can defeat the angles you are trying to create. The covered/uncovered schemes give the offense an additional leverage advantage when they start to do that. Defenses tend to slant or stunt much less against an angle blocking team, and tend to rely more on reading as their defensive linemen attempt to engage and drive back the angle blockers. This allows us to more easily base block defenders as they are now reading rather than attacking. The actual schemes and plays will be discussed in the Lead Series portion of the power chapters, as that series utilizes nothing but covered/uncovered and really is nothing more than an extension to the Power Series. I kept it separate from the power series because I believe it is important to keep the base series (and the angle/wedge blocking portion) simple for new coaches so they can focus completely on the core components.

Why use it? Once you understand the tremendous advantage you have using angle blocking and wedge blocking, you begin to understand that it opens up the ability to utilize drive/base blocking concepts as a changeup scheme when teams start to sit on the line of scrimmage anticipating your angle blocks and wedge blocks. No matter how well your team executes these blocking schemes good defense will adapt over time; the ability to change your blocking schemes while keeping the format simple will be key to your team's long term success. The covered/uncovered schemes utilize our base LEG progression but add a TURN component on the third step and is now used against head-up or covered defenders. This is precisely how we initially teach our LEG blocking progression, and continue to teach it during Every Day Drills (EDDs), after our dynamic warm ups. So in reality, there really is no additional teaching of this scheme, other than the actual plays being taught.

What is 'covered' and 'uncovered'? A "covered" blocker is a blocker with a defender breaking the vertical line of his inside or outside shoulder (Figures 5D and 5E). If a defender splits two blockers due to zero splits the inside defender is covered and the outside defender is uncovered by that specific defender. This is because we always want leverage on the inside defender first and foremost so that we protect our inside gap and we wall off that defender. If a blocker has two defenders splitting him that means he is covered by the inside split defender and the outside defender is ignored as he will cover the next defender or be kicked/walled out. The uncovered rule means that no defender (defensive linemen) is over a blocker as defined by the rules above; this blocker will then follow his "uncovered" assignment. Once he determines he is uncovered, he has to locate the most dangerous man; FIRST DEFENDER AWAY is the rule. The uncovered blocker looks beyond the line (first level) to the second level, seeking the first backer away, if necessary, he may look to the third level and attack the safety. This gives our blockers a great amount of flexibility within each specific scheme, allowing an uncovered blocker help out (or combo) with neutralizing a good defender. Figure 5F illustrates this concept on the backside of a play from the Shift Lead Series.

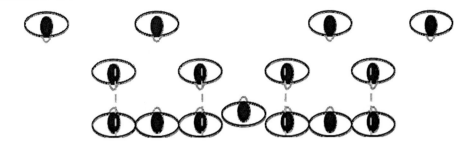

Figure 5D. Example of the covered/uncovered against a 44 split: Above is a good example against a common front I am starting to see a lot on the field a 44 split look using a 2 tech (over guard) and 6 tech (over end). Notice how our center and tackles are uncovered. Often this gives us the ability with our center to double either defensive tackle, block first backer away, or in most cases move up and take a cover 1/3 safety out.

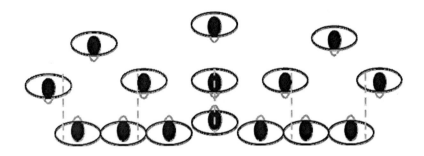

Figure 5E. Example of the covered/uncovered against a 53 look: Above is a good example against a 53 front with their defensive tackles splitting our guards and tackles. Notice that our tackles are considered covered while our guards uncovered. This gives our guard the flexibility to go first defender away and release up field or help out either the center or tackle with his defender.

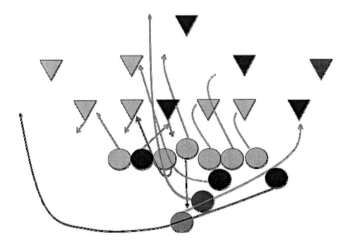

Figure5F. Shift Rip 23 ISO Right: this is a play from our Lead Series and it uses covered/uncovered principles on the backside of the play.

Dealing with Bear Crawlers and Submariners

One of the common challenges when running a compressed formation with tight splits is defenders that bear crawl or submarine on the interior. This really creates two problems for the offense; (1) the bear crawlers cause problems with pullers from the back-side getting caught in the pile, and (2) it causes movement problems for the backs going into the tunnel. You can eliminate a lot of these problems by having the line off the LOS as far as legally possible (must break the plane of the center's hip - belt buckle). This allows the linemen to have some space on the play-side to get their blocks and gives the rest of the offense space to operate on the play-side; however, if you are dealing with athletic defenders that are quick off the ball, submariners and bear-crawlers can still present problems. I have found and developed some simple tactics that allow us to eliminate these defenders as problems.

The easiest solution I have found to neutralize these types of defenders, is to attack them in a slightly different way than executing our traditional TKO/LEG scheme i.e., when our blockers realize they are facing a crawler/submariner they will attack that defender in a alternate way. The blocker will explode into the defender by aiming his face mask at the near rib cage (under the arm pit); he will drive the near forearm into the near shoulder of the defender and the far hand into the near hip of the defender. This allows the blocker to get under the defender and control the center of gravity of the defender. In martial arts, the body has four pivot points (both shoulders and both hips). Basically, if you control two of those pivot points you control the centerline and consequently, the center of gravity of your opponent. This simple adjustment allows us to attack the defender low, explode through him and topple him by driving his center of gravity away from him; this will often result in the defender being toppled or flipped on his back. If a defender in a 3- point stance attempts to bear crawl, then simply drive your hand into his near hip as you step through him and see what happens. Aim for the rib cage and drive the defender's near forearm into his chest to create lift as you drive your hand into his hip to flip the defender's body.

Loaded and Loaded Pressure Fronts

For our purposes, any defense that puts more than eight defenders in the box is considered a loaded front; one of the benefits of using angle blocking concepts is that we are built, as a base, to defeat these types of fronts without calling adjustments at the LOS. When we face these fronts we have to determine if they are pressure fronts and are attempting to blow the play-up behind the LOS. If they are, then we have to adjust our back-side pullers to account for the extra defenders at the LOS. Loaded fronts suggest that there are less defenders at the second and third level, thus there is no need to pull two back-side linemen. Simply adjust, and pull either one or none, to account for the pressure.

If the leakage is occurring on the inside (A/B) of the back-side, then simply adjust such that the BSG becomes the BASE and the BST assumes the BSG's pull rule when necessary. The other alternative is to pull the BST and BSTE, while the BSG stays in as the BASE. This should only be used against BSDE's that are reading, otherwise he could crash down the LOS and follow the pulling TE to the play. Another alternative, if the leakage is at the C gap, is to pull the BSG and BSTE, while the BST executes a fan block to the C gap (rather than having the BSTE shoeshine). In all three cases these are pretty simple adjustments, but it is important to review them in practice occasionally so that the offensive line can easily adapt during a game. Attempting to install these adjustments during a game is not advised. Moreover, simply going through and reviewing specific circumstances and how to adjust to those circumstances, will not give your line the ability to quickly adapt. The need for these adjustments should be anticipated and therefore the adjustments must be practiced as part of the overall offensive line strategy. Furthermore, anticipating the potential need for these adjustments and dedicating some practice time to them will open the lines of communication such that when linemen see a need to adjust they will express that to you as they know you have anticipated the possibility and have developed an answer/solution for it.

Dealing with an Exceptional Defender (need a double team)

The more experience I have with angle blocking the more and more I realize that you don't need double teams to be successful because the TKO scheme actually creates dynamic double and often triple teams as the wall collapses and compresses on the interior defenders. However, there are cases where you need to get two bodies on a defender to move him to the landmark. This is especially true when you are facing a more biologically mature player that has hit puberty early and is already an athletic specimen with genetic gifts.

When I started using SAB full time in 2001 I used a method called Post and Track. This simply meant that if the interior blocker had no immediate threat to his inside gap he could post block the defender that was head up over him to assist the next blocker out. He posted him up and then got back in his track. This worked really well but over time Kenny Mead, a fellow Double Wing coach, modified this play by using a COMBO call with a number to designate which pair will combo block the defender in SAB. I am now using a variation of that COMBO call, wherein we define the blocking assignments by determining which gap in the offense needs to be doubled.

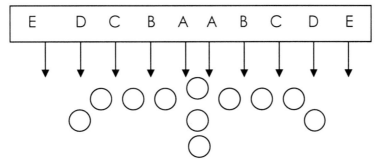

Figure 5G. Gap Method Identification System

By using the gap method (Figure 5G), we can determine which two offensive players must initiate a combo block. When a combo block is called, it simply means that the two blockers will take one half of the defender and drive him to the interior blocker's land mark (this is because the exterior blocker is already at his landmark – near shoulder of next man inside). The two blockers will attack the near arm pit of the defender as the exterior blocker meshes his inside hip with the near hip of the inside blocker. They will drive the defender down the track and into the landmark. When they get to the LOS the interior blocker must determine if he has a threat to his inside gap; if so, he must call off the COMBO call by signal, otherwise he combos the defender to his near landmark.

Combo A – Center/Guard
Combo B – Guard/Tackle
Combo C – Tackle/TE
Combo D – TE/WB (calls off FBI block by WB)

Example #1 Tight Rip 26 Seal Combo C
Example #2 Tight Rip 26 Offset Combo D

With more mature teams and lines that are capable of adjusting on the fly, you can simply tell the interior blocker if there is no threat to his inside gap and the exterior blocker needs help, then he can combo the defender. Once the interior blocker determines that a combo block is appropriate, it is important that he communicate his intention to the exterior blocker in some manner. I let my linemen come up with their own signal system so that it instills a sense of ownership. Again this is approach is viable with older players (above the age of 12).

If an exterior blocker is confronted with an overwhelming defender (i.e. aggressive defender that is a superior athlete) and the COMBO is not a viable option for some reason, then we'll direct our lineman to cut the defender by aiming the far shoulder at a point in front of the far thigh while maneuvering the body across the defenders legs. Typically, once the aggressive player gets toppled a few times, he slows down his charge, thereby allowing the blocker to now make the down block as part of the TKO scheme. Normally when we see an aggressive defender at the line we start calling kicks so we can trap him or we wedge the interior defenders to slow their charge.

Teaching TKO

First you must teach a proper stance to your linemen - it is the base of everything that your linemen will do. Finding the proper stance, one that they are comfortable in and can explode out of throughout the entire game is very important.

The base stance is the Murphy 3-point stance which I learned from Coach Tim Murphy, a fellow Double Wing coach. I feel it is the best stance you can use for the Double Wing. An alternative stance is the modified two point stance which is really something I came up with in 2001 when I needed to make some adjustments due to the type of linemen I had at that time.

Murphy 3-point Stance

1)   Feet are shoulder width apart and balanced
2)   Bend at the knees and hips
3)   Place both elbows on the knees
4)   Place either hand down on the ground in front of the near foot. It should be placed such that there is no forward lean and the vast majority of the weight is over the feet.
5)   Place the other hand in front of the near foot and close the fist as it sits near the down hand so that it is cocked and ready to load and strike.
6)   The head should be up the rear end should be down.

Modified 2-Point Stance

1)   Feet are shoulder width apart and feet are balanced
2)   Bend at the knees and hips
3)   Place both elbows on the knees
4)   Semi-load the arms so that the elbows are past the hips
5)   Head should be up and rear end should be down. The upper torso should be in a slight upward position.

The modified 2-point stance is great for kids that are overweight and/or have weak leg and core strength. Kids like this tend to get into sloppy stances or their stances break down throughout the course of the game. Because the stance is the base of every movement a blocker will execute it needs to be fundamentally sound and it needs to be constant from the start of the game to the finish. The modified 2-point allows the blocker to set in a more up-right position which requires less core and lower body strength to hold that position and it requires less energy (explosive strength) to move out of it. The key to this stance working is for the linemen to get into to a coiled position (meaning they must bend their hips and knees and stay low). Either hand should be able to brush the grass in front of them if they are at the proper level.

Initial Install of the TKO
(excerpts taken from Coaching A Dominant Offensive Line by JJ Lawson)

Once you teach the stance and you feel they are ready to move out of the stance you can install the actual play-side scheme.

Start With the Center

The center will first be shown how he should attack the back-side of the LOS (set the base) by taking two diagonal steps and then stopping to set the landmark. We want him to stop and hold his ground so we can build a diagonal wall with our center as the base of that wall. If he is engaged with a defender he needs to move him two steps and then create a stalemate. If he is not engaged then we want him to stop after two steps so he makes it easy to locate the landmarks for the other TKO blockers. The two steps also allow the BSTE to execute his shoeshine block down to the center's hip without cutting the center or creating an illegal chop block. With our zero splits the center should get a good block on a back-side 1 Tech or 2 Tech against an even front. If the defense is in an odd front then his first two steps are a little more downfield (vertical) so that his downfield shoulder catches some of the NT (Back-side arm pit/chest), making easier for the PSG to contact and drive that NT down to the wall.

The Rest of the Line (TRACK and AT MAN)

The G, T and TE on the play-side each fight to hit their landmark; which is the outside shoulder of the man to their inside. They do not worry about 'who' is in their track, they simply get from point A to point B as fast as possible without letting anyone cross their face or get between them and the man to their inside. Now, if a defender is in their track or enters their track, they will drive him to the landmark point. We want the wall to form starting at the center's pivot and extending downfield. This means that the OG has a track about two yards long, while the OT's track is about three yards long and the TE's track is about 4 yards long, all to get to their landmark. When this is successful, we have a string of 4 OL setting a wall that is almost impossible to break through and stretches about 4 yards downfield.

A great way to give young players a visual idea of how the TKO Wall is supposed to work, is to put a couple of 'defenders' behind a fence gate and point out that the hinge is the Center and then open the gate. When the gate is open 45 degrees, it will effectively 'wall off' the defenders and 'open' the hole for the runner.

The MOAT (Man Outside of the AT MAN)

Play-side blockers who are outside the 'AT' man, should skip through to the second level and then work their way to the top of the wall. Once they get to the second level, the responsibility of these blockers is the first defender to their inside (usually an OLB or ILB). If there is no LB between them and the wall, they should get to the top of the wall, turn toward the back-side and catch anyone who tries coming over the top. Sometimes the LB prevents this, but we try for a perfect wall. This is our ultimate goal. To set a wall starting from the LOS and have it stretch 4-5 yds down the field sealing everything inside toward the middle of the field.

This makes up the entire TKO scheme on the play-side of the line and how we seal off the interior of the defense on the first and second level.

L.E.G Progression Drills (Initial Install for the Offense)

Kneeling Load and Explode Drill

Objective: To develop a proper load and explode technique while developing the lower body strength needed to be a good blocker.

Set up: All players will align on one yard line facing the Head Coach (HC) while the Assistant Coaches (AC) split the line up into small sections to coach up players.

Execution: All players will kneel with the right knee up and arms to the side.
1)   On LOAD, all players will load their upper bodies maintaining numbers to knees and arms loaded with eyes up.
2)   On EXPLODE, all players will unload their body driving the forearms up with fists together coming off the ground straight up such that the heels lift off the ground and the arms are vertical above the head in a split jack position.
3)   On RESET, all players switch legs and take a knee so that their left knee is on the ground.
4)   Repeat sequence.
5)   Work for three to five reps on each leg.

3-Point Stance Load Drill

Objective: To develop a proper load technique out of a 3-point stance. Work on keeping the chest on the knees during the loading phase as they stomp the ground. A 2- point stance can be used as well.

Set up: All players will align on one yard line facing the HC while the AC's split the line up into small sections to coach up players.

Execution: All players on DOWN will get into a 3-point stance.
1)   RIGHT FOOT FIRST – LOAD and all players will execute a proper LOAD step. They will take a short power step as they load their arms and keep their chest on their knees and their heads up.
2)   On RESET all players get back into their 3-point stance ready to go to the left.
3)   Repeat sequence.
4)   Work for three to five reps on each leg.

3-Point Stance Load and Explode Drill

Objective: To develop a proper load and explode technique out of a three point stance. Work on keeping the chest on the knees during the loading phase and unloading through the entire body as the explode foot makes contact with the ground. A two point stance can be used as well.

Set up: All players will align on one yard line facing the HC while the AC's split the line up into small sections to coach up players.

Execution: All players on DOWN will get into a 3-point stance.

    1) RIGHT FOOT FIRST – LOAD and all players will execute a proper LOAD step. They will take a short power step as they load their arms and keep their chest on their knees and their head up.

    2) On EXPLODE all players will unload their body driving the forearms up with fists together coming off the ground straight up so that the heels lift off the ground and the arms are vertical above the head as they take their explode step.

    3) On RESET all players get back into a 3-point stance to work on left foot.

    4) Repeat sequence.

    5) Work for three to five reps on each leg.

3-Point Stance Load, Explode and Go Drill

Objective: To develop a proper load, explode and go technique out of a three point stance. Work on keeping the chest on the knees during the loading phase and unloading through the entire body as the explode foot makes contact with the ground. A two point stance can be used as well.

Set up: All players will align on one yard line facing the HC while the AC's split the line up into small sections to coach up players.

Execution: All players on DOWN will get into a 3-point stance.

    1) RIGHT FOOT FIRST – LOAD and all players will execute a proper LOAD step. They will take a short power step as they load their arms and keep their chest on their knees and their head up.

    2) On EXPLODE all players will unload their body driving the forearms up with fists together coming off the ground straight up so that the heels lift off the ground and the arms are vertical above the head as they take their explode step.

    3) On GO all players will take their next step and every other step as a short power stop as they coil their body and move down the field.

    4) On RESET all players get back into a 3-point stance to work on left foot.

    5) Repeat sequence.

    6) Work for three to five reps on each leg.

We do this drill every day once dynamic warm ups are completed. Once we learn the drills and begin to master them, it should only take 10 minutes to complete the entire sequence. Every player on the team is required to be a good blocker and this is one of our tools to ensure that happens. At this point we move on into the rest of our practice schedule and at some point we will go OFFENSIVE INDYS and split the BACKS and LINES up and have the line work on more specific drills.

Offensive Line Drills

Foot Fire Drill (Taken form CDL by JJ Lawson)

Objective: To teach our players to be comfortable playing low.

• To teach and drill a 6" 'power stomp' with all 7 cleats in the ground. We don't want to see a high kick to get power so keep the steps clean and low.

• To strengthen the core, as well as the arms, legs and inner thighs.

• To increase flexibility and strength in the ankle and instep.

Set Up: Have all the linemen stand on a yard line facing a coach. Make sure they are spread out three to five yards (Figure 5H).

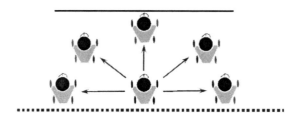

Figure 5H. Hand- and Foot- work for the Foot Fire Drill.

Execution: As you can see from the diagram, we work this drill in several different directions. During each step of this drill we will always move one hand and one foot simultaneously. This is color coded in the diagram. When moving forward we want to move opposite hand and foot together. However, when moving diagonally and horizontally, we move the hand and foot on the same side of the body together.

• On the command 'READY' – players all breakdown.

• On the command 'DOWN' – players get down in a proper 3-point stance.

• On the command '4 POINT' – players put the other hand down in a 4-point stance.

• On the command 'FORWARD ~ STOMP' – players start with RH & LF and take 6" power stomp forward … command 'STOMP' and players move LH & RF, taking a 6" power stomp forward … continue through at least 10-15 forward stomps.

• On the command 'TO THE RIGHT ~ STOMP' – players start with RH & RF and take a horizontal 6" power stomp to the right … command 'STOMP' and players bring their LH & LF back underneath them with a 6" power stomp … again continue through at least 10-15 stomps to the right.

• Repeat this process in all five directions. If your players are lined up in even lines front-to-back and side-to-side, you want them to finish in clean even lines as well.

Shoulder Block Drill (taken from CDL by JJ Lawson)

Objective:

• To teach and drill the L.E.G. blocking progression.
• To teach and drill the perfect fit of the 'contact surface' on the bag.

Set up:

• Align in a proper 3-point stance.
• Slightly offset on the bag with helmet about 6 inches from the bag (Figure 5I).

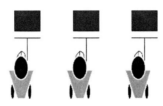

Figure 5I. Alignment and action for the Shoulder Block Drill

Execution:

• On coaches command of LOAD
    1. Players take 3" step while violently loading arms.
    2. Look for a flat back with no rise from the 3-point stance.
• On coaches command of EXPLODE
    1. Players take 6" step while exploding shoulder & forearms into the bag.
    2. Look for a perfect fit of shoulder and forearms on the bag.
• On coaches command of GO
    1. Blockers will begin to stomp and drive bag.
    2. Look for seven cleats in the ground, maintaining good form and firm contact between 'contact surface' and the bag.
    3. When operating at full speed, be sure to block for eight seconds.

Coaching Keys:

This drill can be done in or out of pads, with or without hard contact.

Start at walk-through speed working right then left shoulders. Once you are happy that everyone is getting a good fit on the bag, you can go ½ speed and work your way to full speed repetitions with both shoulders. Try this drill from inside a chute or using a sled.

Try this drill using hand shields and on contact the shield holder releases the shield so that poor technique or failure to maintain contact will result in dropping the shield.

Running Shoulder Block (Taken from CDL by JJ Lawson)

Objective:
• To teach and drill how to block on the run (pulling or blocking down field).
• To teach and drill the LOAD step during the approach to ensure contact.
• To teach and drill the EXPLODE step to ensure a perfect fit on the defender.
• To teach and drill the GO step while they turn their hips to shield the runner.

Set Up:
• Align in a 3-point stance, head up and five yards from the bag (Figure 5J).
• Someone should hold the bag upright so it doesn't just fall on contact.

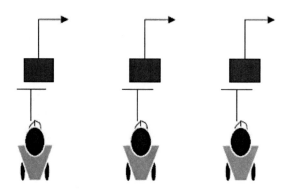

Figure 5J. Alignment and action for the Running Shoulder Block Drill

Execution: On the snap count
1. Players take off low and hard for the bag.
2. 'Shimmy down' with short steps right before contact.
3. Last step before contact is a 6" LOAD step.
4. Look for sinking hips and good hit position.
5. Players should make contact using a 6" EXPLODE step.
6. Players will begin to stomp and drive bag. Call it the GO steps.
7. Look for seven cleats in the ground, maintaining good form and firm contact between shoulder and bag.
8. After several steps, the players should swing their hips to practice sealing the defender away from the runner.

Coaching Keys:

This drill can be done in or out of pads, with or without hard contact.

Start at walk-through speed working right then left shoulders. Once you are happy that everyone is getting a good fit on the bag, you can go 1/2 speed and work your way to full speed repetitions with both shoulders.

Down Block (Taken from CDL by JJ Lawson)

Objective:
• To teach and drill how to block a Gap Defender.
• To teach and drill how to keep a Defender from crossing your face.
• To teach and drill how to get your head across the Defenders far armpit.

Set Up:
• Align in a 3-point stance, offset diagonally one body width from the bag (Figure 5K).
• Someone should hold the bag upright so it doesn't just fall on contact.

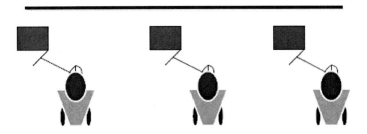

Figure 5K. Alignment and action for the Down Block Drill

Execution:
• On coaches command of LOAD
> 1. Players take a 3" step with near foot while violently loading arms.
> 2. Look for a flat back with no rise from the 3-point stance.

• On coaches command of EXPLODE
> 1. Players take a 6" step with back foot while exploding shoulder & forearms into the bag. Facemask should be aimed at the 'far armpit'.
> 2. Look for a perfect fit of shoulder and forearms on the bag and head across the bag to prevent penetration. This last part is very important as penetration on the play-side is very dangerous to this offense.

• On coaches command of GO
> 1. Blockers will begin to stomp and drive bag down the line.
> 2. Look for seven cleats in the ground, maintaining good form and firm contact between 'contact surface' and the bag.
> 3. When operating at full speed be sure to block for eight seconds.

Coaching Keys:

This drill can be done in or out of pads, with or without hard contact. Start at walk-through speed working Right then Left shoulders. Once you are happy that everyone is getting a good fit on the bag, you can go 1/2 speed and work your way to full speed repetitions with both shoulders. Try this drill using hand shields and on contact the shield holder releases the shield so that poor technique or failure to maintain contact will result in dropping the shield.

Combo Drill (modified from CDL by JJ Lawson)

Objectives:
• To teach and drill how to combo a tough defender.
• To teach the post (inside) blocker to stand up the defender and the track (outside) blocker to drive down on the defender.
• To teach both blockers to squeeze the defender between their helmets and squeeze their hips together to keep the defender trapped between them, as they take him to the post blocker's land mark.

Alignment:
• Align in a 3-point stance, with the bag head up on the post blocker (Figure 5L).
• Someone should hold the bag upright so it doesn't just fall on contact.

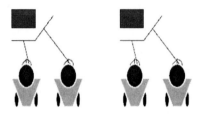

Figure 5L. Alignment and action for the Combo Drill.

Set Up:

• On coaches command of LOAD
    1. Players take 3" step with near foot while violently loading arms.
    2. Look for a flat back with no rise from the 3-point stance.
    3. Each blocker should aim for the near arm pit of the defender.

• On coaches command of EXPLODE
    1. Players take 6" step with back foot while exploding shoulder and forearms into the bag. The post blocker's facemask should be aimed at the armpit on his side while the track blocker's facemask should be aimed at the armpit on his side.
    2. Look for a perfect fit of shoulder and forearms on the bag and heads squeezing the bag together. Also look for the blockers to squeeze their hips together to prevent the defender from splitting the double team.

• On coaches command of GO
    1. Blockers will begin to stomp and drive bag back to the TKO Wall. Often it will be necessary for the post blocker to swing his hips farther toward the track blocker in order to keep from opening a hole to his inside and keep him on his track to his landmark.
    2. Look for seven cleats in the ground, maintaining good form and firm contact between 'contact surface' and the bag. Also look for the blocker's hips to remain together.
    3. When operating at full speed be sure to block for eight seconds.

Coaching Keys:

This drill can be done in or out of pads, with or without hard contact. Start at walk-through speed working right then left shoulders. Once you are happy that everyone is getting a good fit on the bag, you can go 1/2 speed and work your way to full speed repetitions with both shoulders. Try this drill using hand shields and on contact the shield holder releases the shield so that poor technique or failure to maintain contact will result in dropping the shield.

King of the Boards (Taken from CDL by JJ Lawson)

Objective:
• To teach and drill blockers to keep a wide base and drive 'through' the defender and really finish off a block.
• To determine who is your top one-on-one blockers, whether it is due to athletic ability, proper technique or just good old competitive spirit.
• To give the coach a close-up look at the technique and the 'inner fire' of each and every lineman.

Set up:
• Two opponents straddle the board in a proper 3-point stance facing each other with their helmets about eight inches apart (Figure 5M).
• You can use an 8-10 inch wide board or half round dummies for this.
• You also want to stand a blocking dummy behind each competitor.

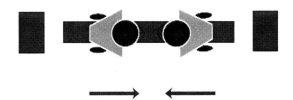

Figure 5M. Alignment and action for the King of the Boards Drill.

Execution:
• On the snap count both blockers will fire off using the L.E.G. steps and attempt to drive his opponent back along the board.
• First player to drive his opponent into the standing dummy is the winner.
• Use a slow whistle to allow pancakes to happen when the loser falls backward over the dummy that his back-side knocks down.
• We like to use a double elimination style tournament at least once a week because kids will always give 100% in a game when they might not during other drills. Repeat until the King claims his crown.

Coaching Keys:

A twist on this drill is to have both players down in a low 4-point stance with their shoulders fit tightly together. Using our foot fire drill technique, each player attempts to drive the other back into the blocking dummy. I like to have the remaining linemen standing on both sides cheering. But you could also have the linemen standing on either side holding hand shields to 'remind' the competitors to stay straddling the board. You may want to have a trophy or a special arm band or hand pad that the winner gets to wear until the next King of the Boards competition.

Wall Drill

Objective:
- To teach the play-side line how to fit and reach their landmarks.
- To develop timing and a uniformed explosive movement.

Set up:
  1.   Put four linemen foot-to-foot as if they are the play-side for the TKO WALL (Figure 5N).
  2.   The coach will face them four yards in front and it helps to have a coach a few yards back as well to watch footwork.

Figure 5N. Alignment and action for the Wall Drill.

Execution:
  1.   On DOWN they get into a 3-point stance.
  2.   On GO they fire off using L.E.G the center sets the base and the rest of the line gets to their landmark using running shoulder blocks as they move on air.
  3.   ON RESET all linemen get back to the line and get into a ready position.

Coaching Keys:

This can be done during game warm-ups as well.

Initially we do this as a walk through, then build up to half speed, and then to full speed.

You can add 'half line' defensive lines (odd/even) with bags to work on forming the wall against fronts as well.

How to Teach Pulling

A key component to our blocking system is pulling. We must be able to effectively pull blockers to the POA. One thing that you have to stress to your linemen is that the offense requires the linemen to pull vertically and not along the LOS like most offenses. I teach this using a progression that first shows our linemen how to move as they pull and then how to block as they move. One of the key elements of this offense is the ability to get more blockers at the POA than the defense has to defend. Typically this can be accomplished in a variety of ways, e.g. using motion, using formation (unbalanced fronts), or by pulling. The YDW uses all of these to get as many players to the point of attack as possible. This not only increases the effectiveness of our power game but it also increases the effectiveness of our misdirection plays and influence plays as well.

Pull and Seal Drill

Objective:
Teaches the pulling linemen how the mechanics of pulling for the seal scheme work.

Set up:
1)   On a yard line, four cones will be set up at a 45 degree angle that is three feet high at the end and five feet wide. This is the simulated wall as it is moving towards the back-side (Figure 5O).
2)   The BSG (near the first cone) will align foot-to-foot with the cone.
3)   When BSG and BST are running this they will be foot-to-foot.

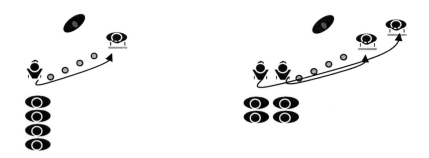

Figure 5O. Alignment and action for the Pull and Seal Drill.

Execution:
1)   At the end of the TKO WALL will be a defender with a shield facing the LOS (about one foot back).
2)   The puller lines up so he is foot-to-foot with the cone. On "DOWN" he immediately gets into a 3-point stance.
3)   On "GO" he drops his near foot as he explodes his near elbow back - both occur at the same time. Then he explodes his far foot forward as he stays low and sprints down the LOS keeping his hips and feet as square as possible to the LOS. He stays tight to the cones (linemen). He should literally brush the cones as he goes up into the tunnel.
4)   As the puller reaches the end of the TKO WALL the coach tells the defender to "STEP" and he will step up and meet the puller delivering a blow with the shield. The puller must LOAD his body, EXPLODE and GO as he drives the defender out of the tunnel (using a running shoulder block).

Once everyone goes through it individually, you should pair them up as a guard and a tackle. They should go through the same routine wherein the guard executes the drill exactly as described above, while the tackle follows him so close that he can put his inside arm on the guard's outside shoulder. There are now two defenders with the other defender just outside of the first defender and slightly back. The tackle must also stay tight to the cones. As the guard makes his block, the tackle must come off his outside shoulder and take the next defender and execute it as the guard does (LEG).

Coaching Keys:

As they develop proficiency with this drill, have one defender align at the top of the tunnel but outside, with another defender inside. The BSG should take the outside defender (outside- in) and the BST should take the inside defender (inside-out).

Pull and Go Drill (This is a Tim Murphy DW Drill)

Objective:
To teach the blocker not to stop and search for a block as he hits the tunnel. If there is no defender he goes vertical and makes a lane for the runner.

Set Up:
Use a similar cone set up as in the Pull and Seal drill, but with an additional three yard box using cones at the end of cone "TKO" wall. Use two defenders in the box (one in the middle and one at the end of the box – Figure 5P).

Execution:
    1)   On DOWN the lineman will get into a good 3-point stance.
    2)   On GO the lineman will fire off, execute a good pull, and get vertical down the tunnel.
    3)   As the lineman hits the tunnel, the coach will signal the first defender to either move left or right out of the box, or hold position. If he moves left or right, the blocker should ignore him and hit the next defender; thereby making a vertical lane for the runner, instead of chasing the defender that vacated.

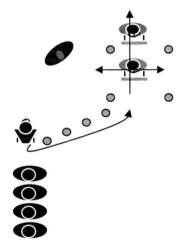

Figure 5P. Alignment and action for the Pull and Go Drill.

Coaching Keys:

You can also do this with BSG and BST while using four defenders. The left defender moves out of the box to the left, while the right defender moves out of the box to the right - they either MOVE or SIT.

Pulling Competition

Objective:

    1)   To teach the pulling linemen to explode off the LOS, get vertical, move into the tunnel, and push vertically to create a vertical lane for the runner.
    2)   Teaches the pulling linemen to be competitive and develops a desire to succeed.

Set Up:

    1)   Set up on a yard line using the basic tunnel cones. Linemen align facing each other, far enough apart to put a three yard square at the end of the tunnels (Figure 5Q).
    2)   A BSG and BST pair will line up on each side.

Execution:

    1)   On DOWN both sides will get into a good 3-point stance.
    2)   On GO they will both fire off and execute a good pull and get vertical.
    3)   Both will attempt to beat the other team into the box and drive the other pair out of the box vertically.
    4)   First team to get to the other side creating a vertical lane is the winner.

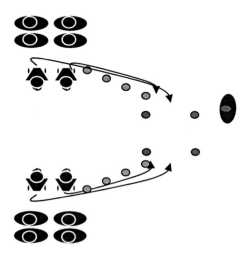

Figure 5Q. Alignment and action for the Pulling Competition Drill.

Coaching Keys:

This gets very competitive at times so be prepared to control the drill.

Pull and Kick Drill

Objective:

    1)   To teach the back-side pulling linemen how to pull in the kick scheme.

Set Up:

    1)   On a yard line using the basic tunnel cone set up, the BSG will align foot-to-foot on the first tunnel cone (Figure 5R).

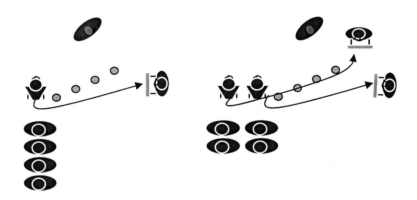

Figure 5R. Alignment and action for the Pull and Kick Drill

Execution:

    1)   On DOWN the linemen will get into a good 3-point stance.

    2)   On GO the BSG will fire off and pull down the LOS at a slight upward angle toward the defender at the end of the line (bottom of the tunnel), aiming for his up field/near arm pit, and kicking him out as he wheels his rear end into the hole (up field) to seal off the defender from the runner.

    3)   Once everyone gets a chance to work on kick outs then pair them up into BSG/BST teams and have them switch every rep so that they both get time kicking out. BSG will kick out and BST will pull and seal inside out.

Coaching Keys:

Remember the BSG kicks out the first defender to cross his face, while the BB leads and blocks inside – out (what the BSG normally does on seal) and the BST pulls and seals inside – out.

Pull and Kick Out First to Show

Objective:
1)   To teach the BSG to kick out the first defender to cross his face.
2)   To teach the BST to pull vertically on the TKO wall and not chase the kick out block so that he can make a vertical lane.

Set Up:
1)   Use the same set up as the Pull and Kick drill.
2)   Have both defenders align together about two yards apart, facing the LOS at the top of the tunnel (Figure 5S).

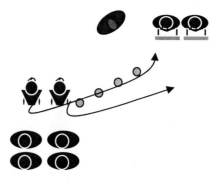

Figure 5S. Alignment and action for the Pull and Kick Out First to Show Drill

Execution:
1)   On DOWN the BSG/BST get into a good 3-point stance.
2)   On GO they fire off. The BSG pulls and looks for the first defender to cross his face. The coach will signal which defender goes down to cross the LOS and the BSG must kick him out using a proper kick out method.
3)   The BST will pull vertically; if the defender gets in his path he will block him (first defender). He will go vertical and not chase the wide defender.

Coaching Key:

This simulates how the BSG will kick out and isolate another defender outside of the kick out and that the BST should not chase a outside defender (that is not his man) and he should go vertical. But if the man is in his tunnel he should take him vertical and drive him out of the lane.

Step Through Drill

Objective:

1)   To teach our Center, Pulling Side Guard (PSG), and Pulling Side Tackle (PST) how to execute the initial footwork to climb the TKO wall and make their blocks.

2)   Teaches the interior line to work as a unit when pulling.

Set Up:

1)   Align a center, PSG, and PST.   Align a defender over PSG and two defenders outside of center to simulate a kick out defender for PSG and seal defender for PST.

2)   At first align the two outside defenders a little wide and as the pullers get good at operating in tight quarters tight up the defenders (Figure 5T).

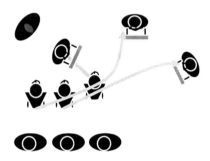

Figure 5T. Alignment and action for the Step Through Drill.

Execution:

1)   On DOWN from CENTER all blockers will get into a good stance.

2)   On SET – GO the center will execute his TKO block and drive to his landmark. You can use a ball to simulate a snap and step as well, once they get the footwork down.   The PSG guard will step through the heels of the center and climb up and execute a kick out on the outside defender. He should LEG as he makes contact. The PST should follow the PSG and has he climbs the center's play side hip he should go vertical and block the defender hitting his inside shoulder and wall him off so that he isolates him away from the edge of the wall (where the WB will be).

3)   Each 3 man group should work for 3 to 5 reps.

Coaching Key:

This simulates the footwork and approach of the center and two pullers so they get used to operating in tight spaces. At first focus on technique and then work on speeding it up so that it happens explosively.

Cut-off/Super Man Drill

Objective:

1)   To teach the BSTE to make a proper (technically sound and safe) cut-off block at the LOS on the back-side. .

Set up:

1)   Line up on a yard line in a good 3-point stance, facing two defenders with bags simulating an interior defenders on the LOS (across from linemen and off-set, Figure 5U).
2)   Start at one yard away and work out to three yards away.
3)   You can work on one, two, three, or four depending on how many bags you have.

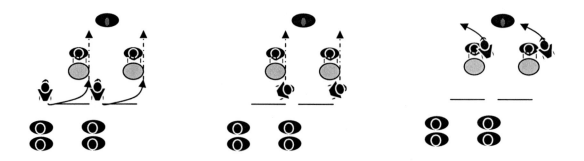

Figure 5U. Alignment and action for the Cut-off/Super Man Drill.

Execution:

1)   On DOWN the linemen will get into a good three point stance.
2)   On GO they will explode off the LOS pushing off on the outside foot and diving towards the Center's near hip as flat as possible.
3)   As soon as they land they will get into a bear crawl and go vertical up the field until they pass the LOS and rise up and turn Back-side and cut-off the first defender coming across the second level. The holders should step the bag one step as they blocker explodes down the LOS.

Alternative:

1)   If you are not comfortable or simply don't like using a diving cut off block (aka: shoeshine) than you can use a severe down block using the exact same aiming point (near hip of the center).

2)   The down block will use the same exact LEG progression as the TKO blocks but his landmark is the near hip of the center.

3)   When he makes contact with a defender he will get his face mask into the far arm pit of the defender and wheel his butt towards the center to cutoff his path to the runner.

Coaching Key:

This is the way we teach the cut-off block. We watch the blocks to make sure they are not aiming for the bags but the center's hip so that they don't hurt a defender on game day by accidentally hitting a knee. We stress aiming for the center's near hip and because we are at depth on the LOS the cut-off works really well for us.

Snapping Drill

Objective:

1)   To teach each lineman how to direct snap (or indirect snap/under center) the ball.

Set up:

1)   Take all of your linemen and put them in pairs with any odd man out working with a pair or a spare coach/parent (Figure 5V).

2)   Have one lineman act as a snapper and one as a back with 4 yards of separation between them.

3)   Direct snap the ball back on the Coaches DOWN SET "GO" and the back catch it.

4)   That back then turns around and becomes the center and the snapper becomes the back. Repeat the process 5 times each.

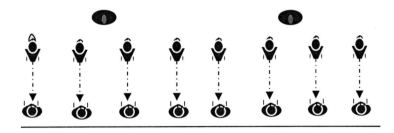

Figure 5V. Alignment and Action for the Snapping Drill.

Execution:

1) The snapper should hold the ball with either one or two hands with the ball out in front of him slightly. He should be in a good two point stance with his head up.

2) On DOWN (eventually the snapper can call down when the coach says ready; once he confirms all snappers and backs are ready). The snapper checks the back for depth.

3) On GO the snapper will snap the ball straight back towards the knees of the back. He should concentrate on snapping the ball on line, so that his knuckles slightly drag the grass; as his forearm makes contact with his inner thigh he releases the ball. The nose of the ball will rise slightly due to the wrist and forearm, so it is important that the snapper rides the top of the grass at the release so the ball stays low.

4) This low direct snap ensures that even a bad snap will simply hit the ground in front of the back and not go over his head.

Coaching Keys:

This is a quick 5 minute drill that allows you to teach all of your linemen how to execute a direct snap and you can do this with the indirect snap (under center as well). The more balls you have the more pairs you can use, so we often ask every one of our linemen to have a regulation ball in their bag with their name on it so we can do this one drill. The purpose of the drill is to ensure every lineman learns the skill of snapping. We do it using a cumulative process, knowing that our starting and backup centers will get a large number of snaps. Moreover, doing this every practice allows our other linemen to gain this skill over time. This way you will never be short a center and will always have a large body of players from which to choose to snap the ball.

Drill Order of Importance

The table below lists the drills and how important they are to the initial install and improving technique. This will give you an idea on how to set-up your practice schedule for your linemen. Basically during OFFENSIVE INDYS the linemen work on these drills; when we go to OFFENSIVE TEAM, we work on schemes as a whole or in half lines to develop timing with the backs and pullers.

Drill	Initial Install	Improvement	Notes
Stance	xxx		
Kneel & L.E. Drill	xxx	XXX	Improves lower body strength and quickness
3-point L.E. Drill	XXX	XXX	
3-point L.E.G Drill	XXX	XXX	
Foot Fire Drill		XXX	Improves lower body and core strength
Shoulder Block Drill		XXX	
Running Shoulder Block Drill		XXX	
Down Block Drill	XXX	XXX	
Combo Block Drill		XXX	
King of the Boards		XXX	
Wall Drill	XXX	XXX	
Pull and Seal	XXX	XXX	
Pull and Go		XXX	
Pulling Competition		XXX	
Pull and Kick	XXX	XXX	
Pull and Kick Out First to Show		XXX	
Step Through Drill		XXX	
Cut-off Drill	XXX	XXX	
Snapping Drill	XXX	XXX	

Chapter 6
Wedge Blocking Concepts

Wedge blocking is our basic scheme to attack the interior (A gaps) and it is a blocking scheme that requires every lineman in the wedge to work as a team. It can, if properly taught and executed, be a powerful blocking scheme that can force a defense to respect the inside running game. Once the defense starts to stack the front to stop the wedge, your offense will realize multiple options of attack to the outside and in the passing game..

At the younger age levels (ages five to eight) this can be the single most effective and devastating scheme against a defense. At the older levels, defenses can adapt and defend it - if it is a stand-alone scheme. However, as a complimentary scheme, incorporated with ABC and perimeter schemes, it becomes an essential component to a very sound and effective blocking scheme combination that allows the offense to attack every gap in devastating manner.

What Is Wedge Blocking?

1. The Wedge is a very simple blocking scheme that can be built into a highly successful series of plays.

2. The line collapses on an apex blocker; the idea is to punch a hole into the first level of the defense by having the blockers burst into the breach with the runner in the middle of the wedge.

3. Builds offensive line unity unlike any other scheme.

4. Sets-up other plays in the series. When the defense sells out on the wedge it opens up other plays.

5. Allows optimal opportunity to interchange linemen.

6. Can be used with a power or deception play. It is surprisingly deceptive.

7. May be used with smaller or weaker players.

8. Demoralizes to the other team.

9. Always an offensive line favorite.

10. Weaker backs can run in the wedge. The backs become interchangeable, as the key component is the line.

Key Points of the Line Running Wedge:

1. Center must fire out on a NT and drive up field.

2. If there is no man over the center he aims for the end zone straight up the field. He fires out and then takes a half step and lets the rest of the line form and drive him up the field. (We don't shift our wedge from odd to even fronts – Center/PSG).

3. The guards, out to the TEs, must step laterally to the inside (slide inside) and get their inside shoulder into the near rib cage of the adjacent lineman. They must also place their outside hand on the near shoulder pad while the inside hand presses on the lower back. It might take the tackle and ends two steps to get fit. They must attempt, at all costs, not to make contact with any defender as they move down inside.

4. As soon as they fit into the wedge they move up field. It should be one instant movement. Slide and move up field as a unified body in two to three steps.

5. If the wedge slows or breaks apart, all the blockers must target a defender and block that defender - like an upward burst of blockers with the runner breaking through the explosion for the open field.

Coaching Keys:

The main reason for keeping the Center as the main POA (if you have the Center and both guards become the apex of the wedge then you are essentially teaching three types of wedges) is that otherwise, the center and guards would be required to identify an ODD/EVEN front, and then identify who should be the apex of the wedge. Furthermore, if you use a guard as the apex, then you must be aware that the back-side now must travel more distance to form the wedge. It is simpler and therefore preferable to teach a CENTER APEX WEDGE and rep it until the line is really good at it.

Challenges to the Wedge

- If the Wedge is not forming fast enough or moving too slow, this may allow perimeter defenders to bring down the runner from behind.
- If the Center (point of the wedge) is not firing off efficiently, this may cause the wedge to falter and fail to form properly. (This is a key problem and must be recognized quickly).
- A key defensive threat to the Wedge is being submarined (or cut) by a NT or A gap defender(s).
- Another key defensive threat is linemen being pulled from the wedge by the defensive line, in an attempt to prevent it from forming.
- If the Wedge is being penetrated and defenders are getting to the ball carrier, this is typically evidence that the Wedge is not forming efficiently, i.e. the wedge blockers must slide and fit into the wedge quickly- Inside shoulder into ribs, inside hand on center of lower back, outside hand to back of inside shoulder. The key component is the shoulder into the ribs. They must get that fit quickly and firmly, the remaining components serve to improve the seal. The TE to OT mesh is very important and can be an area prone to complications. Make sure the TE is meshing quickly as he slides down. The OT to OG is the next spot and the OT must step and mesh quickly as well.

Submarining, Frogging, and/or Bearcrawling Defenders

Submarining – A defender that tries to attack a blocker's legs and trip or collapse him, thereby disrupting the wedge.

Frogging – A defender in a three or four point stance that explodes through the legs of the blocker (looks like a frog as he leaps on all fours).

Bearcrawling – Another tactic where a defender tries to crawl through a gap (normally the A and/or B gap).

These are all handled the same way, as described below.

- "Submarining" defenders can be a real problem initially, the key to discouraging this approach, is to keep attacking with the wedge. A defender throwing himself at the feet of the wedge is ultimately in big trouble. He is going to get run over repeatedly, and by a lot of players.
- Normally a "frogging" defender will do this once or twice, and typically he may stop the wedge for little gain; but it doesn't take long for that defender to realize that he is going to get stomped on and run over if he keeps doing it. Eventually, these defenders realize this is a tactic that cannot be sustained as the wedge running him over conditions him; the key is to stay with the wedge as this will wear out the interior line as they throw themselves at the wedge in an attempt to stop it.
- The wedge integrates the offensive line into a well supported single powerful entity that disintegrates the defensive line, breaking down individual

linemen with time. If you stay with it, by the end of the game the wedge has a wearing down effect and this will benefit your base package. SAB schemes become easier to run; as the defense attempts to stop the wedge they become vulnerable and more easily angle blocked. Jimmy Glasgow, a really good DW youth coach, has a saying "Take the Wedge and you give me the EDGE; take the EDGE and you give me the WEDGE". To attack the EDGE (and PERIMETER) you must develop a legitimate threat to the middle; the WEDGE provides a formidable threat that must be addressed, rendering the defense vulnerable at the EDGE and on the PERIMETER.

- The blockers must keep their KNEES up and legs PUMPING when this occurs. Run the defenders over and condition them to not hit the ground in front of the wedge.

Penetration

- It is important to stress that the guards must mesh with the center correctly and drive the center forward. "Slide inside and drive!" The initial center-guard mesh is all-important to the success of the wedge.
- The Tackle to Guard mesh can cause problems, particularly if the tackles get lazy, are slow, or not executing the footwork correctly. They have a longer step than the guards, so it is important to emphasize taking that slide step inside.
- The TE to Tackle Mesh is where the majority of your penetration problems are going to occur. This is because the slide that the TE must take is long and he must be quick to maintain the mesh. He must slide and drive. You must have a good athlete at TE, as he must get into the wedge as efficiently as the interior linemen even though there is more ground to cover.
- A good rule of thumb is the center can be the least athletic; the farther you move out to the edge the more athletic the player needs to be to fulfill his job.

Linemen Being Pulled from the Wedge

- One adjustment that the defense will commit to executing is having the interior defensive linemen engage either the guard or tackle, and attempt to pull them away from the wedge and thereby disrupt the formation of the wedge.
- It is important to teach the offensive linemen to use the outside arm to stiff arm the defender using one of two techniques.
  - o The first alternative is to drive the palm of the hand into the bottom of the facemask driving the defender's head down into his chest as he moves into the wedge. This creates separation and denies the defender the ability to react to the blockers movements. The strike should be rapid with closed fist knuckles up with the base of the palm striking the bottom of the mask.
  - o The other alternative is to use the same striking method aimed at the inside arm pit of the defender and turn his inside shoulder up field, creating separation at the same time. This makes it nearly impossible for him to pull the blocker as his shoulder is turned up field. Again, the strike should be rapid and aimed at the soft part of the arm pit.

Troubleshooting the Wedge

- It is important to stress the little things for the wedge to be effective.
- Every blocker, except the point (Center), must work to not engage any defender, but instead engage the next man inside and seal the wedge while going up field.
- Linemen in the Wedge must lock their inside shoulder to the outside ribcage to stop penetration as they form and move up field. They must stay connected.
- If the wedge stops, it is dead. It must move forward; when it slows or breaks up, it must explode up field in a burst.
- The runner must stay small in the wedge and explode up field if and when daylight shows.

Key Points to Running the Wedge

- The play of the Center is the key to the success of your Wedge. If your wedge is breaking down quickly, first examine the Center play. Verify that the Center is charging forward and engaging the NT. A common flaw with all young linemen, is a tendency to "stand up" rather than fire out. The Center must fire out following the snap, and get going forward to allow the wedge to form as the entire line moves forward. Otherwise, it will just turn into a self-defeating log jam in the middle.
- If the Center is not slide stepping and allowing the rest of the line to push him on an even front, then he will cause the wedge to break apart before it forms. I always try to place a kid at Center that can do both well, - and he must have a high football IQ. The better your Center, the better your wedge will be.
- The Wedge "Fit" is very important to the success of the wedge as well. It allows the unit of blockers to move as one impenetrable force. The fit is achieved by having the exterior lineman (those outside of the center or pivot man) slide inside (not forward) and fit their inside shoulder into the inside man's ribcage as they get their inside arm up with their hand pressing on the lower back. This locks the players in. As they work up field they must work to get their outside hand onto the inside blocker's shoulder pad (on the near back). The wedge is a very effective blocking scheme, but you must stress the little things, the details, for it to work effectively. The blockers must slide inside and behind the center and lock shoulders quickly as they drive forward. They must get that inside hand on the lower back and press (Mesh). The fewer defenders they engage as they move inside and forward, the more likely an effective and devastating Wedge will form.
- They must lock there inside shoulder to the outside rib cage of the center and allow no penetration to occur. The wedge must always be moving forward. Once it stops the play is dead in the water.
- Once the runner feels the wedge slowing, he must find a crack of daylight and hit it with a burst up field. While in the wedge, the runner must drive into the back of the center and stay small behind him. This reduces the chance of him being seen by the defense and enhances complimentary play actions and misdirection off of the wedge action.

- The footwork is essential for the wedge. The blockers must take a slide step and engage their shoulder into the ribs of the next inside blocker quickly. They have to keep sliding and moving forward until the wedge fully forms. Once it forms they must get their knees high and stay low so that Frogging/Submarining defenders get run over, and defenders trying to slow the wedge by barreling into it are lifted up and back as the wedge drives forward. I am reiterating the fine points for a reason, as you can see, I am a stickler for details, but you have to be when coaching and especially if you expect the wedge to be effective.

Ball Carrier

- The concept of the Wedge is simple, however running the wedge takes a bit of time and practice as it is an art of sorts. It is NOT a dive play; it requires power, patience and acceleration. We start with the Back getting the snap and running right to the back of the Center. He should actually push on the Center's back visible leaning in with the ball-side shoulder. He must STAY IN THE WEDGE until it disintegrates. The ball carrier must be patient and avoid going around either end or looking for an off-tackle bubble. He must stay in the wedge and keep his legs pumping, knees high and moving forward, until the wedge breaks up; then he must sprint to daylight. Stay inside; don't run parallel, it either breaks right up the gut or at a very slight angle. Often the daylight does not appear until 10-15 yards downfield, so he'll need to be patient and stay in the wedge as it churns downfield eating up yardage. Until he sees daylight, he'll need to stay low and push forward. When feeling pressure, he needs keep both hands over the ball.
- We stress to our ball carriers, that if they do not stay in the wedge, they don't carry the ball. Natural inclination is to break it outside or look for the hole. In the wedge there is no hole - it opens up downfield.

Wedge Base Blocking Drills

Wedge Blocking Progression

I use a drill progression to teach my linemen how to block in the wedge scheme. It is a very simple progression that first teaches them how the wedge looks and works, and then teaches them how to form and seal the wedge, and then move it downfield.

Formed Wedge on LOS facing a NT Shows them how the wedge looks and moves. Work for five and then 10 yards (Figure 6A).

1)   The center fires off the ball into the dummy.
2)   The guards mesh into the center and repeat; emphasis that it is now a three on one block.
3)   Add the tackles and repeat the process.
4)   Add the ends and repeat the process.

The preceding steps allow you to trouble shoot the mesh portion of the Wedge, one position at a time. You should repeat the process against a MLB that is four yards back to teach the center how to "slow step" to let the Wedge mesh.

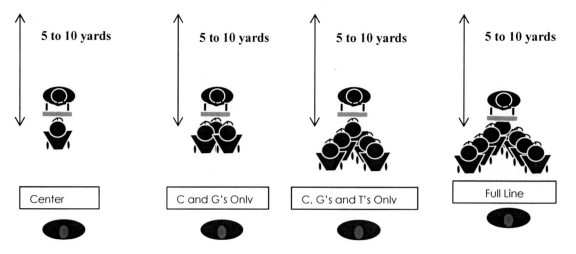

Figure 6A. Formed Wedge and Eyes Wide Shut

Formed Wedge Eyes Wide Shut on LOS facing NT Center's eyes are opened, but others are not. This teaches them to stay together by feel. Work for 10 yards (Figure 6A).

    1)   When initially teaching this you can use the process above.
    2)   Also used when teaching against an even front as well.

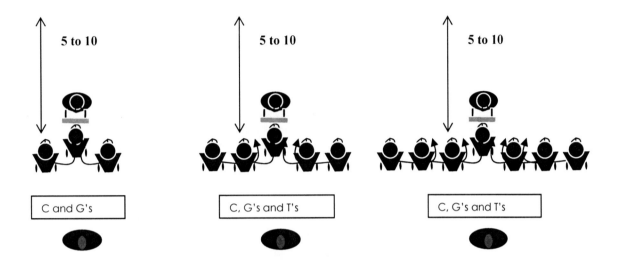

Figure 6B. Forming the Mesh of the Wedge

Forming the Mesh of the Wedge. This teaches the line how to laterally slide into the wedge and move it forward in as few steps as possible. It should look like an explosion inward and upward (Figure 6B).

    1)   Start with the guards meshing with the center; bird dog it, slow motion, full speed.
    2)   Add the tackles as the above. The tackles will likely have to take two lateral steps.
    3)   Add the ends as the above. The ends will likely have to take two to three lateral steps.

Over/Under – Get into the wedge and freeze. Work on first step, second step and then getting into a full mesh.

From LOS – Full speed on NT. Work for 10 yards and then as far as it will go.

From LOS – Full speed on NT Eyes Wide Shut. Work for five yards. If they can go live from a formation and do this drill, then you have an awesome wedge unit.

Wedge - Knees and Feet Up Drill

Objective: To work on getting the wedge to explode forward in a compact form that punches through the defense (Figure 6C).

•   Two blocking bags lined up horizontally on LOS with the top of the bag at the guard's outside hip and then extending towards the TE.

•   Stress getting the Legs and Knees up for the entire group – to include the runner when running the full offense.

•   The bags should roll out of the way as the line collapses inside to form the wedge – if everyone is getting their feet and knees up. Work for 10 yards.

•   Don't let them jump over it. The TE and OT's will try this so be watching for it. Make the entire wedge punches through the gap of the two bags.

•   Start slowly and build up to an explosive sprint so that the wedge explodes through the gap as tightly as possible as an entire unit.

•   The more compact the wedge, the stronger the wedge becomes. It should look like a narrow arrowhead.

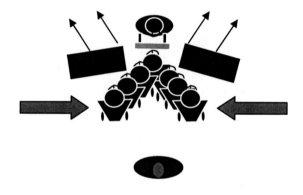

Figure 6C. Wedge – Knees and Feet Up Drill

Explode Drill

- From LOS (5/7 linemen) (Figure 6D) – On "GO" the wedge forms and moves down field, driving full speed on the NT. About 15 yards out, set up three to five defenders with shields. The BB (ball carrier for this drill) stays in the wedge until it slows or shows a crack. Force the Wedge to work for five to 10 yards and then as the BB feels the wedge slowing or he sees a seam/crack of daylight he yells "EXPLODE". On "EXPLODE", the wedge should burst open attacking the downfield defenders.
- The runner must explode up the field into daylight (straight up field). The concept here is to drive the wedge into the defense and past the line backer level. As the unified Wedge punches into the second level, the line explodes and engages any defender down field as the runner breaks up field to the end zone.
- This makes the Wedge a home run play!

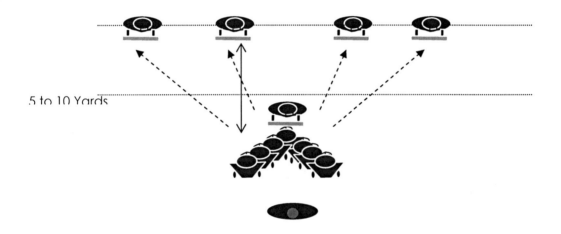

5 to 10 Yards

Figure 6D. Explode Drill

Adjustments

Cut Wedge

- If your mesh between your OG-OT and/or TE-OT is being penetrated due to a hard rush, and you don't have the ability to trap, you can use the Cut Wedge.
- Simply have the TE's and OT's shoeshine to cut-off the defenders as the G-C-G forms the wedge with the back tucked in behind the Center.

Wedge with Five

- You can easily wedge with only the five interior lineman and send the TE's on passing routes, fake-blocking routes, or to block secondary players.

Chapter 7
Perimeter Blocking Concepts

TKO and Wedge blocking will make up about 75% of your offensive blocking schemes, but as teams compress in on your offense in an attempt to stop your interior and off tackle running game, you must have the ability to get outside - particularly when they show you two defenders or less in the perimeters. Having sound and cohesive perimeter schemes that work in conjunction with TKO and WEDGE will make this offense even deadlier and much more effective. The key to being successful with this offense is the ability to determine what the perimeter triangle is doing, thereby enabling you to exploit their weakness immediately. The perimeter itself is an area of great importance; when a defensive end is crashing and the outside backer is sitting on or blitzing the tunnel, often only one defender (the CB) is left to cover the perimeter. As a series based offense we must have the ability to exploit these types of defensive schemes to maximize our offense.

This next chapter discusses (1) the 'monster' sweep blocking concept, (2) how the wide scheme works in the perimeter game and the reverse play, (3) the pin blocking concept (covered/uncovered) used as an alternative to the monster sweep and wide schemes, (4) how we get to the perimeter using the wedge block scheme to influence the defense, and (5) how we block the perimeter of the wedge to get outside.

Bear in mind that most youth defenses are going to be set up to stop the big play in youth football. The toss sweep, quick pitch and the lead QB bootleg are really the home run plays of most youth offenses and for this reason most defenses are set up to stop the sweep to the perimeter and force offenses to drive the field on them with the notion that most teams cannot maintain a consistent drive and be successful from one series to the next. The Double Wing is vastly different in this regard as the focus is on execution and maintaining drives to control the clock. Consequently, defenses that are overly committed to protecting the perimeter (by design) must adjust on the fly (because they often don't scout), or deviate to something that is different from the base defense in order to stop the core plays and the core DW offense. When this occurs, the defense begins to compress hard and fast to the inside (Figure 7A), often leaving only one or two defenders in the perimeter box. This results in opportunities to successfully attack the outside and break ball carriers into the open field. These opportunities must be exploited as they arise in order to fully counter and/or take advantage of what the defense is trying to do. Often, if you can break one or two of these plays in a game, it is enough to break the back of the defense. Timely play calls can also induce mass confusion on their sideline as they attempt to stop the dam from bursting - as you hit them inside, off tackle and outside. Little do they know you are simply reacting to their adjustments and miscalculations.

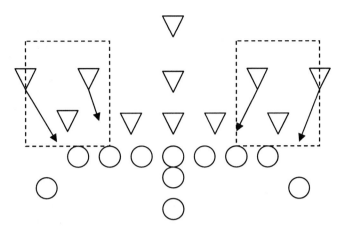

Figure 7A. When you see this will you be ready to handle it?

Monster Sweep Scheme

The monster sweep is one of our core plays and it is nothing more than a power sweep designed to get the ball outside when the defense decides to compress the edge. It relies on pulling the maximum amount of blockers around the edge (Figure 7B) and getting the runner up field through sheer force of numbers, as the defense attempts to compress down on the edge and close off the tunnel.

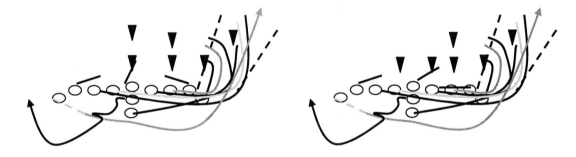

Figure 7B. Monster Sweep against odd (left) and even (right) fronts.

Both of the following must occur for this play to be successful: 1) you must see two or less in the perimeter box as the WB SEAL develops, and 2) at least two of the three perimeter defenders must be vacating their perimeter duties to stop the interior and/or edge play inside (contain, alley, force).

The key block for this play is the PSWB as he must seal the EMLOS to the inside. He has to do this by taking a lateral step with his outside foot so that it aims at the outside hip of the defender. He then must attack the outside arm pit/hip of the defender. As he engages the defender, he must wheel his rear end around to seal the defender inside. When properly executed, the defender has no way of getting outside, since he is now sealed off from the perimeter. It is very rare for a defender to fight our wingback down the line to string the play out because we are not a sweep based team and often by the time we run a sweep play the end is already committing inside. The PSWB must attempt to drive that EMLOS as far inside as possible, as this makes it easier for the play side tackle and guard to pull around and form the rest of the sweep wall.

The next most important block is delivered by the BB. He is the blocker that will read the force defender (corner normally). He must get to that defender ASAP. If the force defender is allowed to compress the play in the backfield, it will blow up. If the force is wide, the BB needs to eat up space quickly and then wall him off. As he makes contact with the force defender, the BB should mirror and then wheel the defender off from the runner and the open field. If the force is off the line of scrimmage and on the outside hip of the EMLOS, then the BB will turn up field and get vertical attacking the outside arm pit of the defender. As he makes contact, he should wheel his butt outside to seal off the force defender. Never call the monster sweep (or any sweep) with a *DE and a CB* on the LOS *outside the EMLOS*; it is a recipe for disaster. Rather, be patient and break the defense down by attacking the middle and edge. As the defense condenses to reinforce the interior – this will open the outside game.

The PSTE, PSG and PST work as a team; the alignment of the next defensive lineman inside of the EMLOS will determine the PSTE's action. If he is head up on the PSTE, then the PSTE should execute a jewel block on that defender. by Aiming his inside shoulder at the outside inner thigh of the defender, the PSTE should literally explode into the inner thigh forcing the defender to protect his lower body and his "jewels". This will cause him to collapse backwards allowing the PST and PSG to fold around him and completely seal off the inside (literally form a TKO wall off the PSTE's near hip). If the next defensive lineman is inside the EMLOS he simply cuts-off (shoe shines) the defender and the PST and PSG fold around him and form the TKO wall.

The Center, when opposed by a NT, must jewel block him to the play-side. If he faces an even front he executes a cut-off to the play-side, at a more up field angle to ensure he doesn't collide with the PSTE. The Center is closer to the LOS and therefore he should go over the top to avoid crossing paths with the PSTE, as the PSTE is set deeper than the Center at the snap. In this case, the Center should be aiming for the near hip of the corner. We simply tell the Center that he cuts-off at his shoulder laterally.

Backside guard and tackle (pulling guard and pulling tackle) will pull play side staying tight to the LOS. If they encounter any leakage, they will plug it up by attacking the far arm pit and wheeling their hips towards the goal line. If engaged by a defender penetrating the line, they must drive that defender back; otherwise they stay flat to the LOS and go vertical as they see the hip of the PSWB, PST, and PSG. As they turn vertical, they create a vertical lane to the end zone, thus the runner has an alley created by the vertical lanes of the guard and tackle along with the boundary. The pulling backside linemen need to scrape the outside hip of the PSWB and go vertical ASAP. If any defender crosses their face, they must drive him to the end zone while wheeling their butt to the inside to wall the defender off.

Finally, the backside tight end will cut off the backside defensive linemen, aiming for the near hip of the Center and then working up field to wall off any backside pursuit. If OVER is called, the PST and BST form the sweep wall; while the PSG and BSG form the vertical lane (essentially the BST and PSG exchange roles).

Half Line Monster Sweep Drill

Objective:

    1)   To develop proper play-side technique and timing on the monster sweep.

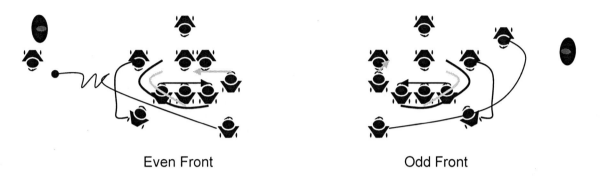

Even Front   Odd Front

Figure 7C. Half Line Monster Sweep Drill

Set up:

    1)   Set up for half line drills as illustrated in above (Figure 7C). One should be ODD and one should be EVEN.
    2)   Should use a Center, PSG, PST, PSTE, PSWB and BB. You run two teams one to each side to maximize reps.

Execution:

    1)   On DOWN all players get into a good stance.
    2)   On GO *defensive* linemen execute GET OFF attempting to penetrate across the LOS while the EMLOS squats on the LOS or crashes inside (either one). The LB will attempt to crash the C gap.
    3)   On GO the *offense* will execute their techniques on the play-side.

Variation:

    1)   Include the QB (in a gun as an extra vertical blocker) and a Safety
    2)   Include TB/motion WB with ball (have him place it on the ground in front of him so on GO he picks it up and runs.

Coaching Keys:

You can do this with cones that are static at first and then add players at half speed, and then full speed. This is a great way to develop the proper mechanics and timing on this play.

WB Wide Reverse Scheme

The reverse scheme is nothing more than the double hand-off counter. In most modern Double Wing team's system the double hand off is an inside hand off attacking the C gap or edge. I have found the normal inside handoff WB counter from the QB to be effective and I just never thought that teaching two plays that do essentially the same thing was an efficient use of time. Instead, I developed the WB reverse using the double handoff in a different way. I use it when I see the back-side defenders flowing hard to seal but also crashing the C gap from the outside to stop the counter and chase the seal from the back-side. When I see these efforts and two defenders or less in the perimeter box, then I realize the opportunity to run the WB reverse and get my countering WB to the outside (Figure 7D).

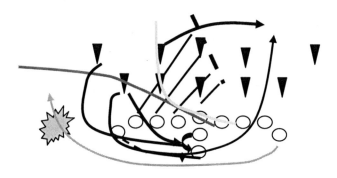

Figure 7D. WB Wide Reverse Scheme

This play is best run when you recognize that the backside EMLOS is collapsing down the LOS chasing the inside hip of the motion WB - this is key. If this is happening, then he is giving up containment and this can be exploited. Secondly, the other two perimeter defenders need to be moving or looking far side reading the flow of the seal. If they are moving flow side then this play is a home run. If they are merely peeking but holding ground, then the play will net you nice yards, but it will have to break away from defenders on the edge to be a homerun.

When the BSG pulls, he must bypass the EMLOS and let him go by (go over the top of him) and then kick out the first defender that he sees outside. The BST pulls and goes vertical staying tight to the wall. If no defender crosses his face, he continues to the end zone to create a vertical lane for the runner. If a defender does cross his face, he attacks the outside arm pit and seals the defender to the backside. The BB and QB get depth as they move backside with the first back (BB in the case of tight) logging the EMLOS and the QB logging the next defender backside which is typically the OLB. These two blocks are key to the success of the play because the EMLOS and OLB and/or CB (if caught inside) are the only defenders that can truly prevent this play from gaining positive yards.

This is a great play to run when the backfield perimeter triangle is over playing the power running game to the away side. Once you see the defensive end vacating inside at a shallow angle and either the OLB or CB vacating their perimeter responsibilities, the defense is vulnerable to the reverse play.

Half Line WB Wide Reverse Drill

Objective: To develop the timing and proper mechanics for the reverse play.

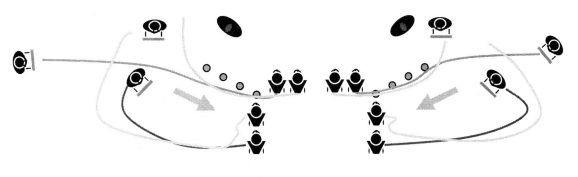

Alley defender wide   Alley defender tight

7E. Half Line WB Wide Reverse Drill.

Set up:

1) Set up for half line drills as illustrated above (Figure 7E). Both groups should have three defenders (FORCE, CONTAIN, and ALLEY) with one having a *tight* ALLEY defender and the other having a *wide* ALLEY defender.
2) The offense should use a BSG, BST, BB and QB. You run two teams one to each side to maximize reps.
3) Once they get the timing down you can add a BSTE and/or WB.
4) Use your multiple backfield alignments to get timing down.

Execution:

1) On DOWN all players get into a good stance.
2) On GO *defensive* linemen follow the coaches hand to signal flow of seal and move accordingly. The PSDE will attack the backfield which will take him the on path that splits the BB and the BSG (same path has if he chased the inside hip of the motion WB).
3) On GO the *offense* will implement their techniques to execute the wide blocking scheme and reverse backfield action.

Variation:

1) Run out of the GUN and swap QB and BB assignments.
2) Have TB run the ball.

Coaching Keys:

You can do this with cones that are static at first and then add players at half speed, and then full speed. This is a great way to develop the proper mechanics and timing on this play. You can rotate players through the drill so that they understand how to handle both looks.

WB Wide Sweep

This is a really nice alternative to the monster sweep. If you are short on practice time and you want to have the full power game installed (interior, edge, and perimeter) then the WB WIDE sweep might be the best alternative. I typically install both, but I feel the monster sweep is the superior sweep scheme and gives me more bang for my buck on the perimeter. However, there are some big differences between the two schemes and I have found that the WIDE SWEEP performs better against certain defensive schemes than the monster sweep. Often the one thing that can really hurt the execution of the monster sweep is an ALLEY defender that is aggressive and can shed blocks breaking down the sweep wall as it being formed by the WB, wall side tackle, and wall side guard. An alternative way to handle this situation, i.e. when you see two in the perimeter box and the OLB is still able to defend the sweep, is to call WIDE SWEEP (Figure 7F). This alternative is particularly effective when an aggressive OLB, having seen the down blocks and the wall form enough times, begins to 'fill' quickly to stop the power play. This renders the OLB vulnerable to being caught inside the wide sweep action. So the down blocks of the TKO wall influence the OLB to fill into the tunnel while the play side wingback logs (walls off) the defensive end. This allows the BSG to pull wide to kick out the force defender while the QB and BB pull and log any other defenders inside or go vertical to the end zone to create a lane for the runner. It is a nice variation on the sweep because you have already taught the blocking scheme; the only thing that really needs to be taught is the variation in the backfield play, which is very similar to the reverse play, though there are differences that need to be addressed. It is a very easy sweep to install; for a new coach it may be preferable to the more powerful monster sweep, at least initially.

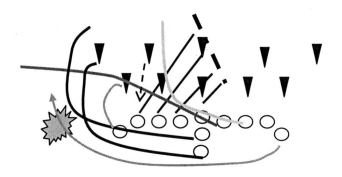

Figure 7F. WB Wide Sweep

The Center to play side will TKO block to their landmarks, opening up the inside of the tunnel which will influence the play side OLB, DE, and CB to collapse the perimeter triangle. The BSG will pull through the center's heels and climb to the second level and kick out the force defender on the outside and drive him to the sideline (go over the top of the EMLOS). If there is no force defender, the BSG will eat up space to ensure there is no contain CB coming down; he'll then turn up field and go vertical to the end zone. The BST will pull and climb the wall, going vertical to the end zone. If any defender crosses his face he will seal them inside. The PSWB will attack the outside arm pit of the defensive end and log/wall him off inside. The QB and BB are responsible for gaining depth and logging the next defenders inside. In the tight formation, the BB will log the next defender past the PSWB and the QB will log the next defender past the BB. If they don't have an immediate threat to wall off, they will go vertical to the end zone to create a lane for the runner. The keys are getting the OLB to fill the edge and getting the DE to crash down into the edge so that both are caught up inside the tunnel isolating the CB one-on-one with the pulling guard thereby giving us two lead blockers.

Half Line WB Wide Sweep Drill

Objective: To develop the timing and proper mechanics for the wide sweep play.

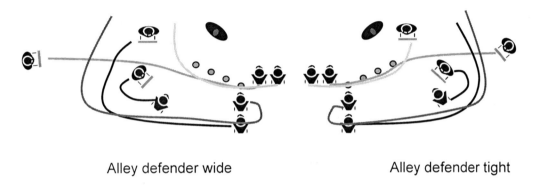

Alley defender wide   Alley defender tight

Figure 7G. Half Line WB Wide Sweep Drill

Set up:

1) Set up for half line drills as illustrated above (Figure 7G). Both groups should have three defenders (FORCE, CONTAIN, and ALLEY) with one group having a *tight* ALLEY defender and the other a *wide* ALLEY defender.
2) Use a BSG, BST, WB, BB, and QB. You should run two teams one to each side to maximize reps.
3) Once they get the timing down you can add a BSTE and/or BSWB.
4) Use your multiple backfield alignments to get the timing down.

Execution:

1) On DOWN, all players get into a good stance.
2) On GO, *defensive* players follow the coaches hand to signal flow of the seal and move accordingly. The PSDE will attack the backfield which will take him on a path that splits the BB and the BSG (same path has if he chased the inside hip of the motion WB).
3) On GO, the *offense* will implement their techniques to execute the wide blocking scheme and reverse backfield action.

Variation:

1) Use Gun formations
2) Use a TB to run the ball (with ball on ground in front of him at snap)

Coaching Keys:

You can do this with cones that are static at first and then add players at half speed, and then full speed. This is a great way to develop the proper mechanics and timing on this play. You can rotate players through the drill so that they understand how to handle both looks.

Pin Blocking Scheme

What Is Pin Blocking?

- Utilizes the Covered/Uncovered concept
- A more aggressive reach blocking technique.
- This scheme can be used as an alternative to our base power sweep in our power series.
- Footwork is not lateral, but vertical allowing the blocker to be aggressive.
- It uses the L.E.G technique with the TURN concept
- Pin block basically tells all the blockers to "PIN" the play-side (outside) shoulder up field by attacking the play side half of the defender's body and then wheeling the hips around so the blocker pins the defender inside.

Key Advantage Points

- Simplifies the reach technique (bucket step/lateral step) to a vertical step that is more aggressive.
- Drives the defender vertically as well as sealing the defender inside.
- Allows us to move from pulling schemes to reach schemes that allow our blockers to get on their defenders much faster.
- Takes advantage of teams attacking our inside gaps due to our ABC and WEDGE concepts.

How it Works

This scheme is used when we need to get the ball to the outside edge without giving the defense a 'pulling' key (Figure 7H). It allows us to hit the outside edge with speed as well as numbers while not pulling the offensive line. It uses the LEG & Turn block to attack the defense in an attempt to pin the play-side shoulder of the play-side defenders while attacking the perimeter. The key to this play is seeing two or less perimeter defenders with only one of them playing contain.

AT MAN – The PSWB is normally the AT MAN unless he is expanded via a tag (LOOSE, BUNCH, TRIPS). The play will be directed at his hip; specifically the outside hip as he pins the first defender inside. The point of attack is the outside hip of the first blocker on the outside of the edge. In a compressed formation that would be the PSWB but in LOOSE, TRIPS, or BUNCH that would be the first blocker on the edge PST or BST (OVER tag)). He uses LEG & TURN or as I like to call it PIN: COVERED/UNCOVERED blocking.

PLAY-SIDE BLOCKER – Every blocker inside the AT MAN to the Center. These blockers must block using the covered/uncovered rule of the PIN block. If it is a LB they must attack the play side arm pit and wheel their hips to the play, effectively cutting off the backer from pursuit. It is important that each play-side blocker takes a good cut off angle to their targeted defender.

BACK-SIDE BLOCKERS – Every blocker on the back-side of the center must use the same rule; if they are 'uncovered' with no backer threatening, they should work up to the next level and cut off the backside corner.

MOAT MAN (Man Outside of AT) – (Force Blocker) – this is normally the BB and his block is determined by the location of the cornerback or last defender on the perimeter. If this defender is wide, the MOAT will kick him out by eating up space quickly, settling down while locking on target, and then driving the defender out to create a vertical seam for the runner. If the cornerback is in close and off the line of scrimmage, the BB will get out wide to attack the outside arm pit of the corner so that he can wall him off.

PIN L.E.G Progression

Note: The PIN L.E.G. Progression is a variation of the L.E.G. progression described in Chapter 5 (page 44), but there are subtle and important differences that should be understood, as we must add the TURN component to this concept, wherein the blockers will 'wheel' their hips when engaging a defender to 'TURN' them inside and seal them off from the perimeter. The steps are as follows:

L - We call the first step the **LOAD STEP** as they have to get that foot up and down fast (literally stomp the ground). They should aim at the outside of the far (outside) toe of the defender with a fast step while staying low (head up, chest on knee). This step will be a little longer than the normal TKO load step but not long enough for the back to rise. The back should not rise up at all on this step. The outside foot of the defender is targeted as it is also the 'near' foot of the defender. They must load their arms on this step quickly (thumbs behind the hips as they cock their arms back at 90 degrees). They must explode out of their stance and into this step with great force.

E - We call the next step the **EXPLODE STEP**; the back foot takes a power step that splits the defender on the inside of his outside thigh. Starting low, the back should raise as the feet, ankles, knees, hips, back, shoulders, elbows and hands explode upward into the body of the defender (chest plate and ribs). It is important to get this second step down as fast as possible as this is the step where first contact is made. The arms/hands should explode into the defender as the foot makes contact with the ground which creates an additional force production via Ground Force Reaction – SYNERGY.

Coaching Keys:

The arms should unload hard into the body so that the defender is literally being punched; with the outside arm ripping the outside funnel of the defender (FUNNEL – outside hip to elbow into the soft part of the arm pit with the heel of the outside hands driving the shoulder up field and back. Aim at the inside forearm into the middle of the breast plate and use that surface to drive the defender up field and back.

The facemask does not make contact with the body. The facemask is a reference aiming at the outside arm pit so that the eyes have a landmark that the body will follow.

G - The next step and every step thereafter is the **GO STEP (unload)**; the near foot takes a short power step to outside hip that is fast and short (get it down quickly and explosively) as they wheel their hips to the outside of the defender putting their bodies in between the defender and the boundary. It is important to maintain a wide base. As they take the step, they should immediately drop their hips by coiling their ankles, knees, hips and lower back. They should then re-elevate as their foot makes contact (a mini-explode step) from the ground up unloading from the feet, ankles, knees, hips, shoulders, arms and hands. They should stay under the defender and literally go through his outside shoulder (not around) and maintain contact as they elevate him. Literally elevating through him driving their hands inward and upward as they drive him vertically up field and inside, pinning not only his outside shoulder but entire body inside.

Run Your Feet!!! – Whether they get the defender's outside shoulder pinned or not, every step must drive towards the outside hip (not around). If they get into a stalemate with a defender, they must keep their feet moving using powerful, explosive, choppy steps. They should never stop moving their feet until the sound of the whistle. Keep all seven cleats on the ground and drive the defender up field.

Coaching Keys:

Use a running shoulder block to engage a LB and take the path through the next outside defensive linemen's near shoulder so that the angle is sharp enough to cut the LB off from the outside.

Attacking the Perimeter with the PIN Blocking Scheme

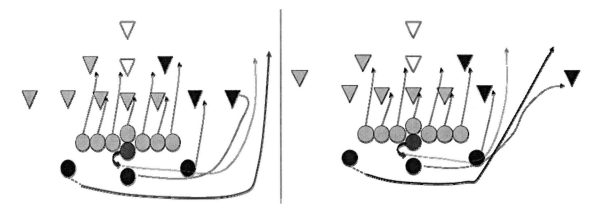

7H. Attacking the Perimeter with the PIN Blocking Scheme. The PIN blocking scheme gives us a method to effectively attack the perimeter without pulling the backside linemen, This variation neutralizes the attempts by the defense to key on the pulling schemes.

The WB has a key block in this scheme as he is the AT MAN in most cases. He must wall off the EMLOS by LEG & TURN so that he pins the defender inside.

The BB also has a key block on the FORCE/OUTSIDE CONTAIN defender (cornerback)-

1) If he is TIGHT: Pin him inside by gaining depth getting wide and wheel blocking him using the LEG & TURN progression (Figure 7H – Left).
2) If he is WIDE: The BB must eat up space as fast as possible, then settle down and wall him off by mirroring his belt buckle and not letting him pass. As he approaches, engage him with a TKO L.E.G progression and remember to wheel your back towards the runner to wall off the defender from the ball (Figure 7H – Right).

This is a very simple COVERED/UNCOVERED scheme. If uncovered, with no backer assignment, the blocker can shift to COMBO with the next blocker play-side, to drive that defender vertical.

Coaching Keys:

I like to add the WB PIN play to our play list when I think a defense is going to read our guards and key on their pulls. I also like to add this when I think I am going to face a defense that is going to have the CONTAIN and FORCE defenders squat down and read. This allows us to get after them quickly and get off the ball with no pull key and still get a lot of players to the POA (QB and BB). And it actually gives you a plus three numbers advantage against most defenses.

Half Line PIN Drill

Objectives:
- To teach the offensive how to execute the PIN play against WIDE and TIGHT perimeters defenders.
- To develop the timing and technique to make the play successful.

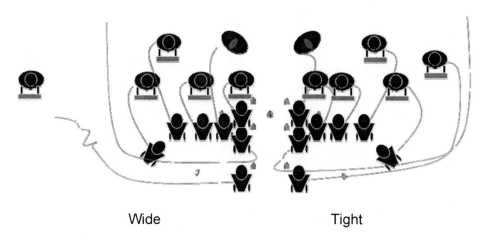

Wide   Tight

Figure 7I. Half Line PIN Drill

Set up:
1) Set up for half line drills as illustrated above (Figure 7I). Both groups should be manned similarly however, one should have a *WIDE* perimeter defender and one the other should have a *TIGHT* perimeter defender.
2) Use a Center, PSG, PST, PSTE, PSWB, QB and BB. You run two teams one to each side to maximize reps.

Execution:
1) On DOWN all players get into a good stance.
2) On GO the *defensive* line executes GET OFF. The LB flows to the play and the force defender works outside, attempting to squeeze the play.
3) On GO the *offense* will execute the PIN scheme using proper technique.

Chapter 8
Shift Power & Lead Series

The Shift series described herein is nothing more than the classic Single Wing straight series using the YDW blocking and play calling structure so that the two concepts easily mesh. The Single Wing is one of the oldest and most productive offensive series in football with a documented history dating back to 1908 when Glen Scobey "Pop" Warner published a correspondence course for football. The ideas were so well received he published a book in 1912 and then later expanded the ideas in a book published in 1927, *Football for Coaches and Players*. A more modern description of the Single Wing, including the Spin series, was published by Ken Keuffel in 1964. Finally, while in retirement Keuffel produced a nice description of the Single Wing in 2004, *Winning Single Wing Football*. Like any good football coach I strive to utilize every piece of information that I get my hands on to create a more improved offense. There is an enormous benefit in my opinion to using the Single Wing approach in conjunction with the YDW because the formations and layered backfield enhance and simplify so many things that we already do. Incorporating the Single Wing allows us to show various looks without having to change the overall structure of the offense. This is and will always be a key concern for me when I start looking at various formation and backfield changes. I always ask myself the following questions when I consider a new formation:

1) Can every core play in my power series be used in this formation with little to no alteration in the basic structure of the play?
2) Can I use my current system of edge tags to alter the perimeter so that I can adapt and isolate the perimeter triangle of the defense?
3) What advantage does it give me that I don't have using my base formation (TIGHT)?
4) Does it give me a leverage or line of force advantage against the defense?

In the next few chapters I will introduce and break down each gun formation that I use, and I will address these questions so that you fully understand the rationale behind my decision to adopt the given formation.

The Single Wing Advantage

1)   Line of force adaption due to each back being at a different level in the backfield.
2)   Leverage advantage can be gained by the offense with the use of non-symmetrical backfield alignments and the use of the 'OVER' call to take advantage of an unbalanced line that is often overlooked by the defense.
3)   Layered backfield allows for the use of cross or misdirection movements due to the backs being at different layers.
4)   Offense has the ability to get the ball from the snapper to multiple backs with one direct snap.

Aligning the backfield of SHIFT

In our Normal (SHIFT) backfield alignment (Figure 8A), the BB is positioned 1 to 2 yards behind the outside hip of play side (wall) guard. The QB aligns 3 to 4 yards back, with backside heel aligned with the play side foot of the center. The TB is positioned 4 to 5 yards back with his play side heel aligned with the backside heel of the center. This is the alignment used for all plays, except the BB running plays (BB WEDGE or BB KICK). When the BB is supposed to get the ball, the alignment is shifted slightly toward back side so that the BB can receive the direct snap. In the BB backfield alignment (Figure 8B), the BB backside heel aligns on play side heel of the center, the QB play side heel aligns to backside heel of center, and TB aligns over the back side guard. This subtle shift affords us the ability to get the ball directly in the hands of the BB while minimizing the chance of the defense recognizing the back field alignment change. It also increases the speed of the play allowing the BB to get into his running lane faster.

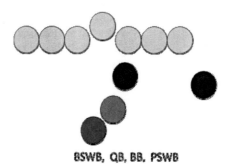

BSWB, QB, BB, PSWB

Figure 8A. Normal Backfield alignment for the SHIFT formation

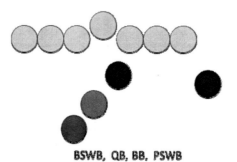

BSWB, QB, BB, PSWB

Figure 8B. BB Play Alignment for the SHIFT formation The BSWB, QB, and BB are slightly shifted toward the backside so that the BB is in a better position to receive the direct snap and quickly enter the running lane or tuck into the wedge.

Shift Formations

1)   Can every core play in my power series be used in this formation with little to no alteration in the basic structure of the play? *Answer - Yes*

2)   Can I use my current system of edge tags to alter the perimeter so that I can adapt and isolate the perimeter triangle of the defense? *Answer – Yes*

3)   What advantage does it give me that I don't have using my base formation (TIGHT)? *Answer – increased speed in running attack (downhill), direct snap gets ball into primary ball carrier's hand, layered backfield increases misdirection.*

4)   Does it give me a leverage or line of force advantage against the defense? *Answer – yes it does, (1) to the strong side edge and perimeter, and (2) when the defense over shifts it gives me an advantage to the weak side as well.*

Summary of the SHIFT Power Series

Interior Power Plays – 10 Wedge Right, 30 Wedge Right (Rip and Liz)

- Use reverse ('XX') action behind it to create deception to hold the perimeter defenders in place on each side.
- QB and BB variants allow you to hit the same spot with two different players increasing the misdirection aspect of the offense.

Edge Plays – Rip 26 Seal Right, Rip 16 Seal Right, Rip 33 Kick Left, Rip 45 Kick Left, Liz 45 Seal Left, Liz 15 Seal Left, Liz 34 Kick Right, Liz 26 Kick Right

- Seal Play (Power Play, e.g. Rip 26 Seal Right, Rip 16 Seal Right, Liz 45 Seal Left, Liz 15 Seal Left)
  - Core play of this offense
  - Must be able to run it anywhere on the field at any time against anything thrown at us.
  - We have a variety of ways of running this play to keep defenses on their toes.
  - TB power play is a pure power play with a maximum amount of blockers. It is our base play.
  - QB power utilizes the TB as a sweep decoy to the perimeter to remove perimeter defenders.

- BB Kick (BB Counter Trap, e.g. Rip 33 Kick Left/ Liz 34 Kick Right)

  - Edge misdirection play that allows us to attack the defense with the pre-flow look of WB power in the opposite direction, WB reverse action in the play direction and hit back inside on the edge with the BB as the perimeters defend power and reverse (XX).
  - BB must hit inside vertically and go north-south quickly.

- WB Kick (WB Counter Trap, e.g. Rip 45 Kick Left, Liz 26 Kick Right)
  - Edge misdirection play that allows us to attack the defense with the pre-flow look of WB power in one direction setting us up to hit back against the flow with an inside counter.
  - WB must hit inside vertically and go north-south quickly.

Perimeter Plays – Rip 28 Monster Sweep Right, Rip 28 Wide Right, Rip 45 Wide Reverse Left, Liz 47 Monster Sweep Left, Liz 47 Wide Left, Liz 28 Wide Reverse Right.

- WB Monster Sweep (Power Sweep, e.g. Rip 28 Monster Sweep, Liz 47 Monster Sweep)

  - Perimeter power play wherein we overwhelm the perimeter with pullers.
  - Must seal the EMLOS to the inside.
  - Best run when you have two in the perimeter triangle and/or you see the EMLOS squatting/crashing to the WB power play.

- WB Wide Reverse (XX outside reverse, e.g. Rip 47 Wide Reverse, Liz 28 Wide Reverse)

  - Perimeter misdirection play. Isolate the interior and perimeter defenders and attempt to attack the backside perimeter triangle (away from power).
  - Key is 2 or less in the perimeter box and EMLOS vacating contain with shallow pinch inside to chase power.
  - Best used against teams that are crashing the backside of power.

- WB Wide Sweep (Rip 28 Wide, Liz 47 Wide)

  - Alternative power perimeter play for monster sweep.
  - If the OLB and CB are filling hard into the tunnel of the TKO wal this is a nice alternative.
  - Good alternative if you are having problems using Monster Sweep due to a good OLB/SS on the play side.

Play Action Passing – Rip Power Pass Right, Liz Power Pass Left, Rip WB Pass Right, Liz WB Pass Left

- Power Pass
  - Run/Pass option
  - Basic flood pattern on the power side.
  - Read low to high (BB flat to WB out).
  - Can teach a peek deep if MOFO (middle of the field open).
  - Run this to the QB's throwing side

A quick reminder on RIGHT/LEFT tags added to the play. This 'side' call is for the linemen and to remind them what side the WALL SIDE lines up on; it has nothing to do with the direction of the play. For instance, on all wedge plays we line up our wall on the right side, so there is no real "tell" to which side the wedge is being run. It is the method I use to notify my wall side where to line up.

Detailed Description of Select Plays
The SHIFT Power Series

<u>Important</u>: A common and essential tactic when using formations wherein multiple players in the backfield could potentially receive the direct snap is the "flash fake". Flash fakes can be executed with or without the ball. Flash fakes are exaggerated actions that attract the attention of the defense. For example, quickly reaching out and then retracting the arms as if a pitch or snap has been received; or deliberately showing the ball while faking a pitch or handoff. When these actions are consistently displayed by the backfield play after play, the defense tends to slow down in an attempt to be sure they are not running away from the play in pursuit of a fake. To maximize the effectiveness of the SHIFT formation, it is important that the entire backfield completely commit to selling their fakes as this is essential element of this offensive series.

<u>Shift Rip 30 Wedge Right</u> (Interior play)

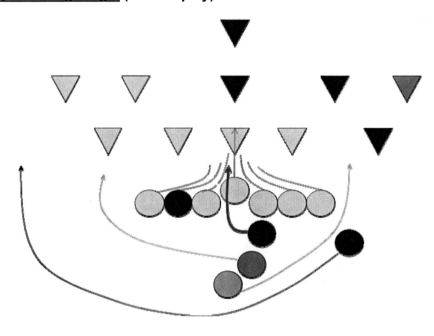

Figure 8C. Shift Rip 30 Wedge Right

Line – Wedge block on Center

BB – Secure the snap and hit the wedge. Find a crease on either side, hit it, and get vertical. Do not go around or under the wedge. Secure the ball and get as many yards you can.

QB – Execute a flash fake and then aim for the inside arm pit of back side defensive end and wall him off.

TB (BSWB) – Execute a flash fake snap, then reverse and attack the inside arm pit of play side defensive end, and wall him off.

WB – Execute a flash fake reverse then attack the perimeter and get vertical.

This is the classic XX or power/reverse action behind the BB wedge creating a split flow that places pressure on both perimeter triangles to defend their edge/perimeter while we attack the interior. Essentially this play isolates the interior as we overwhelm it with the wedge blocking scheme (Figure 8C).

This concept can be used with LOOSE as well, which imposes a different kind of pressure on the strong side (Figure 8D). In this case, pressure results from a passing threat, which forces the perimeter triangle and the safety to cover the possible passing threats both at the perimeter and vertically.

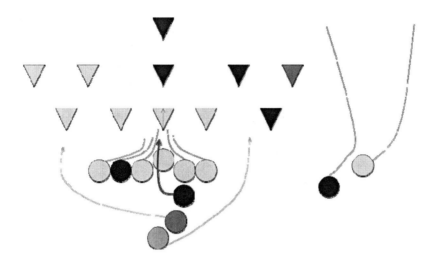

Figure 8D. Shift Loose Rip 30 Wedge Right In this variation, we use LOOSE to threaten the strong side perimeter and isolate the interior defense

Finally, the concept can be used with a NASTY split which offers another variation to threaten the perimeter and isolate the interior without spreading the offense (Figure 8E).

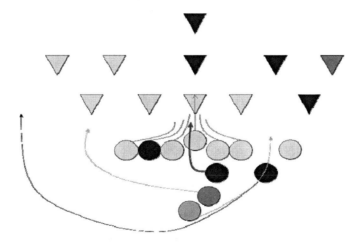

Figure 8E. Shift Nasty Rip 30 Wedge Right Another variation that draws the defense away from the interior by posing legitimate threats to the edge and perimeter.

Coaching Notes:

Can be run using the OVER tag as well.

Opposite is Shift Liz 30 Wedge Right, i.e. the Liz backfield formation mirrors the Rip formation to the left side. Recall that 'Right' only applies to the offensive line and indicates which side the WALL SIDE lines up on.

Shift Rip 10 Wedge Right (Interior play)

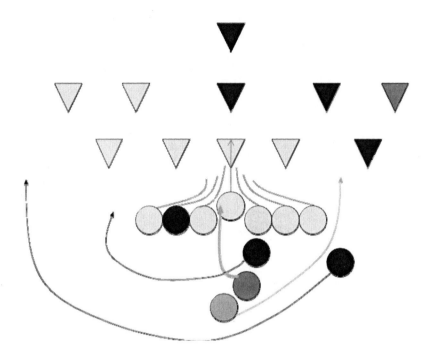

Figure 8F. Shift Rip Wedge Right

Line – Wedge block on center

BB – Cross over and gain depth as if to log the backside defensive end but wall him off to the outside by running through his inside shoulder.

QB – Secure the snap and hit the wedge. Look for a crease on either side, then hit it and get vertical. Do not go around or under the wedge. Secure the ball and get as many yards as you can.

TB (BSWB) – Execute a flash fake snap, then reverse and attack the inside arm pit of play side defensive end and wall him off.

WB – Execute a flash fake reverse then attack the perimeter and get vertical.

This is the classic XX or power/reverse action behind the QB wedge creating a split flow that places pressure on both perimeter triangles to defend their edge/perimeter while we attack the interior. This play works the exact same way the BB Wedge does but it allows us to utilize a power runner type at QB and basically get the ball into another back's hands behind the wedge while the BB provides the backside perimeter threat.

This concept can be used in the LOOSE (Figure 8G) as well by simply placing a different kind of pressure on the strong side. In this case it would be a passing threat forcing the perimeter triangle and the safety to cover the possible passing threat, both at the perimeter and vertically.

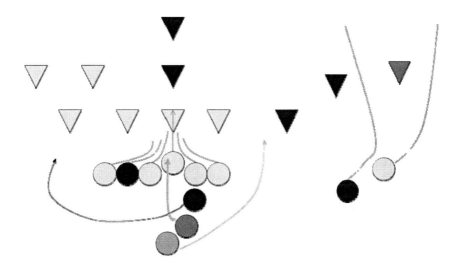

Figure 8G. Shift Loose Rip 10 Wedge Right

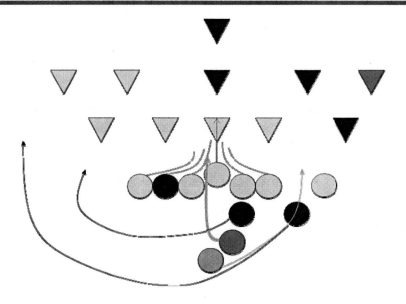

Figure 8H. Shift Nasty Rip 10 Wedge Right

Coaching Notes:

Can be run using the OVER tag as well.

Opposite is Shift Liz 10 Wedge Right.

<u>Shift Rip 26 Seal Right</u> (Edge play)

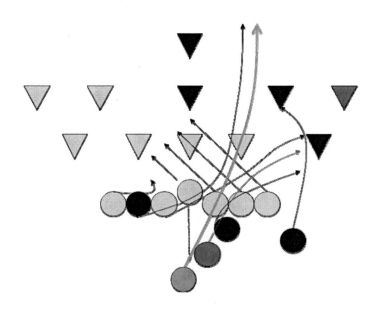

Figure 8I. Shift Rip 26 Seal Right

Line Assignments:

> Wall side – TKO (center to PSTE)
> Pulling Guard – The BSG will pull and kick out the first defender to show above BB and QB
> Pulling Tackle – The BST will pull and move up the wall going vertical to the end zone. Any defender crossing the BST should be engaged and sealed inside.
> Pulling Tight End – Cutoff to the Center's hip. If no one shows climb to linebacker level and cutoff the backside pursuit.

BB – cross over and hug the LOS by aiming for the first play side blocker's inside hip. Kick out the first defender to cross your face. When kicking him out, flip your hips and body into the hole, so you isolate the defender away from the WB as he hits the tunnel.

QB –Execute a flash fake, then cross over step aiming for the heels of the BB; then follow him into the hole and kick out the first defender to show above the BB. *NOTE – if the BB is struggling to kick out a tough defender double team him and let the BSG take the next defender up.*

TB (BSWB) – Secure the snap, then aim for the center's play side hip and get vertical to daylight. Climb the wall and get 5 yards. Once you make it out of the tunnel you make a move and get vertical to the end zone (cutback inside, go vertical, bounce it outside) - do this after breaking past the tunnel. Never let one defender take you down and never let a defender hit you, i.e. you hit him first. Your depth should be 4 to 5 yards but don't hesitate to adjust the depth so that you arrive just behind the BSG and BST as they hit the tunnel. The timing is very important as it will hide your approach into the tunnel.

WB – Take the quickest release to get off the LOS cleanly. Get inside and block the first backer inside (FBI). If the outside backer is flowing to the perimeter or crashing down into the edge, let him go and take the next defender inside (inside backer). Your job is to seal off the linebacker level inside. Drive that backer to the top of the wall - your landmark is the near shoulder of the last blocker on the wall.

This is our base play. You must be able to run this from anywhere on the field against anything the defense throws at you, with any edge or backfield tag you use. It is the base for everything we do in this offense. Though the formation has changed, the idea is the same – we want to attack the edge with overwhelming power and force the defense to adapt to stop the relentless assault. This opens up the rest of the offensive playbook.

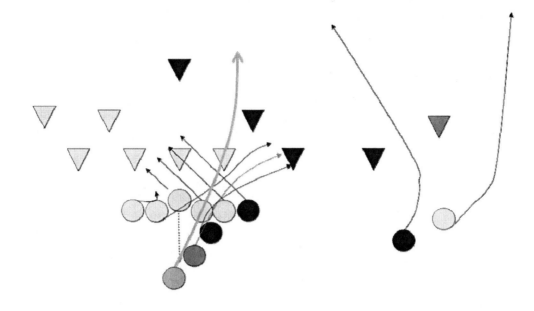

Figure 8J. Shift Loose Over Rip 26 Seal Right

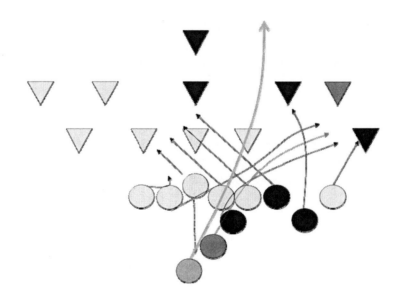

Figure 8K. Shift Nasty Over Rip 26 Seal Right

Coaching Notes:

When we run this play with LOOSE (Figure 8J) or NASTY (Figure 8K), I prefer to use OVER (an unbalanced line) so that I can get a 4 man TKO wall on the play side. If the OVER tag is not used you will only get 3 blockers in the TKO wall.

Opposite is Shift Liz 45 Seal Left.

Shift Rip 16 Seal Right (Edge play)

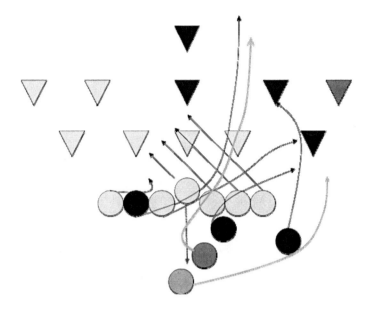

Figure 8L. Shift Rip 16 Seal Right

Line Assignments:

> Wall side – TKO (center to PSTE)
> Pulling Guard – The BSG will pull and kick out the first defender to show above BB and QB
> Pulling Tackle – The BST will pull and move up the wall, then go vertical to the end zone. Any defender crossing BST should be engaged and sealed inside.
> Pulling Tight End – Cutoff to center's hip; if no one shows climb to the linebacker level and cutoff the backside pursuit.

BB – Cross over and hug the LOS by aiming for the first play side blocker's inside hip then kick out the first defender to cross your face. To kick him out, flip your hips and body into the hole so you isolate the defender away from the WB as he hits the tunnel.

QB – Secure the snap, then aim for the Center's play side hip and get vertical to daylight. Climb the wall and get 5 yards. Once you make it out of the tunnel, make a move and get vertical to the end zone (cutback inside, go vertical, bounce it outside). Stay with the blocking until you get 5 yards, make a move only after breaking past the tunnel. Never let one defender take you down and never let a defender hit you; you hit him first. Your depth at the snap should be 4 to 5 yards but don't hesitate to adjust the depth so that you arrive just behind the BSG and BST as they hit the tunnel. The timing is very important as it will hide your approach into the tunnel.

TB (BSWB) – (flash fake), grab cloth with the backside arm as you run to make it look like you have the ball and attack the outside arm pit of the EMLOS to force him to widen and defend your faking. Run like you have the ball and want to score! If you get tackled than you did your job!

WB – Take the quickest release to get off the LOS cleanly, then get inside and block the first backer inside (FBI). If the outside backer is flowing to the perimeter or crashing down into the edge, let him go and take the next defender inside (inside backer). Your job is to seal off the linebacker level inside. Drive that backer to the top of the wall - your landmark is the near shoulder of the last blocker on the wall.

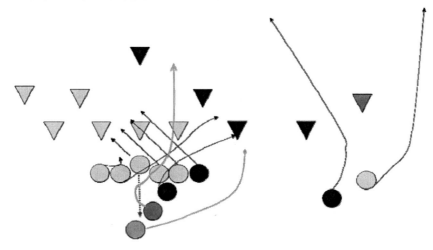

Figure 8M. Shift Loose Over Rip 16 Seal Right

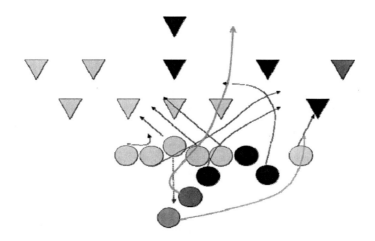

Figure 8N. Shift Nasty Over Rip 16 Seal Right

Coaching Notes:

When we run this play with LOOSE (Figure 8M), NASTY (Figure 8N), BUNCH, or TRIPS, I prefer to include OVER so that I can get a 4 man TKO wall on the play side. If the OVER tag is not used you will only have 3 blockers in the TKO wall. The use of the QB in the power play allows us the ability to use the power play out of TRIPS and BUNCH which moves the both WB's outside to further isolate the perimeter triangle and secondary

Opposite is Shift Liz 15 Seal Left.

Shift Rip 45 Kick Left (Edge play)

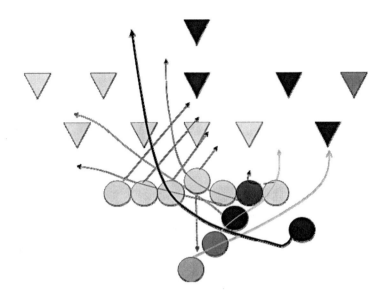

Figure 8O. Shift Rip 45 Kick Left

Line –

> Wall side – TKO (center to PSTE)
>
> Pulling Guard – The BSG will pull and kick out the first defender to cross his face. He should kick him out by flipping his hips and body into the hole to isolate the defender away from the WB as he hits the tunnel.
>
> Pulling Tackle – The BST pulls up the wall and goes vertical to the end zone. Any defender crossing his face should be sealed to the inside with a wall off.
>
> Pulling Tight End – The PTE will cut-off to the Center's hip; if no one shows, he should climb to the next level (linebacker level) and cutoff the backside pursuit.

BB – Jab step to opposite side, mesh with the pulling tackle and kick out the first defender to cross your face above the pulling guard (PG).

QB – Secure the snap, take a short cross step to open belt buckle to WB and make the handoff to him; then carry out the kick block on first defender to cross your face.

TB (BSWB) – Execute a flash fake, then grab cloth with the backside arm as you run to make it look like you have the ball. Attack the outside arm pit of the EMLOS to force him to widen and defend your faking. Run like you have the ball and want to score! If you get tackled then you did your job!

WB – Execute a drop step with inside the foot; then aim for the inside hip of the QB and take the handoff. Secure the ball, and get vertical when you see the first daylight to the end zone. Do not go east-west you must get vertical, Look to get to the boundary after you clear the tunnel.

This is our inside counter play to the WB and a potential home run play. It is a nice backside containment play against an overly aggressive back side perimeter triangle. Faking the power action is a key to the success of this play. The more aggressive the TB and QB are with their run and kick out block, the more likely this play will be successful.

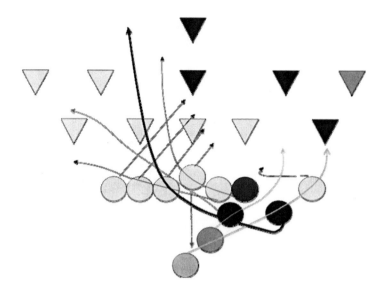

Figure 8P. Shift Nasty Rip 45 Kick Left

Coaching Notes:

This is an outstanding play when you see the backside defenders overplaying or chasing the power play. We'll also run this with NASTY (Figure 8P).

Opposite is Shift Liz 26 Kick Right

Shift Rip 33 Kick Left (Edge play)

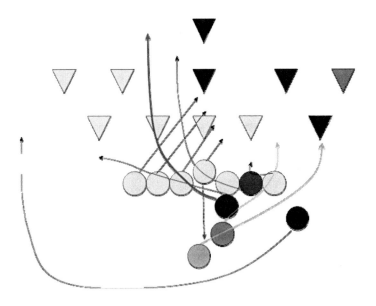

Figure 8Q. Shift Rip 33 Kick Left

Line –

> Wall side – TKO (center to PSTE)
> Pulling Guard – The BSG pulls and kicks out the first defender to cross his face. When he kicks him out, he should flip his hips and body into the hole to isolate the defender away from the WB as he hits the tunnel.
> Pulling Tackle – The BST will pull up the wall and go vertical to end zone. Any defender crossing his face will be sealed him inside with a wall off.
> Pulling Tight End – Cutoff to center's hip; if no one shows climb to the linebacker level and cutoff the backside pursuit.

BB – Jab step to opposite side, mesh with pulling tackle and take the handoff. Get vertical when you see first daylight. Don't get tackled by one defender or brought down by any sort of arm tackle.

QB – Secure the snap, then take a short cross step to open belt buckle to BB. Make a clean handoff to the BB; then execute a kick out block on the first defender to cross your face.

TB (BSWB) – Execute a flash fake (as if receiving the direct snap), then fake a reverse handoff - make sure you rub hips as you go by one another as that will increase the misdirection aspect. Act as though the ball is in the belly with the inside hand, and with the outside hand, fake into the belly of the WB. After the XX fake, grab cloth with the backside arm as you run to make it look like you still have the ball and attack the outside arm pit of the EMLOS to force him to widen and defend your faking. Run like you have the ball and want to score! If you get tackled then you did your job!

WB – Drop step with the inside foot and gain depth. As you move outside of the TB rub hips and cradle fake with the TB. After the XX fake, grab cloth with the backside arm as you run to make it look like you have the ball. Attack the perimeter wide and get vertical to force him to widen and defend your faking. Run like you have the ball and want to score! If you get tackled then you did your job!

This is our inside counter play to the BB and it is a power play as well as a backside containment play against an overly aggressive backside perimeter triangle that is cross keying the WB. Faking the power action and reverse action is the key to the success of this play. The more aggressive the TB, WB, and QB are with their run and kick out block the more likely this play will be successful.

Coaching Notes:

This is an outstanding play when you see the backside defenders overplaying or chasing the power play and cross-keying the far wing back. The BB counter gives us a quick hitting counter trap that we can use out of any edge tag with the BB.

Note that in LOOSE (Figure 8R) we don't have the WB running reverse as it will have no effect on widening the perimeter defenders, rather we attempt to stress the coverage with the loose pair faking outside release fade routes.

Opposite is Shift Liz 34 Kick Right

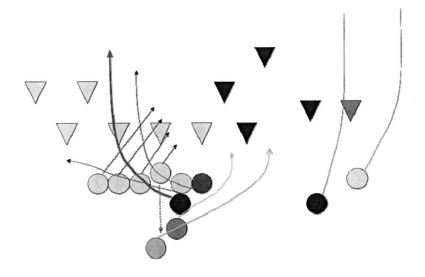

Figure 8R. Shift Loose Rip 33 Kick Left

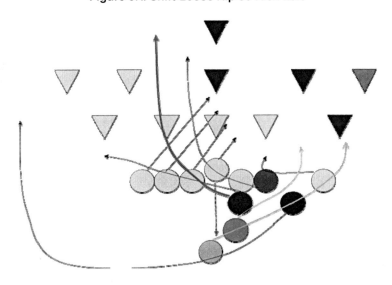

Figure 8S. Shift Nasty Rip 33 Kick Left

Shift Rip 28 Monster Sweep Right (perimeter play)

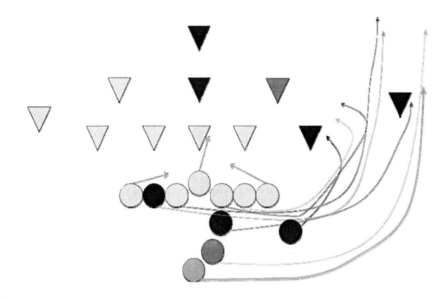

Figure 8T. Shift Rip 28 Monster Sweep Right

Line –

Wall Tight End – Cut off play side to center's hip.

Wall Tackle – Pull around the WTE and WSWB and form a wall by landmarking the outside shoulder of the WSWB.

Wall Guard – Pull around WTE and WSWB and form a wall by landmarking the outside shoulder of the WT.

Center – (NT, i.e. odd front) Jewel block the NT by aiming your far shoulder at the crotch of the defender so that the head goes past the play side hip. If a DT (even front), severe down block, aiming for a point just in front of his far (play side) shoulder while wheeling your butt to the play side.

Pulling Side Guard and Tackle – Pull tight down the LOS and around the perimeter wall, then go vertical to the end zone - creating a vertical lane for the runner. Any defender that crosses your face you should be walled off by attacking his up field arm pit while wheeling your butt towards the runner. Any leakage encountered as you pull down the line should be picked up by cutting it off the same way the center does against an even front.

Pulling Tight End – Cutoff to center's hip; if no one shows climb to the next level (linebacker level).

BB – Cross over, and then get outside and up field quickly. Against a CB that is off the LOS and near the EMLOS, you must come around and attack the outside arm pit and wheel block him. Against a wide CB you must eat up space and then settle down and wall him off to the outside creating an alley for the runner.

QB – Execute a flash fake then cross over and get up field to create a vertical lane for the runner to the end zone. Any defender that crosses your face should be walled off.

TB (BSWB) – Secure the snap and cross over staying flat (parallel) to the LOS until you move past the WSTE; once you see daylight get vertical, make a move (cutback, vertical, bounce) and accelerate up field. The TB will have three vertical blockers going up field near the boundary, so if he can get into the alley between the three vertical pullers and the boundary the chance of a TD is big.

WB – Take a lateral step with the outside foot and attack the outside arm pit of EMLOS; wall him off by wheel blocking and driving him inside as far as you can.

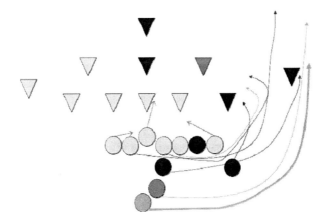

Figure 8U. Shift Over Rip 28 Monster Sweep Right

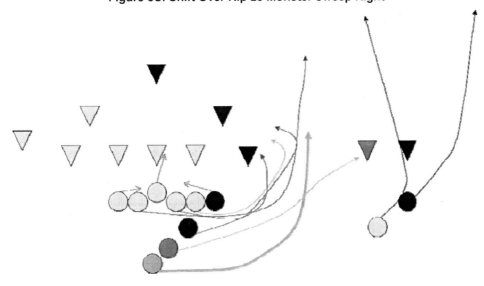

Figure 8V. Shift Loose Over Rip 28 Monster Sweep Right

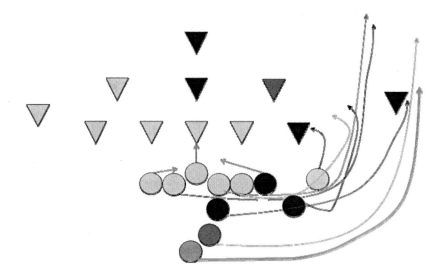

Figure 8W. Shift Nasty Over Rip 28 Monster Sweep Right

This is our WB power sweep and it is based on simply overloading the perimeter with two running backs and four linemen as blockers at the point of attack. Once the defense shows two or less in the perimeter, this is a great way to attack the perimeter and get the ball in space on the outside.

Coaching Notes:

In Shift Loose Over (Figure 8V), our wing back is now a slot along with the split end, so we'll use the BB to log the EMLOS. The key to running the monster sweep or any sweep out of loose, bunch, or trips is to get in the inside lane between the receiver group and the EMLOS. The stress you are placing on the secondary and perimeter defenders to cover pass and play run along with the kick out block by a running back (QB in this case) opens a seam in the perimeter in which to run.

We'll call Nasty or Nasty Over (Figure 8W) when we see the EMLOS staying over or inside of the wall side tight end. When we use the nasty edge tag, we find it best to have the tight end wall off the EMLOS, and have the wing back fold around him to form the wall on the outside shoulder of the tight end. The next lineman inside will cutoff, and the remaining pullers will pull as usual. The next lineman inside will finish the wall while the other lineman or linemen pull and go vertical.

Opposite is Shift Liz 47 Monster Sweep Left

Shift Rip 47 Wide Reverse Left (perimeter play)

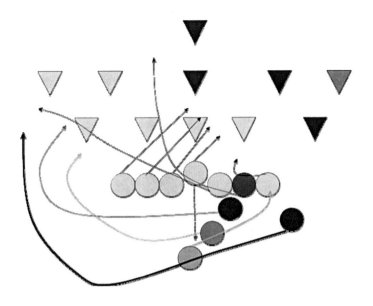

Figure 8X. Shift Rip 47 Wide Reverse Left

Line –

Wall side – TKO (center to PSTE)

Pulling Guard – The BSG will pull and climb as if to seal but go wide and kick out the first defender to cross his face outside (CB). When he encounters the defender, he should kick him out and flip his hips and body into the hole to isolate the defender away from the WB as he hits the tunnel. If facing an athletic corner eat up space, then settle down and wall him off.

Pulling Tackle – The BST will pull up the wall and go vertical to the end zone; any defender crossing his face should be sealed inside with a wall off.

Pulling Tight End – Cutoff to center's hip; if no one shows, climb to the linebacker level and cutoff the backside pursuit.

QB – Execute a flash fake, then cross over and gain enough depth to log the EMLOS and drive him inside. If he is crashing, all you need to do is wall him in for a moment.

BB – Cross over and gain depth under the QB and wall off the next defender inside (OLB normally).

TB – Secure the snap and cross over step, then make an outside handoff to the WB. Following the handoff, aim for the inside arm pit of the BSDE and make a great fake as if running seal. As you reach him - kick him out.

WB – Drop step then get to the outside hip of the TB and take the hand off. Don't rush or sprint into the hand off. Once you get the ball, accelerate to full speed moving outside; once you see daylight get vertical quick. The faster you get vertical the more likely you are to get by the linebacker pursuit. If there is a corner wide, run inside of the BSG's kick out.

This is the classic XX reverse, but with an outside handoff. I use this to pressure the backside perimeter triangle to defend the perimeter or give us the easy score. I call this when I see the BSOLB sitting on the edge for counter and the DE is crashing inside to chase the power play and/or disrupt the edge misdirection plays coming his way. Often the only defender left supporting the perimeter is the CB.

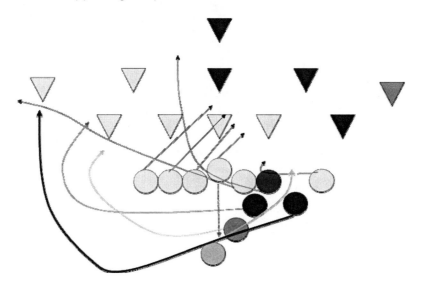

Figure 8Y. Shift Nasty Rip 47 Reverse Left

Coaching Notes:

The nasty tag will hit a lot faster, as the WB is closer to the TB (Figure 8Y). Thus, the timing will need to be developed. Often defenses will really over play the nasty edge tag; having that WB hit a little faster will increase the chance of this being a touchdown for you.

Rip Power Pass Right (Sprint)

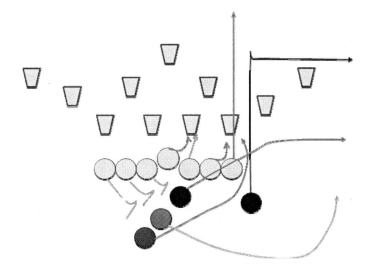

Figure 8Z. Rip Power Pass Right

Line -

> Wall Tackle to Center – Slide to the wall side (Covered/Uncovered). LEM/SSM Pulling Guard to Pulling Tight End – Hinge to the wall side and don't allow any defender inside of you, force any defender encountered to go outside of you and around the hinge wall. KKM

Wall Tight End - Outside release, then go vertical up the middle and pin the safety deep. The ball will only go to you on a MOFO read from the QB/OC.

WB - Outside release, then take 8 to 9 steps and break outside. Accelerate to the sideline until you find and open space. You are the HIGH read (second read) of the QB. If the ball goes to the BB (low read) or the QB runs, turn back over your up field shoulder and wall off the first defender to show (put him on the ground).

BB - Release through the DEMLOS's face to slow his rush so that the TB can get outside and wall the defender inside. Run to the flat and as soon as you get past the DEMLOS get your head around and look for the ball over your down field shoulder. You are the primary read (low read). If the QB runs the ball, turn back over your up field shoulder and wall off the first defender to show (put him on the ground).

TB - Execute a flash fake, then fake sweep to get wide and attack the outside arm pit of first defender to show past the WT.

QB - Secure the snap and gain depth to the wall side (at least 3 to 5 yards of depth). You must threaten the perimeter quickly while looking to throw as soon as you secure the ball. If the BB is open throw to him immediately so he can eat up as much vertical space as possible before the defense recovers. Your read is LOW (BB) to HIGH (WB). If neither is open run the ball. If you see vertical space as your roll out, run the ball. The object is to get positive yards not complete a pass.

You can run a variation of this play that has the WB and WALL TE switch assignments, i.e. the WB runs the vertical route and the WALL TE runs the out. The normal assignment is #1 outside runs the out, #2 runs the vertical, and #3 runs to flat. When running this play out of Loose, Bunch, or Trips, is the routes are #1 vertical, #2 out, and #3 flat.

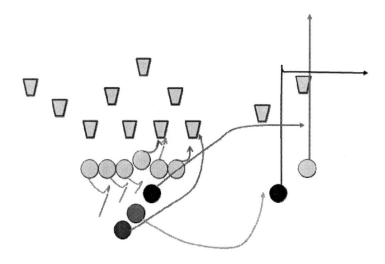

Figure 8AA. Shift Loose Rip Power Pass Right (sprint)

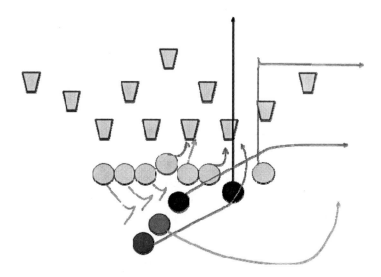

Figure 8BB. Shift Nasty Rip Power Pass Right (sprint)

Coaching Notes:

When we run this play with Loose (Figure 8AA), the normal rule for us is to have the SE run the vertical and the SLOT run the out. Often the BB is wide open as soon as he breaks past the DEMLOS.

When we go Nasty (Figure 8BB) we still use the #1 out, #2 vertical rule.

Remember that you can use OVER to move the PULL TACKLE to the play side, have a tough pass rush on that side. There, he will follow the COVERED/UNCOVERED rule (LEM/SSM).This allows you to pin point additional pass protection (wall or pull side) where it is needed.

NOTE: If the QB or OC sees the MOFO (middle of the field open) meaning there is no FS in the middle of the field, your first read is to the roll and throw it to the WALL TE on the inside shoulder. Throw to where the receiver is going (not at him), so he can catch the ball without slowing down, and run with it to the end zone.

Brief Overview of the Shift Lead Series

Interior Plays – Rip 31/14 Dive Right, Liz 32/13 Dive Left

- Interior power play for this series.
- Use reverse (XX) action behind it to create deception designed to hold the perimeter defenders in place on each side.
- QB and BB plays act as a double dive mini-series with cross action between the QB and BB which confuse the interior LB reads on the backfield.

Edge Plays – Rip 13 ISO Right, Rip 23 ISO Right, Rip 14 Double Right, Rip 24 Double Right, Liz 14 ISO Left, Liz 24 ISO Left, Liz 13 Double Left, Liz 23 Double Left

The ISO Play is a cross blocked play to the pull side (backside) with XX action behind it to hold the perimeter defenders in place while we overwhelm the point of attack.

- Great play to add to the power series as it allows you to attack the pull side immediately and directly (which has the better pullers and makes the cross blocking more effective) when defenses are keying on the WALL side and/or formation strength.
- Solid way of attacking an interior defender playing over the Pulling Guard and attempting to shoot the gap between the pulling guard and center (to chase the puller on pulling plays); the down block of the pull tackle very easy to execute against this defender. It is also a nice way to attack the perimeter triangle on the Pull side when they are sitting on reverse and ready to pursue the XX action.
- We have two ways of running this play to keep defenses on their toes.
- The QB ISO play is a quick power play with full XX action behind it and the BB lead blocking to isolate the first backer inside (ILB often). . Great to use if you have an athletic tough kid at QB.
- The TB ISO play is a pure power play with the BB lead blocking to isolate the first backer inside (ILB often) and QB attacking first defender outside as he hits the hole behind the BB. The WB executes XX action with the TB who is executes a quick counter step, and then attacks the hole as he follows the BB and QB.

The DOUBLE Play is a double team/combo block to the wall side with XX action behind it. Used against even fronts that give us trouble running our angle blocking; particularly when they are sitting their ILB and OLB back as their defensive line absorbs the ABC wall. This play allows us to drive those defenders back into the laps of the backers using our WALL side blockers (our better drive/wall blockers) as double teamers/combo blockers.

Rip 24 Double Right, Rip 14 Double Right, Liz 45 Double Left, Liz 15 Double Left.

- Double plays to the TB allow us to double team the DT and DE with our C/WG and WT/WE. The BB lead blocks and isolates the OLB while the QB walls off the play side CB. The XX action of the TB counter stepping and the WB faking XX action tends to hold the perimeter defenders in place.
- Double plays to the QB have the TB and WB executing XX action to freeze the perimeter defenders in place so there is little need to actually wall off the CB as the QB hits the edge.

Perimeter Plays – Rip 28 Pin Right, Rip 37 Pin Right, Liz 47 Pin Left, Liz 38 Pin Left

- TB Pin Sweep (Power Sweep) (Rip 28 Pin, Liz 47 Pin)
  - Perimeter power play. This play is designed to overwhelm the perimeter by using an aggressive vertical drive step while pinning the outside hip of all play side defenders and keying the last defender outside for a wall off/kick out block.
  - Must seal the EMLOS to the inside, and key the last perimeter defender for wall off/kick out block.
  - Best run when you have two in the perimeter triangle, and/or you see the EMLOS squatting/crashing to the WB power play, as it further isolates the remaining perimeter defenders.

- FB Pin Sweep (counter sweep, e.g. Rip 37 Pin Right, Liz 38 Pin Left)
  - Perimeter misdirection play. Isolates the remaining perimeter defender on the weak side when defenses are shifting to our perceived strength and reducing their backside perimeter to two or less.
  - Key is 2 or less in the perimeter box and EMLOS vacating contain with shallow pinch inside to chase power, power sweep, or the power pass.
  - Best used against teams that are crashing the backside of power, allowing our TB to pin defenders inside while the QB leads for the BB running sweep.
  - Great for teams with a fast athletic BB.
  - Very nice non-pulling misdirection sweep that utilizes a fast BB on the weak side, much the same way we use XX Reverse in our power series.

Play Action Passing – Rip Counter Pass Right, Liz Counter Pass Left

- Drag Pass
  - Run/Pass option
  - Basic high-low drag pattern to power side.
  - Read PSWB corner to BSTE shallow drag (high to low)
  - Run this only if your TB can throw, and only to his throwing side.
  - As a nice backside throwback tag to the TB running a SWING & WHEEL (tagged as TBACK).
- Reverse Pass

- Based off of XX action with WB passing (need a passer at WB)
- Basic high-low drag pattern to the backside (great for over-shifted defenses)
- Read PTE (corner) to WTE (drag) or HIGH to LOW.
- TB runs SWING & WHEEL (tagged TBACK).

A quick reminder on the RIGHT/LEFT tags added to the play. This side call is for the linemen and serves only to remind them on which side the WALL SIDE should line up. It has nothing to do with the direction of the play. For instance, on all wedge plays we line up our wall blockers on the right side. Thus, there is no real "tell" to which side the wedge is being run.

Detailed Description of Select Plays:
The Shift Lead Series

Shift Rip 28 Pin Right

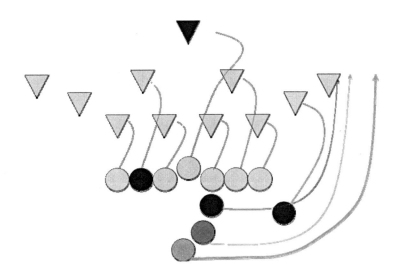

Figure 8CC. Shift Rip 28 Pin Right

PSWB (AT MAN) – If COVERED LEG & TURN (PIN) the defender. If UNCOVERED, take a lateral step to the outside and get vertical engaging the first backer inside by attacking his play side arm pit and walling him off.

PSTE to Center - If COVERED, LEG & TURN (PIN) the defender inside. If UNCOVERED, work to the second level attacking through the near arm pit of the next DLM play side and cut off the first backer inside (FBI). Even if that LB is over the blocker, he still must work through the near arm pit of the near play side DLM as this will be necessary to put him on a good cut off angle to the backer. If the Center has no immediate backer, and the backside ILB/OLB is caught in the wash of the backside cut off, he can release up field to cut off the FS/backside or Cover 2 safety.

BSG to BSTE - Same rules as the play side blockers, but they will work to get vertical much more quickly to cut off the backside secondary pursuit once the runner is play side.

BB – Attack the outside hip of the PSTE and get vertical, going to the end zone. If the corner back is inside, wall him off. If the corner is wide, close distance as quickly as possible, then gather yourself and kick him out. Wall him outside to give the runner a vertical seam inside.

QB – Follow the BB into the edge staying on his outside hip. If the BB moves inside then go vertical to the end zone and wall off any defender crossing your face. If the BB moves outside, cut up field immediately, get vertical to the end zone, and wall off any defender attempting to cross your face.

TB – Secure the snap, cross over and stay flat at cruising speed (60 to 75% of full speed). When you see the daylight in the seam, get vertical and go to the end zone as quickly as possible.

This is a really nice alternative if teams are keying your pulling linemen and/or doing a good job of sitting on the backside. Since there is no 'pull' key, the defense has no initial key to read flow, other than the backfield action. This allows our TB to get to the perimeter with numbers from the backfield, while the edge gets sealed off by the PSTE and PSWB. It is also a really nice alternative if you are having issues with your pullers getting in the way or not getting up field by the time your runner gets into the alley, due to his speed or lack of speed by your pullers in monster sweep and wide.

Coaching Notes:

When running this play with Nasty (Figure 8DD), the PSTE and PSWB simply swap, and the PSTE becomes the AT MAN. When running this play with Loose, the BB will take the EMLOS and log block him so the edge is sealed. The SE and SLOT will release outside and run vertical to drive the defenders away from the seam. The QB will kick out the first defender wide that crosses his face. This allows us to pick up a slot defender that is peeking inside for run.

Opposite: Shift Liz 47 Pin Left

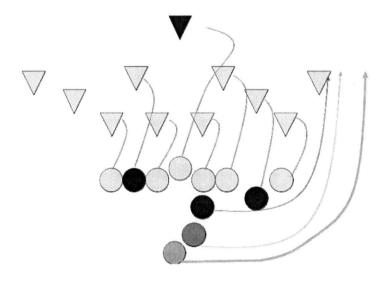

Figure 8DD. Shift Nasty Rip 28 Pin Right

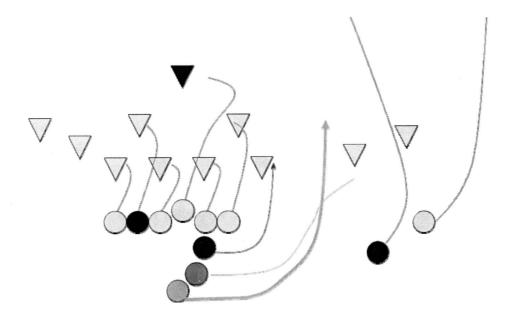

Figure 8EE. Shift Loose Rip 28 Pin Right

Shift Rip 37 Pin Right

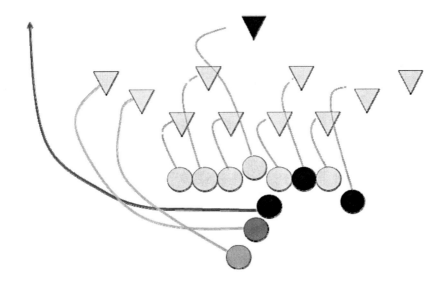

Figure 8FF. Shift Rip 28 Pin Right

PSTE (AT MAN) – If COVERED, LEG & TURN (PIN) the defender. If UNCOVERED, take a lateral step to the outside, and then get vertical engaging the first backer inside by attacking his play side arm pit and walling him off.

PST to Center - If COVERED, LEG & TURN (PIN) defender inside. If UNCOVERED, work to the second level attacking through the near arm pit of the next DLM play side, then cut off the first backer inside (FBI). Even if that LB is over the blocker, he still must work through the near arm pit of the near play side DLM as this will be necessary to put him on a good cut off angle to the backer. If the Center has no immediate backer, and the backside ILB/OLB is getting caught in the wash of the backside cut off, then he can release up field and cut off the FS/backside or Cover 2 safety.

BSG and BSTE - Follow the same rules as the play side blockers, but they will work to get vertical much more quickly to cut off backside secondary pursuit once the runner is play side.

TB – Attack the outside hip of the PSTE and get vertical going to the end zone. If the second level defender (typically OLB) is inside then wall him off.

QB – Follow the TB into the edge staying on his outside hip. If he moves inside, then go vertical to the end zone and wall off any defender crossing your face. If he moves outside, then cut up field immediately, get vertical to the end zone and wall off any defender attempting to cross your face.

BB – Secure the snap, cross over and gain depth until you pass the PULL TE, then stay flat at cruising speed (60 to 75% of full speed). When you see the daylight in the seam, get vertical and go to the end zone as quickly as possible.
This is a great misdirection sweep play when the defense is aligning or shifting over and leaving two or less on the backside perimeter.

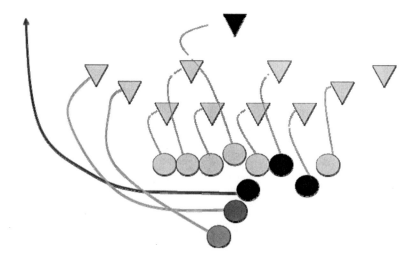

Figure 8GG. Shift Nasty 37 Pin Right

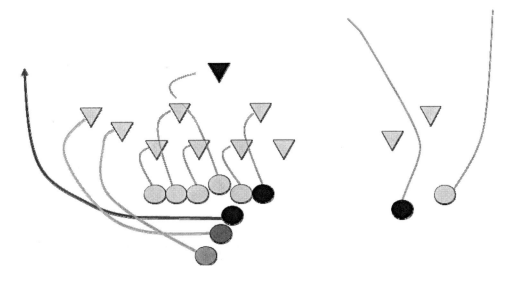

Figure 8HH. Shift Loose 37 Pin Right

Coaching Notes:

When running this play with Nasty (Figure 8GG), the PSTE and PSWB simply swap backside assignments. When running this play with Loose (Figure 8HH), the Slot and SE will run outside release routes to pull the backside perimeter defenders away from the pursuit.

Don't run this play unless the defense is aligning or shifting to strength and thereby over playing the power game. Once they do, they will leave two or less perimeter defenders isolated on the backside, and then you can hit them with this very quick hitting misdirection sweep.

Opposite is Shift Liz 38 Pin Left

Shift Rip 13 ISO Right

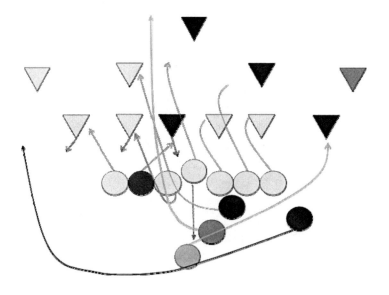

Figure 8ll. Shift Rip 13 ISO Right

Line –

> Pulling Tackle – Block down and drive the first defender inside towards the Center's hip.
> Pulling Guard – Drop your outside foot so it points at 45 degrees, then kick out block the first defender outside that crosses your face (kick out at a 45 degree angle not flat).
> Pulling Tight End – If COVERED, LEG & Turn aiming for the inside arm pit. Wall off with your butt inside as you drive the defender out. If UNCOVERED, then fan block the first defender to cross your face and drive him outside.
> Center – If COVERED, LEG & TURN aiming for the play side arm pit. Wall your butt inside as you drive the defender out. If UNCOVERED, release and block first backer inside; if no backer threat is present, work to cut off the FS or backside COVER 2 safety.
> Wall Guard to Wall Tight End – If COVERED, LEG & TURN aiming for the play side arm pit. Wall your butt to the play side as you drive the defender away. If UNCOVERED, release and cut off the first backer inside; if there is no backer threat, release and cut off the backside secondary pursuit.

BB – Cross over step, then lead into hole and go vertical to the end zone. When encountering any defender attempting to cross your face, LEG & TURN (PIN) him to that side, so the QB can go vertical.

QB – Secure the snap and follow BB into hole. If the BB keeps going vertical cut off his line and head to daylight. If the BB engages a defender, cut to his backside and go vertical to the end zone while working to the near sideline.

TB – Execute a flash fake, fake reverse hand off, and kick out the first defender to cross your face backside (wall side).

WB – Drop step, fake reverse, and then run like you have the football and score a TD. The better the fake, the more likely you can pull the play side perimeter defenders away from the interior. This play is a great alternative when you see the defensive tackle on the pulling side collapsing hard inside to chase the pullers and the next defensive lineman outside is over-playing the reverse. This allows us to essentially cross block the two linemen and open a hole for the BB to isolate and block the first backer to show as the QB follows him into the hole. With the QB and WB faking power and reverse, the play essentially acts as a split flow to force both perimeters to react and respond.

Coaching Notes:

Because this play is run to the pull side, it doesn't matter if it is tagged with Nasty (Figure 8JJ), Loose (Figure 8KK), or any other tag - except for OVER, which would relocate a key blocker away from the play side.

The BB must hit the hole fast, aggressively, and always take on on the first defender encountered on the other side of the LOS, as this block is key to the success of this play.

Opposite: Shift Liz 14 ISO Left

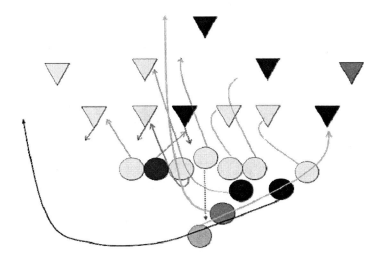

Figure 8JJ. Shift Nasty Rip 13 ISO Right

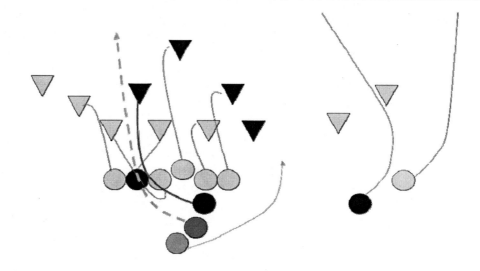

Figure 8KK. Shift Loose Rip 13 ISO Right

Shift Rip 23 ISO Right

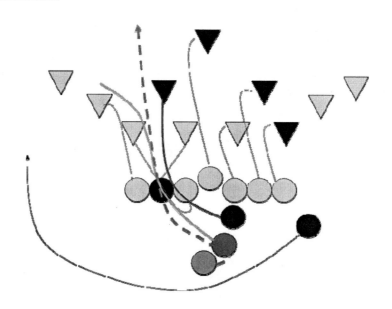

Figure 8LL. Shift Rip 23 ISO Right

Line –

Pulling Tackle – Block down and drive the first defender inside towards the Center's hip.

Pulling Guard – Drop your outside foot so it points at 45 degrees and kick out the first defender outside that crosses your face (kick out at a 45 degree angle not flat).

Pulling End – If COVERED, LEG & Turn aiming for the inside arm pit. Wall off with your butt inside as you drive the defender out. If UNCOVERED, fan block the first defender to cross your face and drive him outside.

Center – If COVERED, LEG & TURN aiming for the play side arm pit. Wall your butt inside as you drive the defender out. If UNCOVERED, release and block the first backer inside; if no backer threat is present, work to cut off the FS or backside COVER 2 safety.

Wall Guard to Wall End – If COVERED, LEG & TURN aiming for the play side arm pit. Wall your butt to the play side as you drive the defender away. If UNCOVERED, release and cut off the first backer inside; if there is no backer threat, release and cut off the backside secondary pursuit.

BB – Cross over step, then lead into the hole and go vertical to the end zone. If any defender attempts to cross your face, LEG & TURN (PIN) him to that side so that the TB can go vertical.

QB – Cross over step, then follow the BB into the hole and cut off his outside hip as he passes the LOS. Wall out the first defender that crosses your face (typically the CB).

TB – Secure the snap, counter step, and hit the hole downhill, reading the BB's block. Break off his backside and get vertical to the end zone.

WB – Drop step, fake reverse then run like you have the football and score a TD. The better the fake, the more likely you can pull the play side perimeter defenders away from the interior.

This play is a great alternative when you see the defensive tackle on the pulling side collapsing hard inside to chase the pullers and the next defensive lineman outside over-playing the reverse. This allows us to essentially cross block the two defenders and open a hole for the BB to attack the first backer he encounters as the QB follows him into the hole. With the QB and WB faking power and reverse, the play essentially acts as a split flow designed to force both perimeters to react and respond.

Coaching Notes:

Since this play is run to the pull side, it doesn't matter if it tagged with Nasty (Figure 8MM), Loose (Figure 8NN), or any other tag - except for OVER, as this will relocate a key blocker away from the play side.

The BB and QB must hit the hole fast, aggressively, and always take on the first defender encountered on the other side of the LOS, as these blocks are key to the success of this play.

Because we run so many power and power sweep plays, it is for a legitimate threat when the TB steps to the strong side, and thus this is an effective method to hold the perimeter defenders in place long enough to overwhelm the pull side.

Opposite: Shift Liz 24 ISO Left

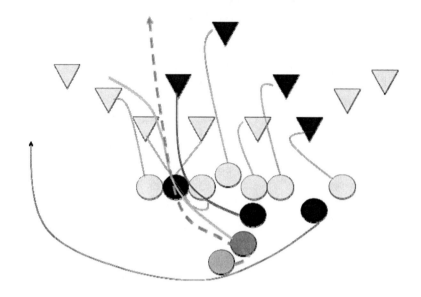

Figure 8MM. Shift Nasty Rip 23 ISO Right

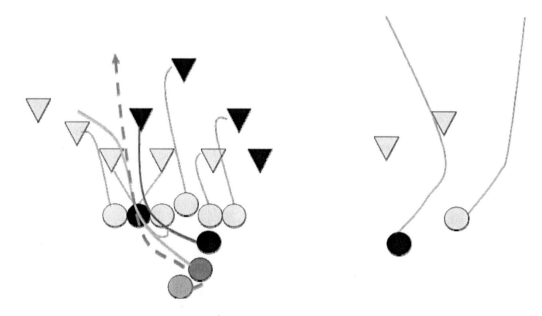

Figure 8NN. Shift Loose Rip 23 ISO Right

Shift Rip 14 Double Right

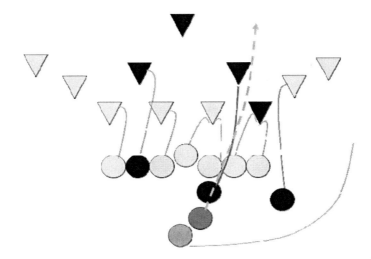

Figure 8OO. Shift Rip 14 Double Right

Line –

> Wall Tight End and Wall Tackle - Combo block the DLM that is covering either of them and drive him straight back. In executing the double team, keep hips together and get near palms into the bottom lip of the breast plate and far palms into the respective arm pit, then drive the defender upward and back.
> Wall Guard and Center - Combo block the DLM that is covering either of them and drive him straight back. In executing the double team, keep hips together and get near palms into the bottom lip of the breast plate and far palms into the respective arm pit, then drive the defender upward and back.
> Pulling Side - Block covered/uncovered (LEG & TURN).

BB – Cross over step, then lead into hole and go vertical to the end zone. If any defender attempts to cross your face, LEG & TURN (PIN) him to that side, so the QB can go vertical.

QB – Secure the snap and follow the BB into hole. If the BB keeps going vertical, cut off his line and go to daylight. If the BB engages a defender, cut to his backside, then go vertical to the end zone while working to the near sideline.

TB – Execute a flash fake, then attack the strong side faking power sweep. Go for the touchdown!

WB – Fire off squeezing inside (tight to the hip of the wall tight end) and wall out the first defender encountered outside of the wall tight end (LEG AND TURN).

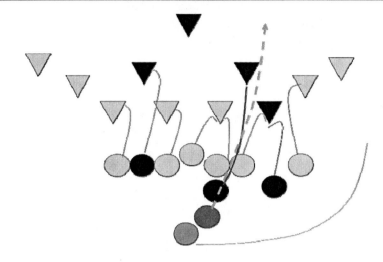

Figure 8PP. Shift Nasty Rip 14 Double Right

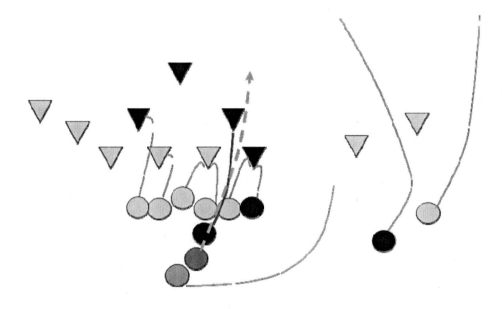

Figure 8QQ. Shift Loose Over Rip 14 Double Right

Coaching Notes:

Since this play is directed to the wall side, it is important to have a four man TKO wall. Note that when we run this play with Nasty (Figure 8PP), the WB picks up the combo block with the WT as the WTE walls out the CB. In Loose (Figure 8QQ), we include OVER to ensure we maintain the four man wall.

The BB must hit the hole fast, aggressively, and always engage the first defender encountered on the other side of the LOS, as this block is a key to the success of this play.

Because we run so many power and power sweep plays, it is more than convincing when the TB fakes the power sweep, i.e. this is an effective method to hold or even pull perimeter defenders away from the edge.

Opposite: Shift Liz 13 Double Left

Shift Rip 31 Dive Right

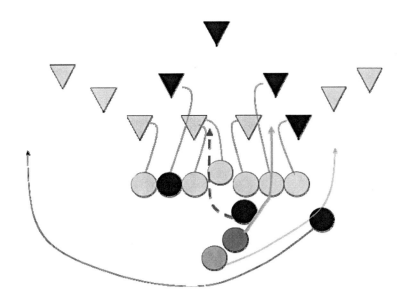

Figure 8RR. Shift Rip 31 Dive Right

Line –

    Wall Tight End to Wall Guard - Block covered/uncovered (LEG & TURN).
    Center and Pull Guard - Combo block the first DLM play side (NT to DT).
    Pulling Tackle and Pulling Tight End - Block covered/uncovered (LEG & TURN).

    Note: If the DLM at the point of attack can be handled with a one-on-one block, the center (even front) or pull guard (odd front) can release to engage the FBI or the safety. We combo block that DLM to create a big hole, so we'll only call for one-on-one if the DLM is easily handled by the one block.

WB - Execute a fake XX reverse.

TB - Execute a flash fake and fake sweep/XX reverse.

QB - Execute a flash fake, cross over step, then attack the wall guard's heels and get vertical. Make it look like you have the ball. Stay away from the pull side.

BB - Secure the snap and get vertical on Center's pull side hip.

Shift Rip 14 Dive Right

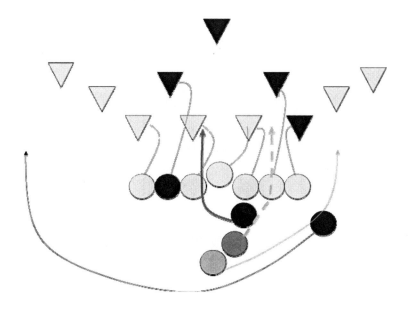

Figure 8SS. <u>Shift Rip 14 Dive Right</u>

Line –

    Center and Wall Guard - Combo block the first DLM play side (NT to DT).

    Note: If the DLM at the point of attack can be handled with a one-on-one block, the center (even front) or pull guard (odd front) can release to engage the FBI or the safety. We combo block that DLM to create a big hole, so we'll only call for one-on-one if the DLM is easily handled by the one block.

    Wall Tackle and Wall Tight End - Block covered/uncovered (LEG & TURN).
    Pulling Guard to Pull Tight End - Block covered/uncovered (LEG & TURN).

WB - Execute a fake XX reverse.

TB - Execute a flash fake and fake sweep/XX reverse.

QB - Secure the snap and get vertical on the Center's wall side hip.

BB - Execute a flash fake, cross over step, then attack the pull guard's heels and get vertical. Make it look like you have the ball. Stay away from the wall side.

Rip Drag Pass Right (Sprint)

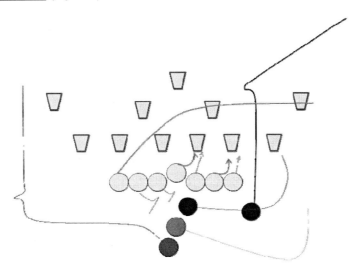

Figure 8TT. Rip Drag Pass Right

Line -

> Wall Tight End to Center – Slide to wall side (Covered/Uncovered). LEM/SSM
> Pulling Guard to Pulling Tackle – Hinge to the wall side and don't allow any defender inside of you, i.e. force any defender encountered to go outside of you and around the hinge wall. KKM

Pulling Tight End - Inside release through the heels of first backer inside and gain depth of 4 to 6 yards. As soon as you pass the Center, start looking for the ball as you are the second read (LOW). If the QB runs the ball, turn back over your up field shoulder and wall off the first defender to show (put him on the ground).

WB - Outside release, take 8 to 9 steps, then break outside at 45 degrees (corner) and accelerate to the sideline until you find open space. You are the HIGH read (first read) of the QB. If the ball goes to the PTE (low read) or the QB runs, turn back over your up field shoulder and wall off the first defender to show (put him on the ground).

TB - Lead step at the pull side DEMLOS, then flatten out and run a Swing (turn and look for the ball, if no ball finish with the Wheel route). If TBACK is added to the play, you are tagged as the primary route. If there is no tag for TBACK, then wall off below the pull tackle hinge.

BB - Gain a little depth, then get to the outside arm pit of the first defender to show past the WTE, and wall him inside.

QB - Secure the snap and gain depth to the wall side (at least 3 to 5 yards of depth). You must threaten the perimeter quickly while looking to throw as soon as you secure the ball. If the WB is open, throw to him immediately so he can eat up as much vertical space as possible before the defense recovers. Your read is HIGH (WB) to LOW (PTE). If neither is open, run the ball. If you see vertical space as you roll out, run the ball. The object is to get positive yards not complete a pass. If tagged with TBACK, gain extra depth, then as you break wide plant and set to throw to the TB. If he is open on the SWING, throw him open. If you see him break to Wheel, throw him open so he can catch the ball and run with it.

This play can be tagged TB (SHIFT RIP DRAG TB PASS RIGHT) to tell the TB and QB to exchange assignments; a great way to get the QB into the throwback, if they are in man coverage.

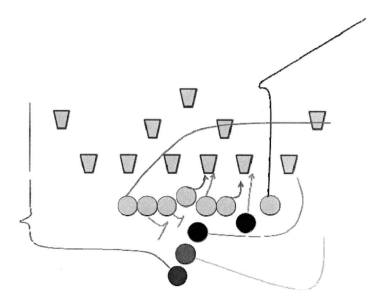

Figure 8UU. Shift Nasty Rip Drag Pass Right

The Loose (Figure 8VV) variation of this play is different because it provides a LOW-HIGH read on the play side with the QUICK OUT by #1 and the CORNER by #2 (smash concept). The drag from backside becomes a #3 read, especially if the corner rolls to the flat and the OLB rolls high to cover the corner - the drag will open in the CURL/HOOK. If the backside corner is covering the PTE, then the TB TBACK becomes a big play with the defense spread out on the other side. The QB must make the low-high read on the run; if he sees neither open, he must look to the drag as it clears past the Center's head.

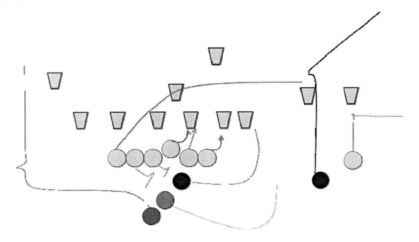

Figure 8VV. Shift Loose Rip Drag Pass Right

Shift Rip Reverse Pass Right (Sprint)

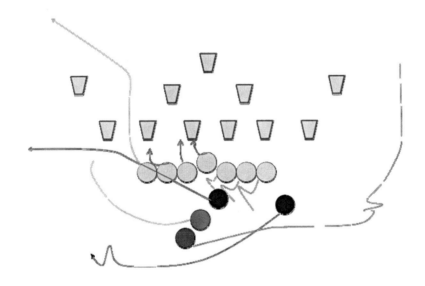

Figure 8WW. Shift Rip Reverse Pass Right

Line -

Wall Tackle to Center – Slide to the wall side (Covered/Uncovered). LEM/SSM Pulling Guard to Pulling Tight End – Hinge to the wall side and don't allow any defender inside of you; i.e. force defenders to go outside of you and around the hinge wall. KKM

Wall Tight End - Release outside, take 8 to 9 steps then break outside at 35 degrees (corner) and accelerate to the sideline until you find open space. You are the HIGH read (first read) of the QB. If the ball goes to the BB (low read) or the WB runs, turn back over your up field shoulder and wall off the first defender to show (put him on the ground).

WB - Drop step, then get to the outside hip of the TB and take the hand off. Don't rush or sprint into the hand off. Once you get the ball, accelerate to full speed and get outside. With the ball secured, get your eyes up field and look for the HIGH (WTE running corner route) and LOW read (BB into flat). If you see the HIGH open throw it immediately, if you see the LOW open throw it immediately, if you see daylight run! If TBACK is added to play, as you get outside, stop plant and throw back to the TBACK so he runs to the ball and vertical. If the Swing is not open, he will run Wheel - so throw him open to the wheel.

TB - Cross over step, then outside hand off to the WB behind the wall side. Flatten out and run a swing route as you break about 3 to 5 yards past the WB's starting spot (turn and look for the ball no ball finish with the wheel route). If TBACK is added to the play, you are tagged as the primary route. If there is no tag for TBACK, wall off below the pull tackle hinge.

BB - Jab step to fake power and run to the flat on the other side. Run through the DEMLOS's far shoulder to slow his rush. As you pass the defender gain speed and get your head around for the ball. If the WB runs, turn back over your up field shoulder and wall in any defender near you (put him on the ground).

QB - Cross over and gain depth to log the DEMLOS.

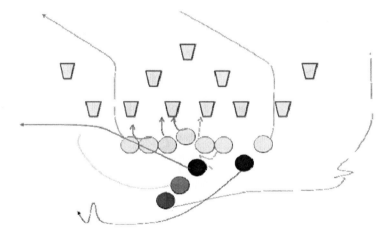

Figure 8XX. Shift Nasty Rip Reverse Pass Left

Coaching Points:

This play is not used with any edge tag other than NASTY (Figure 8XX) or ON, as it expands the WB too far away from the other side to be effective.

You can use OVER to apply additional blocking to the play side if needed.

Chapter 9
Star Power & Lead Series

The Star series is really a modification of the SHIFT series. We move both the TB (inside) and the WB (outside) over to split the wall tight end (WSTE), and we move the BB to the strong side of the QB, at the same depth, splitting the center at 3 to 4 yards. This formation is used to get our BB more involved in the power running game, particularly if we have an athletic power back in our BB position. If we don't, we simply swap the BB and the TB so that we maximize this formation. This gives us a very distinct line of force to the strong edge and perimeter and gives us a very nice bunch passing game as well, i.e. this backfield alignment works really well with the BUNCH/TRIPS edge tags.

Aligning the backfield of STAR

Normal backfield alignment (Figure 9A) for the backs places the QB and BB 3 to 4 yards back aligned with the near foot of both splitting the center. The TB lines up between the tackle and tight end, while the WB aligns on the outside of the tight end; both backs face toward the end zone. The QB and BB are within six inches of each other, such that when the ball is snapped straight back, either back can snatch the ball (depending on the play call) while the other flash fakes. This close proximity helps to create some natural misdirection just as the play is starting forcing the defense to sit and read, or fully commit to their assigned gaps.

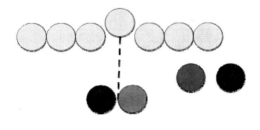

BB, QB, BSWB, PSWB

Figure 9A. Normal Alignment for the Star Series

Star Formations

1.   Can every core play in my power series be used in this formation with little to no alteration in the basic structure of the play? *Answer - Yes*

2.   Can I use my current system of edge tags to alter the perimeter so that I can adapt and isolate the perimeter triangle of the defense? *Answer – Yes*

3.   What advantage does it give me that I don't have using my base formation (TIGHT)? *Answer – More immediate power at the point of attack with which to*

overwhelm the hole, direct snap gets the ball into the primary ball carrier's hands, and the layered backfield increases misdirection.

4. Does it give me a leverage or a line of force advantage against the defense? ANSWER – Yes, it does to the strong side edge and perimeter; when the defense over shifts it gives me an advantage to the weak side as well. In Star we use a double team with our WB/TB or WB/BB on the DEMLOS rather than a kick out. This also opens up our power sweep, as it forces the DEMLOS to recognize the potential for that double team and overplay the inside gap.

Brief Overview of the Star Power Series

Interior Plays – 10 Wedge Right, 30 Wedge Right (Rip and Liz),

- Interior power play for this series.
- Use reverse (XX) action behind it to create deception designed to hold the perimeter defenders in place on each side.
- QB and BB variants allow you to hit the same spot with two different players increasing the misdirection aspect of the offense.

Edge Plays – Rip 36 Seal Right, Rip 16 Seal Right, Rip 23 Kick Left, Rip 45 Kick Left, Liz 35 Seal Left, Liz 15 Seal Left, Liz 24 Kick Right, Liz 26 Kick Right

- Seal Play (Power Play, e.g. Rip 36 Seal Right, Rip 16 Seal Right, Liz 35 Seal Left, Liz 15 Seal Left)
  - Core play of this offense
  - Must be able to run it anywhere on the field, at any time, against any defensive scheme.
  - We have a variety of ways to run this play to keep the defense on their toes.
  - BB power play is a pure power play with a maximum amount of blockers. It is our base play.

- TB Kick (TB Counter Trap, e.g. Rip 23 Kick Left/ Liz 24 Kick Right)
  - Edge misdirection play that allows us to attack the defense with the pre-flow look of WB power in the opposite direction and WB reverse action in the play direction, and then hit back inside, on the edge with the BB as the perimeter defenders converge on power and reverse (XX).
  - BB must hit inside vertically and go north-south quickly.

- WB Kick (WB Counter Trap, e.g. Rip 45 Kick Left, Liz 26 Kick Right)
  - Edge misdirection play that allows us to attack the defense with the pre-flow look of WB power in one direction and then hit back against flow with an inside counter.
  - WB must hit inside vertically and go north-south quickly.

Perimeter Plays – Rip 38 Monster Sweep Right, Rip 38 Wide Right, Rip 37 Wide Reverse Left, Liz 37 Monster Sweep Left, Liz 37 Wide Left, Liz 38 Wide Reverse Right.

- BB Monster Sweep (Power Sweep, e.g. Rip 38 Monster Sweep, Liz 37 Monster Sweep)
  - Perimeter power play. Overwhelm the perimeter with pullers.
  - Must seal the EMLOS to the inside.
  - Best run when you have two in the perimeter triangle and/or you see the EMLOS squatting/crashing to the WB power play.

- BB Wide Reverse (XX outside reverse, e.g. Rip 37 Wide Reverse, Liz 38 Wide Reverse)
  - Perimeter misdirection play. Isolate the interior and perimeter defenders and attempt to attack the backside perimeter triangle (away from power).
  - Key is 2 or less in the perimeter box and EMLOS vacating contain with shallow pinch inside to chase power.
  - Best used against a defense that is crashing the backside of power.

- WB Wide Sweep (Rip 38 Wide, Liz 37 Wide)
  - Alternative power perimeter play for the monster sweep.
  - If the OLB and CB are filling hard into the tunnel of the TKO wall, this is a nice alternative.
  - Good alternative if you are having problems using the Monster Sweep due to a good OLB/SS on the play side.

Play Action Passing – Rip Power Pass Right, Liz Power Pass Left.

- Power Pass
  - Run/Pass option
  - Basic flood pattern on the power side.
  - Read low to high (BB flat to WB out).
  - Can teach a peek deep if MOFO (middle of the field open).
  - Run this to the QB's throwing side

A quick reminder on RIGHT/LEFT tags added to the play. This side call is for the linemen and to remind them what side the WALL SIDE lines up on and has nothing to do with the direction of the play. For instances on all wedge plays we always line up our wall on the right side so there is no real "tell" to which side wedge is being run. It is the method I use to notify my wall side where to line up.

Detailed Description of Select Plays:
The Star Power Series

<u>Star Rip 30 Wedge Right</u> (Interior play)

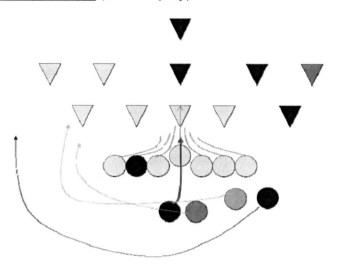

Figure 9B. Star Rip 30 Wedge Right

Line – Wedge block on the Center.

BB – Secure the snap and hit the wedge. Look for a crease on either side, hit it, and get vertical. Do not go around or under the wedge.

QB – Execute a flash fake and go through the heels of the BB and gain depth. Aim for the INSIDE ARM PIT of the far DEMLOS and wall him outside.

TB (BSWB) – Gain depth and block the first defender to show past the far DEMLOS. Wall him outside and away from the wedge.

WB – Execute a flash fake reverse then attack the perimeter and get vertical up field. Make it look like you are scoring.

This is the classic XX or power/reverse action behind the BB wedge creating a split flow that places pressure on both perimeter triangles to defend their edge/perimeter while we attack the interior. Essentially this play isolates the interior as we overwhelm it with the wedge blocking scheme.

Coaching Notes:

Can be run using the OVER tag as well.

Opposite is Star Liz 30 Wedge Right.

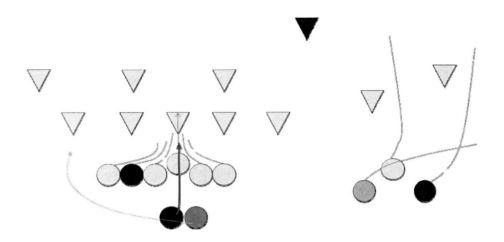

Figure 9C. Star Bunch Rip 30 Wedge Right

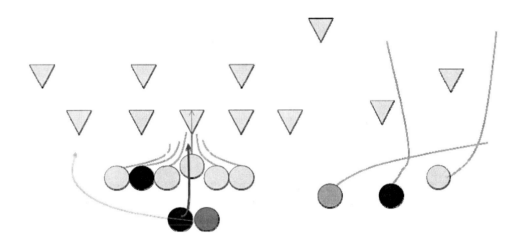

Figure 9D. Star Trips Rip 30 Wedge Right

Star Rip 10 Wedge Right (Interior play)

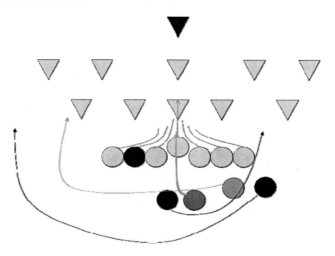

Figure 9E. Star Rip 10 Wedge Right

Line – Wedge block on the Center.

BB – Cross over and gain depth through the heels of the QB, then fake power to the far side. Attack the inside arm pit of the DEMLOS.

QB – Secure the snap and hit the wedge. Look for a crease on either side, then hit it and get vertical. Do not go around or under the wedge. Secure the ball and get as many yards you can.

TB (BSWB) – Gain depth and block the first defender to show past the far DEMLOS. Wall him outside and away from the wedge.

WB – Execute a flash fake reverse, then attack the perimeter and get vertical up field. Make it look like you are scoring.

This is the classic XX or power/reverse action behind the QB wedge creating a split flow that places pressure on both perimeter triangles to defend their edge/perimeter while we attack the interior. This play works the exact same way the BB Wedge does, but it allows us to utilize a power runner type at QB and basically get the ball into another back's hands behind the wedge while the BB assumes the backside perimeter threat.

Coaching Notes:

Can be run using the OVER tag as well.

Opposite is Star Liz 10 Wedge Right.

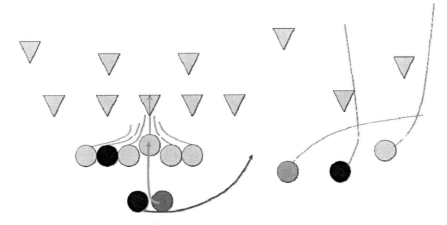

Figure 9F. Star Trips Rip 10 Wedge Right

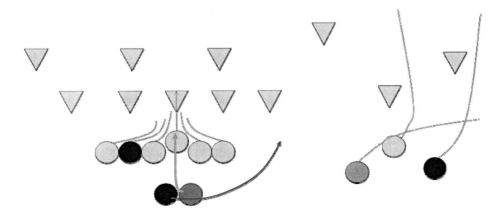

Figure 9G. Star Bunch Rip 10 Wedge Right

Star Rip 36 Seal Right (Edge play)

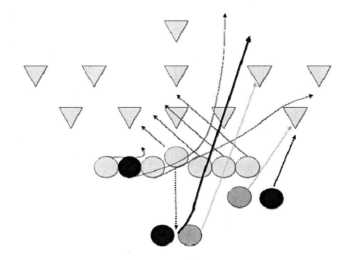

Figure 9H. Star Rip 36 Seal Right

Line –
        Wall side – TKO (center to PSTE)
        Pulling Guard – The BSG will pull and kick out the first defender to show above BB and QB
        Pulling Tackle – The BST pull up the wall and go vertical to the end zone; any defender crossing his face will be sealed inside with a wall off.
        Pulling Tight End – Cutoff to the Center's hip; if no one shows, climb to the linebacker level and cutoff the backside pursuit.

TB/WB – The WB will post block (LEG) the DEMLOS, attacking the center of the breastplate of the defender and the outside arm pit; the TB will attack the inside arm pit. Both will mesh their near hips and COMBO block the DEMLOS driving him out wide as they wall him off.

QB – Execute a flash fake, then cross over step aiming for the heels of the BB. Follow the BB into the hole and kick out the first defender to show above him. It will be the First Backer Inside (FBI) or cornerback.

BB – Secure the snap, then aim for the center's play side hip and get vertical to daylight. Climb the wall and get 5 yards. Once you make it out of the tunnel, make a move (cutback inside, go vertical, bounce it outside) and then get vertical to the end zone. Do not make a move until breaking past the tunnel. Never let one defender take you down and never let a defender hit you; you hit him first. Your depth at the snap should be 4 to 5 yards but don't hesitate to adjust the depth so that you arrive just behind the BSG and BST as they hit the tunnel. The timing is very important as it will hide your approach into the tunnel.

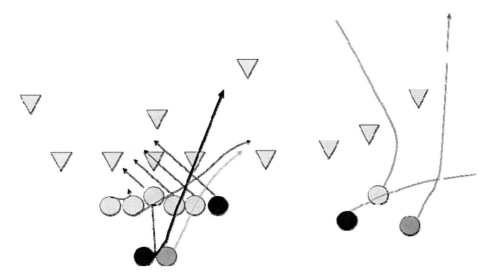

Figure 9I. Star Bunch Over Rip 36 Seal Right

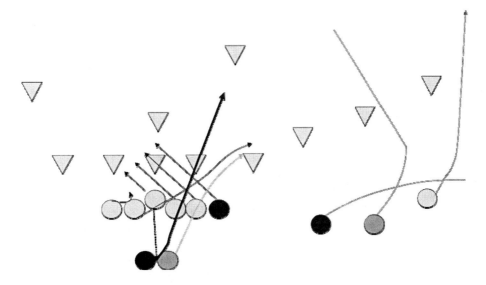

Figure 9J. Star Trips Over Rip 36 Seal Right

Coaching Notes:

I never run this with only 3 blockers on the TKO wall, so I'll include OVER whenever we extend the end with an edge tag (see Figures 9I and 9J).

Opposite is Star Liz 35 Seal Left

<u>Star Rip 16 Seal Right</u> (Edge play)

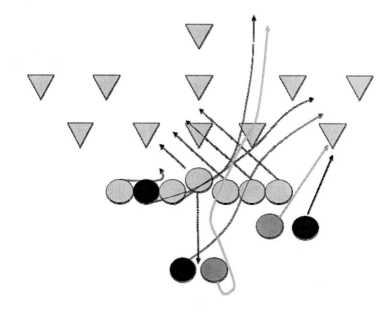

Figure 9K. Star Rip 16 Seal Right

Line –
        Wall side – TKO (center to PSTE)
        Pulling Guard – The BSG will pull and kick out the first defender to show above the BB and QB.
        Pulling Tackle – The BST will pull up the wall then go vertical to the end zone; any defender crossing his face will be sealed inside with a wall off.
        Pulling Tight End – Cutoff to the Center's hip; if no one shows, climb to the linebacker level and cutoff the backside pursuit.

BB – Cross over and hug the LOS by aiming for the inside hip of the first play side blocker, then kick out the first defender to cross your face. When you kick him out, flip your hips and body into the hole so you isolate the defender away from the QB as he hits the tunnel.

QB – Secure the snap and set as if to throw to the strong side deep out, let the BB cross your face, then hit the hole as tight as possible up the wall and get vertical to the end zone. If you cut, take one cut (backside, vertical, outside) and go.

TB/WB – WB will post block (LEG) the DEMLOS attacking the center of the breastplate and the outside arm pit; the TB will attack the inside arm pit. Both will mesh near hips and COMBO block the DEMLOS driving him out wide as they wall him off.

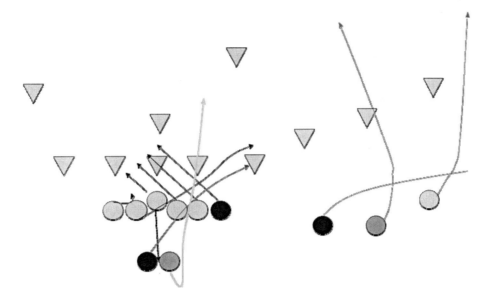

Figure 9L. Star Trips Over Rip 16 Seal Right

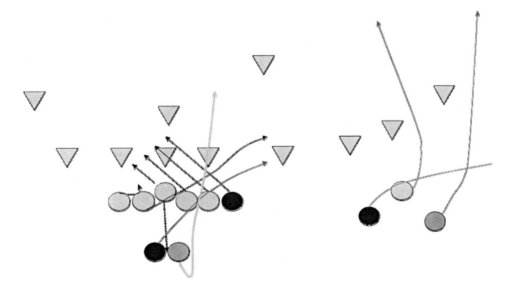

Figure 9M. Star Bunch Over Rip 16 Seal Right

Coaching Notes:

I never run this with only 3 blockers on the TKO wall, so I'll use OVER whenever we extend the end out with an edge tag (see Figures 9L and 9M). This is a great QB draw variation of running power.

Opposite is Star Liz 15 Seal Left.

Star Rip 45 Kick Left (Edge play)

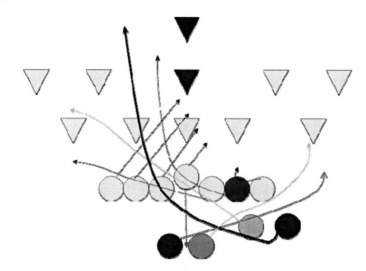

Figure 9N. Star Rip 45 Kick Left

Line –

> Wall side – TKO (Center to PSTE)
>
> Pulling Guard – The BSG will pull and kick out the first defender to cross his face. When he kicks the defender out, the BSG will flip his hips and body into the hole to isolate the defender away from the WB as he hits the tunnel.
>
> Pulling Tackle – The BST pulls up the wall then goes vertical to the end zone; any defender crossing his face will be sealed inside with a wall off.
>
> Pulling Tight End – Cutoff to the Center's hip; if no one shows, climb to the linebacker level and cut off the backside pursuit.

QB – Cross over step then attack the inside arm pit of the DEMLOS and wall him outside.

BB – Secure the snap, take a short cross step to open belt buckle to WB, then make the handoff to him and fake power sweep.

TB (BSWB) – Cross over step and follow pulling tackling into hole; kick out the first defender to show above the pulling guard's kick out.

WB – Drop step with the inside foot then aim for the inside hip of the BB and take the handoff. Secure the ball and get vertical when you see the first daylight to the end zone. Do not go east-west, you must get vertical get up field, then get to the boundary once you clear the tunnel.

Coaching Notes:

This is an outstanding play when you see the backside defenders overplaying or chasing the power or power sweep or power pass play. We don't use the WB Counter in Trips and Bunch as there is not enough flow misdirection to create the backside displacement we are looking for in the play.

This can be run as a SHOVEL pass from the BB to WB by simply adding SHOVEL to the play. Note that a shovel pass is essentially a FORWARD PASS, so if they drop the ball it is simply an incomplete pass.

Opposite is Star Liz 36 Kick Right

Star Rip 23 Kick Left (Edge play)

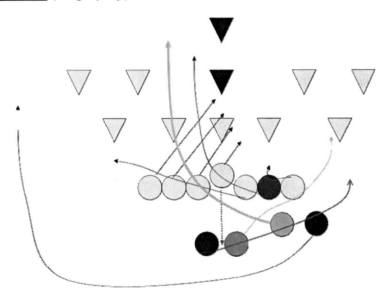

Figure 9O. **Star Rip 23 Kick Left**

Line –

Wall side – TKO (center to PSTE)

Pulling Guard – The BSG will pull and kick out the first defender to cross his face. When he kicks him out, the BSG will flip his hips and body into the hole to isolate the defender away from the WB as he hits the tunnel.

Pulling Tackle – The BST will pull up the wall and go vertical to the end zone; any defender crossing his face will be sealed inside with a wall off.

Pulling Tight End – Cutoff to the Center's hip; if no one shows climb to the linebacker level and cutoff the backside pursuit.

QB – Cross over step and attack the inside arm pit of the DEMLOS and wall him outside.

BB – Secure the snap, take a short cross step to open belt buckle to TB, then make the handoff to him, and fake power sweep.

TB (BSWB) – Drop step with the inside foot then aim for the inside hip of the BB and take the handoff. Secure the ball and get vertical when you see the first daylight to the end zone. Do not go east-west, you must get vertical; get up field and then get to the boundary once you clear the tunnel.

WB – Drop step and fake the XX reverse action to the backside. Make it look real to force the backside edge to widen as the perimeter defenders pursue you and thereby open the hole for the TB.

Coaching Notes:

This is an outstanding play when you see the backside defenders overplaying or chasing the power or power sweep or power pass play. We don't use the TB Counter in Trips or Bunch as there is not enough flow misdirection to create the backside displacement we need for the play to be successful.

This can be run as a SHOVEL pass from the BB to WB by simply adding SHOVEL to the play. Note that a shovel pass is essentially a FORWARD PASS, so if they drop the ball it is simply an incomplete pass.

Opposite is Star Liz 44 Kick Right.

Star Rip 38 Monster Sweep Right (perimeter play)

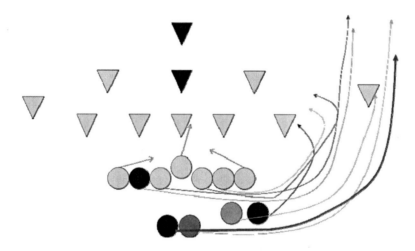

Figure 9P. Star Rip 38 Monster Sweep Right

Line –
> Wall Tight End – Cut off play side to the center's hip.
> Wall Tackle – Pull around the WTE and WSWB then form a wall land marking the outside shoulder of the WSWB.
> Wall Guard – Pull around WTE and WSWB then form a wall land marking the outside shoulder of the WT.
> Center – When facing a NT (odd front), jewel block him by aiming your far shoulder at the crotch of the defender so that your head goes past the play side hip. If facing an even front (DT), severe down block aiming for a point just in front of his far (play side) shoulder and wheel your butt to the play side.

Pulling Side Guard and Tackle – Pull tight down the LOS then pull tight around the perimeter wall and go vertical to the end zone, creating a vertical lane for the runner. Any defender that crosses your face you should be walled him off, i.e. attack his up field arm pit and wheel your butt towards the runner. Any leakage encountered as you go down the line should be picked up by cutting it off the same way the Center does against an even front.

Pulling Tight End – Cutoff to the Center's hip; if no one shows climb to linebacker level.

TB – Cross over then get outside and up field quickly. Against a CB that is off the LOS and near the EMLOS, you must come around to attack the outside arm pit and wheel block him. Against a wide CB, you must eat up space then settle down and wall him to the outside to create an alley for the runner.

QB – Execute a flash fake, cross over, and then get up field to create a vertical lane for the runner to the end zone. Any defender that crosses your face should be walled off.

BB – Secure the snap, then cross over staying flat (parallel) to the LOS until you go past the WSTE. Once you see daylight get vertical and up field, then make a move (cutback, vertical, bounce). Bear in mind you have three vertical blockers going down field near boundary so if you get in the alley between the three vertical pullers and the boundary your chance of a TD is big.

WB – Take a lateral step with the outside foot and attack the outside arm pit of the EMLOS, then wall him off by wheel blocking and driving him inside as far as you can.

Coaching Notes:

This is also used with Trips and Bunch. The key to running the monster sweep or any sweep out of Loose, Bunch, or Trips is to get in the inside lane between the receiver group and the DEMLOS. The stress you are placing on the secondary and perimeter defenders to cover pass and play run, along with the kick out block by a running back (TB in this case) opens a seam in the perimeter, and gives the OC/QB an easy key to identify whether we can fake run and use a play action pass.

Opposite is Star Liz 37 Monster Sweep Left

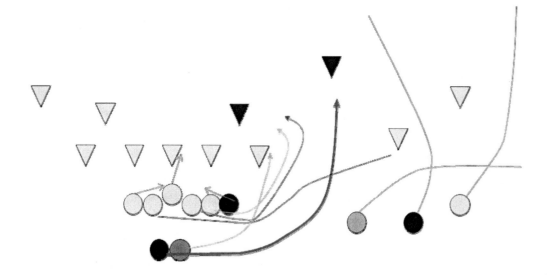

Figure 9Q. Star Trips Rip 38 Monster Sweep Right

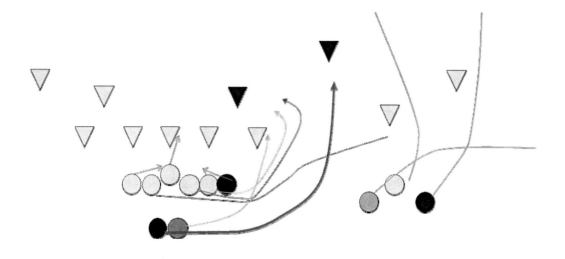

Figure 9R. Star Bunch Rip 38 Monster Sweep Right

Star Rip 38 Wide Right (Perimeter play)

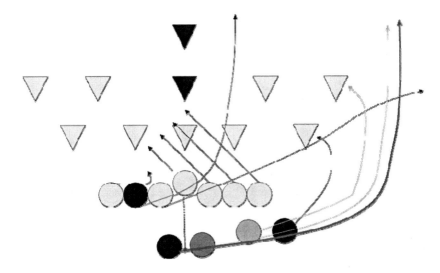

Figure 9S. Star Rip 38 Wide Right

Line –

> Wall side – TKO (Center to PSTE)
>
> Pulling Guard – The BSG will pull and kick out the first wide defender above the BB. If no defender is present outside (CB), he will turn and go vertical to the end zone.
>
> Pulling Tackle – The BST pull up the wall then go vertical to end zone; any defender crossing his face will be sealed inside with a wall off.
>
> Pulling Tight End – Cutoff to the Center's hip; if no one shows, climb to the linebacker level and cutoff the backside pursuit.

TB – Cross over step, gain depth, then get outside of WB's wall off and attack the first defender inside, walling him off.

QB – Execute a flash fake, then cross over step, gain depth and get outside of TB. Get vertical and if any defender crosses your face, wall him inside; otherwise go vertical to the end zone to give the runner a vertical lane.

BB – Secure the snap and cross over staying flat (parallel) to the LOS until you go past the WSTE. Once you see daylight, get vertical and up field, and make a move (cutback, vertical, bounce). Bear in mind that you have a vertical blocker going down field near boundary, so if you can get in that alley between the vertical puller and the boundary your chance of a TD is big.

This is a great sweep against OLB's and CB' s that are filling the alley behind the wall as they will get caught inside and we will have numbers outside for the runner.

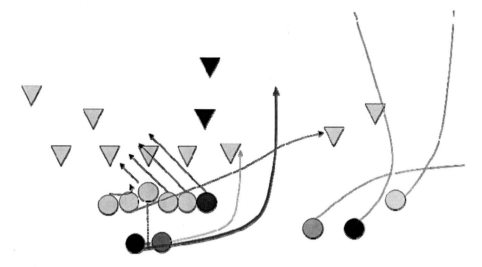

Figure 9T. Star Trips Over Rip 38 Wide Right

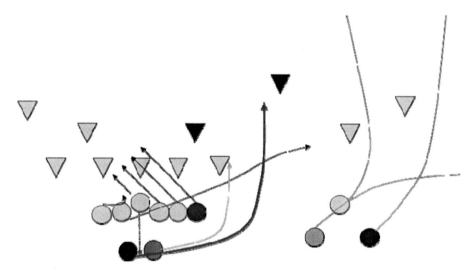

Figure 9U. Star Bunch Over Rip 38 Wide Right

Coaching Notes:

In Star Trips Over (Figure 9T) and Star Bunch Over (Figure 9U), our wing backs are extended along with the split end, thus we use the QB to log the EMLOS. The key to running the WIDE or any sweep out of Loose, Bunch, or Trips is to get in the inside lane between the receiver group and the EMLOS. The stress imposed on the secondary and perimeter defenders to cover pass and play run, along with the kick out block by a running back (QB in this case), opens a seam in the perimeter in which to run.

Opposite is Star Liz 37 Wide Left

Star Rip 47 Wide Reverse Left (perimeter play)

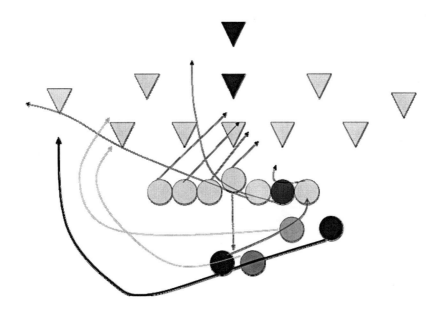

Figure 9V. Star Rip 47 Wide Reverse Left

Line –

    Wall Side – TKO (center to PSTE)

    Pulling Guard – The BSG will pull and climb as if to seal, but then go wide and kick out first outside (CB) defender to cross his face. When kick the defender out, he will flip his hips and body into the hole to isolate the defender away from the WB as he hits the tunnel. When facing an athletic corner, he will eat up space then settle down and wall him off.

    Pulling Tackle – The BST will pull up the wall then go vertical to the end zone; any defender crossing his face will be sealed inside with a wall off.

    Pulling Tight End – Cutoff to the Center's hip; if no one shows climb to the linebacker level and cut off the backside pursuit.

QB – Execute a flash fake, cross over then gain enough depth to log the DEMLOS and drive him inside. If he is crashing all you need to do is wall him in for a moment and push him further inside.

TB – Cross over then gain depth under the QB and wall off next defender inside (OLB normally).

BB – Secure the snap, cross over step, then make an outside handoff to WB. After the exchange, aim for the inside arm pit of the BSDE and make a great fake as if running seal. As you reach the BSDE, kick him out.

WB – Drop step, then get to the outside hip of the TB and take the hand off. Don't rush or sprint into the hand off. Once you get the ball, accelerate to full speed and get outside. Once you see daylight, get vertical quick. The faster you get vertical the more likely you are to get by the linebacker pursuit. If there is a corner wide, run inside of the BSG's kick out.

Coaching Notes:

This play is not used with any sort of edge tag as it takes too long to develop. It can, however, be used with the OVER tag to get an additional blocker.

Opposite is Star Liz 28 Wide Reverse

Star Rip Power Pass Right (Sprint)

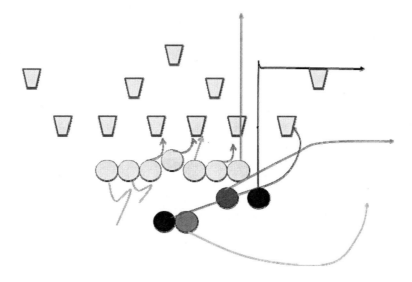

Figure 9W. Star Rip Power Pass Right

Line -
> WT to Center – Slide to wall side (Covered/Uncovered). LEM/SSM
> PG to PTE – Hinge to wall side and don't allow any defender inside of you, rather force him to go outside of you and around the hinge wall. KKMWTE: Outside release and go vertical up the middle then pin the safety deep. The ball will only go to you on a Middle of the Field Open (MOFO) read from the QB/OC.

WB - Outside release and take 8 to 9 steps and break outside and accelerate to the sideline until you find an open space. You are the HIGH read (second read) of the QB. If the ball goes to the BB (low read) or the QB runs, turn back, over the up field shoulder, and wall off the defender to show (put him on the ground).

TB - Release through the DEMLOS's face to slow his rush so that the BB can get outside and wall him inside. Run to the flat; as soon as you get past the DEMLOS, get your head around and look for the ball over your down field shoulder. You are the primary read (low read). If the QB runs the ball, turn back over the up field shoulder and wall off the defender to show (put him on the ground).

BB - Execute a flash fake, then fake sweep, getting wide to attack the outside arm pit of first defender to show past the WT.

QB - Secure the snap and gain depth to the wall side (at least 3 to 5 yards of depth). You must threaten the perimeter quickly while looking to throw as soon as you secure the ball. If the BB is open, throw to him immediately so he can eat up as much vertical space as possible before the defense recovers. Your read is LOW (BB) to HIGH (WB). If neither is open run the ball. If you see vertical space as you roll out, run the ball. The object is to get positive yards not complete a pass.

You can run a variation of this play wherein the WB and WALL TE switch assignments, i.e. the WB runs the vertical and the WALL TE runs the out. The normal assignment is #1 outside runs the out and #2 runs vertical and #3 runs flat. In the case of *Trips* (Figure 9X) or *Loose or Bunch* (Figure 9Y), it is #1 vertical, #2 out, and #3 flat.

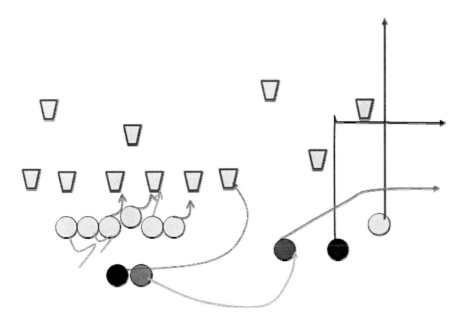

Figure 9X. Star Trips Rip Power Pass Right (sprint)

Coaching Notes:

You can use OVER to place an extra blocker (PULL TACKLE) on the play side, where he will follow the COVERED/UNCOVERED rule (LEM/SSM), This will allow you to adjust if you have a tough pass rush on that side; i.e. this allows you to pin point where you need additional pass protection (wall or pull side).

NOTE: If the QB or OC sees the MOFO (middle of the field open) meaning there is no FS in the middle of the field your first read is to the roll and throw it to the WALL TE on the inside shoulder. Throw to where he is going and not at him so he can catch it and run with it to the end zone.

Opposite Star Liz Power Pass Left (sprint)

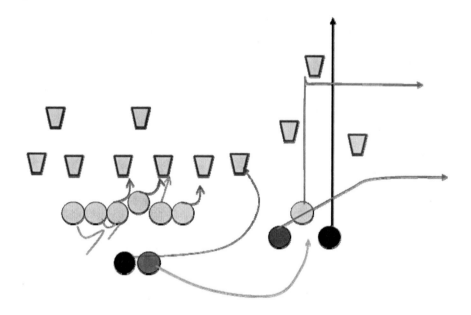

Figure 9Y. Star Bunch Rip Power Pass Right (sprint)

Brief Overview of the Star Lead Series

Interior Plays – Rip 31/14 Dive Right, Liz 32/13 Dive Left

- Interior power play for this series.
- Use reverse (XX) action behind it to create deception and hold the perimeter defenders in place on each side.
- QB and BB plays act as a double dive mini-series with cross action between the QB and BB which confuse the interior LB reads on the backfield.

Edge Plays – Rip 13 ISO Right, Rip 34 Double Right, Liz 14 ISO Left, Liz 33 Double Left

The ISO Play is a cross blocked play to the pull side (backside) with XX action behind it to hold the perimeter defenders in place for a moment while we overwhelm the point of attack.

- Great play to add to the power series as it allows you to attack the pull side immediately and directly (which has the better pullers and makes the cross blocking more effective) when defenses are keying on the WALL side and/or formation strength.
- Solid way of attacking an interior defender playing over the Pulling Guard in an attempt to shoot the gap between the pulling guard and center. As the defender attempts to chase the puller on pulling plays, the down block of the pull tackle becomes very easy to execute. It is also a nice way to attack the perimeter triangle on the Pull side when they are sitting on reverse and ready to pursue the XX action.
- We have two ways of running this play to keep defenses on their toes.
- QB ISO play is a quick power play with full XX action behind it. and the BB lead blocking to isolate the first backer inside (ILB often). Great to use if you have an athletic tough kid at QB.

The DOUBLE Play incorporates a double team/combo block to the wall side with XX action behind it. Used against even fronts that give us trouble running our angle blocking when they are sitting their ILB and OLB back while their defensive line absorbs the ABC wall. This allows us the drive those defenders back into laps of the backers using our WALL side blockers (our better drive/wall blockers) as double teamers/combo blockers.

Rip 34 Double Right, Liz 35 Double Left.

- DOUBLE plays to the BB allow us to double team the DT and DE with our C/WG and WT/WE while the QB lead blocks to isolate the OLB. The XX action of the BB counter stepping and the TB/WB faking XX action, helps to hold the perimeter defenders in place.

Perimeter Plays – Rip 38 Pin Right, Liz 37 Pin Left.

- BB Pin Sweep (Power Sweep, e.g. Rip 38 Pin, Liz 37 Pin)
  - Perimeter power play. Overwhelm the perimeter by using an aggressive vertical drive step and pinning the outside hip of all play side defenders while keying the last defender outside for a wall off/kick out.
  - Must seal the EMLOS to the inside and key the last perimeter defender for a wall off/kick out.
  - Best run when you have two in the perimeter triangle and/or you see the EMLOS squatting/crashing to the WB power play, as this further isolates the remaining perimeter defenders.

Play Action Passing – Rip Drag Pass Right, Liz Drag Pass Left, Rip Reverse Pass Right, Liz Reverse Pass Left.

- Drag Pass
  - Run/Pass option
  - Basic high-low drag pattern to power side.
  - Read PSWB corner to BSTE shallow drag (high to low)
  - Run this only if your TB can throw, and only to his throwing side.
  - As a nice backside throwback tag to the TB running a swing & wheel, tagged as TBACK.

- Reverse Pass
  - Based off of XX action with WB passing (need a passer at WB)
  - Basic high low drag pattern to backside (great for over shifted defenses)
  - Read PTE (corner) to WTE (drag) or HIGH to LOW.
  - TB runs SWING & WHEEL and is tagged TBACK.

A quick reminder on RIGHT/LEFT tags added to the play. This side call is for the linemen and is used to remind them what side the WALL SIDE lines up on; this has nothing to do with the direction of the play. For instance, on all wedge plays we line up our wall side blockers on the right side, so there is no real "tell" to which side the wedge is being run.

Note: DOUBLE and ISO can be run to either the wall or pull side, but I have found that based on the strength of my players, ISO and DOUBLE tend to work best on the pull side. Feel free to experiment, as I have, and try DOUBLE and/or ISO on both sides of your line to see how they work for you.

Star Rip 38 Pin Right

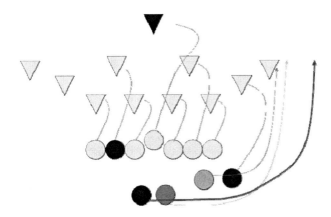

Figure 9Z. Star Rip 38 Pin Right

Line –

> PSTE to Center - If COVERED, LEG & TURN (PIN) the defender inside. If UNCOVERED, work to the second level attacking through the near arm pit of the next Defensive Lineman (DLM) play side, and cut off the first backer inside (FBI). If that LB is over the blocker, he still must work through the near arm pit of the near play side DLM, because this will put him on a good cut off angle. If the Center has no immediate backer and the backside ILB/OLB is getting caught in the wash of the backside cut off, then he can release up field and cut off the FS/backside Cover 2 safety.
>
> BSG to BSTE - Follow the same rules as the play side blockers, but work to get vertical much more quickly to cut off the backside secondary pursuit once the runner is play side.
>
> PSWB (AT MAN) – If COVERED, then LEG & TURN (PIN) the defender. If UNCOVERED, then take a lateral step to the outside and get vertical attacking the first backer inside. Attack his play side arm pit and wall him off.

TB – Attack the outside hip of the PSTE and get vertical toward the end zone. If the corner back is inside, then wall him off; if the corner is wide, cover ground as quickly as possible, then gather yourself and prepare to kick him out, walling him outside to give the runner a vertical seam inside.

QB – Follow the TB into to the edge, staying on his outside hip. If the TB moves inside, then go vertical to the end zone and wall off any defender crossing your face. If he moves outside, turn up field immediately, get vertical to the end zone and wall of any defender attempting to cross your face. The TB will target the CB (likely the widest perimeter defender) and either seal him to the inside or kick him out and wall him off to the outside. Either way, you should turn vertical and take on the next defender that shows.

BB – Secure the snap, cross over and stay flat at cruising speed (60 to 75% of full speed) when you see daylight in the seam, get vertical and go to the end zone as quickly as possible.

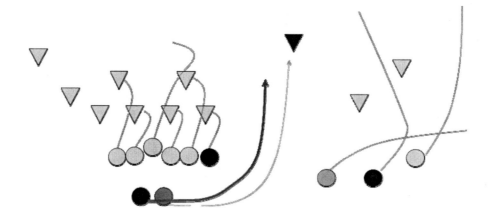

Figure 9AA. Star Bunch Over Rip 38 Pin Right

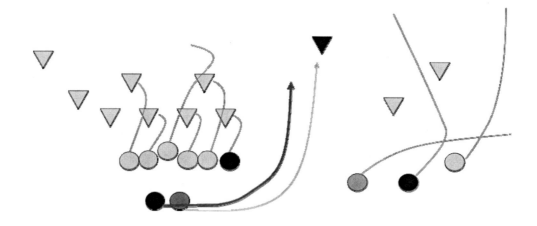

Figure 9BB. Star Trips Over Rip 38 Pin Right

Coaching Notes:

When running this play out of a BUNCH (Figure 9AA) or TRIPS (Figure 9BB) formation, the QB will take the EMLOS and log block him so the edge is sealed. The SE and SLOT will release outside and run vertical to drive the defenders away from the seam while the TB will run a quick out to the sideline to pull his defender away from the ball carrier.

Opposite: Star Liz 37 Pin Left

Star Rip 13 ISO Right

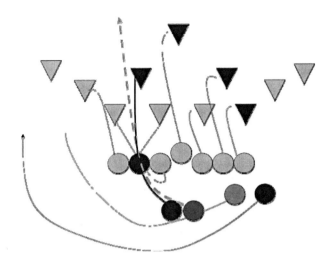

Figure 9CC. Star Rip 13 ISO Right

Line –

    Pulling Tackle – Block down and drive the first defender inside towards the Center's hip.

    Pulling Guard – Drop your outside foot so it points at 45 degrees, then kick out the first defender outside that crosses your face (kick out at a 45 degree angle not flat).

    Pulling End – If COVERED, then LEG & Turn aiming for the inside arm pit and wall off with your butt inside as you drive the defender out. If UNCOVERED, then fan block the first defender to cross your face and drive him outside.

    Center – If COVERED, then LEG & TURN aiming for the play side arm pit and wall your butt inside as you drive the defender out. If UNCOVERED, then release and block the first backer inside; if no backer threat is present, work to cut off the FS or backside Cover 2 safety.

    Wall Guard to Wall End – If COVERED, LEG & TURN aiming for the play side arm pit and wall your butt to the play side as you drive the defender away. If UNCOVERED, then release and cut off the first backer inside; if there is no backer threat, then release and cut off the backside secondary pursuit.

BB – Cross over step, lead into the hole, and go vertical to the end zone. If any defender attempts to cross your face, LEG & TURN (PIN) him to that side so that the QB can go vertical.

QB – Secure the snap and follow BB into hole. If the BB keeps going vertical cut off of his line and go to daylight. If the BB engages a defender, cut to his backside and go vertical to the end zone, working to the near sideline.

TB – Drop step and run through the heels of the QB to gain depth, then work to the outside shoulder of the DEMLOS and wall off the first defender to show.

WB – Drop step, fake reverse and run like you have the football to score a TD. The better the fake, the more of a chance you can pull the play side perimeter defenders away from the interior.

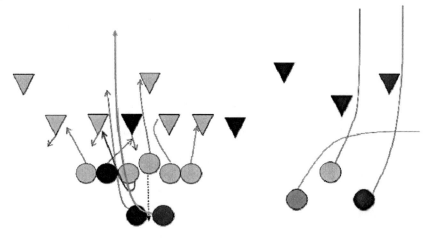

Figure 9DD. Star Bunch Rip 13 ISO Right

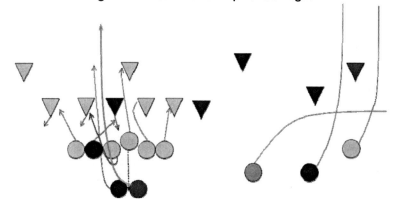

Figure 9EE. Star Trips Rip 13 ISO Right

Coaching Notes:

Since this play is run to the pull side, it doesn't matter if we use Nasty, Loose, or any other tag except for OVER due to the relocation of the PT to the WALL Side which reduces the play side blocking strength.

The BB must hit the hole fast and aggressively; always take on the first defender encountered on the other side of the LOS, as this block is key to the success of this play.

Opposite: Star Liz 14 ISO Left

Star Rip 34 Double Right

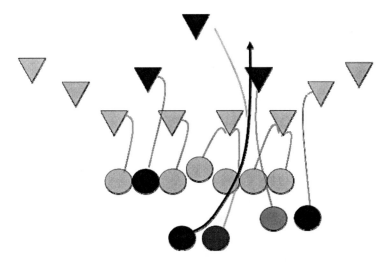

Figure 9FF. Star Rip 34 Double Right

Line –

    Wall Tight End and Wall Tackle - Combo block the DLM that is covering either of them and drive him straight back. Keeping their hips together, each will get their near palm into the bottom lip of the breast plate and their far palm into the respective arm pit, and then drive the defender upward and back.

    Wall Guard and Center - Combo block DLM that is covering either of them and drive him straight back. Keeping their hips together, each will get their near palm into the bottom lip of the breast plate and their far palm into the respective arm pit, and then drive the defender upward and back.

    Pulling Side - Block covered/uncovered (LEG & TURN).

BB – Cross over step, lead into hole, and go vertical to the end zone. LEG & TURN (PIN) any defender attempting to cross your face (to that side) so that the QB can go vertical.

QB – Secure the snap and follow BB into hole. If the BB keeps going vertical cut off of his line and go to daylight. If the BB blocks a defender cut to his backside and go vertical to the end zone while working to the near sideline.

TB – Slide towards the inside hip of the wall tackle, then get vertical and block the first defender to cross your face. Don't let him fill the hole; meet him on his side of the LOS.

WB – Fire off squeezing inside (tight to the hip of the wall tight end), and wall out the first defender outside of the wall tight end you come to (LEG AND TURN).

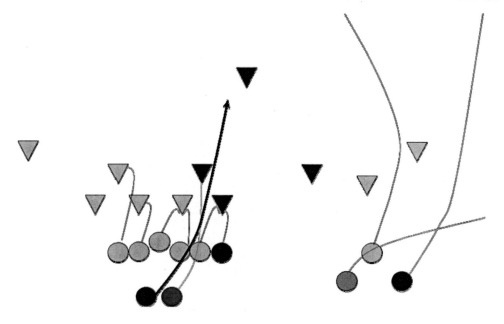

Figure 9GG. Star Bunch Over 34 Double Right

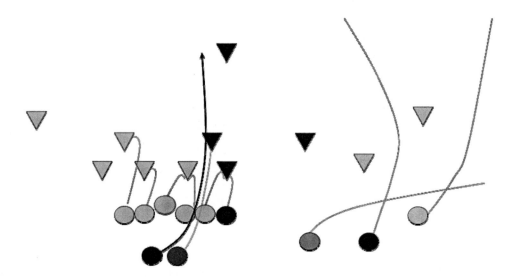

Figure 9HH. Star Trips Over Rip 34 Double Right

Coaching Notes:

Since this play is run to the wall side, it is important to have a four man TKO wall. The BB must hit the hole fast and aggressively and always take on his first block on the other side of the LOS as this block is a key to the success of this play.

Opposite: Star Liz 33 Double Left

Star Rip 31 Dive Right

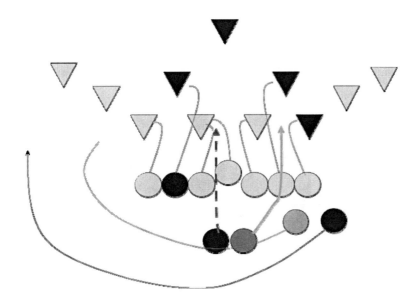

Figure 9II. Star Rip 31 Dive Right

Line –

>   Wall Tight End to Wall Guard - Block covered/uncovered (LEG & TURN).
>   Center & Pull Guard - Combo block the first DLM play side (NT to DT).
>   Pulling Tackle and Pulling Tight End - Block covered/uncovered (LEG & TURN).

>   Note: If the DLM at point of attack can be handled with a one-on-one block, the Center (even front) or Pull Guard (odd front) can release to engage the FBI or the safety, but we usually prefer to COMBO block that DLM to create a big hole - so only block one-on-one if the DLM is easily handled by the one block.

WB - Execute a fake XX reverse.

TB - Execute a flash fake and fake sweep/XX reverse.

QB - Execute a flash fake, cross over step, then attack the wall guard's outside hip and get vertical and make it look like you have the ball. Stay away from the pull side.

BB - Secure the snap and get vertical on Center's pull side hip.

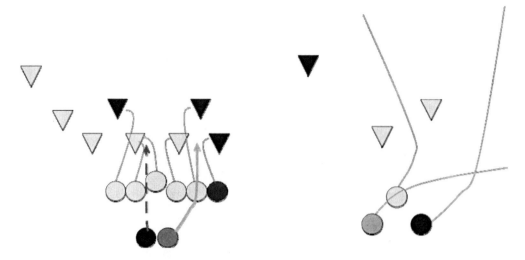

Figure 9JJ. Star Bunch Over Rip 31 Dive Right

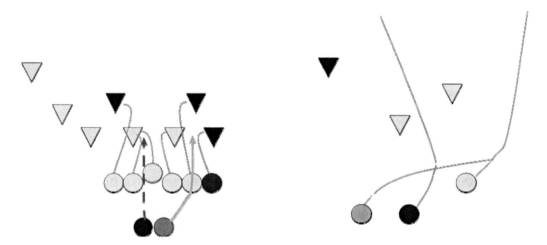

Figure 9KK. Star Trips Over Rip 31 Dive Right

Coaching Notes:

The 31 Dive play can be run with OVER (or without). We have often run it with OVER because the defense would tend to shift their interior away, while leaving the backside perimeter intact. This allowed us to exploit the movement. You can drop the OVER in BUNCH (Figure 9JJ) and TRIPS (Figure 9KK) if you need an additional blocker on the pull side.

Opposite: Star Liz 32 Dive Left

Star Rip 14 Dive Right

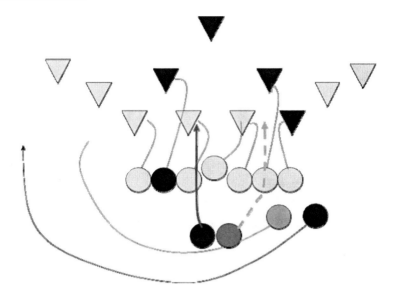

Figure 9LL. Star Rip 14 Dive Right

Line –

    Center and Wall Guard - Combo block first DLM play side (NT to DT).

    Note: If the DLM at point of attack can be handled with a one-on-one block, the Center (even front) or Pull Guard (odd front) can release to engage the FBI or the safety, but we usually prefer to COMBO block that DLM to create a big hole - so only block one-on-one if the DLM is easily handled by the one block.

    The Wall Tackle and Wall Tight End will block covered/uncovered (LEG & TURN). The PULL GUARD to PULL TE will block covered/uncovered (LEG & TURN).

WB - Execute a fake XX reverse.

TB - Execute a flash fake and fake sweep/XX reverse.

QB - Secure the snap and get vertical on the guard's outside hip.

BB - Execute a flash fake, cross over step, then attack the pull guard's heels and get vertical. Make it look like you have the ball. Stay away from the wall side.

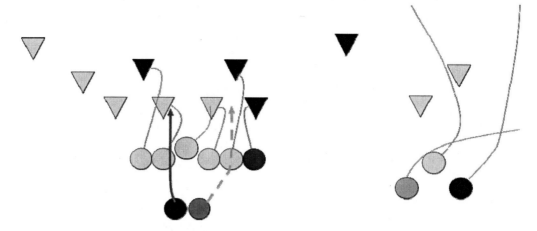

Figure 9MM. Star Bunch Over Rip 14 Dive Right

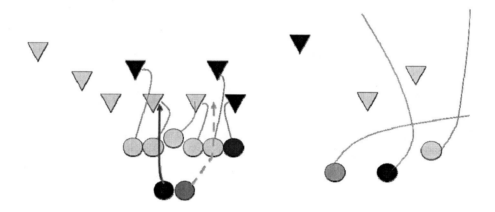

Figure 9NN. Star Trips Over 14 Dive Right

Coaching Notes:

The 14 Dive play can be run with or without OVER when the end is not extended. However, OVER is mandatory with an extended end, e.g. BUNCH (Figure 9MM) or TRIPS (Figure 9NN) or LOOSE. The use of 31 and 14 Dive out of STAR is a great tool for controlling an overzealous defense, i.e. one that is moving its interior line and/or backers to the perceived strength.

Opposite: Star Liz 13 Dive Left

Star Rip Drag Pass Right (Sprint)

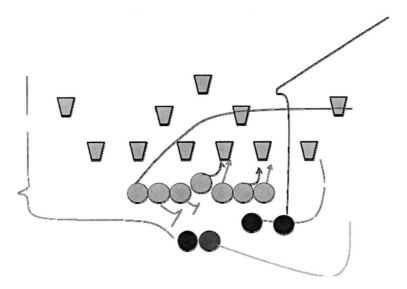

Figure 9OO. Star Rip Drag Pass Right

Line -

Wall Tight End to Center – Slide to the wall side (Covered/Uncovered). LEM/SSM Pulling Guard to Pulling Tackle – Hinge to the wall side. Do not allow any defender inside of you; rather force all defenders to go outside of you and around the hinge wall. KKM

Pulling Tight End - Inside release through the heels of the first backer inside; gain depth of 4 to 6 yards. As soon as you pass the center, start looking for the ball as you are the second read (LOW). If the QB runs the ball, turn back over the up field shoulder and wall off the first defender to show (put him on the ground).

WB - Outside release and take 8 to 9 steps, then break outside at 45 degrees (corner) and accelerate to the sideline until you find open space. You are the HIGH read (first read) of the QB. If the ball goes to the PTE (low read) or the QB runs, turn back over the up field shoulder and wall off the first defender to show (put him on the ground).

BB - Lead step at the pull side DEMLOS and then flatten out and run a swing pattern (turn and look for the ball no ball finish with the wheel route). If TBACK is added to the play, you are the primary route. If there is no TBACK tag, wall off below the pull tackle hinge.

TB - Gain a little depth, then get to the outside arm pit of the first defender to show past the WTE and then wall him inside.

QB - Secure the snap and gain depth to the wall side (at least 3 to 5 yards of depth). You must threaten the perimeter quickly while looking to throw as soon as you secure the ball. If the WB is open throw to him immediately so he can eat up as much vertical space as possible before the defense recovers. Your read is HIGH (WB) to LOW (PTE). If neither is open run the ball. If you see vertical space as you roll out, run the ball. The object is to get positive yards, not complete a pass. If the play is tagged with TBACK, gain extra depth; then as you break wide, plant and set to throw to the BB. If the BB is open on the SWING, throw him open (lead him into open space). If you see him break to the WHEEL, throw him open so he can catch it and run with it.

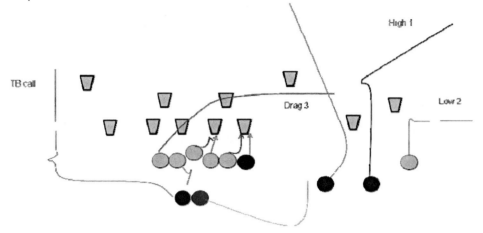

Figure 9PP. Star Trips Over Rip Drag Pass Right

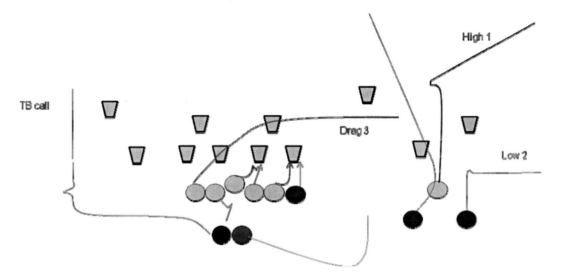

Figure 9QQ. Star Bunch Over Rip Drag Pass Right

Coaching Notes:

The TRIPS (Figure 9PP) and BUNCH (Figure 9QQ) variation of this play are different because it provides a LOW-HIGH read on the play side with the QUICK OUT by #1 and the CORNER by #2 in a smash concept. The drag from backside becomes the #3 read, especially if the corner rolls to the flat and the OLB rolls high to cover the corner, then the drag will open in the CURL/HOOK.

If the backside corner is covering the PTE then the TB (TBACK) becomes a big play with the defense spread out on the other side.

The third receiver from the outside (TB) will run a seam route to drive and pin the near Safety deep to better open the flood route on the outside.

The QB must make the low-high read on the run; if he sees neither open he must look to the drag as it clears past the Center's head. The QB must always run the ball if he sees daylight to the end zone.

Star Rip Reverse Pass Right (Sprint)

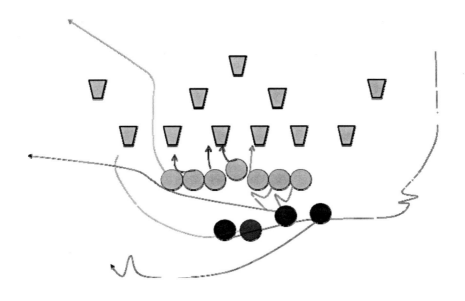

Figure 9RR. Star Rip Reverse Pass Right

Line -
> Wall Tackle to Center – Slide to the wall side (Covered/Uncovered). LEM/SSM Pulling Guard to Pulling Tight End – hinge to the wall side and don't allow any defender inside of you, i.e. force any defender encountered to go outside of you and around the hinge wall. KKM

Wall Tight End - Release outside, take 8 to 9 steps, then break outside at 35 degrees (corner) and accelerate to the sideline until you find open space. You are the HIGH read (first read) of the QB. If the ball goes to the BB (low read) or the WB runs, turn back over the up field shoulder and wall off the first defender to show (put him on the ground).

WB - Drop step, get to the outside hip of the TB, and take the hand off. Don't rush or sprint into the hand off. Once you get the ball, accelerate to full speed and get outside.

With the ball secure, get your eyes up field and look for the HIGH (WTE running corner route) and LOW read (BB into flat). If you see the HIGH read open, throw it immediately; if you see the LOW read open throw it immediately. As always, if you see daylight run! If TBACK is added to the play, as you get outside, stop plant and throw back to the TBACK. Lead him with the pass so that he runs to the ball and vertical. If the SWING is not open, he will run WHEEL, so throw him open to the WHEEL.

BB - Cross over step and give an outside hand off to the WB behind the wall side; then flatten out and run a swing route as you break about 3 to 5 yards past the WB's starting spot (turn and look for the ball no ball finish with the wheel route). If TBACK is added to the play, you are tagged the primary route. If there is no tag for TBACK, wall off below the pull tackle hinge.

TB - Jab step to fake power and run to the flat on the other side. Run through the DEMLOS's far shoulder to slow his rush; as you pass the defender gain speed and get your head around for the ball. If the WB runs, turn back over your up field shoulder and wall off any inside defender that is near you (put him on the ground).

QB - Cross over and gain depth to log the DEMLOS.

Coaching Notes:

You can use OVER to apply additional blocking to the play side when needed.

Star Liz Reverse Pass Left

Chapter 10
Comet Power & Lead Series

The Comet Series is really a variation on the Yale formation of old and the more modern Beast Series by Steve Calande. The base formation for the Comet Series has a balanced line formation with an asymmetric backfield (Figure 10A). The benefit is that we have all of our blockers right at the point of attack and near the LOS, which forces the defense to respond in kind. Often the defense fails to adjust initially, or over compensates. Either way, this formation allows us to take advantage of a disoriented defense until appropriate adjustments are made. I began using this formation because I wanted a simple formation with overwhelming strength. In the base formation, the WB aligns to the outside of the wall tight end, the TB (or QB) aligns on the inside hip of the wall tight end, the BB aligns on the outside hip of the wall guard. The QB (or TB) aligns at a depth 3 to 4 yards. The asymmetric backfield creates a powerful line of force from the QB (or TB) to the TB (QB), with both the WB and BB alongside the leading blocker TB (or QB). You can use OVER to unbalance the line and add even more power at the point of attack for the primary power plays (power, power sweep, and power pass). I have yet to really experiment with other variations (e.g. Loose, Bunch, Trips, etc.), so I am not going to address any other adjustments in this book. However, I believe spreading the formation would likely diminish rather than enhance the advantages inherent in the base formation.

Normal Alignment

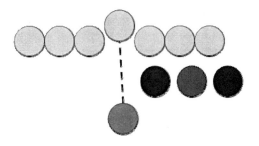

BB, QB, BSWB, PSWB

Figure 10A. The Base Formation for the Comet Series

Comet Formations

1.   Can every core play in my power series be used in this formation with little to no alteration in the basic structure of the play? *Answer - Yes*

2.   Can I use my current system of edge tags to alter the perimeter so that I can adapt and isolate the perimeter triangle of the defense? *Answer – No (more precisely, 'not yet' - OVER can be used but I have not tested the other edge tags with this formation)*

3. What advantage does it give me that I don't have using my base formation (TIGHT)? *Answer – More immediate power at the point of attack to overwhelm the hole, direct snap gets ball into primary ball carrier's hand, having the remainder of the backfield at the point of attack allows us to quickly overwhelm the hole.*

4. Does it give me a leverage or line of force advantage against the defense? ANSWER – *Yes, it does to the strong side edge and perimeter and when the defense over-shifts it gives me an advantage to the weak side as well.*

Brief Overview of the Comet Power Series

Interior Plays – 20 Wedge Right, 30 Wedge Right (Rip and Liz),

- Interior power play for this series.
- Use reverse (XX) action behind it to create deception designed to hold the perimeter defenders in place on each side.
- TB (QB) and BB variants allow you to hit the same spot with two different players increasing the misdirection aspect of the offense.

Edge Plays – Rip 16 Seal Right, Rip 13 Kick Left, Rip 45 Kick Left, Liz 15 Seal Left, Liz 14 Kick Right, Liz 26 Kick Right

- Seal Play (Power Play, e.g. Rip 16 Seal Right, Liz 15 Seal Left)
  - Core play of this offense
  - Must be able to run it anywhere on the field, at any time, against anything the defense tries to do.
  - We have a variety of ways of running this play to keep defenses on their toes.
  - BB power play is a pure power play with a maximum amount of blockers. It is our base play.
  - QB power utilizes the BB as a sweep decoy to the perimeter to remove perimeter defenders and the QB faking pass (much like a delay).

- QB Kick (QB Counter Cutback, e.g. Rip 13 Kick Left/ Liz 14 Kick Right)
  - Edge misdirection play that allows us to attack the defense with the pre-flow look of QB power in the opposite direction and WB reverse action in the play direction, while hitting back inside on the edge with the BB as the perimeter defenders cover power and reverse (XX).
  - BB must hit inside vertically and go north-south quickly.

- WB Kick (WB Counter Trap, e.g. Rip 45 Kick Left, Liz 26 Kick Right)
  - Edge misdirection play that allows us to attack the defense with the pre-flow look of WB power in one direction, while hitting back against flow with an inside counter.
  - WB must hit inside vertically and go north-south quickly.

- BB Kick (BB Counter Trap, e.g. Rip 33 Kick Left/ Liz 34 Kick Right)
  - Edge misdirection play that allows us to attack the defense with the pre-flow look of WB power in the opposite direction and WB reverse action in the play direction, while hitting back inside on the edge with the BB as the perimeters defend power and reverse (XX).
  - BB must hit inside vertically and go north-south quickly.

Perimeter Plays – Rip 18 Monster Sweep Right, Rip 18 Wide Right, Rip 47 Wide Reverse Left, Liz 17 Monster Sweep Left, Liz 17 Wide Left, Liz 28 Wide Reverse Right.

- QB Monster Sweep (Power Sweep, e.g. Rip 18 Monster Sweep, Liz 17 Monster Sweep)
  - Perimeter power play. Overwhelm the perimeter with pullers.
  - Must seal the EMLOS to the inside.
  - Best run when you have two in the perimeter triangle and/or you see the EMLOS squatting/crashing to the QB power play.

- WB Wide Reverse (XX outside reverse, e.g. Rip 47 Wide Reverse, Liz 28 Wide Reverse)
  - Perimeter misdirection play. Isolate the interior and perimeter defenders and attempt to attack the backside perimeter triangle (away from power).
  - Key is 2 or less in the perimeter box and EMLOS vacating contain with shallow pinch inside to chase power.
  - Best used against teams when they are crashing to the backside of power.

- QB Wide Sweep (Rip 18 Wide, Liz 17 Wide)
  - Alternative power perimeter play for the monster sweep.
  - If the OLB and CB are filling hard into the tunnel of the TKO wall this is a nice alternative.
  - Good alternative if you are having problems using the Monster Sweep due to a good OLB/SS on play side.

Play Action Passing – Rip Power Pass Right, Liz Power Pass Left.

- Power Pass
  - Run/Pass option
  - Basic flood pattern on the power side.
  - Read low to high (BB flat to WB out).
  - Can teach a peek deep if MOFO (middle of the field open).
  - Run this to the QB's throwing side

A quick reminder on RIGHT/LEFT tags added to the play. This side call is for the linemen only and is designed to notify the WALL SIDE on which side of the ball they should align.

Detailed Description of Selected Plays:
The Comet Power Series

Comet Rip 30 Wedge Right (Interior play)

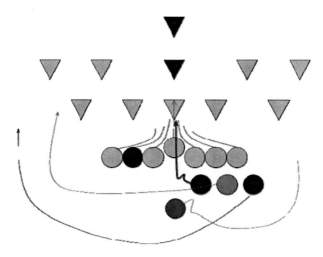

Figure 10B. Comet Rip 30 Wedge Right

Line – Wedge block on the Center.

BB – Secure the handoff (or shovel pass) and hit the wedge. Look for a crease on either side of center, hit it, and get vertical. Do not go around or under the wedge.

QB – Secure the snap and give an inside handoff (or shovel pass) to the BB going into the wedge. Carry out a power sweep fake (rub the inside hip of the reversing WB to fake the XX reverse) by attacking the outside shoulder of the wall side DEMLOS.

TB (BSWB) – Gain depth and block the first defender to show past the far DEMLOS. Wall him outside and away from the wedge.

WB – Execute a flash fake reverse, then attack the perimeter and get vertical up field. Make it look like you are scoring.

This is a really nice play in the COMET series, especially once you establish the power running game of your QB/TB deep. I have used both the hand off and the shovel pass and have found that I prefer the shovel pass. The key to this is to simply have the QB underhand push the ball in front of the BB so he runs into the ball and can quickly secure it as he goes vertical. If he does drop it the play is an incomplete pass and not a fumble; so there is a high reward for very little risk (no fumble) when using the shovel pass.

Coaching Notes:

Opposite is Comet Liz 30 Wedge Right

Comet Rip 20 Wedge Right (Interior play)

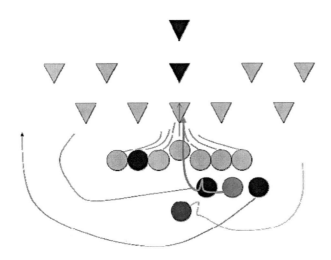

Figure 10C. Comet Rip 20 Wedge Right

Line – Wedge block on the Center

BB – Gain depth and block the first defender to show past the far DEMLOS. Wall him outside and away from the wedge.

QB – Secure the snap and give an inside handoff (or shovel pass) to the TB going into the wedge. Carry out a power sweep fake (rub the inside hip of the reversing WB to fake the XX reverse) by attacking the outside shoulder of the wall side DEMLOS.

TB (BSWB) – Secure the handoff (or shovel pass) and hit the wedge. Look for a crease on either side of the Center; hit it and get vertical. Do not go around or under wedge.

WB – Execute a flash fake reverse, then attack the perimeter and get vertical up field. Make it look like you are scoring.

This is a really a nice play in the COMET series, especially once you establish the power running game of your QB/TB deep. I have used both the hand off and the shovel pass and I have found I prefer the shovel pass. The key to this is to simply have the QB underhand push the ball in front of the TB so he runs into the ball and can quickly secure it as he goes vertical. If he does drop it the play is an incomplete pass and not a fumble; so there is a high reward for very little risk (no fumble) when using the shovel pass. I have found that this play often works better against teams that are really trying to key our BB as it will move them away from the point of attack and put the ball in one of our better runner's hands.

Coaching Notes:

Opposite is Comet Liz 20 Wedge Right.

Comet Rip 16 Seal Right (Edge play)

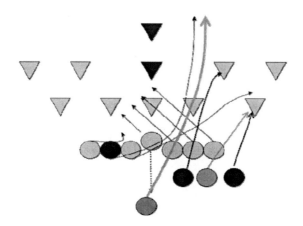

Figure 10D. Comet Rip 16 Seal Right

Line –

Wall Side – TKO (Center to PSTE)

Pulling Guard – Pull and kick out the first defender to show above BB and QB.

Pulling Tackle – Pull up the wall and go vertical to the end zone; if any defender crosses your face, seal him inside with a wall off.

Pulling Tight End – Cutoff to the Center's hip; if no one shows, climb to the linebacker level and cutoff the backside pursuit.

TB/WB – The WB will post block (LEG) the DEMLOS attacking the center of the breastplate of the defender and the outside arm pit; the TB will attack the inside arm pit. Both will mesh near the hips and COMBO block the DEMLOS to drive the defender out wide and wall him off.

BB – Slide step outside, get vertical on the outside hip of the wall side TE, and block the first backer you see. Wall him to the side of his leverage (inside backer pin him inside, outside backer pin him outside).

QB – Secure the snap, aim for the Center's play side hip, and get vertical to daylight. Climb the wall and get 5 yards. Once you make it out of the tunnel, make one move (cutback inside, go vertical, bounce it outside), and get vertical to the end zone. Never let one defender take you down, and never let a defender hit you; you hit him first. Your initial depth should be 4 to 5 yards but don't hesitate to adjust the depth so that you arrive just behind the BSG and BST as they hit the tunnel. The timing is very important as it will hide your approach into the tunnel.

Coaching Notes:

Can be used with the OVER tag to make the line unbalanced and strengthen the line of force to the play side.

Opposite is Comet Liz 15 Seal Left

Comet Rip 45 Kick Left (Edge play)

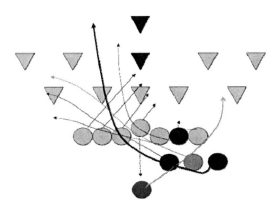

Figure 10E. Comet Rip 45 Kick Left

Line –

  Wall side – TKO (center to PSTE)
  Pulling Guard –Pull and kick out the first defender to cross your face. When you kick him out, flip your hips and body into the hole to isolate the defender away from the WB as he hits the tunnel.
  Pulling Tackle – Pull up the wall, then go vertical to the end zone; any defender crossing your face should be sealed inside with a wall off.
  Pulling Tight End – Cutoff to the Center's hip; if no one shows, climb to the linebacker level and cutoff the backside pursuit.

QB – Secure the snap, take a short cross step to open belt buckle to WB, then make the handoff to him and fake power sweep. This can be done with the shovel pass as well, which will speed up the play and make it look much more convincing to the defense (especially the perimeter defenders as they will initially see the WB go inside, but not near the QB, thus they will often crash down on the QB to kill the power/power sweep).

BB – Cross over step, then attack inside arm pit of the first defender above the DEMLOS and wall him outside.

TB (BSWB) – Cross over step, then follow the BB into the hole and kick out first defender to show above the BB.

WB – Drop step with the inside foot and aim for the inside hip of the BB. Take the handoff, secure it, and get vertical when you see the first daylight to the end zone. Do not go east-west you must get vertical; get up field and then get to the boundary once you clear the tunnel.

Coaching Notes:
This is an outstanding play when you see the backside defenders overplaying or chasing the power/power sweep/power pass play.

Opposite is Comet Liz 26 Kick Right

Comet Rip 23 Kick Left (Edge play)

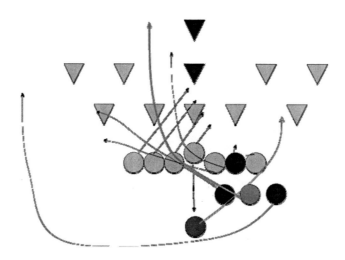

Figure 10F. Comet Rip 23 Kick Left

Line –

Wall Side – TKO (center to PSTE)

Pulling Guard – Pull and kick out the first defender to cross your face. When you kick him out, flip your hips and body into the hole to isolate the defender away from the WB as he hits the tunnel.

Pulling Tackle – Pull up the wall, and then go vertical to the end zone; any defender crossing your face should be sealed inside with a wall off.

Pulling Tight End – Cutoff to the Center's hip; if no one shows, climb to the linebacker level and cutoff the backside pursuit.

QB – Secure the snap, take a short cross step to open belt buckle to TB, then make the handoff and fake a power sweep.

BB – Cross over step, then attack the inside arm pit of the first defender above the DEMLOS and wall him outside.

TB (BSWB) – Drop step with the inside foot and aim for the inside hip of the QB. Take the handoff, secure it, and get vertical when you see the first daylight to the end zone. Do not go east-west, you must get vertical, i.e. get up field and then get to the boundary once you clear the tunnel. This is much better as a shovel pass as it hits much quicker and with better deception.

WB – Drop step and fake the XX reverse action to the backside. Make it look real to force the backside edge to widen with you. This will help open the hole for the TB by forcing the perimeter defenders to widen with you.

Coaching Notes:

This is an outstanding play when you see the backside defenders overplaying or chasing the power, power sweep, or power pass play, while the front side defenders are sitting on the WB reverse and counter.

This can be run as a SHOVEL pass from the BB to WB by simply adding SHOVEL to the play. A shovel pass is a FORWARD PASS, so if they drop the ball it is simply an incomplete pass.

Opposite is Comet Liz 44 Kick Right

Comet Rip 18 Monster Sweep Right (perimeter play)

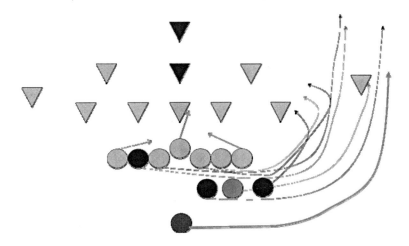

Figure 10G. Comet Rip 18 Monster Sweep Right

Line –
> Wall Tight End – Cut off play side to the Center's hip.
> Wall Tackle – Pull around the WTE and WSWB, then form a wall, land-marking the outside shoulder of the WSWB.
> Wall Guard – Pull around the WTE and WSWB, then form a wall land-marking the outside shoulder of the WT.
> Center – Versus a NT (odd front), jewel block him by aiming your far shoulder at the crotch of the defender so that your head goes past the defender's play side hip. If facing a DT (even front), severe down block by aiming for a point just in front of his far (play side) shoulder. Then wheel your butt to the play side.
> Pulling Side Guard and Tackle – Pull tight down the LOS and around the perimeter wall, and then go vertical to the end zone, creating a vertical lane for the runner. Any defender that crosses your face should be walled off. Attack the defenders' up field arm pit and wheel your butt towards the runner. If you encounter any leakage as you go down the line, cut it off the same way the center does against an even front.

Pulling Tight End – Cutoff to the Center's hip; if no one shows, climb to the linebacker level and cut off the backside pursuit.

TB – Cross over, and then get outside and up field quickly. Against a CB that is off the LOS and near the EMLOS, you must come around and attack his outside arm pit and Wheel block him. Against a wide CB, you must eat up space, and then settle down and wall him to the outside to create an alley for the runner.

BB – Cross over, and then get up field to create a vertical lane for the runner to the end zone. Wall off any defender that crosses your face.

QB – Secure the snap and cross over staying flat (parallel) to the LOS until you go past the WSTE. Once you see daylight get vertical and up field; make one move to daylight (cutback, vertical, bounce). Remember, you have three vertical blockers going down field near boundary, so if you get in the alley between the three vertical pullers and the boundary, your chance of a TD is great.

WB – Take a lateral step with the outside foot and attack outside arm pit of DEMLOS. Wall him off by Wheel blocking and driving him inside as far as you can.

Coaching Notes:

This is a very good play to run with the OVER tag, as it gets one more pulling lineman closer to the perimeter which helps to fully overload the perimeter, especially when the defense is showing 2 or less in the perimeter triangle.

Opposite is Comet Liz 17 Monster Sweep Left.

Comet Rip 18 Wide Right (Perimeter play)

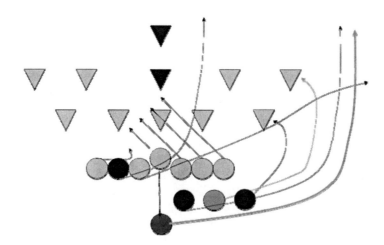

Figure 10H. Comet Rip 18 Wide Right

Line –

Wall Side – TKO (Center to PSTE)

Pulling Guard – Pull and kick out the first defender, wide above the BB. If no defender is present outside (CB), turn and go vertical to the end zone.

Pulling Tackle – Pull up the wall, then go vertical toward the end zone. Wall off any defender crossing your face, sealing him inside.

Pulling Tight End – Cutoff to the Center's hip; if no one shows, climb to the linebacker level and cutoff the backside pursuit.

TB – Cross over, and then get outside and up field quickly. Against a CB that is off the LOS and near the EMLOS, you must come around to attack his outside arm pit and Wheel block him. Against a wide CB, you must quickly close the distance, then settle down and wall him to the outside to create an alley for the runner.

BB – Cross over step, gain depth, and get outside of the TB. Then get vertical and if any defender crosses your face, wall him inside, otherwise go vertical to the end zone to give the runner a vertical lane.

QB – Secure the snap, and cross over staying flat (parallel) to the LOS until you go past the WSTE. Once you see daylight, make a move (cutback, vertical, bounce), then get vertical and up field. Bear in mind you have a vertical blocker going down field near the boundary, so if you get into the alley between the vertical puller and the boundary, your chance of a TD is big.

This is a great sweep against OLB's and CB' s that are filling the alley behind the wall, as they will get caught inside, i.e. we will have numbers outside for the runner.

Coaching Notes:

This can be used with OVER to expand the TKO wall.

Opposite is Comet Liz 17 Wide Left

Comet Rip 47 Wide Reverse Left (perimeter play)

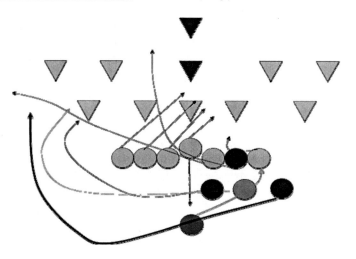

Figure 10l. **Comet Rip 47 Wide Reverse Left**

Line –

> Wall side – TKO (Center to PSTE)
>
> Pulling Guard – Pull and climb as if to seal, but then go wide and kick out the first outside defender (CB) to cross your face. As you kick the defender out, flip your hips and body into the hole to isolate the defender away from the WB as he hits the tunnel. If facing an athletic corner, eat up space then settle down and wall him off.
>
> Pulling Tackle – Pull up the wall, then go vertical toward the end zone. Wall off any defender crossing your face, sealing him inside.
>
> Pulling Tight End – Cutoff to the Center's hip; if no one shows, climb to the linebacker level and cutoff the backside pursuit.

BB – Cross over, then gain enough depth to log the DEMLOS and drive him inside. If he is crashing, all you need to do is wall him in for moment, and push him further inside.

TB – Cross over, and then gain depth under the QB and wall off the next defender inside (OLB normally).

QB – Secure the snap, cross over step, and then make an outside handoff to WB. After the handoff, aim for the inside arm pit of the BSDE and make a great fake as if running seal. As you reach the defender, kick him out.

WB – Drop step, then get to the outside hip of the TB and take the hand off. Don't rush or sprint into the hand off. Once you get the ball, accelerate to full speed and get outside. Once you see daylight, get vertical quick. The faster you get vertical the more likely you are to get by the linebacker pursuit. If there is a corner wide, run inside of the BSG's kick out.

Coaching Notes:

Can be used with OVER to get an additional blocker.

Opposite is Comet Liz 28 Wide Reverse

Comet Rip Power Pass Right (Sprint)

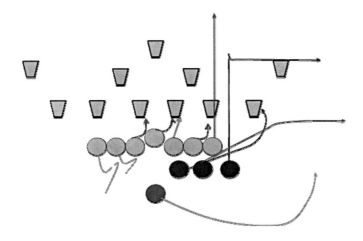

Figure 10J. Comet Rip Power Pass Right

Line -

> Wall Tackle to Center – Slide to the wall side (Covered/Uncovered). LEM/SSM
> Pulling Guard to Pulling Tight End – Hinge to the wall side; don't allow any
> defender inside of you, force all defenders outside and around the hinge wall.
> KKM

Wall Tight End - Outside release, then go vertical up the middle and pin the safety deep. The ball will only go to you on a MOFO read from the QB/OC.

WB - Outside release, then take 8 to 9 steps and break outside. Accelerate to the sideline until you find open space. You are the HIGH read (second read) of the QB. If the ball goes to the BB (low read) or the QB runs, turn back over your up field shoulder and wall off the first defender to show (put him on the ground).

TB - Release through the DEMLOS's face to slow his rush so that the BB can get outside and wall him inside. Run to the flat and as soon as you get past the DEMLOS, get your head around, and look for the ball over your down field shoulder. You are the primary read (low read). If the QB runs the ball, turn back over your up field shoulder and wall off the first defender to show (put him on the ground).

BB - Gain depth, then get wide and attack outside arm pit of first defender to show past the WT (DEMLOS). Wheel your hips to the outside and pin him inside.

QB - Secure the snap and gain depth to the wall side (at least 3 to 5 yards of depth). You must threaten the perimeter quickly while looking to throw as soon as you secure the ball. If the BB is open, throw to him immediately so he can eat up as much vertical space as possible before the defense recovers. Your read is LOW (BB) to HIGH (WB). If neither is open run the ball. If you see vertical space as your roll out, run the ball. The object is to get positive yards, not complete a pass.

You can run a variation of this that has the WB and WALL TE switch assignments, i.e. the WB runs the vertical and the WALL TE runs the out. The normal assignment is #1 outside runs the out, #2 runs the vertical, and #3 runs the flat route. When running this play from Loose, Bunch, or Trips, is the assignments are: #1 vertical, #2 out, and #3 flat.

Coaching Notes:

You can use OVER to get an extra blocker on the play side, if you have a tough pass rush on that side. When moved over, the Pull Tackle will follow the COVERED/UNCOVERED rule (LEM/SSM). In this manner, OVER allows you to pin point where you need additional pass protection (wall or pull side).

NOTE: The Power Pass works really well out of Comet because of the immediate stress you place upon the perimeter defenders on the flood side. If the defense drops into coverage, the QB should see daylight and be able to run the ball. If they collapse to run, the QB should have the BB or WB wide open. In the case of no free safety in the middle, MOFO should be called from the sideline, if you want the QB to throw it deep down the middle.

Opposite Comet Liz Power Pass Left (sprint)

Summary of Plays from the Comet Lead Series

Interior Plays – No viable Dive play as the offset of the BB is too far outside.

Edge Plays – Rip 13 ISO Right, Rip 14 Double Right, Liz 14 ISO Left, Liz 13 Double Left

The ISO Play is a cross blocked play to the pull side (backside) with XX action behind it to freeze the perimeter defenders in place while we overwhelm the point of attack.

- Great play to add to the power series as it allows you to attack the pull side immediately and directly (which has the better pullers and makes the cross blocking more effective) when defenses are keying on the WALL side and/or formation strength.
- Solid way of attacking an interior defender playing over the Pulling Guard and attempting to shoot the gap between the Pulling Guard and the Center. As this defender attempts to hit the gap and chase the puller the down block of the Pull Tackle becomes very easy to execute. It is also a nice way to attack the perimeter triangle on the Pull side; particularly when they are sitting on reverse and ready to pursue the XX action.
- We have two ways of running this play to keep defenses on their toes.
- QB ISO play is a quick power play with full XX action behind it and the BB lead blocking to isolate the first backer inside (ILB often). . Great to use if you have an athletic, tough kid at QB that likes to run inside.

The DOUBLE Play is a double team/combo block to the wall side with no XX action behind it as it is a pure power play. We use this against even fronts that give us trouble running our angle blocking when they are sitting their ILB and OLB back, while their defensive line absorbs up the ABC wall. This allows us to the drive those defenders back into the laps of the backers using our WALL side blockers (our better drive/wall blockers) as double teamers/combo blockers.

Rip 14 Double Right, Liz 13 Double Left.

- DOUBLE plays to the QB allow us to double team the DT and DE with our C/WG and WT/WE, while the QB lead blocks and isolates the OLB.

Perimeter Plays – Rip 18 Pin Right, Liz 17 Pin Left.

- QB Pin Sweep (Power Sweep, e.g. Rip 18 Pin, Liz 17 Pin)
  - Perimeter power play. Overwhelm the perimeter by using an aggressive vertical drive step, pinning the outside hip of all play side defenders, and keying the last defender outside for wall off/kick out.
  - Must seal the EMLOS to the inside and key the last perimeter defender for wall off/kick out.

- Best run when you have two in the perimeter triangle and/or you see the EMLOS squatting/crashing to the QB power play, as it further isolates the remaining perimeter defenders.

Play Action Passing – Rip Drag Pass Right, Liz Drag Pass Left, Rip Reverse Pass Right, Liz Reverse Pass Left.

- Drag Pass
  - Run/Pass option
  - Basic high-low drag pattern to the power side.
  - Read PSWB corner to BSTE shallow drag (high to low)
  - Run this only if your TB can throw and only to his throwing side.
  - As a nice backside throwback tag to the TB running a swing & wheel, tagged as TBACK.

- Reverse Pass
  - Based off of XX action with WB passing (need a passer at WB)
  - Basic high-low drag pattern to the backside (great for over-shifted defenses)
  - Read PTE (corner) to WTE (drag) or HIGH to LOW.
  - TB runs SWING & WHEEL and is tagged TBACK.

A quick reminder on RIGHT/LEFT tags added to the play. This side call is for the linemen only and is designed to notify the WALL SIDE on which side of the ball they should align.

Note: DOUBLE and ISO can be run to either the wall or pull side. I have found that, based on the strength of my players, when I flip my offensive line, ISO works best on the pull side and DOUBLE works best on the wall side. Feel free to experiment, as I have, and use DOUBLE and/or ISO on both sides of your line to see how they work for you.

Detailed Description of Selected Plays:
The Comet Lead Series

Comet Rip 18 Pin Right

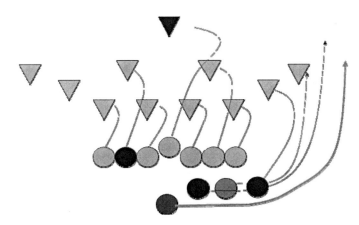

Figure 10K. Comet Rip 18 Pin Right

Line –

>PSTE to CENTER - If COVERED, LEG & TURN (PIN) the defender inside. If UNCOVERED, work to the second level, attacking through the near arm pit of the next DLM play side, and cut off the first backer inside (FBI). If the LB is over the blocker, he still must work through the near arm pit of the near play side DLM as this will put him on a good cut off angle. If the Center has no immediate backer and the backside ILB/OLB is getting caught in the wash of the backside cut off, then he can release up field and cut off the FS or backside Cover 2 safety.

>BSG to BSTE - Follow the same rules as the play side blockers, but they will work to get vertical much more quickly, to cut off the backside secondary pursuit once the runner is play side.

PSWB (AT MAN) – If COVERED, LEG & TURN (PIN) the defender. If UNCOVERED, take a lateral step to the outside, and then get vertical, engaging the first backer inside by attacking his play side arm pit and walling him off.

TB – Attack the outside hip of the PSTE, then get vertical going toward the end zone. If the corner back is inside, wall him off. If the corner is wide, close distance as quickly as possible, gather yourself, and kick him out, walling him outside to give the runner a vertical seam inside.

BB – Follow the TB into to the edge staying on his outside hip. If the TB moves inside, then go vertical to the end zone and wall off any defender crossing your face. If he moves outside, cut off immediately then get vertical to the end zone and wall of any defender attempting to cross your face.

QB – Secure the snap, cross over and stay flat at cruising speed (60 to 75% of full speed). When you see the daylight in the seam, get vertical and go to the end zone as quickly as possible.

Coaching Notes:

This can be run from OVER as well.

Opposite: Comet Liz 17 Pin Left

Comet Rip 13 ISO Right

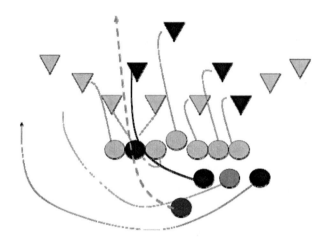

Figure 10L. Comet Rip 13 ISO Right

Line –

Pulling Guard – Drop your outside foot so it points at 45 degrees, then kick out block the first defender outside that crosses your face (kick out at a 45 degree angle, not flat).

Pulling Tackle – Block down and drive the first defender inside toward the Center's hip.

Pulling End – If COVERED, LEG & Turn aiming for the inside arm pit, then wall off with your butt inside as you drive the defender out. If UNCOVERED, Fan block the first defender to cross your face and drive him outside.

Center – If COVERED, LEG & TURN aiming for the play side arm pit then wall your butt inside as you drive the defender out. If UNCOVERED, release and block the first backer inside; if no backer threat is present, work to cut off the FS or backside COVER 2 safety.

Wall Guard to Wall End – If COVERED, LEG & TURN aiming for the play side arm pit, then wall your butt to the play side as you drive the defender away. If UNCOVERED, release and cut off the first backer inside; if there is no backer threat, release and cut off backside secondary pursuit.

QB – Secure the snap and follow the BB into the hole. If the BB keeps going vertical, cut off his line and go to daylight. If the BB engages a defender, cut to his backside and go vertical to the end-zone while working to the near sideline.

TB – Execute a flash fake, fake reverse hand off and kick out the first defender to cross your face backside (wall side).

WB – Drop step, fake reverse, then run like you have the football and score a TD. The better the fake, the more likely you can pull the play side perimeter defenders away from the interior.

BB – Cross over step, then lead into the hole and go vertical to the end zone. If any defender attempts to cross your face, LEG & TURN (PIN) him to that side, so the QB can go vertical.

Coaching Notes:

Opposite is Comet Liz 14 ISO Left

Comet Rip 14 Double Right

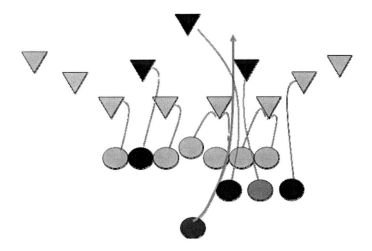

Figure 10M. Comet Rip 14 Double Right

Line –

> Wall Tight End and Wall Tackle - Combo block the DLM that is covering either lineman and drive him straight back. Keep hips together, get near palms into the bottom lip of the breast plate and far palms into the respective arm pit, then drive the defender upward and back.
>
> Wall Guard and CENTER - Combo block the DLM that is covering either lineman and drive him straight back. Keep hips together; get near palms into the bottom lip of the breast plate and far palms into the respective arm pit, then drive the defender upward and back. Pulling Side - Block covered/uncovered (LEG & TURN).

BB – Cross over step, then lead into the hole and go vertical to the end zone. If any defender attempts to cross your face, LEG & TURN (PIN) him so that the QB can go vertical.

QB – Secure the snap and follow the BB into the hole. If the BB continues going vertical, cut off his line and head to daylight. If the BB engages a defender, cut to his backside and go vertical to the end zone while working to the near sideline.

TB – Slide towards the inside hip of the Wall Tackle, then get vertical and block the first defender to cross your face. Don't let him fill the hole, meet him on his side.

WB – Fire off squeezing inside (tight to the hip of the wall tight end) and wall out the first defender outside of the Wall Tight End (LEG AND TURN).

Coaching Notes:

The BB must get into the hole quickly, so don't hesitate to scoot him over a tad to help him get into the hole quicker.

You can tag this with BLAST and all three backs (BB, TB, WB) will form a wedge on the TB and blow up the OLB ahead of them. This is a great way to run this play on short yardage and goal line situations.

Opposite: Comet Liz 13 Double Left

Comet Rip Drag Pass Right (Sprint)

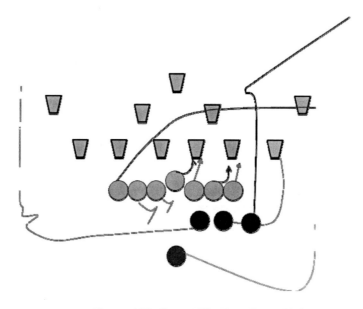

Figure 10N. Comet Rip Drag Pass Right

Line -

> Wall Tight End to Center – Slide to the wall side (Covered/Uncovered). LEM/SSM
> Pulling Guard to Pulling Tackle – Hinge to the wall side; don't allow any defender
> inside of you, force any defender encountered to go outside of you and around the
> hinge wall. KKM

Pulling Tight End - Inside release through the heels of first backer inside as you gain depth of 4 to 6 yards. As soon as you pass the Center, start looking for the ball as you are the second read (LOW). If the QB runs the ball, turn back over your up field shoulder and wall off the first defender to show (put him on the ground).

WB - Outside release, then take 8 to 9 steps and break outside at 45 degrees (corner). Accelerate to the sideline until you find open space. You are the HIGH read (first read) of the QB. If the ball goes to the PTE (low read) or the QB runs, turn back over your up field shoulder and wall off the first defender to show (put him on the ground).

BB - Lead step at the pull side DEMLOS, then flatten out and run a Swing (turn and look for the ball, if no ball then finish with the Wheel route). If TBACK is added to the play, you are tagged as the primary route. If there is no tag for TBACK, wall off below the Pull Tackle hinge.

TB - Gain a little depth and get to the outside arm pit of the first defender to show past the WTE, and then wall him inside.

QB - Secure the snap and gain depth to the wall side (at least 3 to 5 yards of depth). You must threaten the perimeter quickly while looking to throw as soon as you secure the ball. If the WB is open throw to him immediately so he can eat up as much vertical space as possible before the defense recovers. Your read is HIGH (WB) to LOW (PTE). If neither is open, run the ball. If you see vertical space as you roll out, run the ball. The object is to get positive yards, not complete a pass. If tagged with TBACK, gain extra depth, then as you break wide, plant and set to throw to the BB. If he is open on SWING, throw him open. If you see him break to Wheel, throw him open so he can catch it and run with it.

Comet Rip Reverse Pass Right (Sprint)

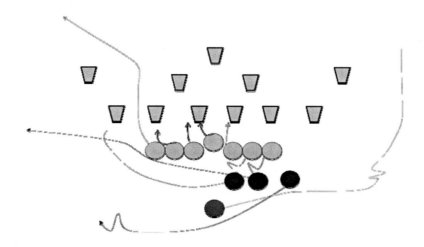

Figure 10O. Comet Rip Reverse Pass Right

Line -

> Wall Tackle to Center – Slide to the wall side (Covered/Uncovered). LEM/SSM
> Pulling Guard to Pulling Tight End – Hinge to the wall side; don't allow any
> defender inside of you, i.e. force any defender encountered to go outside of you
> and around the hinge wall. KKM

Wall Tight End - Release outside, take 8 to 9 steps and break outside at 35 degrees (corner). Accelerate to the sideline until you find open space. You are the HIGH read (first read) of the QB. If the ball goes to the BB (low read) or the WB runs, turn back over your up field shoulder and wall off the first defender to show (put him on the ground).

WB - Drop step, then get to the outside hip of the TB and take the hand off. Don't rush or sprint into the hand off. Once you get the ball, accelerate to full speed and get outside. Once you secure the ball, get your eyes up field and look for the HIGH (WTE running corner route) and LOW read (BB into flat). If you see the HIGH open throw it immediately, if you see the LOW open throw it immediately, if you see daylight run! If TBACK is added to play, as you get outside, stop, plant, and throw back to the TBACK so he runs to the ball and vertical. If the Swing is not open, he will run Wheel, so throw him open to the Wheel.

QB - Cross over step, then outside hand off to the WB behind the wall side. Then flatten out and run a swing route as you break about 3 to 5 yards past the WB's starting spot (turn and look for the ball, if no ball, finish with the Wheel route). If TBACK is added to the play, you are tagged the primary route. If there is no tag for TBACK, wall off below the pull tackle hinge.

TB - Jab step to fake power and run to the flat on the other side. Run through the DEMLOS's far shoulder to slow his rush. As you pass the DEMLOS gain speed and get your head around for the ball. If the WB runs, turn back over your up field shoulder and wall in any inside defender near you (put him on the ground).

BB: Cross over and gain depth to log the DEMLOS.

Coaching Point:

You can use OVER to apply additional blocking to the play side if needed.

Opposite is Comet Liz Reverse Pass Left

Chapter 11
Nova Power & Lead Series

The Nova formation is based on the Hugh Wyatt direct snap Wildcat formation. However, the basic structure is slightly different. I think the formation is an ingenious direct snap variation of the Double Wing and the more I use it, the more advantages I see. When compared to the classic tight formation, and even the shift formation I am currently using as my base, the advantages offered by the Nova formation are unique. The one thing you should remember about this formation is that it is essentially the tight formation with a direct snap. There are very few, if any, modifications required to duplicate the tight formation power series. Unlike the other formation variations where RIP/LIZ is defining the formation strength, with the Nova formation RIP/LIZ is actually stating formation strength *and motion*. The QB uses a spin technique and pitches the ball to the motion WB. Following the WB motion, the QB (back nearest the motion) will spin towards the motion to pitch, or fake pitch, to the motion back. This is a big difference between the Wyatt Wildcat and the Nova. Coach Wyatt does not run a classic power play out of the Wildcat as he opts to hand off and boot back-side. I want my power scheme, and more specifically the QB lead, to be part of every formation I use in my system; uniformity in the formations I use is very important. The LOFs are aimed at the EDGE and the PERIMETER with two backs on each side of the formation - making it a well balanced, symmetric attack formation.

Aligning the backfield of Nova

The QB and BB will align 4 yards deep, hip-to-hip splitting the center (Figure 11A). The BB will always align to the strength call (RIP to the right, LIZ to the left). Wingbacks will align so that their heels are in line with the toes of the QB and BB, and they will be half an arm length away from the last man on the line of scrimmage (tight end or tackle). This alignment will allow the motion WB to take his normal RIP/LIZ motion (cross under, side step, forward step).

Note: I did not include pictures of the NASTY and LOOSE plays as the edge tags are the same as in SHIFT.

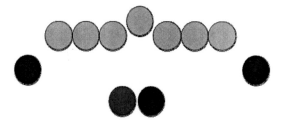

BSWB, QB, BB, PSWB

Figure 11A. The Base Nova Formation

QB Spin Footwork

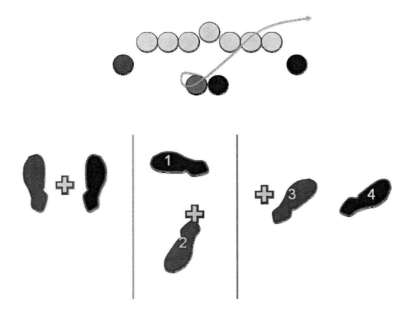

Figure 11B. The QB Spin Footwork

The QB will spin for the majority of the plays in this formation, see Figure 11B above. The plus sign represents the QB's starting point. The blue foot is his left foot, and the red foot is his right foot. Figure 11B illustrates a RIP Motion spin (spinning towards the left wingback as he goes into RIP motion). At the snap and secure, the QB will take his right foot and cross step to the left (step 1), as he does this his left foot will step back and turn towards the motion wingback (step 2). The left foot will act as the pivot and complete the spin (step 3), as the right will come around and land facing the left perimeter (step 4).

Nova Formations

1.   Can every core play in my power series be used in this formation with little to no alteration in the basic structure of the play? *Answer - Yes*

2.   Can I use my current system of edge tags to alter the perimeter so that I can adapt and isolate the perimeter triangle of the defense? *Answer – Yes*

3.   What advantage does it give me that I don't have using my base formation (TIGHT)? *Answer – Increased speed in the running attack (downhill), direct snap allows the pullers a clear line of access to the play side. QB spin action creates additional misdirection in the backfield and distorts keys.*

4.   Does it give me a leverage or line of force advantage against the defense? ANSWER – Yes, it does to the strong side edge and perimeter. When the defense over-shifts it gives an advantage to the weak side as well.

Brief Overview of the Nova Power Series

Power Series

Interior Plays – 10 Wedge Right, 30 Wedge Right (Rip and Liz),

- Interior power play for this series.
- Use reverse (XX) action behind it to create deception designed to hold the perimeter defenders in place on each side.
- QB and BB variants allow you to hit the same spot with two different players increasing the misdirection aspect of the offense.

Edge Plays – Rip 26 Seal Right, Rip 16 Seal Right, Rip 33 Kick Left, Rip 45 Kick Left, Liz 45 Seal Left, Liz 15 Seal Left, Liz 34 Kick Right, Liz 26 Kick Right

- Seal Play (Power Play, e.g. Rip 26 Seal Right, Rip 16 Seal Right, Liz 45 Seal Left, Liz 15 Seal Left)
  - Core play of this offense
  - Must be able to run it anywhere on the field, at any time, against any defensive tactic.
  - We have a variety of ways to run this play to keep defenses on their toes.
  - TB power play is a pure power play with a maximum amount of blockers. It is our base play.
  - QB power utilizes the TB as a sweep decoy to the perimeter to neutralize perimeter defenders.

- BB Kick (BB Counter Trap, e.g. Rip 33 Kick Left/ Liz 34 Kick Right)
  - Edge misdirection play that allows us to attack the defense with the pre-flow look of WB power in the opposite direction and WB reverse action in the play direction, and then hit back inside on the edge with the BB, as the perimeters defend power and reverse (XX).
  - BB must hit inside vertically and go north-south quickly.

- WB Kick (WB Counter Trap, e.g. Rip 45 Kick Left, Liz 26 Kick Right)
  - Edge misdirection play that allows us to attack the defense with the pre-flow look of WB power in one direction and then hit back against flow with an inside counter.
  - WB must hit inside vertically and go north-south quickly.

Perimeter Plays – Rip 28 Monster Sweep Right, Rip 28 Wide Right, Rip 45 Wide Reverse Left, Liz 47 Monster Sweep Left, Liz 47 Wide Left, Liz 28 Wide Reverse Right.

- WB Monster Sweep (Power Sweep, e.g. Rip 28 Monster Sweep, Liz 47 Monster Sweep)
  - Perimeter power play. Overwhelm the perimeter with pullers.
  - Must seal the EMLOS to the inside.

- Best run when you have two in the perimeter triangle and/or you see the EMLOS squatting/crashing to the WB power play.

- WB Wide Reverse (XX outside reverse, e.g. Rip 47 Wide Reverse, Liz 28 Wide Reverse)
  - Perimeter misdirection play. Isolate the interior and perimeter defenders and attempt to attack the backside perimeter triangle (away from power).
  - Key is 2 or less in the perimeter box and EMLOS vacating contain with shallow pinch inside to chase power.
  - Best used against teams when they are crashing the backside of power.

- WB Wide Sweep (Rip 28 Wide, Liz 47 Wide)
  - Alternative power perimeter play for monster sweep.
  - If the OLB and CB are filling hard into the tunnel of the TKO wal this is a nice alternative.
  - Good alternative if you are having problems using Monster Sweep due to a good OLB/SS on play side.

Play Action Passing – Rip Power Pass Right, Liz Power Pass Left, Rip WB Pass Right, Liz WB Pass Left

- Power Pass
  - Run/Pass option
  - Basic flood pattern on the power side.
  - Read low to high (BB flat to WB out).
  - Can teach a peek deep if MOFO (middle of the field open).
  - Run this to the QB's throwing side

A quick reminder on the RIGHT/LEFT tags added to the play. This side call is for the linemen only, and is designed to remind them on which side of the ball the WALL SIDE should align. Thus, these tags do not necessarily indicate the direction of the play.

Rip/Liz Motion

The WB executes this when given the motion signal. He takes a cross over step with his outside foot behind his inside foot, sliding inside as he does. He then steps forward with his inside foot aiming at the AT MAN'S outside hip. He should get the pitch just under the Back-side C gap. The pitch is going to come from the side and not from in front of him like the TIGHT formation. The QB will execute his spin and push the ball in front of the WB so that as he takes his third step he will run into the ball as he goes towards the AT MAN (Figure 11C).

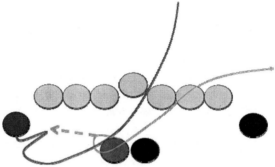

Figure 11C. Illustration of Rip/Liz Motion from the Nova Formation.

Detailed Description of Selected Plays:
The Nova Power Series

Nova Rip 30 Wedge Right (Interior play)

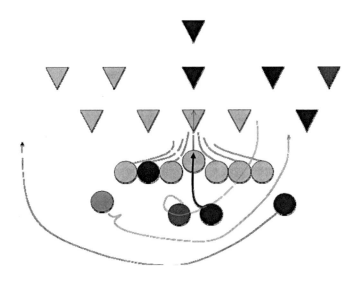

Figure 11D. **Nova Rip 30 Wedge Right**

Line – Wedge block on the Center

BB – Secure the snap and hit the Wedge. Look for a crease on either side, then hit it and get vertical. Do not go around or under the Wedge. Secure the ball and get as many yards you can.

QB – Execute a flash fake, and then aim for inside arm pit of back side defensive end and wall him off.

TB (BSWB) – Rip motion and execute a flash fake pitch and reverse, then attack the inside arm pit of the play side defensive end and wall him off.

WB – Execute a flash fake reverse, and then attack perimeter and get vertical up field.

This is the classic XX or power/reverse action behind the BB wedge creating a split flow that places pressure on both perimeter triangles to defend their edge/perimeter while we attack the interior. Essentially this play isolates the interior as we overwhelm it with the Wedge blocking scheme.

This concept can be used in the LOOSE as well, which simply places a different kind of pressure on the strong side. In this case, it would be a passing threat forcing the perimeter triangle and the safety to cover both at the perimeter and vertically.

Coaching Notes:

Can be used with the same edge tags as SHIFT, i.e. Loose and Nasty.

Opposite is Nova Liz 30 Wedge Right

Nova Rip 10 Wedge Right (Interior play)

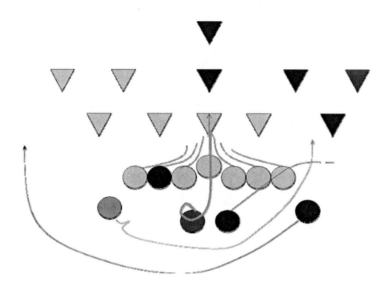

Figure 11E. Nova Rip 10 Wedge Right

Line – Wedge block on the Center

BB – Cross over and gain depth as if to log the backside defensive end but wall him off on the inside by running through his inside shoulder.

QB – Secure the snap and hit the Wedge. Look for a crease on either side, then hit it and get vertical. Do not go around or under the Wedge. Secure the ball and get as many yards you can.

TB (BSWB) – Rip motion and execute a flash fake pitch and reverse, then attack the inside arm pit of the play side defensive end and wall him off.

WB – Execute a flash fake reverse, then attack the perimeter and get vertical up field.

This is the classic XX or power/reverse action behind the QB Wedge creating a split flow that places pressure on both perimeter triangles to defend their edge/perimeter while we attack the interior. This play works the exact same way as the BB Wedge, but it allows us to utilize a power runner type at QB and basically get the ball into another back's hands behind the Wedge while the BB assumes the backside perimeter threat.

This concept can be used in the LOOSE as well, which simply places a different kind of pressure on the strong side. In this case it would be a passing threat forcing the perimeter triangle and the safety to cover both at the perimeter and vertically.

Coaching Notes:

Can be used with the same edge tags as SHIFT, i.e. Loose and Nasty.

Opposite is Nova Liz 10 Wedge Right.

Nova Rip 26 Seal Right (Edge play)

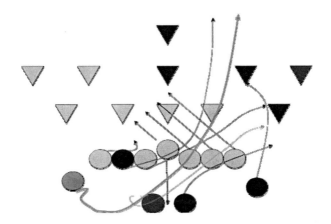

Figure 11F. Nova Rip 26 Seal Right

Line –
>   Wall Side – TKO (Center to PSTE)
>   Pulling Guard – The BSG will pull and kick out the first defender to show above BB and QB
>   Pulling Tackle – The BST will pull up the wall and go vertical to the end zone, any defender crossing his face will be sealed inside with a wall off.
>   Pull Tight End – Cutoff to Center's hip; if no one shows, climb to the linebacker level and cutoff the backside pursuit.

BB – Cross over and hug the LOS by aiming for the first play side blockers inside hip. Kick out the first defender to cross your face. When kicking him out, flip your hips and body into the hole so you isolate the defender away from the WB as he hits the tunnel.

QB – Spin and pitch the ball to the TB, then cross over step aiming for the heels of the BB and follow him into the hole. Kick out the first defender to show above the BB.
NOTE – if the BB is struggling to kick out a tough defender, double team him and let the BSG take the next defender up.

TB (BSWB) – Rip motion and secure the pitch, aim for the Center's play side hip and get vertical to daylight. Climb the wall and get 5 yards. Once you make it out of the tunnel, make one move (cutback inside, go vertical, bounce it outside), and get vertical to the end zone. Never let one defender take you down, and never let a defender hit you - you hit him first. Your initial depth should be 4 to 5 yards, but don't hesitate to adjust the depth so that you arrive just behind the BSG and BST as they hit the tunnel. The timing is very important as it will hide your approach into the tunnel.

WB – Take the quickest release to get off the LOS cleanly, then get inside and block the first backer inside (FBI). If the outside backer is flowing to the perimeter or crashing down into the edge, let him go and take the next defender inside (inside backer). Your job is to seal off the linebacker level inside. Drive that backer to the top of the wall. Your landmark is the near shoulder of the last blocker on the wall.

Coaching Notes:

When running this play from either NASTY or LOOSE, I prefer to include OVER so that I can get a 4 man TKO wall on the play side. If the OVER tag is not used you will only have 3 blockers in the TKO wall.

Opposite is Nova Liz 45 Seal Left.

Nova Rip 16 Seal Right (Edge play)

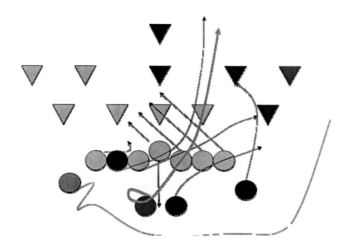

Figure 11G. Nova Rip 16 Seal Right

Line –

> Wall side – TKO (Center to PSTE)
> Pulling Guard – The BSG will pull and kick out the first defender to show above the BB and QB
> Pulling Tackle – The BST will pull up the wall, then go vertical to the end zone. Any defender crossing his face will be sealed inside with a wall off.
> Pull Tight End – Cutoff to Center's hip; if no one shows climb to the linebacker level and cutoff the backside pursuit.

BB – Cross over and hug the LOS by aiming for the first play side blockers inside hip. Kick out the first defender to cross your face. When you kick him out, flip your hips and body into the hole so you isolate the defender away from the WB as he hits the tunnel.

QB – Secure the snap, aim for the Center's play side hip and get vertical to daylight. Climb the wall and get 5 yards. Once you make it out of the tunnel, make one move (cutback inside, go vertical, bounce it outside) and get vertical to the end zone. Never let one defender take you down, and never let a defender hit you - you hit him first. Your initial depth should be 4 to 5 yards, but don't hesitate to adjust the depth so that you arrive just behind the BSG and BST as they hit the tunnel. The timing is very important, as it will hide your approach into the tunnel.

TB (BSWB) – Execute a flash fake, grab cloth with the backside arm as you run to make it look like you have the ball. Attack the outside arm pit of the EMLOS to force him to widen and defend your faking. Run like you have the ball and want to score! If you get tackled then you did your job!

WB – Take the quickest release to get off the LOS cleanly, then get inside and block the first backer inside (FBI). If the outside backer is flowing to the perimeter or crashing down into the edge, let him go and take the next defender inside (inside backer). Your job is to seal off the linebacker level inside. Drive that backer to the top of the wall. Your landmark is the near shoulder of the last blocker on the wall.

Coaching Notes:

When running this play from either NASTY or LOOSE, I prefer to include OVER so that I can get a 4 man TKO wall on the play side.

Opposite is Nova Liz 15 Seal Left

Nova Rip 45 Kick Left (Edge play)

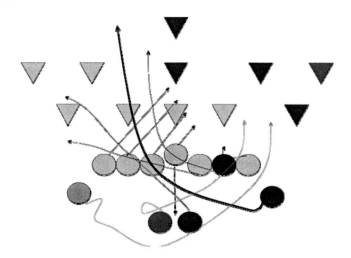

Figure 11H. Nova Rip 45 Kick Left

Line –

>Wall Side – TKO (Center to PSTE)
>Pulling Guard – The BSG will pull and kick out the first defender to cross his face. When kicking out the defender, the BSG will flip his hips and body into the hole to isolate the defender away from the WB as he hits the tunnel.
>Pulling Tackle – The BST will pull up the wall then go vertical to the end zone. Any defender crossing his face will be sealed inside with a wall off.
>Pull Tight End – Cutoff to the Center's hip, if no one shows, climb to the linebacker level and cutoff the backside pursuit.

BB – Jab step to the opposite side, mesh with pulling tackle and kick out the first defender to cross your face above the pulling guard (PG).

QB – Secure the snap, spin, take a short cross step to open belt buckle to WB and make a handoff to him. Then execute a kick out block on the first defender to cross your face. Let the WB cross your face and slow down for the handoff.

TB (BSWB) – Rip motion, execute a flash fake, and grab cloth with the backside arm as you run to make it look like you have the ball. Attack the outside arm pit of the EMLOS to force him to widen and defend your faking. Run like you have the ball and want to score! If you get tackled then you did your job!

WB – Drop step with the inside foot and aim for the inside hip of the QB. Take the handoff, secure it, and get vertical when you see the first daylight to the end zone. Do not go east-west; you must get vertical, up field and to the boundary after you get out of the tunnel.

Coaching Notes:

This is an outstanding play when you see the backside defenders overplaying or chasing the power play. We don't use the WB Counter in Loose as there is not a enough flow misdirection to create the backside displacement we are looking for in the play. We will use it with Nasty.

Opposite is Nova Liz 26 Kick Right

Nova Rip 33 Kick Left (Edge play)

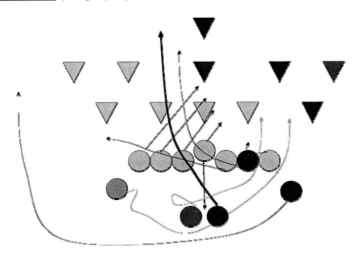

Figure 11I. Nova Rip 33 Kick Left

Line –

    Wall side – TKO (Center to PSTE)

    Pulling Guard – The BSG will pull and kick out the first defender to cross his face. When kicking out the defender, the BSG will flip his hips and body into the hole to isolate the defender away from the WB as he hits the tunnel.

    Pulling Tackle – The BST will pull up the wall, and then go vertical to the end zone. Any defender crossing his face will be sealed him inside with a wall off.

    Pull Tight End – Cutoff to the Center's hip; if no one shows, climb to the linebacker level and cutoff the backside pursuit.

BB – Secure the snap and jab step to opposite side, mesh with the pulling tackle and get vertical when you see first daylight. Don't get tackled by one defender or any sort of arm tackle.

QB – Spin, then take a short cross step and get by the BB as he jab steps. Attack vertically up the field off the Pull Tight End's outside hip.

TB (BSWB) – Rip motion, execute a flash fake, then fake a reverse handoff (make sure you rub hips as you go by one another as that will increase the misdirection aspect). After the XX fake, grab cloth with the backside arm as you run to make it look like you have the ball. Attack the outside arm pit of the EMLOS to force him to widen and defend your faking. Run like you have the ball and want to score! If you get tackled then you did your job!

WB – Drop step with the inside foot and gain depth. As you move outside of the TB, rub hips and cradle fake with the TB. After the XX fake, grab cloth with the backside arm as you run to make it look like you have the ball. Attack the perimeter wide and get vertical to force the defender to widen to defend your faking. Run like you have the ball and want to score! If you get tackled then you did your job!

This is our inside counter play to the BB. It is a power play, and a backside containment play against an overly aggressive backside perimeter triangle that is cross keying the WB. Faking the power action and reverse action is the key to the success of this play, and the more aggressive the TB, WB, and QB are with their run and kick out block the more likely this play will be successful.

Coaching Notes:

This is an outstanding play when you see the backside defenders overplaying or chasing the power play and cross keying the far wing back. The BB counter gives us a quick hitting counter trap that we can use out of any edge tag with the BB.

Note that in LOOSE we don't have the WB running reverse as it will have no effect on widening the perimeter defenders, instead we attempt to stress the coverage with the loose pair faking outside release fade/seam routes.
Opposite is Nova Liz 34 Kick Right.

Nova Rip 28 Monster Sweep Right (perimeter play)

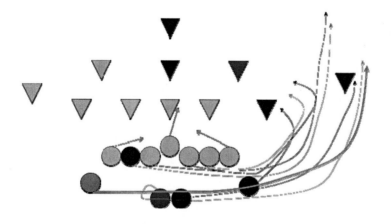

Figure 11J. Nova Rip 28 Monster Sweep Right

Line –

> Wall Tight End – Cut off play side to the Center's hip.
> Wall Tackle – Pull around the WTE and WSWB, and then form a wall, land-marking the outside shoulder of the WSWB.
> Wall Guard – Pull around the WTE and WSWB, and then form a wall land- marking the outside shoulder of the WT.
> Center – Versus a NT (odd front), jewel block him by aiming your far shoulder at the crotch of the defender so that your head goes past the play side hip. Versus a DT (even front), severe down block aiming for a point just in front of his far (play side shoulder), and then wheel your butt to the play side.
> Pulling Side Guard and Tackle – Pull tight down the LOS and pull tight around the perimeter wall. Then go vertical to the end zone, creating a vertical lane for the runner. Any defender that crosses your face should be walled off by attacking his up field arm pit and then wheeling your butt towards the runner. Any leakage encountered as you go down the line should be picked up by cutting it off the same way the Center does against an even front.
> Pull Tight End – Cutoff to the Center's hip; if no one shows, climb to the linebacker level.

BB – Cross over, and then get outside and up field quickly. Against a CB that is off the LOS and near the EMLOS, you must come around and attack the outside arm pit and wheel block him. Against a wide CB, you must close distance quickly, then settle down and wall the defender to the outside to create an alley for the runner.

QB – Execute a flash fake, then cross over and get up field to create a vertical lane for the runner to the end zone. Any defender that crosses your face should be walled off.

TB (BSWB) – Secure the snap and cross over staying flat (parallel) to the LOS until you go past the WSTE. Once you see daylight, make a move (cutback, vertical, bounce), and then get vertical and up field. Bear in mind you have three vertical blockers going up field near boundary, so if you get in the alley between the three vertical pullers and the boundary, there is a good chance you'll score a TD.

WB – Take a lateral step with the outside foot and attack outside arm pit of EMLOS. Wall the defender off by wheel blocking and driving him inside as far as you can.

This is our WB power sweep; it is based on simply overloading the perimeter with two running backs and four linemen as blockers at the point of attack. Once the defense shows two or less in the perimeter, this is a great way to attack the perimeter and get the ball into space on the outside.

Coaching Notes:

We run this play from Nasty or Nasty Over when we see the EMLOS staying over or inside of the wall side tight end. When we go into the Nasty edge tag, it is best to have the tight end wall off the EMLOS and have the wing back fold around him to form the wall on the outside shoulder of the tight end. The next lineman inside will finish the wall while the other lineman or linemen pull and go vertical.

In Shift Over Loose, since our wing back is now a slot (with a split end), we use the BB to log the EMLOS. The key to running the monster sweep or any sweep out of loose is to get in the inside lane between the receiver group and the EMLOS. The stress you are placing on the secondary and perimeter defenders to cover pass and play run, along with the kick out block by a running back (QB in this case), opens a seam in the perimeter in which to run.

Opposite is Nova Liz 47 Monster Sweep Left

Nova Rip 28 Wide Right (Perimeter play)

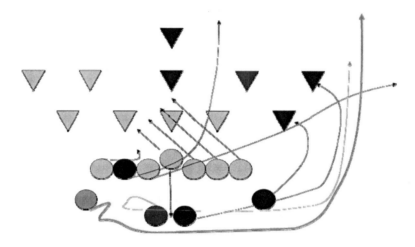

Figure 11K. Nova Rip 28 Wide Right

Line –

        Wall Side – TKO (Center to PSTE)

        Pulling Guard – The BSG will pull and kick out the first wide defender above the BB. If no defender is present outside (e.g. CB), turn and go vertical to the end zone.

        Pulling Tackle – The BST will pull up the wall and go vertical to the end zone. Any defender crossing your face should be sealed inside with a wall off.

        Pull Tight End – Cutoff to the Center's hip; if no one shows, climb to the linebacker level and cutoff the backside pursuit.

BB – Cross over step, gain depth, and get outside of WB's wall off. Then attack the first defender inside and wall him off.

QB – Execute a flash fake, cross over step, gain depth, and then get outside of BB and get vertical. If any defender crosses your face, wall him inside; otherwise go vertical to the end zone to give the runner a vertical lane.

TB (BSWB) – Secure the snap and cross over staying flat (parallel) to the LOS until you go past the WSTE. Once you see daylight, make a move (cutback, vertical, bounce), then get vertical and up field. . Bear in mind that you have a vertical blocker going down field near boundary, so if you get in the alley between the vertical puller and the boundary your chance of scoring is great.

This is a great sweep against OLB's and CB's that are filling the alley behind the wall, as they will get caught inside which will give us numbers outside for the runner.

Coaching Notes:

When we run this play from Nasty, we often use OVER to get the full four-man TKO wall, while the WB and WTE block the FBI and DEMLOS, respectively.

In Shift Over Loose, since our wing back is now a slot (with a split end), we use the BB to log the EMLOS. The key to running the WIDE (or any sweep) out of Loose, Bunch, or Trips is to get in the inside lane between the receiver group and the EMLOS. The stress you are placing on the secondary and perimeter defenders to cover pass and play run along with the kick out block by a running back (QB in this case) opens a seam in the perimeter in which to run. in.

Opposite is Nova Liz 47 Wide Left

Nova Rip 47 Wide Reverse Left

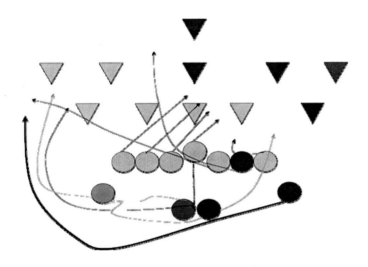

Figure 11L. Nova Rip 47 Wide Reverse Left

Line –

Wall side – TKO (Center to PSTE)

Pulling Side – The BSG will pull and climb as if to seal, but then go wide and kick out the first outside defender (e.g. CB) to cross his face. When you kick the defender out, flip your hips and body into the hole so you isolate the defender away from the WB as he hits the tunnel. If facing an athletic corner, quickly close distance, and then settle down and wall him off.

Pulling Tackle – The BST will pull up the wall and go vertical to the end zone. Any defender crossing his face will be sealed inside with a wall off.

Pull Tight End – Cutoff to the Center's hip; if no one shows, climb to the linebacker level and cutoff the backside pursuit.

QB – Execute a flash fake, then cross over and gain enough depth to log the EMLOS and drive him inside. If he is crashing; all you need to do is wall him in for moment.

BB – Cross over and gain depth under the QB; wall off the next defender inside (OLB normally).

TB – Secure the snap, cross over step, and then make an outside handoff to WB. Following the handoff, aim for the inside arm pit of the BSDE, and make a great fake as if running seal. As you reach the defender, kick him out.

WB – Drop step, and then get to the outside hip of the TB and take the hand off. Don't rush or sprint into the hand off. Once you get the ball, accelerate to full speed and break outside. Once you see daylight get vertical quick. The faster you get vertical the more likely you are to get by the linebacker pursuit. If there is a corner wide, run inside of the BSG's kick out.

This is the classic XX reverse, but with an outside handoff. I use this play to place pressure on the backside perimeter triangle to defend the perimeter or give us the easy score. I call this play when I see the BSOLB sitting on the edge for a counter while the DE is crashing inside (1) to chase the power play or (2) trying to disrupt the edge misdirection plays coming his way. Often the only defender left supporting the perimeter is the CB.

Coaching Notes:

The Nasty tag will hit a lot faster as the WB is closer to the TB, thus the timing will need to be developed. Often defenses will really over play the Nasty edge tag, so having that WB hit a little faster will increase the chance of this being a touchdown for you.

Opposite: Nova Liz 28 Wide Reverse Right

Nova Rip Power Pass Right (Sprint)

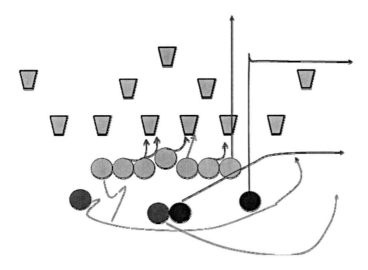

Figure 11M. Nova Rip Power Pass Right

Line -
> Wall Tackle to Center – Slide to the wall side (Covered/Uncovered). LEM/SSM
> Pulling Guard to Pull Tight End – Hinge to the wall side; don't allow any defender
> inside of you, rather force defenders to go outside of you and around the hinge
> wall. KKM

Wall Tight End - Outside release, then go vertical up the middle and pin the safety deep.
The ball will only come to you on a MOFO read from the QB/OC.

WB - Outside release, then take 8 to 9 steps and break outside. Accelerate to the sideline
until you find and open space. You are the HIGH read (second read) of the QB. If the ball
goes to the BB (low read) or the QB runs, turn back over your up field shoulder and wall
off the first defender to show (put him on the ground).

BB - Release through the DEMLOS's face to slow his rush so that the TB can get outside
and wall him inside. Run to the flat, and as soon as you get past the DEMLOS, get your
head around and look for the ball over your down field shoulder. You are the primary read
(low read). If the QB runs the ball, turn back over your up field shoulder and wall off the
first defender to show (put him on the ground).

TB: Flash fake and fake sweep, get wide and attack the outside arm pit of first defender
to show past the WT.

QB: Secure the snap and gain depth to the wall side (at least 3 to 5 yards of depth). You
must threaten the perimeter quickly, while looking to throw as soon as you secure the ball.
If the BB is open, throw to him immediately so he can eat up as much vertical space as
possible before the defense recovers. Your read is LOW (BB) to HIGH (WB). If neither is

open run the ball. If you see vertical space as you roll out, run the ball. The object is to get positive yards not complete a pass.

You can run a variation of this that has the WB and WALL TE switch assignments; i.e. the WB runs the vertical and the WALL TE runs the out. The normal assignment is #1 outside runs the out, #2 runs the vertical, and #3 runs the flat route. When running the play from Loose, Bunch, or Trips, #1 runs the vertical, #2 the out, and #3 the flat route.

Coaching Notes:

You can use OVER to move your PULL TACKLE to the wall side where will follow the COVERED/UNCOVERED rule (LEM/SSM). This will provide an extra blocker on the play side, if you have a tough pass rush on that side. Thus, you can use OVER to pinpoint where you need additional pass protection (wall or pull side).

NOTE: If the QB or OC sees the MOFO (middle of the field open), meaning there is no FS in the middle of the field, your first read is the WALL TE. Throw to the inside shoulder, but lead the receiver, i.e. throw to where the receiver is going (not at him) so he can catch it on the run and continue to the end zone.

Brief Overview of the Nova Lead Series

Interior Plays – Rip 31/14 Dive Right, Liz 32/13 Dive Left

- Interior power play for this series.
- Use reverse (XX) action behind it to create deception that is designed to hold the perimeter defenders in place on each side.
- QB and BB plays act as a double dive mini-series with cross action between the QB and BB which confuse the interior LB reads on the backfield.

Edge Plays – Rip 13 ISO Right, Rip 23 ISO Right, Rip 14 Double Right, Rip 24 Double Right, Liz 14 ISO Left, Liz 24 ISO Left, Liz 13 Double Left, Liz 23 Double Left

The ISO Play is a cross blocked play to the pull side (backside) with XX action behind it that is designed to hold the perimeter defenders in place while the point of attack is overwhelmed.

- Great play to add to the power series as it allows you to attack the pull side immediately and directly (which has the better pullers and makes the cross blocking more effective) when defenses are keying on the WALL side and/or formation strength.
- Solid way of attacking an interior defender playing over the Pulling Guard and attempting to shoot the gap between the Pulling Guard and Center to chase the puller on pulling plays. In this case, the down block of the Pull Tackle is very easy to execute. It is also a nice way to attack the perimeter triangle on the Pull side when they are sitting on reverse and ready to pursue the XX action.
- We have two ways of running this play to keep defenses on their toes.
- The QB ISO play is a quick power play with full XX action behind it and the BB lead blocking to isolate the first backer inside (ILB often). . Great to use if you have an athletic tough kid at QB.
- The TB ISO play is a pure power play with the BB lead blocking to isolate the first backer inside (ILB often) and the QB attacking the first defender outside as he hits the hole behind the BB. The WB executes XX action while the TB executes a quick counter step and then attacks the hole following the BB and QB.

The DOUBLE Play is a double team/combo block to the wall side with XX action behind it. Used against even fronts that give us trouble running our angle blocking; when they are sitting their ILB and OLB back while their defensive line absorbs up the ABC wall. This allows us to drive those defenders back into the laps of the backers using our WALL side blockers (our better drive/wall blockers) as double teamers/combo blockers.

Rip 24 Double Right, Rip 14 Double Right, Liz 45 Double Left, Liz 15 Double Left.

Youth Double Wing II: The Gun!

- DOUBLE plays to the TB allow us to double team the DT and DE with our C/WG and WT/WE. The BB lead blocks and isolates the OLB while the QB walls off the play side CB. The XX action of the TB counter stepping and the WB faking, helps to hold the perimeter defenders in place.
- Double plays to the QB have the TB and WB executing XX action to further hold the perimeter defenders in place. So there is little need to actually wall off the CB as the QB hits the edge.

Perimeter Plays – Rip 28 Pin Right, Rip 37 Pin Right, Liz 47 Pin Left, Liz 38 Pin Left

- TB Pin Sweep (Power Sweep, e.g. Rip 28 Pin, Liz 47 Pin)
  - Perimeter power play. Overwhelm the perimeter by using an aggressive vertical drive step, pinning the outside hip of all play side defenders, and keying the last defender outside for wall off/kick out.
  - Must seal the EMLOS to the inside and key the last perimeter defender for wall off/kick out.
  - Best run when you have two in the perimeter triangle and/or you see the EMLOS squatting/crashing to the WB power play, as it further isolates the remaining perimeter defenders.

- FB Pin Sweep (counter sweep, e.g. Rip 37 Pin Right, Liz 38 Pin Left)
  - Perimeter misdirection play. Isolates the remaining perimeter defender on the weak side when defenses are shifting to our perceived strength and reducing their backside perimeter to two or less.
  - Key is 2 or less in the perimeter box and EMLOS vacating contain with shallow pinch inside to chase power/power sweep/power pass.
  - Best used against teams that are crashing the backside of power and allowing our TB to pin them inside while the QB leads for the BB running sweep.
  - Great for teams with fast and athletic BB's.
  - Very nice non-pulling misdirection sweep that utilizes a fast BB on the weak side much the same way we use XX Reverse in our power series.

Play Action Passing – Rip Counter Pass Right, Liz Counter Pass Left

- Drag Pass
  - Run/Pass option
  - Basic high low drag pattern to power side.
  - Read PSWB corner to BSTE shallow drag (high to low)
  - Run this only if your TB can throw and only to his throwing side.
  - A nice backside throwback to the TB running a swing & wheel when tagged with TBACK.

- Reverse Pass
  - Based off of XX action with WB passing (need a passer at WB)
  - Basic high-low drag pattern to the backside (great for over-shifted defenses)

- Read PTE (corner) to WTE (drag) or HIGH to LOW.
- A nice backside throwback to the TB running a swing & wheel when tagged with TBACK.

A quick reminder on the RIGHT/LEFT tags added to the play. This side call is for the linemen only, and is designed to remind them on which side of the ball the WALL SIDE should align. Thus, these tags do not necessarily indicate the direction of the play.

Nova Rip 28 Pin Right

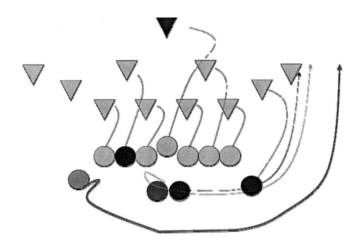

Figure 11N. Nova Rip 28 Pin Right

Line –

PSTE to CENTER - If COVERED, LEG & TURN (PIN) the defender inside. If UNCOVERED, work to the second level attacking through the near arm pit of the next DLM play side. and then cut off the first backer inside (FBI). Even if that LB is over the blocker, he should still work through the near arm pit of the near play side DLM as this will put him on a good cut off angle. If the Center has no immediate backer, and the backside ILB/OLB is getting caught in the wash of the backside cut off, them he can release up field and cut off the FS/backside Cover 2 safety.

BSG to BSTE - Follow the same rules as the play side blockers, but work to get vertical much more quickly, and then cut off the backside secondary pursuit once the runner is play side.

PSWB (AT MAN) – If COVERED, LEG & TURN (PIN) the defender. If UNCOVERED, take a lateral step to the outside and then get vertical attacking the first backer inside. Attack the defender's play side arm pit and wall him off.

BB – Attack the outside hip of the PSTE and then get vertical toward the end zone. If the corner back is inside and wall him off. If the corner is wide, close distance as quickly as possible, then gather yourself and kick him out. Wall him outside to give the runner a vertical seam inside.

QB – Follow the BB into to the edge staying on his outside hip. If the BB moves inside and go vertical toward the end zone and wall off any defender crossing your face. If the BB moves outside, cut off immediately, and then get vertical toward the end zone and wall off any defender attempting to cross your face.

TB – Secure the snap, cross over, and stay flat at cruising speed (60 to 75% of full speed). When you see daylight in the seam, get vertical and go to the end zone as quickly as possible.

Coaching Notes:

When running this play from Nasty, the PSTE and PSWB simply swap so that the PSTE becomes the AT MAN.

From Loose, the BB will take the EMLOS and log block him so the edge is sealed. The SE and SLOT will release outside and run vertical to drive the defenders away from the seam. The QB will kick out the first wide defender that crosses his face outside. This allows us to pick up a slot defender that is peeking inside for run.

Opposite is Nova Liz 47 Pin Left

Nova Rip 37 Pin Right

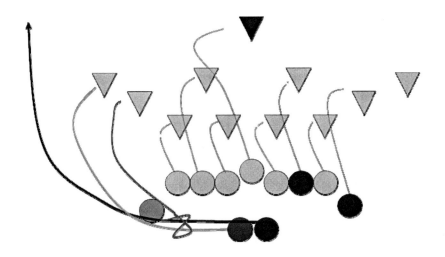

Figure 11O. Nova Rip 37 Pin Right

Line -
> Pull Tight End (AT MAN) – If COVERED, LEG & TURN (PIN) the defender. If UNCOVERED, take a lateral step to the outside and get vertical attacking the first backer inside. Attack the defender's play side arm pit and wall him off.
> Pulling Tackle to Center - If COVERED, LEG & TURN (PIN) the defender inside. If UNCOVERED, work to the second level attacking through the near arm pit of the next DLM play side, and then cut off the first backer inside (FBI). Even if that LB is over the blocker, he should still work through the near arm pit of the near play play sideside DLM as this will put him on a good cut off angle. If the Center has no immediate backer, and the backside ILB/OLB is getting caught in the wash of the backside cut off, them he can release up field and cut off the FS/backside Cover 2 safety.
> Wall Guard to Wall Tight End - Follow the same rules as the play side blockers, but work to get vertical much more quickly, and then cut off the backside secondary pursuit once the runner is play side.

TB – Attack the outside hip of the PTE and get vertical toward the end zone. If the second level defender (typically OLB) is inside, wall him off.

QB – Follow the TB into to the edge staying on his outside hip. If the TB moves inside, then go vertical toward the end zone and wall off any defender crossing your face. If the TB moves outside, then cut off immediately, and get vertical toward the end zone. Wall off any defender attempting to cross your face.

BB – Secure the snap, cross over, and gain depth until you pass the PTE. Stay flat at cruising speed (60 to 75% of full speed) until you see daylight in the seam, then get vertical and to the end zone as quickly as possible.

Coaching Notes:

When running this play from Nasty, the PSTE and PSWB simply swap backside assignments.

When running from Loose, the slot and SE run outside release routes to pull the backside perimeter defenders away from pursuit. The key to this play is 2 or less on the backside perimeter.

Opposite is Nova Liz 38 Pin Left

Nova Rip 13 ISO Right

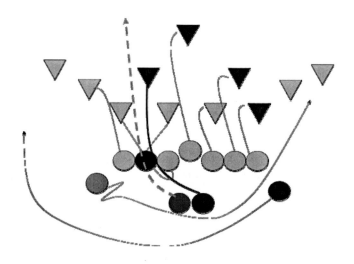

Figure 11P. Nova Rip 13 ISO Right

Line –

Pulling Guard – Drop your outside foot so it points at 45 degrees, then kick out block the first defender outside that crosses your face (kick out at a 45 degree angle not flat).

Pulling Tackle – Block down and drive the first defender inside towards the Center's hip.

Pulling End – If COVERED, LEG & Turn aiming for the inside arm pit, and then wall off with your butt inside as you drive the defender out. If UNCOVERED, fan block the first defender to cross your face and drive him outside.

Center – If COVERED, LEG & TURN aiming for the play side arm pit, and then wheel your butt inside as you drive the defender out. If UNCOVERED, release and block the first backer inside; if no backer threat is present, work to cut off the FS or backside COVER 2 safety.

Wall Guard to Wall End – If COVERED, LEG & TURN aiming for the play side arm pit, and then wheel your butt to the play side, as you drive the defender away. If UNCOVERED, release and cut off the first backer inside; if there is no backer threat, release and cut off the backside secondary pursuit.

BB – Cross over step, then lead into the hole and go vertical to the end zone. If any defender attempts to cross your face, LEG & TURN (PIN) him to that side so that the QB can go vertical.

QB – Secure the snap and follow the BB into the hole. If the BB continues going vertical, cut off his line and head to daylight. If the BB engages a defender, cut to his backside and go vertical to the end zone as you work to the near sideline.

TB – Execute a flash fake, fake reverse hand off, and then kick out the first defender to cross your face backside (wall side).

WB – Drop step, fake reverse and run like you have the football. The better the fake, the more likely you can pull the play side perimeter defenders away from the interior. This play is a great alternative, when you see the defensive tackle on the pulling side collapsing hard inside to chase the pullers while the next defensive lineman outside is over-playing the reverse. This allows us to essentially cross block these two defenders to open a hole for the BB. The BB may then isolate block the first backer as the QB follows him into the hole. With the TB and WB faking power and reverse, this play acts as a split flow to force both perimeters to react and respond.

Coaching Notes:

Since this play is run to the pull side, it doesn't matter if this is run from Nasty, Loose, or any other tag - except for OVER, which would move a key blocker (PT) away from the play side, to the WALL Side. The BB must hit the hole fast, aggressively, and always take on the first block on the other side of the LOS, as this block is a key to the success of this play.

Opposite: Nova Liz 14 ISO Left

Shift Rip 23 ISO Right

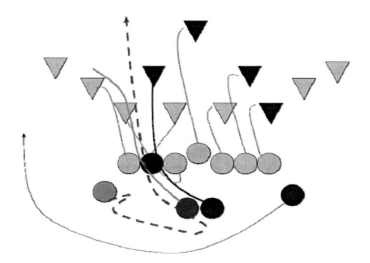

Figure 11Q. Shift Rip 23 ISO Right

Line –

> Pulling Guard – Drop your outside foot so that it points at 45 degrees, and then kick out the first defender outside that crosses your face (kick out at a 45 degree angle not flat).
>
> Pulling Tackle – Block down and drive the first defender inside towards the Center's hip.
>
> Pulling End – If COVERED, LEG & Turn aiming for the inside arm pit, and then wall off with your butt inside as you drive the defender out. If UNCOVERED, Fan block the first defender to cross your face and drive him outside.
>
> Center – If COVERED, LEG & TURN aiming for the play side arm pit, and then wheel your butt inside as you drive the defender out. If UNCOVERED, release and block the first backer inside; if no backer threat is present, work to cut off the FS or backside COVER 2 safety.
>
> Wall Guard to Wall End – If COVERED, LEG & TURN aiming for the play side arm pit, and then wheel your butt to the play side, as you drive the defender away. If UNCOVERED, release and cut off the first backer inside; if there is no backer threat, release and cut off the backside secondary pursuit.

BB – Cross over step, then lead into the hole and go vertical to the end zone. Any defender attempting to cross your face, LEG & TURN (PIN) him to that side so that the QB can go vertical.

QB – Cross over step, and then follow the BB into the hole. Cut off his outside hip as he passes the LOS and wall out the first defender that crosses your face(typically the CB).

TB – Secure the snap, counter step, and then hit the hole downhill reading the BB's block. Break off his backside and get vertical to the end zone.

WB – Drop step, fake reverse, and run like you have the football. The better the fake, the more likely you can pull the play side perimeter defenders away from the interior. This play is a great alternative when you see the defensive tackle on the pulling side collapsing hard inside to chase the pullers while the next defensive lineman outside is over-playing the reverse. This allows us to essentially cross block the two defenders and open a hole for the BB to isolate block the first backer encountered as the QB follows him into the hole. With the QB and WB faking power and reverse respectively, it acts as a split flow to force both perimeters to react and respond.

Coaching Notes:

Since this play is run to the pull side, it doesn't matter if this is run from Nasty, Loose, or any other tag - except for OVER, which would move a key blocker (PT) away from the play side, to the WALL Side. The BB and QB must hit the hole fast, aggressively and always take on your first block on the other side of the LOS, as this block is key to the success of this play.

Because we run so many power and power sweep plays, it is quite convincing when the TB steps to the strong side, and thus this action tends to hold the perimeter defenders in place long enough to overwhelm the pull side.

Opposite: Nova Liz 44 ISO Left

Nova Rip 14 Double Right

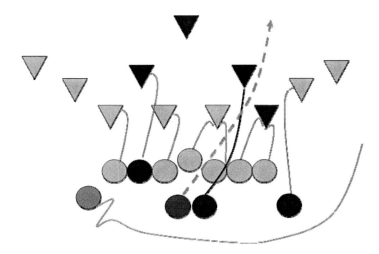

Figure 11R. Nova Rip 14 Double Right

Line –
Wall Tight End and Wall Tackle - Combo block the DLM that is covering either, and drive him straight back. Keep hips together, get near palms into the bottom lip of the breast plate and the far palms into the respective arm pit, and then drive the defender upward and back.
Wall Guard and CENTER - Combo block the DLM that is covering either, and drive him straight back. Keep hips together, get near palms into the bottom lip of the breast plate and the far palms into the respective arm pit, and then drive the defender upward and back.
Pulling Side - Block covered/uncovered (LEG & TURN).

BB – Cross over step, then lead into the hole and go vertical to the end zone. Any defender attempting to cross your face, LEG & TURN (PIN) him to that side so that the QB can go vertical.

QB – Secure the snap and follow the BB into the hole. If the BB continues going vertical, cut off his line and head to daylight. If the BB engages a defender, cut to his backside and go vertical to the end zone as you work to the near sideline.

TB – Slide towards the inside hip of the Wall Tackle, get vertical, and block the first defender to cross your face. Don't let him fill the hole; meet the defender on his side of the LOS.

WB – Fire off squeezing inside (tight to the hip of the wall tight end) and wall out the first defender you encounter outside of the Wall Tight End (LEG AND TURN).

Coaching Notes:

Because this is run out to the wall side it is important to have a four man TKO wall. The BB must hit the hole fast and aggressively and always take on his first block on the other side of the LOS as this block is key to the success of this play. Because we run so many power and power sweeps it is more than convincing for the TB to fake the power sweep to hold or even pull the perimeter defenders away from the edge.

Opposite: Nova Liz 13 Double Left

Nova Rip 31 Dive Right

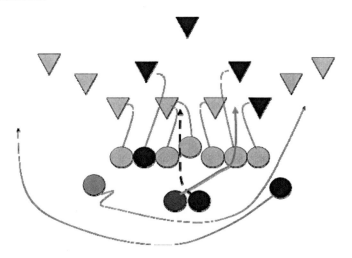

Figure 11S. Nova Rip 31 Dive Right

Line –

  Wall Side - The WTE to WG will block covered/uncovered (LEG & TURN).
  Center and Pull Guard - Combo block the first DLM play side (NT to DT).
  Pull Tackle and Pull Tight End - Block covered/uncovered (LEG & TURN).

  Note: If the DLM at point of attack can be handled with a one-on-one block, the Center (even front) or Pull Guard (odd front) can release to the FBI or the safety. Remember, we combo block that DLM to create a <u>big</u> hole, so we only go one-on-one if the DLM is easily handled by the one block.

WB - Fake XX reverse.

TB - Execute a flash fake and fake sweep/XX reverse.
QB - Execute a flash fake, cross over step, and attack the Wall Guard's heels. Get vertical and make it look like you have the ball. Stay away from the pull side.
BB: Secure the snap and get vertical on Center's pull side hip.

Nova Rip 14 Dive Right

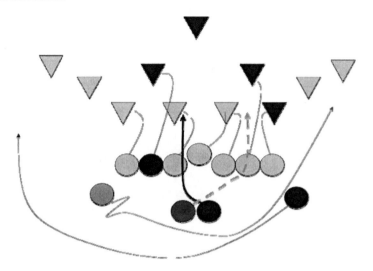

Figure 11T. Nova Rip 14 Dive Right

Line –

    Center and Wall Guard - Combo block first DLM play side (NT to DT).

    Note: If the DLM at point of attack can be handled with a one-on-one block, the Center (even front) or Pull Guard (odd front) can release to the FBI or the safety. Remember, we combo block that DLM to create a <u>big</u> hole, so we only go one-on-one if the DLM is easily handled by the one block.

    Wall Tackle and Wall Tight End - Block covered/uncovered (LEG & TURN).
    PULL GUARD to PULL TE - Block covered/uncovered (LEG & TURN).

WB - Execute a fake XX reverse.

TB - Execute a flash fake and fake sweep/XX reverse.

QB - Secure the snap and get vertical on the Center's wall side hip.

BB - Execute a flash fake, cross over step, and then attack the Pull Guard's heels and get vertical. Make it look like you have the ball. Stay away from the wall side.

Nova Rip Drag Pass Right (Sprint)

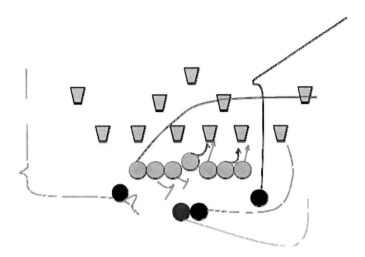

Figure 11U. Nova Rip Drag Pass Right

Line -

Wall Tight End to Center – Slide to the wall side (Covered/Uncovered). LEM/SSM Pulling Guard and Pulling Tackle – Hinge to the wall side. Don't allow any defender inside of you; rather force all defenders to go outside of you and around the hinge wall. KKM

PTE: Inside release through the heels of first backer inside and gain depth of 4 to 6 yards. As soon as you pass the Center, start looking for the ball as you are the second read (LOW). If the QB runs the ball, turn back over your up field shoulder and wall off the first defender to show (put him on the ground).

WB: Outside release and take 8 to 9 steps. Break outside at 45 degrees (corner) and accelerate to the sideline until you find open space. You are the HIGH read (first read) of the QB. If the ball goes to the PTE (low read) or the QB runs, turn back over your up field shoulder and wall off the first defender to show (put him on the ground).

TB: Lead step toward the pull side DEMLOS, and then flatten out and run a swing (turn and look for the ball, if no ball, finish with the wheel route). If TBACK is added to the play, you are tagged as the primary route. If there is no tag for TBACK, wall off below the pull tackle hinge.

BB: Gain a little depth, and then get to the outside arm pit of the first defender to show past the WTE and wall him inside.

QB: Secure the snap and gain depth to the wall side (at least 3 to 5 yards of depth). You must threaten the perimeter quickly, while looking to throw as soon as you secure the ball. If the WB is open, throw to him immediately so he can eat up as much vertical space as possible before the defense recovers. Your read is HIGH (WB) to LOW (PTE). If neither is open, run the ball. If you see vertical space as you roll out, run the ball. The object is to get positive yards, not complete a pass. If tagged with TBACK, gain extra depth and as you break wide plant and set to throw to the TB. If he is open on SWING throw him open; If you see him break to Wheel, throw him open - so he can catch it and run with it.

Nova Rip Reverse Pass Right (Sprint)

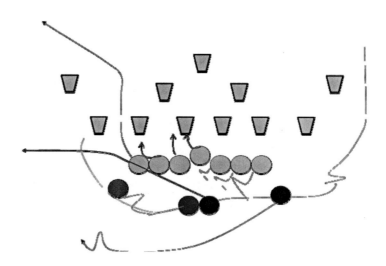

Figure 11V. Nova Rip Reverse Pass Right

Line -

> Wall Tackle to Center – Slide to the wall side (Covered/Uncovered). LEM/SSM Pulling Guard to Pull Tight End – Hinge to the wall side; Don't allow any defender inside of you; rather force all defenders to go outside of you and around the hinge wall. KKM

Wall Tight End - Release outside, take 8 to 9 steps and break outside at 35 degrees (corner). Accelerate to the sideline until you find open space. You are the HIGH read (first read) of the QB. If the ball goes to the BB (low read) or the WB runs, turn back over your up field shoulder and wall off the first defender to show (put him on the ground).

WB - Drop step, get to the outside hip of the TB, and take the hand off. Don't rush or sprint into the hand off. Once you get the ball, accelerate to full speed and get outside. Once you secure the ball, get your eyes up field and look for the HIGH (WTE running corner route) and LOW reads (BB into flat). If you see the HIGH open, throw it immediately; if you see the LOW open, throw it immediately; if you see daylight - run! If TBACK is added to play, as you get outside, stop plant and throw back to the TBACK. Lead him so that he runs to the ball and vertical. If the Swing is not open, he will run Wheel, so throw him open to the Wheel.

TB - Cross over step and outside hand off to the WB behind the wall side. Then flatten out and run a swing route as you break about 3 to 5 yards past the WB's starting spot (turn and look for the ball no ball finish with the wheel route). If TBACK is added to the play, you are tagged as the primary route. If there is no tag for TBACK, wall off below the pull tackle hinge.

BB - Jab step to fake power, and then run to the flat on the other side. Run through the DEMLOS's far shoulder to slow his rush. As you pass the defender, accelerate and get your head around for the ball. If the WB runs, turn back over your up field shoulder and wall in any inside defender near you (put him on the ground).

QB - Cross over and gain depth to log the DEMLOS.

Coaching Point:

This play is not used with any edge tag other than NASTY or ON, as the other tags will spread the WB too far away from the other side to be effective.

You can use OVER to apply additional blocking to the play side, when needed.

Chapter 12
Alternative Plays for the Power Series

I don't consider the following to be a part of the respective base power series, but I do think they are plays that can enhance a specific group of kids and play an important role in the power series as you develop your system with your kids. There are three specific plays that I consider solid alternatives that can be added to the basic power series to enhance the package based on the talent you face and the types of defense you are going to see.

Traditional BB KICK "Trap" to Flow Side

For the educated and/or experienced Double Winger, you will notice that we use a Counter Trap (trap going away from the flow of power – Figure 12A) instead of the traditional trap play to the BB going towards the direction of flow (Figure 12B). The reasoning is pretty simple; I have always had more success with the counter trap game than the traditional play side trapping game. I have included the BB Kick (trap) in the alternative play list because although I don't consider it a base play within our series, I do consider it a very relevant part of our system. We use it when I see a defense that is going to give up the flow side A/B gaps by overplaying power and power sweep from the inside linebacker position. One of the key concepts when running our trapping game, is that we use it in conjunction with our wedge play. Reading the defensive line, we wedge; attacking defensive line, we trap using the trapping method I describe on page 48 of this manual.

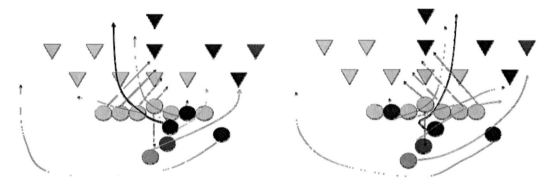

Figure 12A – Shift Rip 33 KICK LT
BB Counter Trap against flow

Figure 12B – Shift Rip 34 KICK RT
BB Trap with flow

With the Counter Trap, the purpose of the play is to attack an aggressive outside backer on the backside while kicking out a defensive end that is reading the Wing Back Reverse. The perimeter pressure applied via the Wing Back Reverse, forces the defensive end to open up, and the kick out by the backside guard opens the hole. The key is the backside backer reacting to either the front side flow of power going the other way, or the backside reverse action of the far wingback - which creates an alley over the backside interior we can exploit with a quick hitting blocking back behind that kick out block along with the pulling tackle sealing the top of the wall off.

With the traditional trap, the intent of the play is to attack the alley created when (1) the backside linebacker is sitting on counter/reverse, (2) the inside backer and play side backer are over-playing the power, power sweep, and/or power pass action thus, creating a seam in the play side interior that we can exploit (Figure 12C).

Obviously the key to both of these plays, is the combination of aggressive defensive tackles or defensive ends we can trap, as well as overly aggressive backers looking to stop the edge/perimeter play on their side (or in the case of counter trap on the other side as well), which results in the backers vacating their gap responsibility.

You can easily replace the BB counter trap with the more traditional BB trap play in your base series, or as I have done in the past, you can install the counter trap at the beginning of the season and as the season progresses you can install the traditional BB trap to further enhance your misdirection game.

TB KICK "Cutback" Play

This play was really popularized by the Calande Double Wing, but he used the far wingback to WHAM block. While that may have worked for him, I have found that this tactic applies to many players to the hole when they may better be applied to threatening the vertical pass on the far side, or attacking the near side perimeter with the wingback faking reverse. I have played with both variations and I have found that I really like the use of the XX action behind the cutback in compressed formations; and the threat of the vertical pass on the far side in expanded formations (loose, bunch, trips), as it blends naturally into my present system. The way I teach this play is very simple, whether we are in a compressed formation or an expanded formation, the TB (BSWB) will take a cross over step, and then a lead step getting his hips turned the opposite direction he is going. He will then cut back into the kick out lane on the backside.

In a compressed formation with the wingback faking reverse, we have the TB take the steps and keep the ball in his belly. The drop step and reverse action of the wingback and the turning of the tail back, helps to really sell the reverse action to the backside perimeter and they naturally expand to defend what they perceive to be a reverse play. The additional action of the quarterback and the blocking back heading towards the backside helps to solidify the reverse for the defense, and they often sell out to stop the reverse by closing down the perimeter. In doing so, they often open an alley on the edge. With the pulling guard kicking out the first defender to show (DEMLOS typically) and the blocking back and quarterback kicking out the second and third defenders respectively, a huge hole can be opened in the backside edge as the tailback cuts back and goes vertical.

In an expanded formation like Loose, Bunch, or Trips, we attempt to (1) stretch the defense out and isolate their backside perimeter players away from the core of the offense and (2) force them to respect the strong side power game of our power, power sweep, and/or power pass game. The play initially looks like power. As the blocking back and quarterback turn backside to kick out the first, second, and third level with the pulling guard; the running back simply cuts back into the weak side of the defense.

The key to calling this play is when we don't think our typical misdirection game of WB KICK and BB KICK will have enough power to overcome the perimeter defenders sitting on counter and reverse. We need to exploit that edge to keep the strong side perimeter defenders honest in their attack of our offense.

FAN Pass (called Fade Pass in the <u>YDW: Winning Youth Offense book</u> page 39)

This is a play I have used a great deal against bump and run, i.e. press cover teams, because it puts the cover guy on the TB (BSWB) in a real bind as he is naturally picked by his own teammates. This often forces the corner on the fan side to either rotate over, take the TB coming out of the backfield running the swing route, or stay on the wingback running the fade route. Often he is going to stay with his cover rule and that puts the ball in one of our best player's hands with a high percentage pass. This is a very flexible play and can be run out of any of our edge tags.

The pass protection can very simple by using wall protection (see <u>YDW: Winning Youth Offense</u>) or you can use the more advanced deuce pass protection. The quarterback secures the snap, sets facing the swing route and if he is open he throws it immediately; if he is covered, he resets and throws the ball to the wingback running the fade route.

If the defense is leaving the middle of the field open (MOFO), we will call MOFO and tell the QB to read INSIDE-OUTSIDE on the wall tight end running seam and the wingback running the Fade route.

Key Point to Remember

Something to always keep in mind is to never add too much. Never add for the sake of having this or that play simply because it looks good or you think you can run it effectively. There should always be a very precise reason why you run any specific play. For example I run the plays in the power series because they complement each other in a very meaningful way. The power play is our base play to the edge (off tackle), the power sweep allows us to attack a perimeter triangle that is specifically trying to shut down the edge and close off the power play. The power pass allows us to attack a perimeter triangle that is placing all of its resources to stopping the edge and perimeter running game (power and power sweep). Meanwhile the various forms of the wedge allow us to attack into the interior of the defense that is either soft, and/or isolated from the perimeter defenders due to our play calling. The misdirection component of our power series allows us to attack the backside defenders (specifically the perimeter defenders) when they are vacating their responsibilities too quickly in an effort to better support the other side of the defense facing the power game (power, power sweep, and/or power pass). When they do that, we have the Blocking Back Kick, the Wing Back Kick, and the Wing Back Reverse, that give us the means to punch a hole into an already soft spot in the defense. Adding additional plays will reduce the level of execution in all the plays you have, so you must be careful about what you add and ask the question: Does this play have a specific purpose and provide a benefit to what I am doing?

SHIFT Rip 34 Kick Right Trap

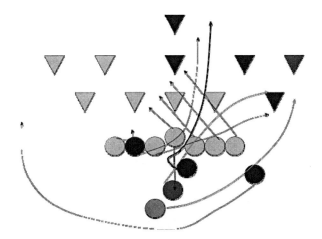

Figure 12C. SHIFT Rip 34 Kick Right Trap

Line –

Wall side – TKO (Center to PSTE)
Pulling Side – The BSG pulls and kicks out the first defender to cross his face. When he kicks him out, he will flip his hips and body into the hole to isolate the defender away from the WB as he hits the tunnel.
Pulling Tackle – The BST will pull up the wall, and go vertical to the end zone; any defender crossing his face will be sealed inside with a wall off.
Pulling Tight End – Cutoff to the Center's hip; if no one shows, climb to the linebacker level and cutoff the backside pursuit.

BB – Slide step in front of the snap and secure the ball. Sit and let the pullers cross your face; when the pulling guard crosses your face get vertical on the outside hip of the pulling tackle (if in OVER simply climb the wall tightly).

QB – Execute a flash fake, and then kick out the second level defender above the BSG's kick out (same as seal play).

TB (BSWB) – Execute a flash fake then fake a reverse handoff, (make sure you rub hips as you go by one another as that will increase the misdirection aspect). After the XX fake, grab cloth with the backside arm as you run to make it look like you have the ball. Attack the outside arm pit of the EMLOS to force him to widen to defend your faking sweep. Run like you have the ball and want to score! If you get tackled, then you did your job!

WB – Drop step with the inside foot and gain depth. As you move outside of the TB, rub hips and execute a cradle fake with the TB. After the XX fake, grab cloth with the backside arm as you run to make it look like you have the ball. Attack the perimeter wide and get vertical to force the defender to widen to defend your faking. Run like you have the ball and want to score! If you get tackled then you did your job!

Shift Nasty Over Rip 34 Kick Right Trap

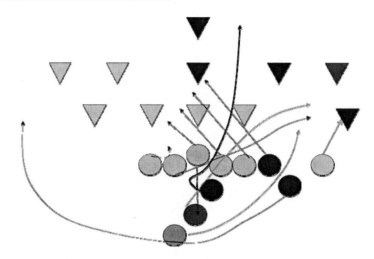

Figure 12D. Shift Nasty Over Rip 34 Kick Right Trap

Shift Loose Over Rip 34 Kick Right Trap

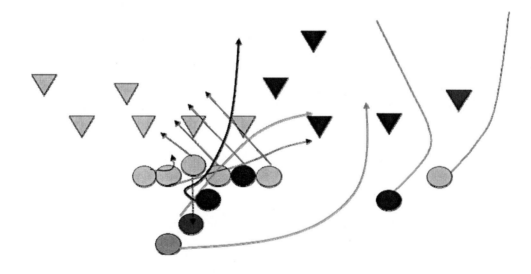

Figure 12E. Shift Loose Over Rip 34 Kick Right Trap

Star Rip 34 Kick Right Trap

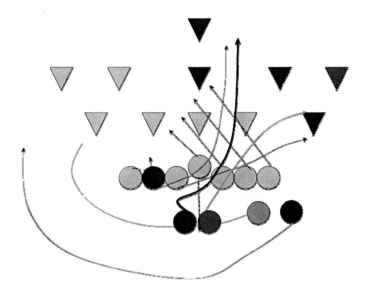

Figure 12F. Star Rip 34 Kick Right Trap

Star Trips Over Rip 34 Kick Right Trap

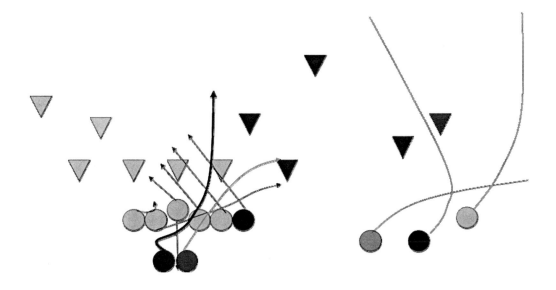

Figure 12G. Star Trips Over Rip 34 Kick Right Trap

Star Bunch Over Rip 34 Kick Right Trap

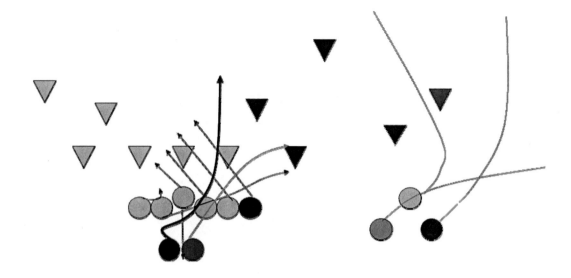

Figure 12H. Star Bunch Over Rip 34 Kick Right Trap

Comet Rip 34 Kick Right Trap

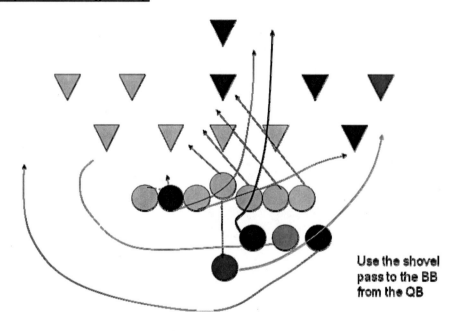

Use the shovel pass to the BB from the QB

Figure 12I. Comet Rip 34 Kick Right Trap

Nova Rip 34 Kick Right Trap

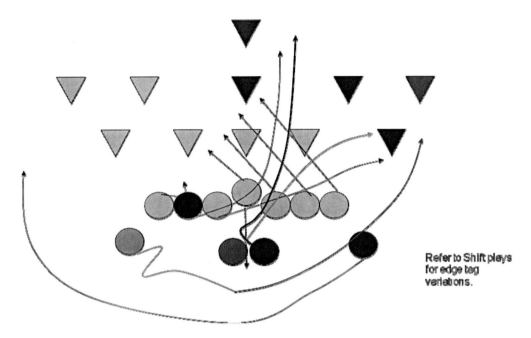

Refer to Shift plays
for edge tag
variations.

Figure 12J. Nova Rip 34 Kick Right Trap

Shift Rip 25 Kick Left Cutback

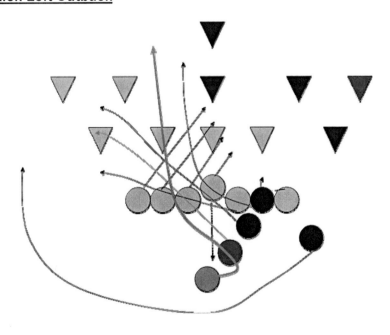

Figure 12K. Shift Rip 25 Kick Left Cutback (see description below)

Line –
> Wall Side – TKO (center to PSTE)
> Pulling Side – The BSG will pull and kick out the first defender to cross his face. As he kicks the defender out, he will flip his hips and body into the hole to isolate the defender away from the WB as he hits the tunnel.
> Pulling Tackle – The BST will pull up the wall and go vertical to the end zone; any defender crossing his face will be sealed inside with a wall off.
> Pulling Tight End – Cutoff to the Center's hip; if no one shows, climb to the linebacker level and cutoff the backside pursuit.

BB – Jab step to the opposite side, then kick out the first defender to cross your face above the quarterback's kick out.

QB – Execute a flash fake, then jab step to the opposite side and kick out the first defender to cross your face above the pulling guard's kick out. The combination of the QB and BB allows us to kick out a LB filling into the tunnel.

TB (BSWB) – Secure the snap, then take a cross over step and a lead step while getting your hips turned in the opposite direction you're going. Then cut back into the kick out lane on the backside. Keep the ball in your belly as you face the WB who is faking XX action, i.e. let the WB sell the reverse.

WB – Drop step with the inside foot and gain depth. As you move outside off the TB, rub hips and cradle fake as you go by him. After the XX fake, grab cloth with the backside arm as you run to make it look like you have the ball. Attack the perimeter wide, and then get vertical to force the defender to widen to defend your faking. Run like you have the ball and want to score! If you get tackled then you did your job!

Shift Nasty Rip 25 Kick Left Cutback

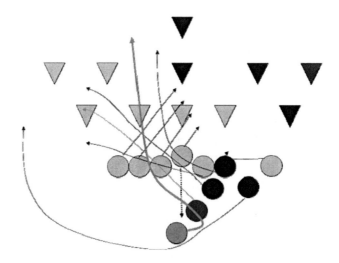

Figure 12L. Shift Nasty Rip 25 Kick Left Cutback

Shift Loose Rip 25 Kick Left Cutback

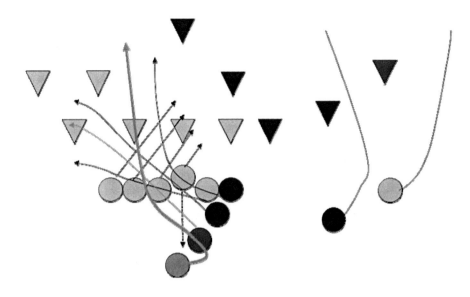

Figure 12M. Shift Loose Rip 25 Kick Left Cutback

Star Rip 25 Kick Left Cutback

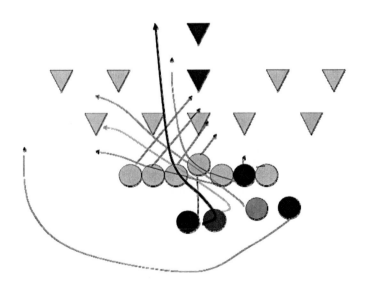

Figure 12O. Star Rip 25 Kick Left Cutback

Star Trips Over Rip 35 Kick Left Cutback

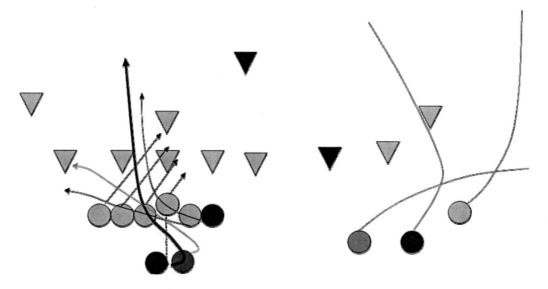

Figure 12P. Star Trips Over Rip 35 Kick Left Cutback

Star Bunch Over Rip 35 Kick Left Cutback

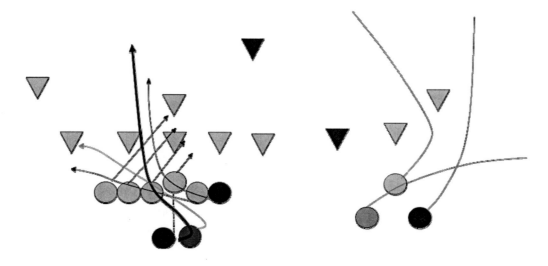

Figure 12Q. Star Bunch Over Rip 35 Kick Left Cutback

Comet Rip 15 Kick Left Cutback

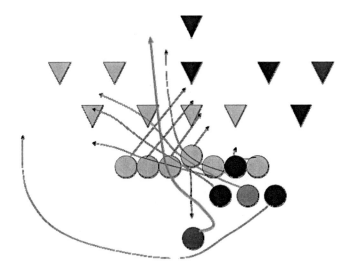

Figure 12R. Comet Rip 15 Kick Left Cutback

Nova Rip 25 Kick Left Cutback

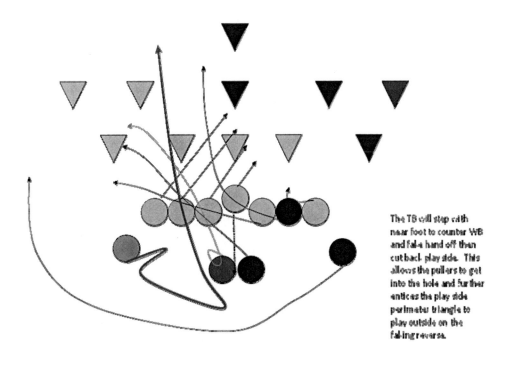

The TB will step with near foot to counter WB and fake hand off then cutback play side. This allows the pullers to get into the hole and further entices the play side perimeter triangle to play outside on the faking reverse.

Figure 12S. Nova Rip 25 Kick Left Cutback

Shift Rip Fan Pass Right

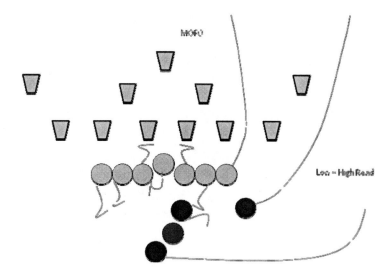

Figure 12T. Shift Rip Fan Pass Right (see description below)

Line -

Center - If UNCOVERED, and no backer is over, the Center will (1) double (SSM) with an OG that needs help on either side, or (2) work to the backside OT that needs help inside, by dropping and helping on the inside shoulder of the OT. The Center should be taught to use a code word to inform the OT he will get help. If Covered, LEM.

Wall and Pull Guard - If UNCOVERED, Kick Kick Mirror (KKM) with the outside foot first and then drive hips inside, towards center. If COVERED, LEM.

Wall and Pull Tackle - If UNCOVERED, Kick Kick Mirror (KKM) with the outside foot first and then drive hips inside, towards center. If COVERED, LEM.

Pull TE If UNCOVERED, Kick Kick Mirror (KKM) with the outside foot first and then drive hips inside, towards center. If COVERED, LEM.

BB: Double the near side edge rusher with the Wall Tackle, or in the case of an overload/hanger, pick up the first defender to show on the outside hip of the near tackle. Always help to the outside shoulder. If the rusher is coming aggressively you can cut him (Texas NCAA rules not NFHS rules). The BB will move to meet him as he normally does, but just as contact is made he will take his outside shoulder and cross body cut the DE from outside in.

QB: Quickly drop, throwing foot first, getting good distance from the LOS. Set up facing the low read (Swing route). If he is open, throw to an open spot in front of his path so he can catch and run. If he is covered, reset quickly to the High read (fade), and throw to the outside shoulder so he can catch it on the run.

TB: Rip motion, then hand fake the pitch. Run hard to sell the toss until you cross the QB. Then get a little depth, and get to the flat as you run the Swing route.

RWB: Outside release to get width, and then execute a fade with max speed to get separation. When you pass the LBs, look for the ball over your outside shoulder.

Wall TE: Outside release and run right up the seam. Find open space to the inside. Accelerate until you pass the LB level and get separation, then look to your inside shoulder. Your job is to run off the near-side safety.

Coaching Keys:

The QB must make a good shoulder and hip fake, and then stay in the pocket. He must set his feet to the receiver and throw the ball quickly!

You can use OVER to move the Pull Tackle to the side you need additional protection.

TAG – Delay – tells the BSTE to run a 'delay fade'; the QB will now throw the ball to him after he fakes to the right side. the QB will then simply turn and throw to the BSTE on a short fade.

"Tight Rip Fan Pass Right Delay". The Pull tight end will Kick Kick and Go (run his route).

Shift Loose Rip Fan Pass Right

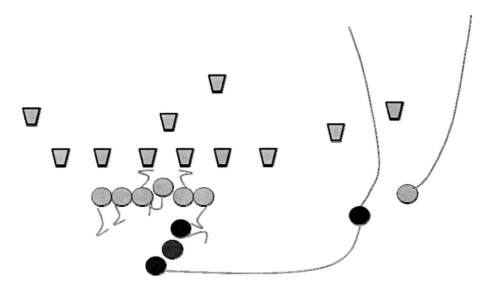

Figure 12U. Shift Loose Rip Fan Pass Right

Shift Loose Rip Fan Pass Right

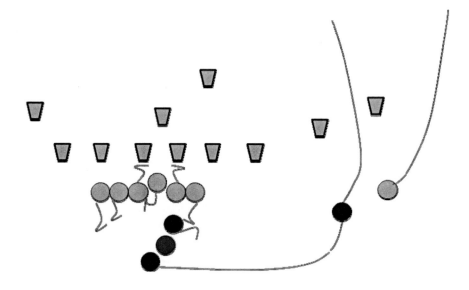

Figure 12V. <u>Shift Loose Rip Fan Pass Right</u>

Star Rip Fan Pass Right

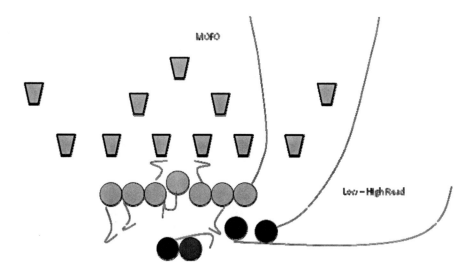

Figure 12W. Star Rip Fan Pass Right

Star Bunch Rip Fan Pass Right

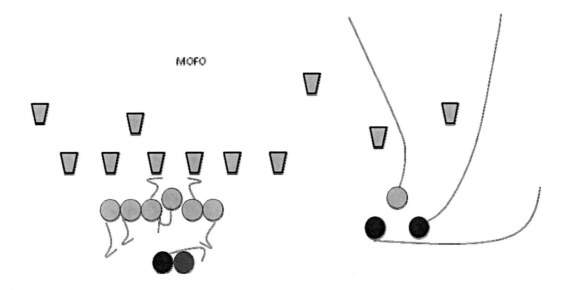

Figure 12X. Star Bunch Rip Fan Pass Right

Star Trips Rip Fan Pass Right

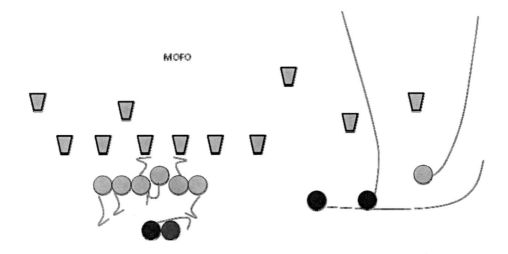

Figure 12Y. Star Trips Rip Fan Pass Right

Comet Rip Fan Pass Right

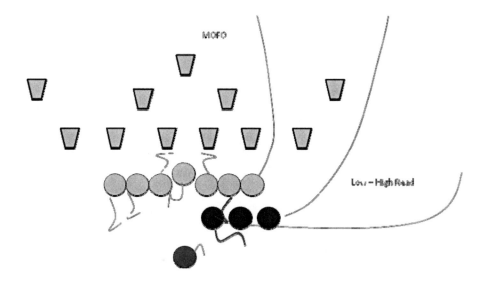

Figure 12Z. Comet Rip Fan Pass Right

Nova Rip Fan Pass Right

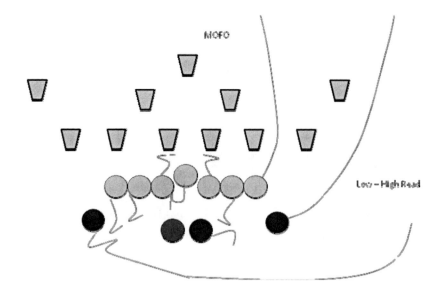

Figure 12AA. Nova Rip Fan Pass Right

Chapter 13
Tornado Series

The Tornado series is a by-product of my experiments with the Fly series and the document that John Teed authored in 2003. I also incorporated elements of the Single Wing Spin series made famous by Charles Caldwell. I started really experimenting with this out of the Eagle series (the 2x2 spread series I utilize), but I found it was actually a much more effective offensive approach from the Shift formation. I have yet to use this from the Star, Comet or the Nova formations; honestly, I have really never considered it out of these formations because I feel it is very effective out of the Shift direct snap formations.

Key Elements:

1) A QB that spins 360 degrees and always attacks towards the strength of the formations and opposite the flow of the WB faking reverse.

2) WB will always fake reverse or we will actually run the reverse.

3) The majority of the plays require the BB to flow to the backside, to create a false key when we run plays to the QB and TB to the strong side.

4) The only pass play is the FLY audible to the SE running the FADE.

5) We motion the wing back (slot) when he is in LOOSE, so that we can maintain the proper timing between the WB, the spinning QB, and the mesh of the BB moving weak side. Motion can also be used to refine the timing of the mesh when we are in SHIFT.

Brief Overview of the Tornado Series

Perimeter – Shift Rip 28 Wide Right Tornado, Shift Loose Over Rip 28 Wide Right Tornado, Shift Liz 47 Wide Left Tornado, Shift Loose Over Liz 47 Wide Left Tornado, Shift Rip 47 Wide Left Reverse Tornado, Shift Loose Rip 47 Wide Left Reverse Tornado, Shift Liz 28 Wide Right Reverse Tornado, Shift Loose Over Liz 28 Wide Right Reverse Tornado.

Edge – Shift Rip 33 Kick Left Tornado, Shift Loose Rip 33 Kick Left Tornado, Shift Liz 34 Kick Right Tornado, Shift Loose Liz 34 Kick Right Tornado, Shift Rip 16 Kick Right Tornado, Shift Loose Over Rip 16 Kick Right Tornado, Shift Liz 15 Kick Left Tornado, Shift Loose Over Liz 15 Kick Left Tornado

Interior – Shift Rip 30 Wedge Right Tornado, Shift Loose Rip 30 Wedge Right Tornado, Shift Liz 30 Wedge Left Tornado, Shift Loose Liz 30 Wedge Left Tornado.

Audibles

Fly - Audible to the Split End in Loose when the QB or TB is carrying the ball. Audible is used when we see the corner playing man but looking inside.

Speed - Audible that tells the QB and TB to run a speed option to the strong side when we have a play going the other way (key breaker – influence play). QB spins and reads the DEMLOS.

Shift Rip 30 Wedge Right Tornado (Interior)

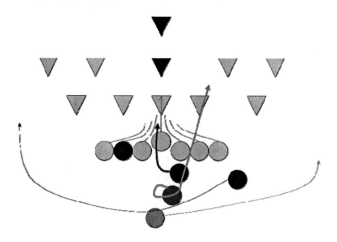

Figure 13A. Shift Rip 30 Wedge Right Tornado

Line – Wedge block on the Center

BB – Secure the snap and hit the Wedge. Look for a crease on either side, then hit it and get vertical. Do not go around or under the Wedge. Secure the ball and get as many yards you can.

QB – Execute a flash fake, spin and aim for outside hip of wall side TE. Get vertical, up the field as you threaten the edge.

TB (BSWB) – Execute a flash fake snap, and run a power sweep as if you have the ball. Take it for a touchdown.

WB – Execute a flash fake reverse, and mesh with the QB as he spins. It is important that the timing of this play happens so that you mesh with the QB as he is facing away from the LOS and the TB goes by you to run power sweep.

In LOOSE, the WB (SLOT) will go into sprint motion and slow down only to adjust to ensure he meshes with the QB at the proper time. Otherwise it is at full speed.

The WB can also go in motion in the normal (base) SHIFT formation if necessary to maintain proper timing. In this case, the WB would get into sprint motion on READY. Again timing of the mesh is essential.

The mesh is very important. The WB should always rub his outside hip with the QB's belt buckle or near hip (depending on the QB's rotation). This increases the misdirection aspect of the mesh and makes it nearly impossible for a defense to discern who has the ball for the next two to three steps.

Shift Loose Rip 30 Wedge Right Tornado

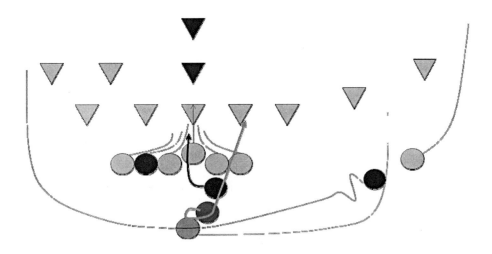

Figure 13B. Shift Loose Rip 30 Wedge Right Tornado

Audibles

In *SHIFT LOOSE*:

FLY audible – Tells the BB to execute a flash fake and fake wedge while the QB takes the snap, spins, sets his feet and throws to the outside shoulder of the SE running the fade down the field. We call this audible when we see the 'cover man' in man coverage looking inside and not actually playing his coverage. You can spot this when you run LOOSE edge tags, and see the coverage not playing the SE down the field.

In either *SHIFT* or *SHIFT LOOSE*:

SPEED audible – Tells the BB to execute a flash fake and fake wedge while the QB takes the snap, spins and gets into the pitch relationship with the TB (BSWB). He keys the first defender past the DEMLOS (who we see chasing the play flat down the LOS – which is our key to call this audible). He then attacks the inside hip of the defenders (typically the OLB), and if the OLB comes at the QB he pitches the ball ASAP to the TB. If he sits or floats to the TB the QB quickly gets vertical.

Shift Rip 33 Kick Left Tornado

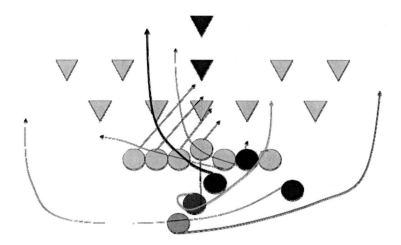

Figure 13C. Shift Rip 33 Kick Left Tornado

Line –

Wall Side – TKO (Center to PSTE)

Pulling Side – The BSG will pull and kick out the first defender to cross his face. As he kicks the defender out, he will flip his hips and body into the hole to isolate the defender away from the WB as he hits the tunnel.

Pulling Tackle – The BST will pull up the wall and then go vertical to end zone. Any defender crossing his face will be sealed inside with a wall off.

Pulling Tight End – Cutoff to the Center's hip; if no one shows, climb to the linebacker level and cutoff the backside pursuit.

BB – Secure the snap and get vertical on the outside hip of the pulling tackle. Don't run east-west, get north-south quickly and out of the tunnel.

QB – Execute a flash fake, spin and aim for outside hip of Wall Side TE. Then get vertical up the field as you threaten the edge.

TB (BSWB) – Execute a flash fake snap and run power sweep as if you have the ball. Take it for a touchdown.

WB – Execute a flash fake reverse and mesh with the QB as he spins. It is important that the timing of this play happens so that you mesh with the QB as he is facing away from the LOS and the TB goes by you to run power sweep.

In LOOSE, the WB (SLOT) will go into sprint motion and slow down only if necessary to adjust to ensure he meshes with the QB at the proper time. Otherwise, he should remain at full speed.

The WB can also go in motion in the normal (base) SHIFT formation if necessary to maintain proper timing. In this case, the WB would get into sprint motion on READY. Again timing of the mesh is essential.

The mesh is very important. The WB should always rub his outside hip with the QB's belt buckle or near hip (depending on the QB's rotation). This increases the misdirection aspect of the mesh and makes it nearly impossible for a defense to discern who has the ball for the next two to three steps.

Shift Loose Rip 33 Kick Left Tornado

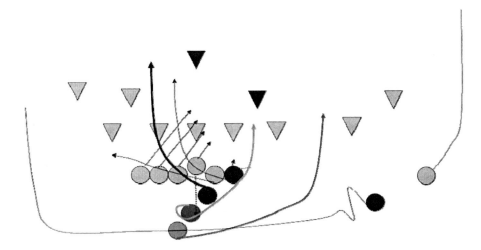

Figure 13D. Shift Loose Rip 33 Kick Left Tornado

Audibles

In *SHIFT LOOSE*:

FLY audible – Tells the BB to execute a flash fake and fake wedge while the QB takes the snap, spins, sets his feet and throws to the outside shoulder of the SE running the fade down the field. We call this when we see the 'cover man' in man coverage, but looking inside and not actually playing his coverage. You can spot this when you run LOOSE edge tags, and see the coverage not playing the SE down the field.

In either *SHIFT* or *SHIFT LOOSE*:

SPEED audible – Tells the BB to execute a flash fake and fake wedge while QB takes the snap, spins and gets into a pitch relationship with the TB (BSWB). He keys the first defender past the DEMLOS (who we see chasing the play flat down the LOS – which is our key to call this audible). He then attacks the inside hip of the defenders (typically the OLB). If the OLB comes at the QB he pitches the ball ASAP to the TB; If the LB sits or floats to the TB, the QB quickly gets vertical.

Shift Rip 16 Kick Right Tornado

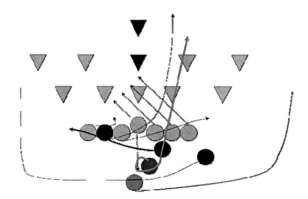

Figure 13E. Shift Rip 16 Kick Right Tornado

Line –

      Wall Side – TKO (Center to PSTE)
      Pulling Side – The BSG will pull and kick out the first defender to cross his face. As he kicks out the first defender, he will flip his hips and body into the hole to isolate the defender away from the WB as he hits the tunnel.
      Pulling Tackle – The BST will pull up the wall, go vertical to end zone, and any defender crossing his face will be sealed inside with a wall off.
      Pulling Tight End – Cutoff to the Center's hip; if no one shows, climb to the linebacker level and cutoff the backside pursuit.

BB – Cross over and kick out the first defender to cross your face. Make him pay!

QB – Secure the snap, spin, and get vertical up the wall as tight as you can.

TB (BSWB) – Execute a flash fake snap and run a power sweep as if you have the ball. Take it for a touchdown.

WB – Execute a flash fake reverse, and then mesh with the QB as he spins. It is important that the timing of this play be precise so that you mesh with the QB as he is facing away from the LOS and the TB goes by you to run power sweep.

In LOOSE, the WB (SLOT) will go into sprint motion and slow down only if necessary to adjust to ensure he meshes with the QB at the proper time. Otherwise, he should remain at full speed.

The WB can also go in motion in the normal (base) SHIFT formation if necessary to maintain proper timing. In this case, the WB would get into sprint motion on READY. Again timing of the mesh is essential.

The mesh is very important. The WB should always rub his outside hip with the QB's belt buckle or near hip (depending on the QB's rotation). This increases the misdirection aspect of the mesh and makes it nearly impossible for a defense to discern who has the ball for the next two to three steps.

Shift Loose Over Rip 16 Kick Right Tornado

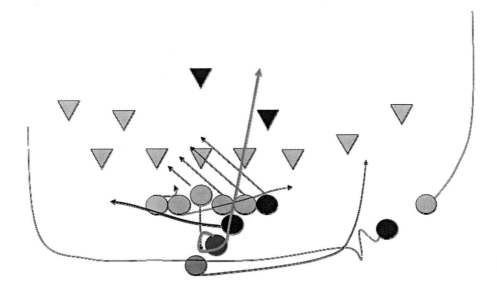

Figure 13F. Shift Loose Over Rip 16 Kick Right Tornado

Audibles

In *SHIFT LOOSE*:

FLY audible – Tells the BB to execute a flash fake and fake wedge while the QB takes the snap, spins, sets his feet and throws to the outside shoulder of the SE running the fade down the field. We call this when we see the 'cover man' in man coverage, but looking inside and not actually playing his coverage. You can spot this when you run LOOSE edge tags, and see the coverage not playing the SE down the field.

In either *SHIFT* or *SHIFT LOOSE*:

SPEED audible – Tells the BB to execute a flash fake and fake wedge while QB takes the snap, spins and gets into a pitch relationship with the TB (BSWB). He keys the first defender past the DEMLOS (who we see chasing the play flat down the LOS – which is our key to call this audible). He then attacks the inside hip of the defenders (typically the OLB). If the OLB comes at the QB he pitches the ball ASAP to the TB; If the LB sits or floats to the TB, the QB quickly gets vertical.

Shift Rip 28 Wide Right Tornado

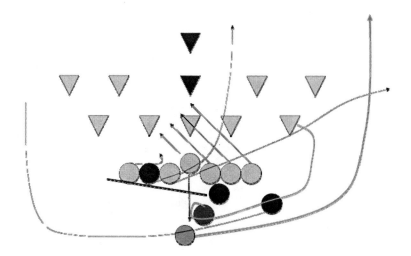

Figure 13G. Shift Rip 28 Wide Right Tornado

Line –

> Wall Side – TKO (Center to PSTE)
> Pulling Guard – The BSG pull and kick out the first wide defender above the BB. If no defender is present outside (CB), the BSG will turn and go vertical to the end zone.
> Pulling Tackle – The BST will pull up the wall, and then go vertical to end zone. Any defender crossing his face will be sealed inside with a wall off.
> Pulling Tight End – Cutoff to Center's hip; if no one shows, climb to the linebacker level and cutoff the backside pursuit.

BB – Cross over and kick out the first defender to cross your face. Make him pay!

QB – Execute a flash fake, spin, and get out wide as you gain depth. Attack the outside arm pit of the unblocked defender outside and wall him outside. As you attack his outside arm pit, log him.

TB (BSWB) – Secure the snap and cross over staying flat (parallel) to the LOS until you go past the WSTE. Once you see daylight, get vertical.

WB – Execute a flash fake reverse and then mesh with the QB as he spins. It is important that the timing of this play be precise, so that you mesh with the QB as he is facing away from the LOS and the TB goes by you to run power sweep.

In LOOSE, the WB (SLOT) will go into sprint motion and slow down only if necessary to adjust to ensure he meshes with the QB at the proper time. Otherwise, he should remain at full speed.

In LOOSE, the TB will run in between the alley created by the log block of the QB, the kick out of the Pulling Guard, and the SE running fade.

Shift Loose Over 28 Wide Right Tornado

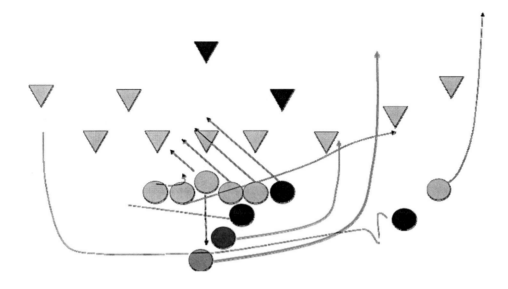

Figure 13H. Shift Loose Over 28 Wide Right Tornado

Audibles

In *SHIFT LOOSE*:

FLY audible – Tells the BB to execute a flash fake and fake wedge while the QB takes the snap, spins, sets his feet and throws to the outside shoulder of the SE running the fade down the field. We call this when we see the 'cover man' in man coverage, but looking inside and not actually playing his coverage. You can spot this when you run LOOSE edge tags, and see the coverage not playing the SE down the field.

In either *SHIFT* or *SHIFT LOOSE*:

SPEED audible – Tells the BB to execute a flash fake and fake wedge while QB takes the snap, spins and gets into a pitch relationship with the TB (BSWB). He keys the first defender past the DEMLOS (who we see chasing the play flat down the LOS – which is our key to call this audible). He then attacks the inside hip of the defenders (typically the OLB). If the OLB comes at the QB he pitches the ball ASAP to the TB; If the LB sits or floats to the TB, the QB quickly gets vertical.

Shift Rip 47 Wide Left Reverse Tornado

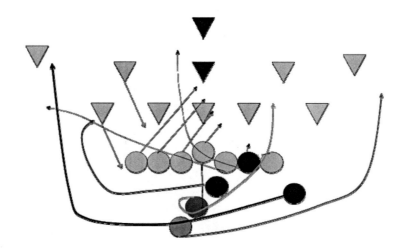

Figure 13l. Shift Rip 47 Wide Left Reverse Tornado

Line –

Wall Side – TKO (Center to PSTE)

Pulling Side – The BSG will pull and climb as if to seal, but then go wide and kick out the first defender to cross his face outside (CB). As he kicks the defender out, he will flip his hips and body into the hole to isolate the defender away from the WB as he hits the tunnel. If facing an athletic corner, the BSG will close distance quickly, then settle down and wall him off.

Pulling Tackle – The BST will pull up the wall and go vertical to the end zone. Any defender crossing his face will be sealed inside with a wall off.

Pulling Tight End – Cutoff to the Center's hip; if no one shows, climb to the linebacker level and cutoff the backside pursuit.

BB – Cross over and gain some depth and then get to the outside arm pit of the first unblocked defender outside and log him by walling him inside.

QB – Secure the snap and start your spin. As you turn your back to the LOS, mesh with the WB and hand the ball off to him. Complete your spin and attack the outside hip of the pull side TE faking the power.

TB (BSWB) – Execute a flash fake snap and run power sweep as if you have the ball. Take it for a touchdown.

WB – Secure the hand off from the QB and maintain speed. It is important that the timing of this play is precise so that you mesh with the QB as he is facing away from the LOS and the TB goes by you to run power sweep. Gain a little depth and let the pulling guard get by to secure your alley. Get vertical as you pass the log block of the BB.

In LOOSE, the WB (SLOT) will go into sprint motion and slow down only if necessary to adjust to ensure he meshes with the QB at the proper time. Otherwise, he should remain at full speed.

The WB can also go in motion in the normal (base) SHIFT formation if necessary to maintain proper timing. In this case, the WB would get into sprint motion on READY. Again timing of the mesh is essential.

The mesh is very important. The WB should always rub his outside hip with the QB's belt buckle or near hip (depending on the QB's rotation). This increases the misdirection aspect of the mesh and makes it nearly impossible for a defense to discern who has the ball for the next two to three steps.

Shift Loose Rip 47 Wide Left Reverse Tornado

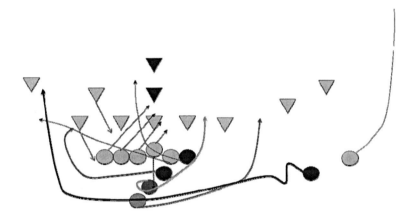

Figure 13J. Shift Loose Rip 47 Wide Left Reverse Tornado

Audibles

In *SHIFT LOOSE*:

FLY audible – Tells the BB to execute a flash fake and fake wedge while the QB takes the snap, spins, sets his feet and throws to the outside shoulder of the SE running the fade down the field. We call this when we see the 'cover man' in man coverage, but looking inside and not actually playing his coverage. You can spot this when you run LOOSE edge tags, and see the coverage not playing the SE down the field.

In either *SHIFT* or *SHIFT LOOSE*:

PITCH audible – Tells the BB to execute a flash fake and fake wedge while QB takes the snap, spins and gets into a pitch relationship with the TB (BSWB). He keys the first defender past the DEMLOS (who we see chasing the play flat down the LOS – which is our key to call this audible). He then attacks the inside hip of the defenders (typically the OLB). If the OLB comes at the QB he pitches the ball ASAP to the TB; If the LB sits or floats to the TB, the QB quickly gets vertical.

Chapter 14
Uncovered Passing Concepts

The next two chapters are dedicated to the sideline audibles I use after the base play is called, our team aligns, and I see an opportunity to quickly take advantage of a defense that has misaligned or over-adjusted to our formation strength and perceived pre-snap flow. Once I get a sense for how a defense is aligning pre-snap, I also want to get a feel for how the defense is reacting post-snap. The post-snap reaction is a true perimeter triangle read and a true indication of what is happening on the perimeter. Thus, this is what should drive offensive adjustments.

The uncovered passing concept is one the easiest ways to quickly adapt and attack a defense that is unwilling to cover your Loose, Trips, or Bunch sets in a balanced manner. It gives you a simple way of forcing the defense to respect every eligible player on the field and, consequently it forces the defense to cover the entire field. Often when a Double Wing coach runs his play list, he is constrained to running the called play and then adapting to the defense's lack of adjustments or misalignments. Below are several examples I have seen from various defenses that did not cover down on our expanded sets. Figure 14A is an example of our SHIFT LOOSE OVER LIZ set and how a 44 split defense misaligned; the near side OLB did not cover down on the loose pair, leaving a 2-on-1 misalignment. Often this happens because teams get fixed on stopping our power, power sweep, and/or power pass game and forget or neglect to actually cover the threats on the perimeter. In the second figure, FIGURE 14B, you see the STAR TRIPS OVER RIP formation and an example of what often occurs once we get our power game rolling from that set. The defense is unwilling to expand out their inside backer or free safety, leaving us free to exploit a 3-on-2 misalignment.

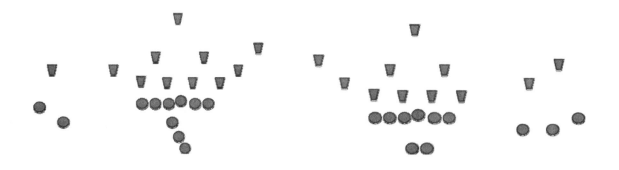

Figure 14A. SHIFT LOOSE OVER LIZ   Fig 14B. STAR TRIPS OVER RIP

Advantages of Using the Uncovered Passing Concept

1)   It allows you to quickly get the ball to the open receiver on the perimeter in a position to get vertical into an open field and maximize yards after the catch. Whether you have an elite receiver or an average play you can always get positive yards with very little work.

2)   It allows you to quickly adapt to a defense that is not covering down on the expanded sets out on the perimeter (2-on-1 and 3-on-2) giving you a key numbers advantage.

3)   It gives you the flexibility in your power, power sweep, and/or power pass game by appearing to be one step ahead of the defense in your playing calling. This will often force the defense to play a very 'vanilla' base defense.

Uncovered Rules

1)   Whenever the coaching staff sees a 2-on-1 situation (or 3-on-2 in the case of Trips or Bunch) on either loose pair, we will audible to an uncovered pass to get the ball immediately to a receiver on that side. 2-on-1 meaning 2 receivers to 1 defender within 6 yards of the loose pair.

2)   BROKEN/BLENDER means throw to the slot receiver right now. (BR = right, BL = left, can be any code word you choose)

3)   ROOK/LOOK means throw to split end right now. (R = right, L = left, can be any code word you choose)

4)   The receiver not called releases and gets leverage position on the defender to screen him off from the called receiver (MDM). It is like a basketball pick; get position on the defender so that your butt is facing the receiver and your numbers are facing the defender, and then mirror him as long as possible.

5)   The receiver must catch the ball and then get vertical and outside immediately. Get as many yards as possible.

Uncovered Passing Concepts and Formations

1)   Eagle (2x2) Spread formation (2-on-1)
2)   Loose edge tag (2-on-1)
3)   Trips edge tag (3-on-2)
4)   Bunch edge tag (3-on-2)

Uncovered Pass to the Split End

Example 1: The called play is SHIFT LOOSE OVER RIP 26 SEAL RIGHT in Figure 14C below; offensive coordinator sees that the slot defender is not covering down, giving us a 2-on-1 look. OC calls SE uncovered audible (for us that is "ROOKIE-ROOKIE") and the QB and the loose pair, acknowledge the sideline audible. The QB calls for the snap and everyone executes the called play - except for the quarterback and the loose pair, as they will execute the audible.

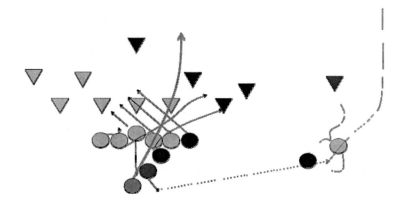

Figure 14C. SHIFT LOOSE OVER RIP 26 SEAL RIGHT - Split Uncovered Audible Called from Sideline.

Example 2: Here the called play is STAR TRIPS OVER RIP 36 SEAL RIGHT (Figure 14D); the offensive coordinator sees that the slot defender is not covering down and therefore the defense is giving us a 3-on-2 look. The OC calls the SE uncovered audible (i.e. "ROOKIE-ROOKIE"). The QB and the Trips group acknowledge the sideline audible and the QB calls for the snap. Everyone executes the called play, except for the quarterback and the Trips group, as they will execute the audible.

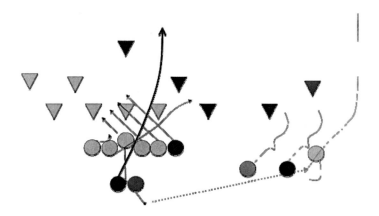

Figure 14D. STAR TRIPS OVER RIP 36 SEAL RIGHT - Split Uncovered Audible from Sideline

Example 3: The called play is STAR BUNCH OVER RIP 36 SEAL RIGHT (Figure 14E); the offensive coordinator sees that the slot defender is not covering down and is therefore giving us a 3-on-2 look. The OC calls SE uncovered audible (i.e. "ROOKIE-ROOKIE"). The QB and the Bunch group acknowledge the sideline audible and the QB calls for the snap. Everyone executes the called play, except for the quarterback and the Bunch group, as they will execute the audible.

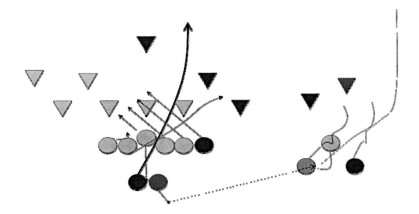

Figure 14E. STAR BUNCH OVER RIP 36 SEAL RIGHT - Split Uncovered Audible from Sideline

Uncovered Pass to the Slot

Example 1: The called play is SHIFT LOOSE OVER RIP 26 SEAL RIGHT (Figure 14F); the offensive coordinator sees that the slot defender is not covering down and is therefore giving us a 2-on-1 look. The OC then calls the SLOT uncovered audible (i.e. "BROKEN-BROKEN"). The QB and loose pair acknowledge the sideline audible and the QB calls for the snap. Everyone executes the called play, except for the quarterback and the loose pair, as they will execute the audible.

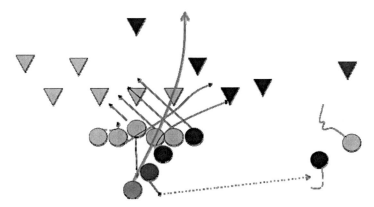

Figure 14F. SHIFT LOOSE OVER RIP 26 SEAL RIGHT - Slot Uncovered Audible from Sideline

Example 2: Here the called play is STAR TRIPS OVER RIP 36 SEAL RIGHT (Figure 14G); the offensive coordinator sees that the slot defender is not covering down and is therefore giving us a 3-on-2 look. The OC then calls the SE uncovered audible (i.e. "BROKEN-BROKEN"). The QB and the Trips group acknowledge the sideline audible and the QB calls for the snap. Everyone executes the called play except for the quarterback and the Trips group, as they will execute the audible.

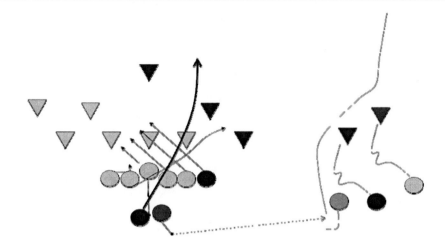

Figure 14G. STAR TRIPS OVER RIP 36 SEAL RIGHT - Slot uncovered audible from sideline

Example 3: The called play is STAR BUNCH OVER RIP 36 SEAL RIGHT (Figure 14H); the offensive coordinator sees that the slot defender is not covering down and is therefore giving us a 3-on-2 look. Thus, the OC calls the SE uncovered audible (i.e. "BROKEN - BROKEN"). The QB and the Bunch group acknowledge the sideline audible and the QB calls for the snap. Everyone executes the called play, except for the quarterback and the Bunch group, as they will execute the audible.

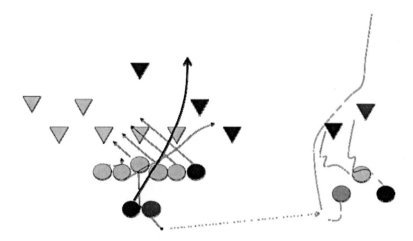

Figure 14H. Slot uncovered audible from sideline

Installing and Developing the Uncovered Pass

This is actually very simple and what I have done in the past (and the present) is totally dependent on the freedom I have to run my practices. If there are restrictions on time, I have to account for this when we consider installing the uncovered passing game.

One of the main benefits of developing the uncovered passing game is that it contributes to the development of basic passing and receiving skills. Moreover, you not only develop proper passing and receiving fundamentals, but a sense of timing between your passers and your receivers. It develops a sense of confidence between the passers and the receivers as well, and that is just as important as the fundamentals you are developing. The uncovered pass is very simple and one of the most basic passes the passer can make. It has a high percentage of success and allows you to develop confidence in your passer. It also is a very basic route for the receiver, since the only movement by the receiver is that he simply drops his inside foot and presents his numbers to the passer. The passer can then immediately throw the ball to the up field shoulder of the receiver, so he can turn and run vertically. Cumulatively, these advantages make the uncovered pass a great way to also work on basic pass/receiving skills at the same time you install the uncovered passing concepts.

> 1) If there are no time restrictions on the individual practices, I simply require all my receivers and my passers to arrive 15 minutes early to practice suited up and ready to go. We begin our uncovered pass progression and work on that for about 10 to 12 minutes prior to practice starting.
> 2) If there is a time restriction on the individual practices, I work on it during INDIVIDUAL BACKS time when we are working on the passing game.
> 3) I always get the initial installation done in the preseason so that the practice methods are understood and we maximize the limited amount of time we have during the season.

Uncovered Pass Progression

> 1) Two-sided Uncovered Pass: On Static Defenders
> 2) Two-sided Uncovered Pass: On Defenders
> 3) Two-sided Uncovered Pass: On Defenders (3-on-2)

Two-sided Uncovered Pass: On Static Defenders

Purpose: To install the uncovered passing concept with the passer and receiver pairs and develop the basic receiver and passer fundamentals that are essential to a successful passing game.

Setup: Six cones, arranged as illustrated in Figure 14I below. A wingback (slot) and an end will pair up and work together. We try to get at least four pairs with two pairs working on each side with a passer.

Execution: The coach will monitor and make correction but we are looking to maximize reps and time. One pair will work as a set of defenders and one set as the receivers. The slot defender will line up and then move inside towards the near cone. The QB will simply turn, set his feet, and fire the ball quickly and accurately at the receiver's upfield shoulder. The receiver will secure the ball first, and then quickly turn and get vertical on the butt of his blocking receiver. The blocker will release and get position on the remaining defender so that his butt is facing the receiver and his numbers are facing the defender. He will position himself between the defender and the receiver. Each receiver group will execute a SLOT uncovered pass, and then switch pairs (i.e. defenders become receivers, receivers become defenders). Then each receiver group will execute a SPLIT END uncovered pass, and switch pairs. Repeat this process three times and then the QBs will switch sides to get in three more reps throwing in the opposite direction (i.e. The QB initially throwing right, will now throw left). Finally, the receiver pairs will switch sides (left to right) and repeat the entire process, with the receivers now catching passes from the opposite direction (i.e. receivers initially catching passes from the right will now catch passes from the left). This will give the quarterbacks a total of twenty four passes to each receiver pair (twelve passes to each receiver – 3 from each QB, from each side of the field).

The defenders will simply align and remain still, providing a static target for the blocker position himself against and the receiver to run away from.

The receiver will align with this inside foot up, as this is the base receiver stance. On the snap the receiver will drop his inside foot and present his numbers to the passer. As he turns to the QB, he will quickly get his hands up and ready them for catching the ball.

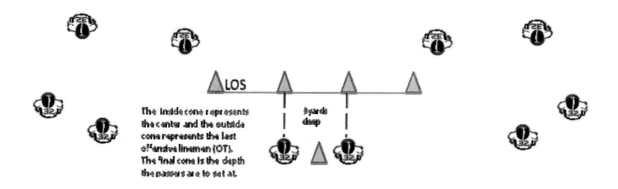

Figure 14I. Uncovered Pass Progression: On Static Defenders

Two-sided Uncovered Pass: On Defenders

Purpose: To further develop the uncovered passing concept with the passer and receiver pairs using live defenders, and to develop the basic receiver and passer fundamentals that are essential to a successful passing game.

Setup: Six cones arranged as illustrated in Figure 14J below. A wingback (slot) and an end will pair up and work together. We try to get at least four pairs with two pairs working on each side with a passer.

Execution: The coach will monitor and make corrections but we are looking to maximize reps and time. One pair will work as a set of defenders and one set as the receivers. The slot defender will line up and then move inside towards the near cone. The QB will simply turn, set his feet, and fire the ball quickly and accurately at the receiver's up field shoulder. The receiver will secure the ball first, and then quickly turn and get vertical on the butt of his blocking receiver. The blocker will release and get position on the remaining defender so that his butt is facing the receiver and his numbers are facing the defender. He will let the defender come to him as he mirrors the defender. It is like a basketball pick, but physical contact is made and it is aggressive as the blocker mirrors the defender as long as possible. The eyes of the defender will tell the blocker where the defender intends to go. Each receiver group will execute a SLOT uncovered pass, and then switch pairs (i.e. defenders become receivers, receivers become defenders). Then each receiver group will execute a SPLIT END uncovered pass, and switch pairs. Repeat this process three times and then the QBs will switch sides to get in three more reps throwing in the opposite direction (i.e. The QB initially throwing right, will now throw left). Finally, the receiver pairs will switch sides (left to right) and repeat the entire process, with the receivers now catching passes from the opposite direction (i.e. receivers initially catching passes from the right will now catch passes from the left). This will give the quarterbacks a total of twenty four passes to each receiver pair (twelve passes to each receiver – 3 from each QB, from each side of the field).

The defenders will align and play soft coverage on their primary read.

The receiver will align with this inside foot up, as this is the base receiver stance. On the snap the receiver will drop his inside foot and present his numbers to the passer. As he turns to the QB, he will quickly get his hands up and ready them for catching the ball.

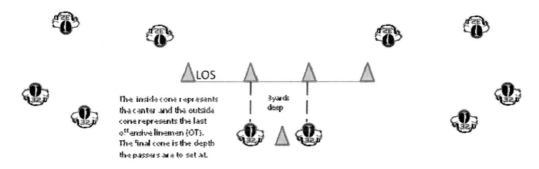

The inside cone represents the center and the outside cone represents the last offensive linemen (OT). The final cone is the depth the passers are to set at.

Figure 14J. Uncovered Pass Progression: On Defenders

Two-sided Uncovered Pass: On Defenders 3-on-2

Purpose: To further develop the uncovered passing concept with the passer and receiver pairs for bunch and trips using live defenders, and to develop the basic receiver and passer fundamentals that are essential to a successful passing game.

Setup: Six cones arranged as illustrated in Figure 14K below. Two wingbacks (slot) and an end will pair up and work together in a Trips formation on one side and a Bunch formation on the other side. We try to get at least four pairs with two pairs working on each side with a passer.

Execution: The coach will monitor and make corrections but we are looking to maximize reps and time. One pair will work as a set of defenders and one set as the receivers. The slot defender will line up and then move inside towards the near cone. The QB will simply turn, set his feet, and fire the ball quickly and accurately at the receiver's up field shoulder. The receiver will secure the ball first, and then quickly turn and get vertical on the butt of his two blocking receivers. The blockers will release and get position on the remaining defenders so that their butts are facing the receiver and their numbers facing the defenders. They will let the defenders come to them as they mirror the defenders. It is like a basketball pick, but physical contact is made and it is aggressive as the blocker mirrors the defender as long as possible. The eyes of the defender will tell the blocker where the defender intends to go. Each receiver group will execute a SLOT uncovered pass, and then switch pairs (i.e. defenders become receivers, receivers become defenders). Then each receiver group will execute a SPLIT END uncovered pass, and switch pairs. Repeat this process two times and then the QBs will switch sides to get in two more reps throwing in the opposite direction (i.e. The QB initially throwing right, will now throw left). Finally, the receiver pairs will switch sides (left to right) and repeat the entire process, with the receivers now catching passes from the opposite direction (i.e. receivers initially catching passes from the right will now catch passes from the left).

The defenders will align and play soft coverage on their primary read.

The receiver will align with this inside foot up, as this is the base receiver stance. On the snap the receiver will drop his inside foot and present his numbers to the passer. As he turns to the QB, he will quickly get his hands up and ready them for catching the ball.

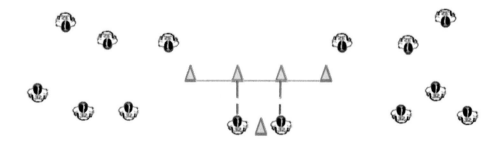

Figure 14K. Uncovered Pass Progression: On Defenders 3-on-2

Receiver Basic Fundamentals

Receiver Rules:

1)   The inside foot is up if you are a slot or split end. Feet are staggered with a shoulder width length between the inside foot heel and the outside foot toe.
2)   You are looking inside until the ball is snapped so you can see the QB. This is so he can confirm that you see and acknowledge any audible.
3)   Facemask is over the nose and the arms are cocked and below the chin.
4)   The Slot must align his inside foot to the toe of the outside foot of the SE. In the case of bubble and wheel routes he can align up to 1 yard deep behind the outside foot of the SE. He aligns 2 to 3 yards away from the SE.
5)   LOOSE SE aligns 8 to 15 yards depending on play. On running plays they should align 12 to 15 yards out to get maximum separation of the perimeter defenders. On any outside or vertical passing route, align the loose pair closer to the passer. Any inside passing route align the loose pair farther out, to give the inside route more space to operate in.
6)   SE must always check with the LINE JUDGE

Receiver Stance:

1)   Inside foot up.
2)   The SE must check with the Ref on his side to confirm he is on the LOS. The Slot's inside foot should be at the depth of the heel of the outside foot of the SE or a little deeper (6").
3)   Head up, slight bend in the knees, hips bent.
4)   Hands up in front of the chest or just outside of the rib cage with elbows in near the ribcage.
5)   Toes pointed up field and feet shoulder width apart, not narrow or wide.

Catching Mechanics and Fundamentals:

Whenever a receiver catches the ball, the hands must be spread; thumbs out, fingers spread, soft like a net (hands and fingers should naturally wrap around the ball as it makes contact). Relaxed hands catch balls, stiff hands will cause the ball to bounce (hard surface). Relaxed hands absorb the energy of the ball.

a.   If the ball is above the chest, the thumbs are together and make a soft net (don't tense/stiffen hands)
b.   If ball is below the chest the pinkies are together and make a soft net (don't tense/stiffen hands)
c.   If the ball is over the shoulder the pinkies and forearms are together and make a soft net.
d.   Secure ball and get vertical.

Final Thoughts on Uncovered Passing Concepts:

- Uncovered Passing Game: Whenever the defense presents a 1-on-2 (or 3-on-2) situation on either perimeter, we will get the ball to one of the receivers while the other blocks the MDM (Most Dangerous Man). The receiver must catch the ball and get vertical to the end zone as quickly as possible.
- The Uncovered Passing Game is a simple way of building a timing relationship between our QB's and receivers as the pass and the body mechanics for the receiver are very simple. It builds confidence in both our QB and receivers while allowing them to enhance proper passing/catching techniques.
- With uncovered passing, we want to get the ball to the best receiver on that perimeter, so we have the ability to get the ball to either the SE or SLOT.
- Remember this gives us the ability to attack a defense dynamically, pre-snap, when they misalign on our perimeter players.

Chapter 15
Key Breakers and Influence Audibles

This is the final chapter on our immediate adjustment audibles, i.e. audibles that we call from the sideline when we see misalignments in the defense pre-snap. Our 'key breaker' / 'influence audibles' are a set of audibles that allow us to attack a defense that is keying our wall side and pullers. The vast majority of defenses will naturally key the pullers in our offense to the direction of the play. Most offensive coordinators fear defenses finding keys that can give away the direction of the play, but I find it gives me information on the defense's mindset as well. Recall that uncovered passing concepts (Chapter 14) allow us to attack a defense that is not respecting our perimeter players when we have them expanded (e.g. Loose, Bunch, Trips). The threat of the uncovered passing audible forces the defense to play us balanced across the entire front. Similarly, the key breaker/influence audibles allow us to attack a defense that is predicting our plays based on our blocking schemes (e.g. wall side and pullers). In essence, we will key on what they are using to key on us and thereby use their attempts to key certain features of our offense against them. The combination of power, misdirection, play action passing, the ability to modify our backfield, the ability to modify our perimeter, use uncovered pass concepts, and key breaker / influence audibles - in conjunction with a no-huddle system in a very simple manner - allows us to keep a defensive coordinator on his toes. Moreover, it forces a defense to play with discipline and better than average execution in their defensive scheme. It takes the Double Wing philosophy and gives it a few additional weapons that allow it to appear as if we are doing a lot of things, when in fact, we are doing only a few more things that make the whole system appear much more complex.

At a Nike Coach of the Year clinic, at which I spoke, I was watching a presentation being given by a high school defensive coordinator and listening to him discuss how his linebackers key the offense. His exact comment was, "Running backs are like girl friends they will lie to you but pulling linemen are like your mom they never lie to you. When a lineman pulls, that means the play is always going that way." Honestly a lot of little bells went off at this point because the coach was saying something that many defensive coordinators and coaches have always impressed on their defenders - that pullers will take you to the play – which, is why defensive line coaches teach their defensive linemen to get in the "pocket" of the puller and find the ball (essentially chasing the puller to the ball). If that is the case, then we as offensive coordinators have to take this obvious "key" and use it against the defense in a meaningful way so that we force defenders to start doubting their keys; in some cases, keys they have been taught from day one. Once the defense begins doubting their leys, the ability to execute their defense is greatly reduced, as they are no longer reacting based on the instincts instilled and reinforced by coaching but rather they begin waiting for the play to develop to avoid over-reacting. Thus, key breakers and influence audibles give our offense an important advantage, whether the defense is actually reading the false key or simply sitting on their assignments longer than normal to verify what they are actually seeing. In the end, defenses play their base scheme with individual defenders delaying their reaction to the ball to ensure they don't misread the flow and direction.

It is important to understand the perimeter triangle concept (Chapter 3) and how to read it, both pre-snap and post-snap, to really maximize the advantage of the key breaker / influence audibles.

Why call a Key Breaker / Influence Audible from the Sideline?

1) Defense is keying the wall side.
2) Defense is keying the pulling linemen.
3) Defense has two or less on the backside perimeter.
4) Defense is vacating a specific space we can attack.

Why Use the Audibles?

1) A very simple way of attacking flaws in the defense immediately.
2) Allow us to adapt instantly to various threats that would cause our called play to fail.
3) Allow us to move the ball while creating confusion in the defense.
4) Defense has 2 or less in the backside perimeter.
5) Secondary supporting run and not defending pass.
6) Defense vacating a second or third level to fill a gap in the first level.

What are the Key Breaker / Influence Audibles?

1) Razzle
2) Boot
3) Waggle
4) Jump
5) Fly

How Do We Call Audibles?

1) Our QB, after the offense lines up in formation, will always check with the sideline unless the sideline yells "run it" which tells him to get the play off now.
2) First: The QB checks with the sideline and the OC (offensive coordinator) shouts an audible. Nearest offensive player echo's it to the middle of the field. Everyone runs the original play - except those involved in the audible.
3) Second: For more mature QB's who are able to handle calling it on their own, we let him call audibles. There is a teaching progression involved with the development of the QB calling his own audibles. Often at first, once a game is in hand we will tell him that he can call a certain audible on his own, if he sees it open. We grade him from series to series based on whether or not the audible was called and whether it was it the right thing to do. Most often we start with the uncovered audible because that is a very easy teaching progression for the QB and Receivers.

Razzle Audible

Why? *We observe 2 or less in the backside perimeter pre-snap or post-snap. The backside defensive end is attacking with a very shallow angle to cut off the ball as it flows away.*

What is it? *It is really the WB KICK REVERSE in the backfield, while the line executes the called play (typically SEAL, WIDE, MONSTER SWEEP, POWER PASS, or WEDGE) the other way.*

Rules for Calling It:

1)   When we see 2 or less on the backside perimeter triangle due to defenses over shifting to our formation strength/motion we can call this audible.

2)   When we suspect that the backers are keying our pulling linemen and the wall side (if you flip your line) we will run this play.

3)   Can only be used in compressed formations with no 'expanded' edge tags. (no Loose, Bunch, or Trips).

4)   Putting your line in OVER going the other way is often further enticement and will get the defense to really shift to that side. So if you see them doing this run the RAZZLE!

Figures 15A and 15B illustrate two examples of the Razzle audible but you can run it from COMET and NOVA as well, as long as you don't use any expanded edge tags (LOOSE, BUNCH, TRIPS). As you can see it puts a lot of pressure on a defense that decides to go 2 or less on the backside perimeter and presume to think our wall side and pullers will send them to the play.

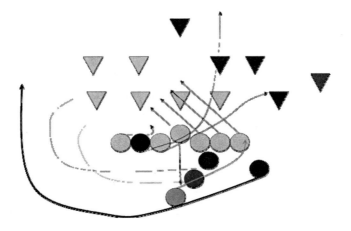

Figure 15A – Shift Rip 26 Seal Right (RAZZLE)

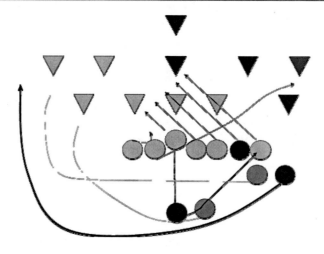

Figure 15B – Star Rip 36 Seal Right (RAZZLE)

Boot Audible

Why? *When we see 2 or less on the backside perimeter triangle due to defenses over-shifting to our formation strength/motion we can call this audible. When we suspect that the backers are keying our pulling linemen and wall side, we will run this play. When we see that the BSDE is coming inside shallow/down the line to chase our power, power sweep, and/or power pass we will run this play, as this leaves only the CB in a position to play both run and pass on the perimeter. The BSDE is unblocked so it is important that you discern that he is chasing the flow and not containing the QB, as this is a naked bootleg.*

What is it? *As mentioned above, it is essentially a naked bootleg with a two receiver flood using the pull tight end and the BB to force the two (or less) remaining defenders to cover three players (one runner and two receivers). It is always a run first, pass second play. If the QB sees daylight he should tuck the ball and get vertical. The Pull TE takes an inside release through the outside shoulder of the first defender inside. He then takes 5 to 7 steps and breaks to the outside at 45 degrees. He then looks for the ball over his outside shoulder. The BB will run through the outside shoulder of the DEMLOS and into the flat; looking for ball over his outside shoulder* (see Figures 15C and 15D).

Rules for Calling It:

1)   When we see 2 or less on the backside perimeter triangle due to the defense over-shifting to our formation strength/motion we can call this audible. Naked bootleg!!!
2)   When we suspect that the backers are keying our pulling linemen and wall side (if you flip your line) we will run this play.
3)   When we see that the BSDE is coming inside shallow/down the line to chase our power, power sweep , or power pass we will run this play, as this leaves only the CB in a position to play run and pass on the perimeter. The BSDE is

unblocked so it is important that you discern that he is chasing the flow and not containing the QB.

4)   Can be used in expanded or compressed formations, so it is a little better audible in that regard as compared to WAGGLE. It actually works better with the use of LOOSE, BUNCH and TRIPS, as these tags spread the defense out and away.

5)   We are trying to isolate the backside corner and force him to play run (QB) or pass (LOW – BB flat to HIGH – BSTE corner).

6)   Putting your line in OVER going the other way is often further enticement and will get the defense to really shift to that side.

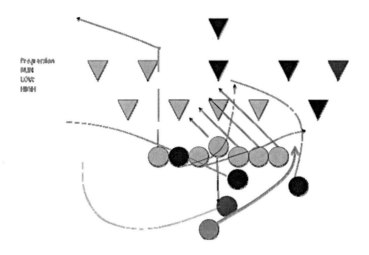

Figure 15C – Shift Rip 26 Seal Right (BOOT)

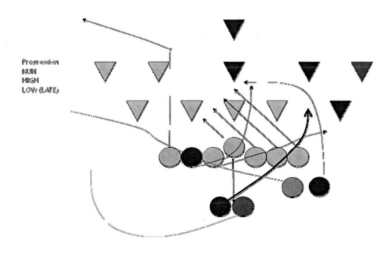

Figure 15D – Star Rip 36 Seal Right (BOOT)

Waggle Audible

Why? *When we see 2 or less on the backside perimeter triangle due to the defense over-shifting to our formation strength/motion we can call this audible. When we suspect that the backers are keying our pulling linemen and wall side (if you flip your line) we will run this audible. When we see that the BSDE is coming inside shallow/down the line to chase our power, power sweep, and/or power pass, we will run this play, as this leaves only the CB in a position to play run and pass on the perimeter.*

What is it? *It is a bootleg with the BB logging the DEMLOS while the PULL TE runs a corner route and the WB runs a shallow drag route. This creates a RUN-HIGH-LOW read for the QB going away from flow with a two receiver flood using the Pull Tight End and the WB to force the two (or less) remaining defenders to cover three players (one runner and two receivers). It is always a run first, pass second play. If the QB sees daylight, he should tuck the ball and get vertical. The Pull TE takes an inside release through the outside shoulder of the first defender inside, and then takes 5 to 7 steps and breaks to the outside at 45 degrees. He should then look for the ball over his outside shoulder. The WB will run through the FBI's heels as he acts as if he is going to block him. He wants to climb so that he comes out on the waggle side at about 4 to 6 yards of depth (see Figures 15E and 15F).*

Rules for Calling It:

1)	When we see 2 or less on the backside perimeter triangle due to the defense over-shifting to our formation strength/motion we can call this audible.
2)	When we suspect that the backers are keying our pulling linemen and wall side (if you flip your line) we will run this audible.
3)	When we see that the BSDE is coming inside shallow/down the line to chase our power, power sweep, and/or power pass, we will run this play, as this leaves only the CB in a position to play run and pass on the perimeter.
4)	Can only be used in compressed formations with no 'expanded' edge tags (no Loose, Bunch, or Trips).
5)	We are trying to isolate the backside corner and force him to play run (QB) or pass (BSTE high to WB low – late).
6)	Putting your line in OVER going the other way is often further enticement and will get the defense to really shift to that side.

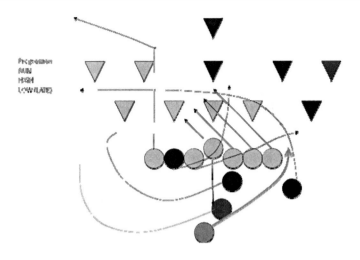

Figure 15E – Shift Rip 26 Seal Right (Waggle)

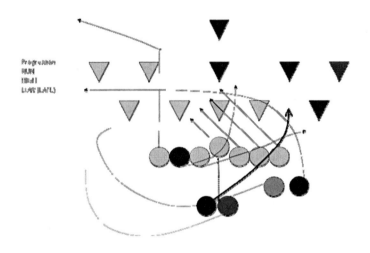

Figure 15F – Star Rip 36 Seal Right (Waggle)

Jump Audible

Why? *This is nothing more than the old fashion single wing jump pass used as a key breaker/influence play that attacks inside linebackers that are filling fast to stop the power, power sweep, and/or power pass plays. Often when this does happen, the backside OLB is either sitting on the counter/reverse or filling his backside gap hard as well.*

What is it? *It is based on the classic jump pass that the single wing utilizes in their offensive arsenal. We use it as an audible on the backside as it simplifies the concept for our kids and only requires two kids to learn the play* (see Figures 15G and 15H).

Rules for Calling It:

1)   Used against linebackers that are playing the line aggressively and are not focused on covering our BSTE.

2)   Defenses will often fast flow and collapse to our strong side when they see POWER FLOW (power, power sweep, and/or power pass); this often causes the BSLB and ILB's to flow to the strength leaving a gap in the shallow middle.

3)   TB takes a lead step towards hole, gets his eyes on the space occupied by the MLB/ILB at pre snap. He then jumps up and throws the ball, if the backer vacates (attack the LOS). If the backer holds ground, the TB will land and get to the hole for any positive yards.

4)   This is a really nice goal line play when we expect the defense to play a loaded pressure front and come right at the LOS. Often with no FS or secondary support this throw is pretty easy to make.

5)   TB (BSWB) must sell the run initially to get the defense to collapse, so the BSTE has a clear space for the ball.

6)   TB must get the ball on his ear ready to throw prior to jumping. He jumps, and then as he gets vertical and sees the lane, he throws the ball.

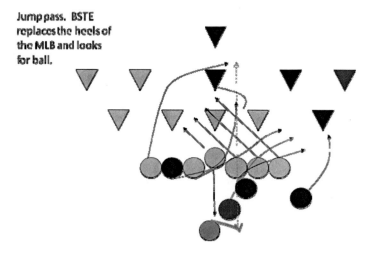

Figure 15G – Shift Rip 26 Seal Right (JUMP)

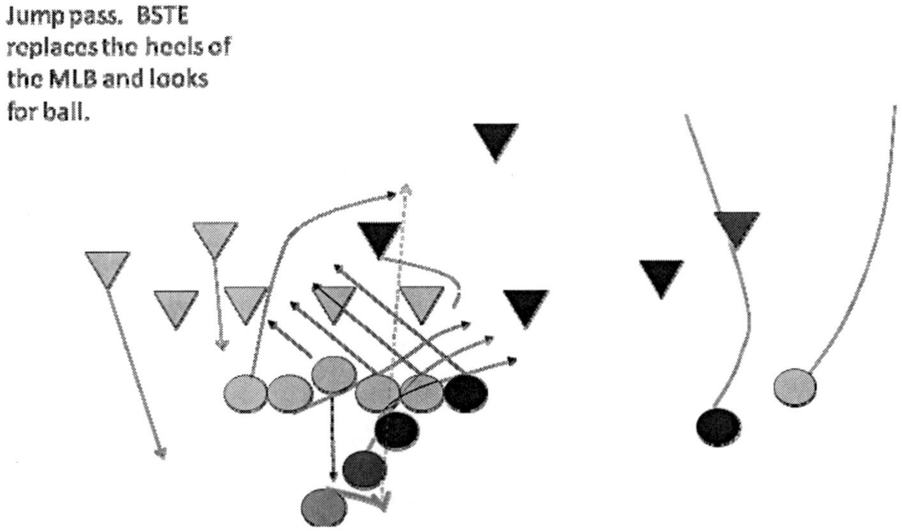

Jump pass. BSTE
replaces the heels of
the MLB and looks
for ball.

Figure 15H – Shift Loose Over Rip 26 Seal Right (Jump)

Fly Audible

Why? *Used when we see the coverage defenders committed to stopping run and not covering the pass.*

What is It? *It is a combination of a fade and a seam route with the QB making an outside – inside read; if MOFO (middle of the field open) throw the inside seam route* (see Figures 15I and 15J).

Rules for Calling It:

1)   Unlike the uncovered concept we run this when we see press / 'bump and run' defenders peeking in to the backfield and not actually playing the receiver.
2)   Can snap it to either the TB (BSWB) or the QB, whoever is the best passer. Requires a lead step to sell run, then set and throw. Read the field as you take the lead step.
3)   Ball must be gone in under 2 seconds to ensure it is a legal play (to avoid ineligible receivers downfield) as we are running this with any play called (run or pass).
4)   Great short yardage audible or when you expect to face loaded fronts.

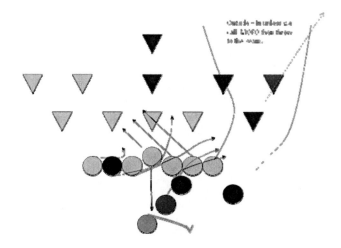

Figure 15I – Shift Rip 26 Seal Right (FLY)

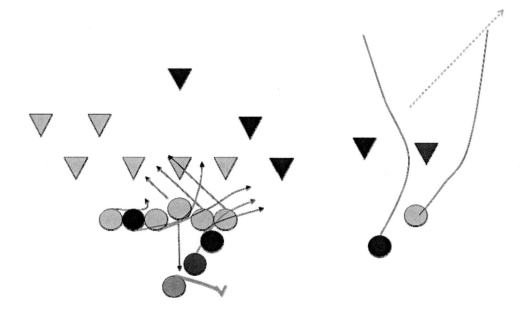

Figure 15J – Shift Loose Over Rip 26 Seal Right (FLY)

Chapter 16
Buck Wedge Series

This is a modification of the classic split flow series in the YDW that puts pressure on both perimeters of the defense and the interior at the same time, forcing the defense to protect all three areas at once. This simple series has been a staple of my offense for six seasons and has been very successful for my teams and teams that run my offense throughout the country, especially at the younger age levels. Because of the edge pressure and misdirection component, it puts a lot of stress on the defense to play disciplined defense in all three sections (left and right perimeter as well as the interior). I use this series with younger teams and wedge teams (back up player's series), as well as a complimentary series for my offense. It is used only out of the SHIFT formation as it is the most versatile direct snap formation we use. I have only used this with the base formation and have never used this with any edge tags.

The key component to the Buck Wedge Series is that all the ball carriers and the line carry-out great fakes. The longer and better the fakes, the more likely those defenders will not react to the actual ball carrier. A good fake can often pull one or two defenders away from the ball, so stress great faking and this series will carry you a very long way. Don't forget the passing game, and the effect it will have on the defense as they stack the LOS while attempting to defend the perimeters and the interior. Once they start slamming up to the LOS to stop the run, it will be very easy to get a receiver behind the defense to make a big play. The main play is the BB wedge play; about 60% of the snaps in this series should go to the BB.

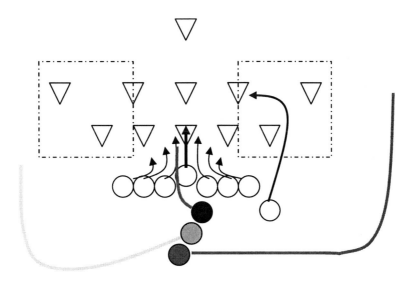

Figure 16A – Shift Rip Buck Wedge Series

The keys to this series, are (1) the Wedge relentlessly firing off and gaining yards every time the series is run. This must happen whether you are actually running behind the Wedge or not. And, (2) the backs must deliver convincing fakes to the perimeter on every play. Both of these elements are absolutely essential to the overall success of the play.

Once the defense commits to stopping the run it allows you to exploit the passing lanes down field. A good rule to follow is 'if you attack the perimeters with the run, then you have to exploit the vertical lanes in the passing game'. The QB must sell the perimeter attack and he must attack the LOS as he does, i.e. he must force a decision by the perimeter defenders and the secondary to commit to the run.

The QB's movement is much easier in the SHIFT formation compared to the TIGHT formation because he doesn't have to make a handoff, as the ball is directly snapped to the BB, QB, and TB. This puts much more immediate pressure on the defense to react to the areas the buck series attacks. The one key element in this series is that all three backs (BB, QB, and TB) must flash fake and act as if they have the ball on every snap in the buck series. They need to explode from their position after they flash fake and force the defenders to react to them at once. What often happens is the WB and TE go unnoticed and the passing game opens up very quickly as you start to hammer them (1) inside with BB wedge, (2) on the strong perimeter with the TB sweep, and (3) on the weak perimeter with the QB naked boot.

I recommend the Buck Series to young teams because the run blocking is all wedge blocking. Even the sweep blocking is essentially wedge blocking with the play side being ARC blocked for the sweep. The QB bootleg is further reinforced with an actual run-pass action using the Drag pass concept. Pass blocking is simply WALL pass protection as we use the backfield to wall off the edge for the QB and WB.

SHIFT RIP 30 WEDGE RIGHT BUCK

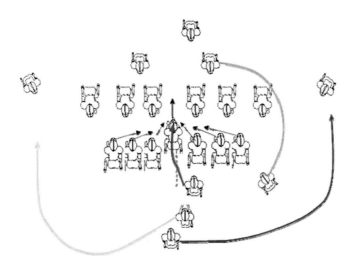

Figure 16B. SHIFT RIP 30 WEDGE RIGHT BUCK

Line: TE to TE Wedge block

BB: Secure the snap and get vertical into the Center's back and the Wedge. Drive the Center forward. If you see a crease on either side of the Center between the Guards get vertical and get out of the Wedge. Never go around the Wedge or delay getting into the Wedge. Always go forward.

QB: Execute a flash fake and run the boot action to the backside gaining depth until you get past the Pull Tight End, and then get vertical and run for a touchdown. Flash fake, grab cloth with the outside arm, and get your eyes on the first perimeter defender you see as you run for daylight. The eyes help to sell the fake as a defender will often attack a ball carrier looking at him, as he expects the ball carrier to be watching a defender as he attempts to run away from the defense.

TB: Execute a flash fake and run the sweep action to the front side staying flat until you pass the WB.   Flash fake, grab cloth with the outside arm, and get your eyes on the first perimeter defender you see as you run for daylight.   The eyes help to sell the fake as a defender will often attack a ball carrier looking at him as he expects the ball carrier to be watching a defender as he attempts to run away from the defense.

WB: Outside release, and then work up field and inside to block the FBI. If you encounter a backer attacking the LOS, let him go and move inside to the next backer. If you encounter a backer moving out wide to play the sweep fake, let him go and move inside as well. If there is no backer inside (because he filled the LOS), climb and block the near safety.

SHIFT RIP 28 WEDGE RIGHT ARC BUCK

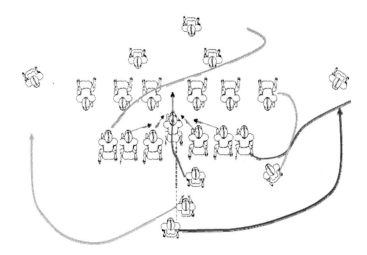

Figure 16C. SHIFT RIP 28 WEDGE RIGHT ARC BUCK

Line - OT to OT Wedge block.

WALL TE - Pull underneath the WB's wall block and kick out the first defender to cross your face. If the CB is out wide eat up grass as quickly as possible and wall that CB out. If the CB is inside and off the LOS, pull under the WB, and then get vertical to attack the outside armpit and wall the CB inside.

PULL TE - Step inside as if executing the Wedge but climb to the heels of the far backer. Get up field and on the far side of the deep defender and then get vertical to the end zone. If the deep defender (safety) attempts to cross your face wall him inside.

BB - Execute a flash fake and get vertical into the Center's back and the Wedge. Drive the Center forward. If you see a crease on either side of the Center between the Guards, get vertical and get out of the wedge. Never go around the wedge or delay getting into the wedge. Always go forward. You must sell the fake as if you really have the ball in the Wedge, so go all the way to the end zone, if you are not tackled and the play is still live.

QB - Execute a flash fake and run the boot action to the backside gaining depth until you get past the Pull Tight End. Then get vertical and run for a touchdown. Flash fake, grab cloth with the outside arm, and get your eyes on the first perimeter defender you see as you run for daylight. The eyes help to sell the fake as a defender will often attack a ball carrier looking at him as he expects the ball carrier to be watching a defender as he attempts to run away from the defense.

TB - Secure the snap and get to 75% of full speed; when you see daylight as you pass the WB's wall block get vertical and accelerate to full speed.

WB - Outside release and wall block the DEMLOS. Attack the outside arm pit and get your hips turned quickly to the perimeter.

Shift Rip 17 Wall Right Drag Pass Buck

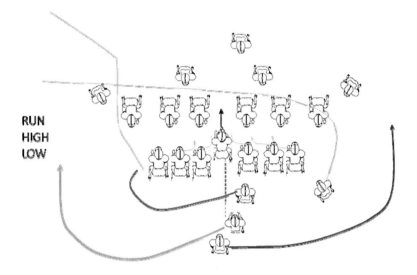

Figure 16D. Shift Rip 17 Wall Right Drag Pass Buck

Line -
> Pull Tackle to Wall Tight End - WALL PASS PROTECTION, i.e. If COVERED, LEM – Shift inside (load explode mirror – on third step get hips inside); if UNCOVERED, SSM inside (slide inside, slide, mirror). .
> Center - Fire off the ball and get vertical for two steps. If facing a NT (odd front) LEM. When facing an even front (no NT) SSM to QB boot.

This is our base WALL PASS PRO, which is designed to sell Wedge to the defense and eliminate inside penetration. This is a very simple method of selling the wedge action while sealing off the inside from penetration.

Pull Tight End - Outside release and get vertical. On your 6th step, cut to the outside at 45 degrees and run to the sideline. Look for the ball over your outside shoulder.

BB - Execute a flash fake (this will freeze the interior defenders, or better yet, get them to bite vertically). Cross over, gain depth, and get to the outside arm pit of the first defender to show and wall him inside. Your block is very important as this will allow the QB more time to get outside and make the RUN-PASS read.

QB - Secure the snap and run the boot action to the backside gaining depth until you get past the Pull Tight End, and then get vertical and run for a touchdown. Sell the run as you gain depth and get wide. Once you go vertical look for DAYLIGHT FIRST, then make the HIGH READ of the Pull Tight End running the corner route, and then the LOW READ of the WB running the shallow drag.

TB - Execute a flask fake and run the sweep action to the front side staying flat until you pass the WB. Flash fake, grab cloth with outside arm, and get your eyes on the first perimeter defender you see as you run for daylight. The eyes help to sell the fake as a defender will often attack a ball carrier looking at him as he expects the ball carrier to be watching a defender as he attempts to run away from the defense.

WB - Outside release, and then run through the heels of the near inside backer and gain depth. Your depth should be 4 to 6 yards as you get to the other side. Get your eyes over your inside shoulder and look for the ball as you pass the Center's far shoulder.

Shift Rip 47 Wedge Right Drag Pass Buck

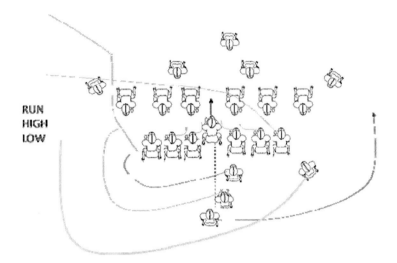

Figure 16E. Shift Rip 47 Wedge Right Drag Pass Buck

Line -

Pull Tackle to Wall Tackle - WALL PASS PROTECTION, i.e. If COVERED, LEM – Shift inside (load explode mirror – on third step get hips inside); if UNCOVERED, SSM inside (slide inside, slide, mirror). .
Center - Fire off the ball and get vertical for two steps. If facing a NT (odd front) LEM. When facing an even front (no NT) SSM to QB boot.

This is our base WALL PASS PRO, which is designed to sell Wedge to the defense and eliminate inside penetration. This is a very simple method of selling the wedge action while sealing off the inside from penetration.

Pull Tight End - Outside release and get vertical. On your 6th step, cut to the outside at 45 degrees and run to the sideline.   Look for the ball over your outside shoulder.

Wall Tight End - Inside release and run through the heels of the near inside backer and gain depth. Your depth should be 4 to 6 yards as you get to the other side of the LOS. Get your eyes over your inside shoulder and look for the ball as you pass the Center's far shoulder.

BB - Execute a flash fake (this will freeze the interior defenders, or better yet, get them to bite vertically). Cross over, gain depth, and then get to the outside arm pit of the first defender to show and wall him inside. Your block is very important as this will allow the WB more time to get outside and make the RUN-PASS read.

QB - Execute a flash fake (this will freeze the interior defenders, or better yet, get them to bite vertically). Cross over, gain depth, and then get to the outside arm pit of the first unblocked defender past the BB and wall him inside. Your block is very important as this will allow the WB more time to get outside and make the RUN-PASS read.

TB - Secure the snap and make outside hand off to WB running the reverse.   Then grab cloth with the outside arm, and get your eyes on the first perimeter defender you see as you run for daylight. The eyes help to sell the fake as a defender will often attack a ball carrier looking at him, as he expects the ball carrier to be watching a defender as he attempts to run away from the defense.

WB - Drop step and execute the XX reverse handoff. Secure the ball, and then gain depth and width quickly.   Sell the run as you gain depth and get wide. Once you go vertical look for DAYLIGHT FIRST, then the HIGH READ of the Pull Tight End running the corner route, and then the LOW READ of the WB running the shallow drag.

Appendix I
Creating a Simple but Effective No Huddle System

I have not bothered to use a huddle in four years, with the reason being that it is essentially a waste of time. It takes time from your already full practice schedule to work on and develop the proper huddle mechanics. It eats up precious time from the play clock and it has absolutely no bearing on the outcome of the game or what will happen on the score board. When I first decided to go no-huddle, I thought long and hard about the advantages and disadvantages compared to a typical huddle system. Honestly I don't see the down side, and I see no real disadvantage to a no-huddle system. The advantages however are numerous and I think once you see what I see, you will agree.

1) Absolute control of the tempo during your offensive possessions.
2) The ability to manage both the play clock and game clock from the sideline pre- and post- snap.
3) The high tempo of a no-huddle system allows us to gain additional levels of conditioning (mental, emotional, and physical) that non no-huddle teams don't get in practice. Defenses often wear down in all three areas when they move at a pace to which they are not accustomed.
4) The ability to force the defense to properly manage their timeouts. Defenses can end up wasting timeouts trying to reduce an offense's momentum, readjust or correct misalignments and mistakes that their defense is making on the field, and fix personal issues.
5) The ability to force the defense to properly manage their rotation of back up defenders. A missing player on the field, to many players on the field, the wrong players on the field, all can be issues that can typically be easily addressed when an offense uses a typical huddle scheme, but the defense must be nearly perfect when facing a no-huddle scheme that can alter the tempo.
6) There is no mental or emotional stress on the offense during 2 minute phases of the game because the offense is used to moving at that tempo. On the other hand, it places additional stress on the defense that is compounded by the fact that the offense is used to operating at that level.
7) It is an efficient use of personnel and time, during both practice and in the game.

These are the seven key reasons I use the no-huddle. Obviously the ability to further apply stress to the opposing defense is a key reason why I use the no-huddle, but it is aforementioned reasons that make the no-huddle so effective in my opinion.

Elements for the No-Huddle

1) All offensive players have a three panel wrist coach
2) We use a color coded overlapped grid system
3) We verbally call the formation, strength, and wall side as well as edge tags.
4) The play is called via the color coded grid system.
5) The offensive coordinator calls the formation and play from the sideline and the nearest offensive players echo the play in to the rest of the team.
6) Center is responsible for getting the offense to the line and calling "DOWN"
7) QB is responsible for checking for an adjustment audible for the sideline and snapping the ball.

Three Different Tempos

Slow – slow the game down, eat up the clock, maximize our time of possession. We look to get to the 5 second mark (when the official starts to manually count down from 5 seconds to 0 seconds using a hand signal). This offers us a 5 second buffer but on average we get to about 3 seconds prior to snap. We aim for 21 to 23 seconds.

Normal – normal play call. We don't rush but our goal is to get our offense to the line and in the proper formation and ready to run the play. We aim for 14 to 20 seconds per play.

Fast – hurry up/2 minute offense. We want the offense to quickly get to the line and get set in the proper formation and get the play off. We have coded system built into the grid that the QB will run, and we will reiterate from the sideline as they hurry to the line. We aim for 6 to 10 seconds of time.

Managing the Tempo of the Game

Superior to Average Opponent –

1) *Normal Pace* to minimize mistakes and gain composure. To evaluate the perimeter triangle, coverage alignments, and schemes. To put the defense at ease. Best to use when the score difference is +/- 12 points.
2) *Fast Pace* to increase emotional and mental stress of defense. To increase the chance of a defensive mistake or misalignment. To increase the amount of time we have on the game clock. To increase the amount of offensive snaps we have increasing the likelihood of increased scoring. To decrease the chance of defensive rotations and substitutions. Use it when the defense brings in backups, after a defensive injury, after a defensive time out, after a defensive penalty, after a turnover change of possession, after an official's timeout. Go to full time use when we are down by 15 or more points at any time. Go to full time use when we are down by 6 or more points if in the 4th quarter.
3) *Slow Pace* when we are up by 21 or more points in the first half and by 13 or more points in the second half to increase our time of possession and decrease the game clock. If we are down by 24 or more points in the fourth quarter and we are not effectively moving the ball.

Below Average Opponent –

1)   *Normal Pace* to minimize mistakes and gain composure. To evaluate the perimeter triangle, coverage alignments, and schemes. To put the defense at ease. Best to use when the score difference is +/- 12 points.

2)   *Fast Pace* to gain a scoring leverage so we can control the tempo of the game. Once we are up by 21 points we will no longer use it.

3)   *Slow Pace* to control the time of possession and reduce the game clock to ensure that the score does not get out of hand.

How the Paces Work

Normal Pace

1)   OC (offensive coordinator) calls the FORMATION, EDGE TAG, and WALL or the entire play (if he has it ready) and the offense gets to the line of scrimmage.

2)   QB and Center are responsible for getting everyone to the line.

3)   OC calls the Play. Center checks that the offense is ready and calls DOWN. QB takes charge of offense.

4)   QB checks for an adjustment audible (uncovered pass, key breaker/influence audible).

5)   QB snaps the ball and the offense executes the play.

Example 1 –

The prior play ends and the whistle blows the play dead. The center and quarterback are both getting the offense up and moving to the sideline. The nearest offensive player to our sideline is looking and listening for the next play as is the center and quarterback. OC shouts out SHIFT LOOSE OVER RIP RIGHT twice (telling the offense we want a SHIFT formation with a LOOSE and OVER TAG and we are aligned with strength to the right and wall to the right). The offense moves into position correctly and gets ready for the center to call DOWN. OC calls SHIFT LOOSE OVER RIP BLUE 1 twice. The near end echoes it twice to the rest of the team. They all look at their wrist coach and the center calls DOWN and the team gets set. The OC, who has been watching the defense align so he can count the perimeter triangle, sees that the defense is neutral (3 in the perimeter triangle on each side). The QB turns to check for any adjustments and the OC shouts RUN IT twice. QB calls snap count and runs the play SHIFT LOOSE OVER RIP 26 SEAL RIGHT (as indicated on the wrist coach).

Example 2 -

The prior play ends and the whistle blows the play dead. The center and quarterback are both getting the offense up and moving to the sideline. The nearest offensive player to our sideline is looking and listening for the next play, as is the center and quarterback. The OC shouts out STAR OVER LIZ GREEN 6 twice (telling the offense we want a STAR OVER LIZ 35 SEAL LEFT). The near end echoes the call twice to the rest of the team. The offense moves into position correctly and gets ready for the center to call DOWN. Center sees everyone in position and calls down. The OC who has been watching the defense align so he can count the perimeter triangle sees that the defense is soft on the backside as they have over shifted (2 in the perimeter triangle). QB turns to check for any adjustments and OC shouts RAZZLE RAZZLE twice. The QB calls snap count and the entire line use 36 SEAL LEFT but the backfield runs RAZZLE to the right via the call the coach has made.

EXAMPLE 2 above is typically how we call the play, as I want have that play ready when the previous play is over, i.e. I will call the whole thing if I have it ready.

FAST PACE

> 1)   OC will shout FAST- FAST to indicate the transition into a hurry up.
> 2)   Center and QB will make sure all players are getting up to the LOS as OC calls the play.
> 3)   There are two methods. One is to simply call the COLOR with the formation/edge tag and the QB will take charge of the play calling as that specific color grid will have a set of 4 plays to call in a row. The formation and edge tag will not change.   The other method, which requires the OC to have the play ready after each snap count, is to call the play like a NORMAL PACE with the entire play called.
> 4)   OC calls the play and the near offensive player echoes it in.
> 5)   CENTER calls down as soon as everyone gets to the line. Remember the QB and CENTER are pushing to get everyone to the line.
> 6)   QB checks with OC for an adjustment call.
> 7)   QB calls snap count to get the ball off.
> 8)   The offense will repeat steps 3 to 8 until we score, lose possession, or the coach calls NORMAL-NORMAL or SLOW-SLOW.

Example 3 –

The prior play ends and the OC calls FAST-FAST. The QB and CENTER hurry everyone up to the LOS. OC calls SHIFT LOOSE OVER RED-RED and the near tight end echoes the call to the rest of the team. QB checks his wrist coach and sees the 1st RED play and calls RED 18 – RED 18 (the team knows it is SHIFT LOOSE OVER RIP POWER PASS RIGHT). QB checks with OC for adjustment and OC is calling RUN IT-RUN IT. QB calls snap count and runs the play.

Example 4 –

The play in Example 3 ends; the QB immediately gets up and checks his wrist coach and yells 2nd RED play. The center is calling for everyone to get to the LOS and yelling SHIFT LOOSE OVER – SHIFT LOOSE OVER as the OC echoes it from the sideline. QB calls RED 20 – RED 20 (the team checks wrist coach and sees RIP 26 WIDE RIGHT) so the play is SHIFT LOOSE OVER RIP 26 WIDE RIGHT. The QB turns to check and see if the OC has an adjustment audible and the OC sees the OLB on the loose side is not covering down the slot and he shouts BROKEN-BROKEN and the QB and loose pair acknowledge it (tap helmet or butt) and the QB calls the snap count and the QB and loose pair run uncovered slot pass while the rest of the team execute the Rip 26 wide right.

Slow Pace

    1)   OC will call SLOW-SLOW and from that point the team will get up and group up about 10 yards behind the ball.

    2)   OC will call the FORMATION-EDGE TAG-WALL SIDE and they will get lined up. The OC will then call the play and the offense will check their wrist coach.

    3)   OC will let the play clock count to 7 to 10 seconds and yell RUN IT.

    4)   CENTER will call DOWN and QB will immediately check with OC for adjustment call.

    5)   OC will call RUN IT or call the audible.

    6)   QB will call the snap count and run the play.

Example 5 -

Prior play ends and the OC calls SLOW-SLOW and the QB and CENTER get everyone up to the LOS with no real rush. OC calls SHIFT LOOSE OVER RIGHT twice and the near tight end echoes the call to the rest of the team. Offense waits for the OC to call the play. OC calls SHIFT LOOSE OVER GREEN 41 (which is RIP 13 ISO LEFT). OC watches play clock countdown to about 10 seconds and shouts RUN IT twice and near TE echoes the call. CENTER calls DOWN and QB checks with QB for any adjustment call. OC calls RUN IT RUN IT. QB calls snap count and runs play.

Example 6 –

Following the previous play, the QB and CENTER get everyone to the LOS, again not rushing them. OC calls SHIFT OVER LEFT twice and offense aligns waiting for the play to be called in. OC watches play clock get to about 10 seconds and calls BLUE 1 (LIZ 45 SEAL LEFT) twice and CENTER calls DOWN and QB checks with OC who saw the backside corner playing run all the way and now sees 2 in the perimeter triangle. He calls BOOT-BOOT and the QB acknowledges and he snaps the ball and runs the play.

All the above examples are actual examples from games I have called this past season and really highlight how effective this system is as it gives us complete control of the tempo of the game while we are on offense. Coupled with our defensive scheme it gives us the ability to really control the tempo and manage the game and play clock in a very simple manner.

Getting It Installed

During Offensive Team time when we do PERFECTION DRILLS and AIR DRILLS and once the offense has a good feel for each drill, we start to rep situations within the drills and will call FAST-FAST, SLOW-SLOW or NORMAL-NORMAL, and run those situations like a game. Repetition of game situations and developing an understanding of how to control the pace of the game, gives our team the additional confidence and knowledge that we are always capable of winning a game or at the very least controlling the game.

Wrist Coach Grid System

I use a three panel wrist coach and it is a required part of the uniform. You can find really good deals on them on the internet by simply searching for a three panel wrist coach. If you have local dealer you can give him those links and see if he can price-match or give you a better deal if you buy them in bulk. It has never been an issue to get our players to acquire them.

I use EXCEL to set these grids up and often I simply send the EXCEL spreadsheet out to the team. Each tab is numbered and I set up a series of tabs with different sequences so that if we are concerned with a specific opponent noting our calls during their scouting visits we will change our panels up. I have three tabs as of now and typically I start with TAB 1 and at midseason we switch to TAB 2 and during the playoffs we switch to TAB 3. If we think an opponent has deciphered one of our TABs, we simply switch to a different one. Once you see how we set it up, you'll it is pretty simple to develop them. I use a superscript X, XX, or XXX to indicate the FAST-FAST series of plays I want run. So that when I call RED X RED X, that means run all superscript^X play in numeric order. This gives us the ability to set up all of our plays quickly. I use a set of four plays for X, XX, and XXX. One set is a power set, one set is a misdirection set, and one is a pass heavy set. Bear in mind we can use audibles to quickly adapt and adjust our FAST-FAST sub-series. That is three subseries for each color or a total of twelve sub-series for our FAST-FAST PACE. It gives us endless possibilities for attacking a defense. Obviously, even though we have this big list, a lot of these plays will not be installed early in the season. However, as the season progresses we will have installed all of the plays that our team executes well. This is the actual wrist coach from our 2009 season.

As you can see below, there are multiple listings of our key plays, so it is just about impossible to figure out this play call list in one game. Especially if the OC is using multiple colors and numbers. This makes it very difficult for a defensive coaching staff to figure it all out.

TAB 1

	RED		RED		RED
1	Rip 26 Seal RT	16	Rip 26 Seal RT	31	Liz 45 Seal LT
2	Rip 28 Wide RT	17	Rip 28 Wide RT	32	Liz 47 Wide LT
3	Rip 28 MSTR SWP RT	18	Rip Power Pass RT	33	Liz Power Pass LT
4	Rip Power Pass RT	19	Rip 30 Wedge RT	34	Liz 30 Wedge LT
5	Rip 30 Wedge RT	20	Rip 10 Wedge RT	35	Liz 10 Wedge LT
6	Rip 10 Wedge RT	21	Rip 33 Kick LT	36	Liz 34 Kick RT
7	Rip 33 Kick LT	22	Rip 45 Kick LT	37	Liz 26 Kick RT
8	Rip 45 Kick LT	23	Rip 31 Dive RT	38	Liz 14 ISO LT
9	Rip 47 Wide LT REV	24	Rip 14 Dive RT	39	Liz 24 ISO LT
10	Rip 13 ISO RT	25	Rip 13 ISO RT	40	Liz 47 Pin LT
11	Rip 23 ISO RT	26	Rip 23 ISO RT	41	Liz 38 Pin RT
12	Rip Drag Pass RT	27		42	
13	Rip Reverse Pass RT	28		43	
14	Rip 28 Pin RT	29		44	
15	Rip 37 Pin LT	30		45	

	BLUE		BLUE		BLUE
1	Liz 45 Seal LT	16	Liz 45 Seal LT	31	Rip 26 Seal RT
2	Liz 47 Wide LT	17	Liz 47 Wide LT	32	Rip 28 Wide RT
3	Liz 47 MSTR SWP LT	18	Liz Power Pass LT	33	Rip Power Pass RT
4	Liz Power Pass LT	19	Liz 30 Wedge LT	34	Rip 30 Wedge RT
5	Liz 30 Wedge LT	20	Liz 10 Wedge LT	35	Rip 10 Wedge RT
6	Liz 10 Wedge LT	21	Liz 34 Kick RT	36	Rip 33 Kick LT
7	Liz 34 Kick RT	22	Liz 26 Kick RT	37	Rip 45 Kick LT
8	Liz 26 Kick RT	23	Liz 32 Dive LT	38	Rip 31 Dive RT
9	Liz 28 Wide RT REV	24	Liz 13 Dive LT	39	Rip 14 Dive RT
10	Liz 14 ISO LT	25	Liz 14 ISO LT	40	Rip 28 Pin RT
11	Liz 24 ISO LT	26	Liz 24 ISO LT	41	Rip 37 Pin LT
12	Liz Drag Pass LT	27		42	
13	Liz Reverse Pass LT	28		43	
14	Liz 47 Pin LT	29		44	
15	Liz 38 Pin RT	30		45	

	GREEN		GREEN		GREEN
1	Rip 26 Seal RT	16	Liz 45 Seal LT	31	
2	Rip 28 Wide RT	17	Liz 47 Wide LT	32	
3	Rip Power Pass RT	18	Liz Power Pass LT	33	
4	Rip 30 Wedge RT	19	Liz 30 Wedge LT	34	
5	Rip 10 Wedge RT	20	Liz 10 Wedge LT	35	
6	Rip 33 Kick LT	21	Liz 34 Kick RT	36	
7	Rip 45 Kick LT	22	Liz 26 Kick RT	37	
8	Rip 31 Dive RT	23	Liz 32 Dive LT	38	
9	Rip 14 Dive RT	24	Liz 13 Dive LT	39	
10	Rip 13 ISO RT	25	Liz 14 ISO LT	40	
11	Rip 23 ISO RT	26	Liz 24 ISO LT	41	
12	Rip 36 Seal RT	27	Rip 16 Seal RT	42	
13	Rip 38 Wide RT	28	Liz 15 Seal LT	43	
14	Liz 35 Seal LT	29	Rip 18 Wide RT	44	
15	Liz 37 Wide LT	30	Liz 17 Wide LT	45	

The open slots are for special plays or additional plays. For example, I use those slots for our Eagle (2x2) series (detailed discussion of the Eagle series is beyond the scope of this book, though the formation is presented in Chapter 4, pages 33-34). You can dumb down this audible system to meet your needs and can easily adapt this for younger kids by simply using your play calling.

Appendix II
Creating a Dynamic Warm-Up Program

One of the most important coaching responsibilities, is the development our young athletes. We really must help our players become better athletes in general, not just better football players. Often we as coaches overlook that important aspect of our job and I am sad to say the only people that suffer are the kids we train (or don't train depending on how you look at it). It has taken me about fifteen years and a lot of reading, additional education and certification, as well as experimenting, training players, and field learning. What I have found is that if we as coaches take the time to develop and foster basic athletic skills from the onset of their training, once these basic skills are established, you have a great foundation for your players to develop into superior athletes. Global coordination, explosive strength, balance, stability, agility, and quickness are keys to giving a young athlete the opportunity to reach that genetic ceiling and maximize his athletic potential. I have found that the study of functional development, adolescent development, functional anatomy, and kinesiology are great starting points as a youth coach. I have come to realize there is no such thing as a uncoordinated child or a wimpy kid. It really boils down to one question: "Are you willing to invest the time to actually develop your kids into warriors?" If so, it starts with turning each of your players into the best athletes they can be.

Before you is a complete layout of my thought process on dynamic warm ups as well as my philosophy on how I believe to properly train kids to maximize that all important genetic ceiling.

Key Points

From the age of six to puberty is the best window to work on athletic development and sports specific skills (depending on if it is a male or female, the age of puberty can vary from 10 to 15, we will focus on males 11 to 16). The reason being that the child's brain is very adaptable and open to learning new skills in the pre-adolescent stage of their life due to plasticity, the ability to adapt to stimuli – this includes the CNS (central nervous system), PNS (peripheral nervous system), and the NMS (neuromuscular system) and local skeletal muscle systems.

Adaptation and plasticity are very important aspects in coordination development in childhood athletes (pre-adolescent). As we move from pre-adolescence to adolescence to fully mature, the plasticity (ability to adapt) decreases. The human body can always adapt to new stimulus but the window for adaption is much bigger in pre-adolescent than adolescents and even bigger when compared to fully mature adults (25 and older). This is basically due to the hormones and changes that occur in a young person's body with the onset of puberty. The same changes that start the process of maturation and growth also initiate the closing of the "window to adaptation". As an infant, and up to the time when a child reaches puberty, the window to adaptation is wide open. Children literally absorb all sorts of information around them and adapt it to their needs; as they reach puberty and begin to mature, that window begins closing until adulthood (mature), at which point the window is about three quarters closed. Yes, as an adult you can adapt to stimulus and change - but not as quickly or efficiently. As you start to decline that window closes even further to the point it is nearly shut but not all the way closed. Yes you can still adapt to new changes but it takes longer for that adaptation to occur. In short, kids adapt much quicker than adults; often the younger the child the more quickly they adapt.

I use my dynamic warm-ups as much more than a method to warm up the body to optimum body temp. It is a method to warm-up not only the skeletal muscle tissue, but also the CNS (central nervous system), PNS (peripheral nervous system), and the NMS (neuromuscular system); as well as stretch all the muscles involved in the dynamic warm up properly (in motion), develop strength in the stabilizer and synergy muscles in all three planes of movement, and prepare the entire body for additional work (body and mind). There is now enough long term evidence to support the proposition that dynamic warm-ups reduce joint and muscle related injuries. This is because the warm-ups help to develop proper propreceptive awareness (body awareness - which is the leading cause of injury in most athletes in my opinion).

Because it is a method of properly warming up/stretching/and preparing the body for an increased work load, it is a prime time to work on basic movement skills (global coordination skills). These skills are required for every athlete to function and perform at a high level. I feel as a youth coach it is my job to develop this aspect of every athlete that plays for me. It is both a selfish act (in that there is a tangible benefit for me as a coach to have better athletes) and an act of responsibility on my part.

Adaption is a cumulative effort. Adaption does not occur over night or even in the course of a month, three months, or a year. Proper habits are not formed in a short span of time but instilled over a long period of time. All of this is dependent on the individual athlete and several key factors like environment of learning and living, genetic ceiling, biological maturity (physical growth, emotional growth, and adaption), hydration, nutrition and most importantly interest (it is well established that a kid that is interested in running, sports, and exercise is going to adapt more quickly than a child being forced to participate - the neurological and physiological development studies in this area are very fascinating).

As coaches, we always want to maximize our efforts and get the most out of every drill we utilize. The DYNAMIC WARM UP is a period for me to develop my athletes over the long term by developing proper GLOBAL COORDINATION SKILLS like linear movement skills, lateral movement skills, and multi-directional skills. Obviously in football the multi-directional skills are the most important, but if we are concerned with developing well rounded athletes, then all three GLOBAL COORDINATION SKILLS are important. To this point (the selfish part of me), I am always faced with limited talent and how to best utilize that talent and more importantly the talent in the middle and bottom of my roster. I have found that if I can increase the athletic potential of the middle and bottom of the roster and maximize my full roster by the end of the season (play offs), that I have a distinct advantage over my competition when they fail to effectively develop their talent whether due to lack of commitment or understanding. Again the training is cumulative, i.e. I realize that it will not happen quickly, but over the long term (over the full length of the season) and into the remaining seasons I will be maximizing the talent on my team.   More importantly, I am setting up the framework for each of these young athletes to develop into better athletes as they grow into adults.

Global Coordination Development (Brian Grasso – President and Founder of IYCA)

The key ingredient to working with pre-adolescent and early adolescent athletes is providing global stimulation from a movement perspective. Younger athletes must experience and eventually perfect a variety of motor skills in order to ensure both future athletic success and injury prevention. Developing basic coordination through movement stimulus is a must, with the eventual goal of developing sport-specific coordination in the teenage years. Coordination itself, however, is a global system made up of several synergistic elements and not necessarily a singularly defined ability. Balance, rhythm, spatial orientation and the ability to react to both auditory and visual stimulus have all been identified as elements of coordination. In fact, the development of good coordination is a multi-tiered sequence that progresses from skills performed with good spatial awareness but without speed to skills performed at increased speeds and in a constantly changing environment. As Joseph Drabik points out, coordination is best developed between the ages of 7 - 14, with the most crucial period being between 10 - 13 years of age.

1. The specific advantages of a dynamic warm-up, by comparison with the more traditional 'sit and stretch' routine, are as follows:

2. Because it involves continuous movement, it maintains warmth in your body and muscles. I have found that many athletes drop their core temperature by 2-3° after sitting and stretching for 10-15 minutes;

3. It prepares the muscles and joints in a more sport specific manner than static stretching.

4. It enhances coordination and motor ability as well as revving up the nervous system – benefits which are particularly important for younger athletes who are still 'learning their bodies.

5. Finally, and possibly most importantly, it prepares the mind for the workout ahead.

6. Proper mental preparation for any sport is vital and, in my considerable experience with teams and groups, I have found that while many sit-and-stretch routines are an excuse for daydreaming, the dynamic warm-up forces athletes to focus and concentrate on the task at hand."

(Article Source: http://EzineArticles.com/?expert=Brian_Grasso)

Stretching

Flexibility – the range of motion that is available at a given joint of the body while at rest.

Flexibility is related to the extensibility of all the soft tissue including muscles, tendons, ligaments, joint capsules, and fascia that surround the bone structures and joint structures. It should be noted that flexibility is variable and pre-determined by gender and genetics; however since we don't know the true ceiling of most athlete's genetic pre-disposition to flexibility we must first put a well rounded flexibility program in place so that athlete can reach that ceiling and maximize his or her potential.

More often the not if you go to a football practice the first thing you see is the coaching staff lining up the players into neat lines or circles and then having the athletes do static stretching. This comes from the good old days of when we were players and our coaches really didn't know any better. However times, and more importantly our knowledge of the human body and how it functions, have changed and we know that the muscles in the body operate in a chain or series of muscles working together not in isolation as science assumed in the past. A major muscle contracting (agonist) induces the opposite muscle (antagonist) to relax or stretch all the while also getting additional help from synergist muscles and the stability muscles (deep muscles around the joint structures involved in the movement). Static stretching has its place but it is not before a practice and it is certainly not before you are getting your players ready to conduct full speed drills without warming up the body structure correctly.

If we look at a football player in a functional mode then we can notice right off the bat that the body we are viewing is in an upright, dynamically moving position rather than a static position holding a stretch or one that is lying prone and holding a stretch. Our body moves through three planes of motion (sagittal, coronal, and vertical) and if our warm up and stretching are not accounting for the multiple planes of motion then our stretching routine is not going to be effective. Also, we must account for how the body moves (kinesiology), e.g. even while simply walking the muscles are accelerating, stabilizing, and decelerating the body. This movement is dynamic (always changing and moving) in nature. The majority of all sports movements are accomplished in an upright posture. Doing static stretches in a seated or supine posture doesn't prepare the body for proper movement while accounting for body weight, gravity, and ground reaction forces. Static stretching has its place, but if you're attempting to increase flexibility and reduce injuries due to sports specific movements, then dynamic stretching before a workout or practice makes much more sense. During the cool down phase is when static stretching makes much more sense in the practice schedule. This is when muscles need to be realigned (and reset from a neuromuscular perspective).

Planes of Motion

Sagittal – plane bisects the body from the front to back, into right and left symmetrical halves. Flexion and extension motion will occur on this plane.

Coronal – plane bisects the body from side to side dividing it into front and back halves. Lateral flexion, abduction, and adduction motions occur on this plane.

Transverse – plane divides the body into superior (upper) and inferior (lower) halves. Rotational movements will occur in this plane.

Muscle Contractions and Movements:

When muscles cause a limb to move through the joint's range of motion, they usually act in the following cooperating groups:

1. *Agonists*: These muscles cause the movement to occur. They create the normal range of movement in a joint by contracting. Agonists are also referred to as *prime movers* since they are the muscles that are primarily responsible for generating the movement.

2. *Antagonists*: These muscles act in opposition to the movement generated by the agonists and are responsible for returning a limb to its initial position.

3. *Synergists*: These muscles perform, or assist in performing, the same set of joint motion as the agonists. Synergists are sometimes referred to as *neutralizers* because they help cancel out, or neutralize, extra motion from the agonists to make sure that the force generated works within the desired plane of motion.

4. *Fixators(stabilizers)*: These muscles provide the necessary support to assist in holding the rest of the body in place while the movement occurs. Fixators are also sometimes called *stabilizers*.

For example, when you flex your knee, your hamstring contracts and to some extent, so does your calf and lower buttocks. This basic movement causes several other things to occur in and around that knee. Meanwhile, your quadriceps are inhibited (relaxed and lengthened) so as not to resist the flexion. In this example, the hamstring serves as the agonist, or prime mover; the quadriceps serves as the antagonist; and the calf and lower buttocks serve as the synergists. Agonists and antagonists are usually located on opposite sides of the affected joint (like your hamstrings and quadriceps, or your triceps and biceps), while synergists are usually located on the same side of the joint near the agonists. Larger muscles often call upon their smaller neighbors to function as synergists.

The following is a list of commonly used agonist/antagonist muscle pairs:

1. pectorals/latissimus dorsi (pecs and lats)
2. anterior deltoids/posterior deltoids (front and back shoulder)
3. trapezius/deltoids (traps and delts)
4. abdominals/spinal erectors (abs and lower-back)
5. left and right external obliques (sides)
6. quadriceps/hamstrings (quads and hams)
7. shins/calves
8. biceps/triceps
9. forearm flexors/extensors

Kinetic Chains

A kinetic chain is a grouping of body parts that are inter-linked. Just as links of a chain keep it connected and working, body parts affect other body parts. For example, forces in the foot and ankle can affect body parts such as the knees, the hips and the lower back. There are eight functional chains of movement that involve the muscles, fascial components, and skeletal structure that transfer and translate movement throughout the body. These functional chains are structurally connected, such that the whole body can be considered in terms of series of chains. These chains can be described as the front chain, back chain, lateral chains on the sides (left and right) and two diagonal chains in the front and back. These chains incorporate prime movers, synergy, and stabilizer muscles to facilitate efficient movement. With the physical chains come the control mechanisms that help manage and distribute work throughout the body. These are made up of components of the nervous system (central and peripheral). The kinetic chains are force connections throughout the body that the central and peripheral nervous system use to make movement efficient.

Dynamic Stretching and Warm Ups

Dynamic stretching involves stretching while performing a specific movement pattern (fundamental or sports specific). It utilizes movements that are controlled, which allow the individual to mimic and prepare for the movement patterns that will follow the warm up period. Dynamic warm-ups and stretching, helps to set the proprioceptors of the muscles, ligament, and joint capsules, while allowing the muscles to strengthen eccentrically. Dynamic stretching includes stretching in all three planes of motion. This is a huge benefit in preparing, strengthening, and developing the joint structures and supporting structures like the major muscles, stability muscles, and synergy muscles, along with the joint capsules. Static stretching is simply not sufficient to accomplish these important aims. This means that you, as a coach, are not preparing your young charges correctly for what you are about to do in a full speed practice. One of the major reasons why young athletes are prone to major injuries to their joint capsules is that during growth spurts the soft tissue (muscle, ligaments, tendons, and fascia) are already stressed and elongated; applying additional stress means the areas that are the weakest are going to fail first. Most knee (and all lower body joint injuries) injuries occur because of linear and rotational force being applied to the knee at the same time. Football players don't move in straight lines they execute cuts, jump cuts, spins, and lateral movements that are explosive in nature. All of this force being generated is moving in and out of those joint capsules via ground force reaction and your body's natural ability to move energy throughout the body via synergy muscles and stabilizer muscles to maintain movement economy and efficiency via kinetic chains.

The activation of the movement system correctly prior to sport performance or practice has been found crucially important. I have been researching and developing optimal warm-up and movement preparation programs for young athletes for years. The science and research support these concepts, and frankly I have seen the benefits for ten years and have no doubt it works.

Proprioception (from Latin proprius, meaning "one's own" and perception) is the sense of the relative position of neighboring parts of the body.

- proprioception - the ability to sense the position and location and orientation and movement of the body and its parts wordnetweb.princeton.edu/perl/webwn
- proprioceptor - special nerve endings in the muscles and tendons and other organs that respond to stimuli regarding the position and movement of the body wordnetweb.princeton.edu/perl/webwn
- proprioceptive - of or relating to proprioception wordnetweb.princeton.edu/perl/webwn
- Specialized sensory receptors located inside muscles, joints, and tendons that monitor the length and tension of the musculotendonous complex. In doing so, they proceed the central nervous system with information concerning kinesthetic sense www.infitpt.com/glossary.html

In the book Progressive Plyometrics For Kids written by Donald A. Chu and Avery D. Faigenbaum in 2006 they made this statement about dynamic warm ups:

"Despite the universal practice of pre-event static stretching, little evidence exists that static stretching has a favorable impact on muscle performance or injury rates in children and teenagers. On the other hand, pre-event dynamic warm-up activities that are designed to elevate body temperature, excite the neuromuscular system, and maximize ranges of motion have been shown to positively influence muscle performance in children and teenagers. In addition, since a variety of movement skills can be practiced during warm ups, participants have another opportunity to practice fundamental movement skills."

Dynamic Warm Up and Getting the Entire Systems Ready for Work

This is another great article on the subject and I think it will help to shed some additional light on the subject matter. Specifically, how the dynamic warm up helps to train a young athlete and additionally the amount of additional fundamental training and time saving that can occur with a sound dynamic program in place.

I really want reinforce how important this subject is and how much it can help you has a coach to have a properly set up warm up program in place and what ALL THE REAL BENEFITS are to you as a youth football coach.

This piece is written by Tommi Paavola, M.S., C.S.C.S. runs Youth Fitness and Conditioning Programs in New Jersey, US and develops systems for athletic development. Website for more information http://www.discovermovement.com.

1. "Traditional" vs." the New Warm-up"

Anyone who has been involved in sports has some kind of mental association with warming up. My memories are mostly about running around the field and sitting down on the ground afterwards for some static stretches. The stretches were always the same, the hurdler-stretch and other reach-down movements. Generally speaking, I remember my youth sport warm-ups being boring, inefficient and not stimulating for the mind or the body. It was just something we had to do. In fact I believe now that the term "warm-up" is outdated as the pre-sport or pre-workout activity is about so much more than just "warming up."

Active and dynamic warm-ups and movement preparation routines are replacing the old mentally and physically more passive warming-up practices. The general idea of (just) elevating the body temperature by slow jogging, followed by a few static stretches, is being revolutionized by a more focused and involved movement preparation.

An athlete spends between 10-20 minutes a day preparing the body for the competition or practice. This time accumulates slowly but surely and functions not only as a primer for the sport performance but as an opportunity to learn and develop various motor skills.

The activation of the movement system correctly prior to sport performance or practice has been found crucially important. We have been researching and developing optimal warm-up and movement preparation protocols for years.

2. 368 - The simple system of human movement

In order to reproduce a great warm-up that really works, we need some sort of a system. Without a pattern or a system, all of our warm-ups will be random and we will never be able to predict the outcome of the warm-up reliably.

The Dynamic Warm-Up Method aims at creating the desired physiological adaptation as reliable as possible every time. Our simplified concept of human movement helps us in approaching the warm-up systematically and comprehensively. This concept is called 368.

The 368-system gives a simplified biomechanical idea of human anatomy in relation to integrated movement. Learning more than 700 muscles with their functions in relation to everyday training seems like an impossible task for most of us. That is why observing the body in the following way can be helpful:

3 PLANES: The movement occurs in three planes, sagittal, frontal and transverse. In lay terms, this translates into forward/backward, side to side and rotational movement, respectively.

6 STATIONS: The human body can be described in six levels or stations:

1. Foot and ankle

2. Knee

3. Hip

4. Lumbar spine

5. Thoracic spine

6. Cervical spine

8 CHAINS: The muscles and fascial components together form functional units that translate movement throughout the body and are structurally connected making the whole body into "one big muscle". These chains are the front chain, back chain, lateral chains on the sides and the diagonal chains in the front and in the back.

The 368-concept helps us executing the warm-up systematically as well as in observing the movement in real-time. And how does the 368 actually do this?

> 1. By reminding us to warm-up and activate the body in all three planes as all of the sports and activities occur in multi-planar environment.
> 2. By making sure that each of the body parts have been "checked" and "turned on" the right way.
> 3. By guiding us in terms of movement patterns instead of individual muscles.

3. "Turning on" the body-wide systems in the warm-up

Cardiovascular System

One of the main goals of warm up in sport practice has always been "to increase the core temperature". That is what "warming up" sounds like anyway. Many functions of the body operate better as the internal temperature of the body rises as a result of physical activity. Stimulating the cardiovascular system is most definitely a part of any warm-up protocol.

Neuromuscular System

The objective of the warm-up is to "start the engines" in terms of neurological and musculoskeletal system as well. This is where the old school warm-up often falls short as the optimal muscle activation will most likely not be a result from slow jogging and static stretches. Activating the nervous system means that we will optimize the sequence of how the muscles work together. Turning on the receptors requires motion. That is why sitting down to passively stretch your muscles is normally not the best approach to elevating acute performance.

Metabolic/Hormonal system

Different activities call for different approach in warming up. A power lifter might warm up completely differently than a marathon runner. And a rower would certainly not use the same warm-up as a pistol shooter. The intensity level of the warm-up depends on the desired acute response. The metabolic system and hormone activity can be regulated/stimulated by the nature of the warm-up.

Mental/Psychological System

The mind has to be stimulated and active starting from the first moment of the warm-up. You can NOT cheat the body into proper adaptation if the mind is not involved and challenged. Whether the warm-up routine is slow or fast by nature the level of focus and concentration correlates directly with the physiological results of the warm-up.

4. WARM-UP: Invaluable practice time for the fundamentals

Until recently the quality of the warm-up has not been considered an important factor in athlete's development but more or less a necessary protocol that needs to be done in order to start the "real practice." However, this couldn't be further from the truth. The first 10 minutes of the practice could actually become the most important phase in the session. Think about it, not only are you in the most receiving state to learn and develop skills but you also set the tone for everything else done after the warm-up. It would a waste of time not to take advantage of the warm-up routines that can accumulate to hundreds of hours of training time on a yearly level.

Imagine how much more could be achieved in your warm-up if all these elements are incorporated in a well structured system and performed automatically in the beginning of each session. We can easily turn "the least inspiring" phase of the workout into the most exciting and essential component of our training.

5. Sport specific warm-up

So how do we prepare the body for a specific activity?

How do we know what movements to include and which stations or chains to concentrate on?

Developing a sport specific warm-up or an activation routine will require at least a basic understanding of the sport movement.

Some sports require more emphasis of postural activation during the warm-up as the others might need to focus on specific myofascial chains in the body. A cyclist that sits in a "flexed hip"-position could probably use a concentrated effort on making sure that also the back side (read; glutes) would stay active during the ride. A 'thrower' or a soccer player might have to place particular emphasis on making sure that the diagonal front chain that crosses over the body and the abdominal wall, is active and ready for the rapid stretch-shortening action to occur.

By analyzing the sport movement in terms of three planes, six stations and eight chains, the warm-up activation routine is much easier to put into practice.

We also need to design the warm-up based on the metabolic and systemic requirements of the sport. For example, a shot put athlete's single performance takes about 2 seconds whereas a triathlete keeps going for hours. We would not want design a warm-up for the shot put athlete that would tire him out and take away from his 100% maximal effort. We also would not want to send a triathlete on his/her way without making sure that the core temperature has been increased to the point where the oxygen uptake and delivery are at their optimal pre-activity level. So, depending on the dominant energy systems in each sport we might choose quite a different approach of preparing for the activity.

6. 32 Warm-up studies to prove the point

Journal of Strength and Conditioning Research published a review called *Effects of Warming up on physical performance; A systematic review with meta-analysis.*

This review basically searched as many scientific articles as possible that investigated the effects of warming up in humans on performance improvement in physical activity. The results were interesting.

- 92 different warm-up combinations were assessed

- 79% of the warm-ups improved performance

- 17% showed a <u>negative impact</u> upon performance

- The degree of performance improvement varied from <u>1% to 20%</u>

The study revealed quite a few fascinating details that you may want to read yourself. In terms of optimizing the performance it is crucial to think about the conclusions of this study. Why?

- It is possible to actually decrease performance by warming up

- It is clear that not all the warm up protocols are equal (1% vs. 20%)

- It is obvious that a correct warm up system can make a BIG difference in sports performance (practice or competition)

The review discusses some of the problems in the warm-up that decreased performance. Poor protocols did not include movements or activities specific to the performance task or they were too vigorous for example for an explosive performance (vertical jump). Overall, the poor warm-up protocols were inappropriate for the activity.

So what are some of the take-home-message from the scientific reviews?

1. Different activities require a different warm-up protocol
2. Sport specific "needs analysis" is important when designing a warm-up
3. Timing, intensity and volume are essential variables to be considered in the warm-up routine

7. The Dynamic Warm-up Method

As we have already found out, a general warm-up with general variables is not the most effective way of preparing the movement system for activity. However, we believe it is possible to create a system that re-produces the best possible sequence of movements and actions in order for the optimal state of performance to be created. The system can function as a basic structure and each sport can be individually inserted into the system with its own variables.

The Dynamic Warm-Up Method has 7 stages:

• Emotional calibration - Creating an emotionally sound training environment

- This means observing the athlete and finding out the emotional and mental state. If the athlete is anxious, nervous or disturbed, the coach should first listen and help unload any burdens in order to decrease the anxiety level. This is of course just a normal act of care and compassion but can be built into a system as well.

• Focus/Concentration

- The first movements of the workout and the warm-up set the stage for everything else. Choosing the exercise or movement to start with should immediately engage the athlete in a state of focus and concentration. For youth athletes this can be a fun activity that requires coordination and effort, such as multi-planar jumping jacks. An older athlete may often move directly to the Dynamic Flexibility. Selection of the focus factor exercises should favor the safest possible exercise alternatives while providing enough mental stimulation and physical challenge.

• Dynamic flexibility/Mobility

- Dynamic flexibility movements are active and aimed at stimulating and starting up the proprioception, the neural control of the movement system. This means that the body engages in the movements that go through different ranges of movements in different angles and planes. Dynamic flexibility exercises can be performed both in vertical as well as in horizontal position. Examples of dynamic flexibility exercises are lunges with various arm drivers, broomstick rotations, hip circles or single leg reaches.

- Stabilizer Activation

- This phase targets the neuromuscular units that control and stabilize different joints of the body. The first stabilizer that needs to be awake is the center, the core of the body that stabilizes the lumbar spine first and foremost and then spreads out down to the hip and up to the scapular region. Depending on the sport activity, more emphasis can be given to the joints that particularly require stability in a given movement. A runner might be more interested in the ankle and hip stability as a swimmer should include the shoulder and scapular stability activation in the warm-up sequence.

- Prime Mover Activation (Fundamental Movement Pattern Activation)

- Progressively everything moves towards a total integration in the body. The prime mover activation can be defined as *rehearsal or practice of the fundamental movement patterns*, such as squat, lunge, push, pull, rotation etc. This stage can be performed with external resistance to increase the recruitment in the bigger muscle groups.

- Elastic Elements Activation (Short-Stretching Cycle)

- The efficiency of movement depends on the ability of the muscle-tendon unit (and fascia) to store elastic energy in itself. The better all the muscular-fascial chains of the body are able to store and release the energy, the more effective and economical the movement will be. The stretch shortening -cycle can only store energy for a short amount of time and performing a few rapid repetitions of jumps, throws, hops etc. will make sure that the elastic element are active and functioning properly.

- Task-specific Movement Activation

- And finally the athlete should exercise the actual sport movement that he/she is about the practice or perform. All the systems are brought back into an integrated action as the task-specific skill combines all the previous stages and makes the movement more sub-conscious and hopefully automatic and reflexive. At this final stage the athlete should arrive at a state of performance that is approximately 20% higher than about 10 minutes prior.

I hope that this report will help you with your pursuit of better function and higher performance whether you are an athlete yourself or a dedicated coach helping others in reaching their true potential."

Article Source: http://EzineArticles.com/?expert=Tommi_Paavola

What is in a Good Dynamic Warm-Up Program

Warming-up or movement preparation increases the core body temperature (typically by about 3 degrees), activates the nervous system, actively elongates the muscles and stabilizers, and builds technique and effectiveness of movement. These exercises work in building functional joint mobility, dynamic flexibility, functional strength, and stabilizer strength.

The movements start slowly and progress in to explosive movements that activate your body's athletic systems essential for a high level of football competition and practice. This set of exercises also includes lower body plyometrics, for lower body explosiveness as well.

I use two specific types of warm ups for our team. One is an athletic development and global coordination warm up we do at the beginning of practice. This warm up focuses on a full athletic movement warm up and is also designed to be a global coordination and functional movement development program that works over the course of the season. The other is a 'sport specific' warm up based on fundamentals of football.

> 1)   Athletic Development and Global Coordination Warm Up
> 2)   Football Fundamentals (Stance, Blocking, Tackling, Shedding, Pursuit, and Ball Handling)

Athletic Development and Global Coordination Warm-Up

> 1)   Should not take more than 15 minutes and typically the warm up takes only 10 minutes once you get into regular season.
> 2)   Use basic movement patterns and advance as the season goes on to more advance movements.
> 3)   Linear, lateral, backwards, multidirectional, and full body movements are all used.
> 4)   Each movement is done slowly at first and we progressively increase in speed as the warm up progresses.
> 5)   Proper movement that is slow and deliberate to start with so that you develop proper movement patterns as well as stabilizer and core strength.
> 6)   As movements are mastered speed can be increased. Typically 50 to 75% at a first as the athlete progresses speed increases to 60 to 85%.

Team Dynamic Warm-Up Progression

All players line up on the goal line and spread across the field so they are double arms interval apart from boundary to boundary. If team is crowded and can't achieve this they simply take every even player and step back and form a second line right behind the first.

They will move 15 yards there and back for a total of 30 yards of movement for each exercise. Each line will move there and back and if a second line is present they will move to the rear and the next line will move up and prepare for the exercise just performed. If you need to save time you can cut it down to 10 yard there and back for a total of 20 yards and that will shave about 2 to 3 minutes of the total warm up.

When you initially begin conducting your dynamic warm ups you need to teach basic running form and movement economy as well as how to quickly recover in between reps. These are important functions that every one of your athletes will need to know to maximize his performance on the field.

Running Form:

1)   Standing arm turnover: have the athletes cock their arm at 90 degrees and practice rotating their arms properly. Practice 2 to 3 sets of 15 seconds so that the coaches correct improper form.

2)   Run in place: add the lower body with a focus on proper arm rotation and form as well as lower body form (no feet landing outward, knee drive, heel drive, relaxed form). Practice 2 to 3 sets of 15 seconds as above.

3)   It is good to do this the entire first week of practice on the front end of warm ups to fix any basic run form issues.

4)   Below you will find more detail on running form and ways to fix some basic problems.

Basic Linear Speed Techniques

The first rule you should always apply to coaching is not to "over coach" an athlete. The second rule is to not teach an "unnatural movement technique". I see a lot of so called knowledgeable speed coaches over teaching techniques and teaching incorrect movement techniques that do not fit the athlete's natural movement patterns. This can cause more problems and damage, so be aware of this caveat at all times.

Figure II-A

Linear Actions you are looking for in the athlete:

Tall action: This means erect; running on the ball of the foot (not toes or heels) with full extension of the back, hips, legs as opposed to "squatting down low" when running. Developing and stressing proper posture while in movement and static is fundamental to creating a good running form. See Figure II-A above.

Relaxed action: This means move easily, as opposed to tensing and "working hard" to move. Let the movements of running flow; the athlete should look like a wheel in motion with the hips and torso being the hub of the wheel. Keep the hands relaxed, the shoulders low, and the arms swing rhythmically to the sides.

Smooth action: This means float across the top of the ground. All motion should be forward not up and down or to the side. Leg action should be efficient and rhythmic. The legs should move easily under the body in a constant even pattern like a moving wheel. With the forward leg and arm (opposite arm) pulling and the rear leg and arm pushing the body towards the target.

Drive action: This means push from an extend rear leg (very important), rear elbow drive with a high forward knee drive followed by a strike of claw foot action just behind the body's center of gravity (COG),

Proper Sprint Technique (Movement Economy):

Head and neck are aligned with the body. You should have straight line from the head, neck, back, and rear leg. The head and neck should be relaxed; by simply letting the jaw hang will help reduce tension in the head and neck area. This tension can cause the shoulders, arms, and back to tense as well so it is imperative to relax the jaw and neck muscles. It will cause restricted arm movement; which reduces speed. The eyes are looking straight ahead past the finish point.

The arms should be relaxed with elbows bent near or at 90 degrees. Swing should come from the shoulder and should be in line and straight; it should never cross the body at all but instead be motioning down field at the finish. The fingers should go just above the midline of the chest and go jus behind the hip. Arm swing should be in concert with the lower body. When the right arm goes completely forward (elbow pointed down and up field) at the same time the left foot (rear foot) is coming off the ground (from ball of foot). The left arm is coming back with the elbow pointed back and slightly up as the right leg is going forward (knee is lifting). As knee is driven forward, the arm on the opposite side of the body is also driven forward from a position behind the body. The arms move forward in front of the body until the hands are about shoulder high. The arm should never leave the flexed position (often runners swing the arm out at the back). The amount of the opening and closing of the angle should be fairly small. The elbows should never be away from the body but almost brush the ribcage (staying in line with the direction).

There is a myth that the hands should be straight out (as if shaking some ones hand) is in fact a fallacy and should not be listened to. When you keep your hand straight you tense the muscles in the palm and this causes the muscles in the forearm to tense as well which in turn cause the muscles around the elbow to tense causing the elbow to lift from the body or run in a less smooth manner.   Instead the hands want to be in a curled position naturally. Meaning the fingers should curl into the palm as if wrapped around a roll quarters and the thumb should rest just over the index finger.

Let the body lean forward naturally but don't bend over. The body should have a slight forward tilt with the head, neck, back, hips, and back leg inline. At the acceleration phase (starting) there is going to be more forward 'lean'. The athlete should be looking down in front of him, which in turn creates additional lean to create a shorter stride (faster shorter steps = more power). As the athlete accelerates and the body begins to lift to a natural lean, the head comes up and looks past the finish line.

Run on the balls of the feet and not the toes or heels. The ball should strike the ground and stay on the ground for just an instant as the leg turns over and drives (pushes) off the ground. This is a key point as a lot of young runners run on their toes which causes excessive braking or a loss of power (push) due to inadequate contraction of the calf muscles when the ball of the foot strikes the ground

The foot should land directly underneath the sprinter. An over-stride will result in the foot landing in front of the center of gravity, which will cause braking. Under striding causes a lot of fast movement and energy expenditure without covering enough ground. A key point is that the body leans at about 60 degrees (approximation) and if a line is drawn through the body from the head to the foot and the line becomes baseline the forward thigh of the runner should be at or near 130 degrees to that baseline. This means the knee needs to drive forward (not upward) to create the pulling force necessary to increase speed.

Keep the head and trunk still and the entire body relaxed. The body (specifically muscles) is more receptive to neuromuscular commands from the brain when it is relaxed. Furthermore the torso and core must be relaxed as it must move in multiple directions as the body increases in speed.   When the right arm is back the left leg is back that means the right shoulder is forward and the left hip and lower back is moving backward. This means the torso is twisting and in doing so if the torso is tensed there is a bigger chance of muscle pulls in the torso area (specifically the lower back and rear shoulders). Also the more tense the torso, the less flexible it becomes. This reduces not only neuromuscular control, but also decreases speed as the body cannot create additional force through the torso.

Rotating the shoulders creates sideward-motion forces, which detract from the force needed to propel you directly forward as quickly and forcefully as possible.

Part of good technique is to relax the trunk, arm, and antagonists of the stride movements. Energy is often wasted to keep accessory muscles contracted and the body rigid, and wasted energy equals decreased speed. Use relaxation to be as efficient as possible and recover as quickly as possible.

Now bear in mind if you are football player and you carry the ball (QB, RB, WR) you need to understand how to carry a ball and run as well. Simply follow the above techniques and lock the ball into the inside of the elbow by turning the hand upward with the palm of the hand on the front tip and the bottom tip in the inner elbow and press the open part of the ball against the front of the chest so your elbow can still swing freely. Simple press the ball and the fingers lay on the top of the football keeping it locked in. The ball comes in and is locked by turning the hand inward and pressing the ball into the body and the other hand going over the ball to cover it when you expect any type of contact from the defense. Do not let the ball affect your technique. Also you must be aware of your gear (helmet and pads altering your technique). So work on perfecting running technique while in gear with a ball.

Rapid Recovery:

This is very simple but often used method with youth teams. At any point that an athlete is able to rest he should immediately relax and start taking in deep breathes, pause, and let them out slowly to flood the body oxygen and start the process of flushing the body of lactic acid, which only occurs with the increase of oxygen into the blood stream. It is very important to relax and breath if only for few seconds as those moments will accumulate over the course of the game and practice. Fatigue cause a reduction in performance and in focus and the fastest way to minimize that is to develop a habit of recovery and relaxing as much as possible between plays and drills.

Beginning of the Season Warm Up (10 to 15 minutes)

Form Run: 50% effort focus on form and technique
Run: 75% effort
Sprint: 100% max effort

Players must pause for a few seconds on all HOLD and LUNGE movements.

1) Linear
   a. Form run there and back
   b. High knee hold there and heel to butt hold back
   c. High Knees there and butt kickers back
   d. Forward lunge there and drum majors back
   e. Form run there and back
2) Lateral
   a. Shuffle there and back
   b. Tapioca there and back
   c. Carioca there and back
   d. Lateral Lunge there and back
   e. Lateral Run there and back
3) Backward
   a. Backwards lunge and run back
   b. Backwards run and run back
   c. Back pedal and run back
4) Upper Body
   a. Bear stomp and sprint back
   b. Bear crawl and sprint back
   c. Inch worm and sprint back

Veteran Warm up (10 to 12 minutes)

1) Linear
   a. Form Run there and back
   b. High knee hold there and heel to butt hold back
   c. High Knees there and butt kickers back
   d. Forward lunge there and drum majors back
   e. Frankenstein and form run back
   f. Power Skip and form run back
2) Lateral
   a. Shuffle there and back
   b. Tapioca there and back
   c. Carioca there and back
   d. Lateral Lunge there and back
   e. Shuffle and on GO cross over and form run there and repeat back
3) Backward
   a. Backwards lunge and run back
   b. Backwards run and run back
   c. Back pedal and run back
   d. Back pedal, rotate, and sprint there and back
4) Upper Body
   a. Bear stomp and sprint back
   b. Bear crawl and sprint back
   c. Inch worm and sprint back
   d. Lateral bear crawl there and back
   e. Crab walk
   f. Backwards bear crawl

Football Fundamentals Warm up

Once the athletic development warm-up is completed we allow our players to quickly grab water and recover for a few minutes (stressing proper recovering methods). The next three segments are designed to not only warm up the players and get them ready to execute football stances and techniques but also get them in the right emotional and mental state to continue to execute at a high level throughout the remainder of practice. The goal is to get them working on developing the basic fundamentals (blocking, tackling, and defensive shedding) as a group and focused on proper stance, technique, intensity, and aggression. It also allows our entire coaching staff to fix problems in their basic fundamentals and techniques right at the beginning of the practice while making sure the kids know we are looking for those corrections during practice.

We have them pair up and face each other on each side of the goal line. We try to even up the pairs so there is a good level of competition. It is important to swap out the pairs often as well. It does you no good if your best athletes are always pairing up together and your weakest players are pairing up. It is important that all your athletes are being challenged so make sure the pairs are nearly equal but also providing some quality competition. This alone builds up emotional and mental toughness and it forces players in a very natural way to bring out that much needed aggression and intensity that is needed in practice and during a game. How often have you seen a football team come out cold or not focused. We don't have that issue because our pre-game warm-ups are exactly what you see on these pages.

Offensive Line Stance and Blocking (5 minutes)

    1)   INITIAL INSTRUCTION: Offensive line stance: review, hold for small amount time, recover, repeat for 2 to 5 reps. Each pair will mirror each other so they can see good and bad stances (based on coaches' corrections). We have them face each other so that they can see a good stance or see other players being corrected on problems in their form. This helps to reinforce what we are looking for in their stances.

    2)   INITIAL INSTRUCTION: LEG progression. LOAD step first, EXPLODE step second. GO step third. Each pair will work on their LEG facing each other. Move at ½ speed at first and slowly move to one on one live blocking. My preference is a few LOAD steps left and right, a few LOAD-EXPLODE steps to the right and left, and full one on one blocking seeing who can drive their one back.

    3)   EVERY DAY DRILL: As the season moves on we will start repping LEG & TURN to the left and right for a few reps and PIN to the left and right one on one.

    4)   EVERY DAY DRILL: Again as the season moves on we will work on pass protection as a team: LEM and SSM and KKM with one defender and one pass blocker rep each one to the left and right.

Tackling (5 minutes)

    1)   INITIAL INSTRUCTION: LEG TACKLING: pairs will have one act as a ball carrier simulating the holding of a football on either side. The other will act as a defender and they will rotate each rep.

    2)   INITIAL INSTRUCTION: From a hitting position: LOAD arms, drop hips, eyes on arm pit of the ball.

    3)   INITIAL INSTRUCTION: From hitting position: LOAD as above and EXPLODE up and into arm up as the arms explode up and wrap the defender up. Attempt to drive the ball up and away from the body. You have to bite the arm pit (not literally) of the ball carrier that requires you to drop your hips on load low enough to come up into the arm pit.

    4)   INITIAL INSTRUCTION: From the hitting position: LOAD as above, EXPLODE as above, and GO through the ball carrier in this case as he explodes he will lift and drive the ball carrier back a few steps (echo of whistle). 2 through 4 will be done with the ball carrier static so that the defender can learn the proper technique of biting the arm pit and wrapping up.

    5)   EVERY DAY DRILL: Once this progression is taught you can move to the ball carrier on GO driving forward and attempting to drive through the tackle using step 3 and 4.

    6)   EVERY DAY DRILL: The next step is they get into their normal defensive stance (3 point for defensive linemen, 2 point balanced for CB, OLB and MLB, and 2 point staggered for DE and have them rep the tackling with a ball carrier attempting to go through the tackler (make sure it is straight through and not around).

    7)   EVERY DAY DRILL: Finally you can have the ball carrier spin, juke, cut, or go through to practice tackling against a moving target.

8) EVERY DAY DRILL (EDD): The first game week we are doing 2 or 3 reps against a GO THROUGH BALL CARRIER in stances and 2 or 3 reps with a MOVING BALL CARRIER. Bear in mind they are operating double arms distance from each other so the tackling distance is small and the movement is in a very confined space.

Defensive Shedding (5 minutes)

1) INITIAL INSTALL: one player will be a defender and the other player will be a blocker. The blocker will get in a kneeling stance on both knees so that his body is straight from the knees to the top of his head. On down he will get his body into a loaded position. The defender will get into a six point stance with the fingers spread on the ground, knees on the ground, and toes on the ground. On GO the defender will explode through his hips going up and forward as he quickly drives his palms into the breast plate of the blocker and attempt to drive him back. Make sure the defender's head is up, elbows are slightly bent and inside. The contact should be explosive and should drive the blocker back and the impact should be heard as a short explosive pop. This teaches the basic punch the defenders will need to know if they get caught up by a blocker. After each rep they switch jobs and repeat. 2 to 5 reps should be performed to reinforce the technique.

2) INITIAL INSTALL: The next step is to get both players off the ground and into hitting positions. One player will act as a blocker and the other will be a defender. On DOWN both players will get into a balanced hitting position (basic linebacker stance) and on GO the blocker will attempt to LEG block into the defender at about ½ speed and the defender will execute the punch as quickly as possible and slide to left or right quickly. The contact should drive the blocker back as the defender moves to the side. Again 2 to 5 reps should be performed to reinforce the technique.

3) INITIAL INSTALL: The next step is to teach a basic PUNCH AND RIP to the left and right. This is our basic shed technique it is the starting point for any other shed technique we teach. With the pairs both in hitting positions one will be a blocker and one will be a defender. On GO the blocker will attempt to block (LEG) the defender aggressively and the defender will explode into the defender and initiate an explosive punch into the breast plate of the blocker and then immediately rip to the direction indicated by the coach (ball, stack call, etc). The rip should be executed as a PUNCH – RIP - GO(dip the ripping shoulder and explode the hand and elbow through the funnel (ribcage-elbow-armpit) and the ripping foot should step across the outside of defender's far heel as he steps past the blocker (play behind his heels). The near hand pull the chest of the blocker towards him as he is ripping through to help get past the defender. Rep it 2 to 5 times each.

4) INTIAL INSTALL – Once we teach the PUNCH & RIP we teach a SPEED RIP (no punch then get in the hole by ripping through). 2 to 5 reps each.

5) INITIAL INSTALL – PUNCH & SWIM (used against a blocker that is play low or is shorter than the defender). Same as the PUNCH & RIP

except after you make the explosive punch you swim the opposite arm over quickly and as it falls the arm drives the blocker past as the near hand pulls him past. The swim must be fast and explosive as it goes up and over.

6)   INITIAL INSTALL – SPEED SWIM as PUNCH & SWIM except no punch is made. Rep 2 to 5 times.

7)   INITIAL INSTALL – BULL RUSH (used when a blocker is flat footed and reading or waiting).   The defender will make explosive contact but instead of simply punching he will unload into the blocker and attempt to get him back on his heels and drive him straight back as he attempts to drive his shoulder pads up high (we say rip his pop his helmet off with his shoulder pads like popping a soda cap off a bottle – POP IT OFF).

8)   EVERY DAY DRILL – Once we establish our basic shed moves we will start teaching our team more advance moves. Using basic wrist, elbow, and shoulder clubs in combination with rip, swim, and bull rush as well as spin moves. What we try to do is teach a broad spectrum of defensive shed moves and we then let each defender practice the ones they are good at. Obviously as coaches we will guide them in which ones they will excel in. Typically it is good for each defender to know the basic PUNCH & RIP, SPEED RIP, and BULL RUSH and from there we might expand a player's quiver of moves. Most kids have enough with those three but I feel it is important to show them some new moves every once in awhile, as the season progresses so they don't get board and often the new moves help to reinforce the old moves. 4 to 6 reps each.

9)   Make sure you have the coaching staff act as landmarks for their pairs so that the defenders can attack a "target" behind the blockers. I have my entire coaching staff take 2 to 4 pairs each and they monitor those pairs and while acting as their landmark.

Final Thoughts on Football Fundamental Warm ups

After the initial techniques are taught (initial install), we want our players to be physical and give all out effort - both the offensive and defensive players. Again, the benefits of the aforementioned approach are derived as a cumulative effect; over time our players develop fundamentally as we push our players to become physically, mentally and emotionally tough. Again it is all about turning our kids into warriors on that football field.

Practice Warm Up with Global Athletic Development and Football Fundamentals

1st Week

    1)   Dynamic Warm Ups: 15 minutes
    2)   Blocking Progression Warm up: 10 minutes
    3)   Tackling Progression Warm up: 10 minutes
    4)   Defensive Shed Progression Warm Up: 10 minutes

Remainder of Pre-Season

    1)   Dynamic Warm Ups: 10 minutes
    2)   Blocking Progression Warm Up: 10 minutes
    3)   Tackling Progression Warm Up: 5 minutes
    4)   Defensive Shedding Progression: 5 minutes

In Season/ Pre-Game Warm Ups

    1)   Dynamic Warm Ups: 10 minutes
    2)   Blocking Progression Warm Up: 5 minutes
    3)   Tackling Progression Warm ups: 5 minutes
    4)   Defensive Shedding Progression: 5 minutes

Brief Description of Movements

Linear – warms up the body in the sagittal plane for the most part.

Form Run - a run at 50% using correct linear form.

High Knees – a jog stressing the knee lift portion. The knee should attempt to go above the belly button. Maintain proper linear form at all times. This stretches the hamstring and all the stability and synergy muscles associated with the hamstring. High knee hold is a slower technique that is more about balance, stability, and stretching.

Butt Kickers – a jog stressing the heel lift portion. The heel should make contact with the butt. Maintain proper linear form at all times. This stretches the quadriceps and all the stability and synergy muscles associated with the quads. Butt kicker hold is a slower technique that is more about balance, stability, and stretching.

Drum Major – this is at a fast walk. One leg is raised and is rotated inward so that the heel of the foot strikes the hand of the opposite arm near the belt buckle. The heel should go as high as possible crossing the midline. This stretches the hip flexors and gluteus and all the stability and synergy muscles associated with the hip flexors and gluteus.

Fast Skips – this is basically skipping at a fast rate using good linear form. Start with a slow longer skip and work towards a fast rapid skip with the feet touching the ground and quickly coming off the ground. Stretches and warms up the muscles in the foot, ankle, and shin.

Frankensteins – at a walk the athlete will kick up his leg as straight as possible so that it goes above his chin with his hands out straight ahead of him like Frankenstein. It is very good exercise for balance and core stability while also stretching the hamstring, gluteus, and lower back.

Straight Leg Bounding – Sometimes called Russian skips. The legs are straight using a good linear. The feet should have very little ground contact and work for the feet to get good height off the ground. This is another good movement for the hamstrings and gluteus.

Forward Lunges - Take a long step out and lean forward so that the back leg is straight and the front leg is at 90 degrees with the knee behind the ankle and then sit down into the lunge. This stretches the pelvis muscles, inner muscles around the hip joint, quadriceps, and hip muscles. It also stretches the hamstring of the front leg as well. All the stability and synergy muscles are being warmed up and stretched as well. Make sure the upper torso is upright at all times. Have them do this slowly so that they get a good stretch with a pause at the bottom.
Lateral – warms up and stretches the body in the coronal and transverse planes.

Walking Shuffle – This is nothing more than a shuffle at a walk. It is the first exercise we do in our lateral warm up. Make sure you are using correct lateral form at all times. The feet do not touch or cross over. The hips and knees are bent and the body is low to the ground but not bent at the waste. This stretches the hip and pelvis muscles as well as the groin muscles and all the stability and synergy muscles involved.

Shuffle – This is a faster version that further warms up the muscles and stretches them. Both feet are moving and the athlete should glide over the ground.

Walking Crossover – This is nothing more than a carioca at a walk. The back foot cross over as far as possible causing the front knee to slightly bend. This warms up and stretches the hip flexors, lower back, and pelvis and all of the associated stability and synergy muscles.

Tapioca – This is a fast short cross over steps using good lateral movement form. This really stretches the hip flexors and gluteus as well as the lower back muscles and all of the associated stability and synergy muscles.

Carioca – This is a longer cross over step using good lateral movement. This further stretches the hip flexors and gluteus as well as the lower back muscles and all of the associated stability and synergy muscles.

Shuffle and Touch – This is nothing more than a shuffle with the upper body staying low and on every second shuffle the hands touch the ground in between the feet while the head stays up. This further stretches the lower back, gluteus, and hamstrings as well as all the normal muscles being stretched during the shuffle. Knees an hips are bent to keep the body low.

Lateral Run – This is running laterally with the rear leg being in front at all times. Good lateral movement form is important. This stretches all the leg muscles, hip flexors, pelvis, and lower back muscles as well as the stability and synergy muscles involved in the coronal and transverse planes.

Lateral Lunge – Does the same thing as the walking lunge but in the coronal plane. Make sure the upper torso is upright and this is done as a slow pace with a pause at the bottom.

Upper Body – This warms up the upper body in the sagittal plane but it adds body weight and ground force reaction.

Bear Stomp – A bear crawl at a walk. The butt should be down and the knees stay off the ground. The hand and foot should forcefully stomp the ground as they walk. It stretches and warms up the muscles in the arm, shoulder, upper back, and chest along with the stability and synergy muscles. It also warms up the core as the body stabilizes on two appendages and moves.

Bear Crawl – A full speed version of the bear walk. Further warms up and develops the upper body; also good for developing coordination in the four appendages and body awareness.
Backwards Bear Crawl - A full speed version going backwards. Further warming -up and developing the upper body; also good for developing coordination in the four appendages and body awareness.

Lateral Bear Crawl - A full speed version of the bear walk laterally with the near side arm and leg moving first. Further warms up and develops the upper body; also good for developing coordination in the four appendages and body awareness.

Crab Walk – This is performed on all fours with the butt facing the ground. This basically works out and stretches all the muscles that the bear crawl does but in reverse order.

Spider man – This is a more complex bear crawl. The athlete basically starts in the prone position with the arms and legs away from the body. He then lifts his body off the ground and crawls (like spider man).   This is a much more complex movement that further develops body awareness and coordination.

Inch Worm – place your hands down in front of your feet and walk out on your hands until you are in a push up position and then walk in with your feet keeping them straight at all times. Repeat to the finish line. Great way to warm-up the upper body, core and upper body joint stabilizer as well.

Backwards Walk – This simply walking backwards. The athlete is warming up and stretching all the muscles that a form run or a linear exercise would except in reverse. This is a complex movement that helps to teach and master backwards movement.

Backwards Run – Running Back wards applying good linear form and leaning slightly forward. Your eyes are forward at all times and you simply look for the last marker out of the corner of your eyes.

Slow Back Pedal – The chin is over the knee and the hips and knees are bent so you are low. The heels of the feet drive back in short slow steps as you pump your arms. Done at 50% of the normal speed.

Back Pedal – As above but at full speed.

Backwards Lunges - Take a long step back and lean forward so that the back leg is straight and the front leg is at 90 degrees with the knee behind the ankle and then sit down into the lunge. This stretches the pelvis muscles, inner muscles around the hip joint, quadriceps, and hip muscles. It also stretches the hamstring of the front leg as well. All the stability and synergy muscles are being warmed up and stretched as well. Make sure the upper torso is upright at all times. Have them do this slowly so that they get a good stretch with a pause at the bottom.

Appendix III
Team Drills for Practice and Development

This appendix is set up to show a few additional drills that I use to develop the execution and timing in the offense as well as correct technique and execution flaws of player. The full team drills allow us to develop timing and execution for our plays and series as well as practice specific situations during a game. It allows us to develop our team's sense of tactical cohesion and unity. Half line drills allow us to develop the proper execution and angles for specific plays as well as isolate and correct problems with individual players and positions.

Team Drills

1. Perfection Drill
2. Power Hour Drill
3. Half Line: Pull Side Puller Drills (BSWB/QB Seal, BB/WB Kick, WB Wide)
4. Half Line: Pull Side Lead Drills (QB ISO, BSWB ISO, BB PIN)
5. Half Line: Wall Side Lead Drills (QB Double, BSWB PIN)

Team Drills Explanation

Perfection Drill

Purpose – To rep plays on air so that we can focus on strictly execution and technique for each play. It is also used to develop our no huddle and audible system as well as develop situational awareness.

Set up – (Figure III-A) Offense on the five yard line and the offensive coordinator aligns on the boundary to simulate game time with one coach acting as a line judge on each side and the line coach as a back judge. Each play is run and all position coaches monitor their players and correct flaws in their technique immediately and on the fly. For each successful run (no mistakes at any positions) they gain five yards and for each successful pass they gain ten yards. We work to the goal line and if any mistake is made we move back to the starting point. Quality reps that maximize time are very important so we work for five reps a minute. At the beginning of the season you are going to only get two reps a minute but as the team's confidence and effort increase the reps per minute will decrease. At first your focus should be on working on teamwork, timing, and execution. Once those are established we work on fine tuning the mechanics of our no huddle and our audible system. Basic things like receivers always checking if they are on the LOS with the line judges and the center and quarterback making sure everyone is aligned properly are key components you have to be checking on. Once all of those are established we also work on our tempo components as well.

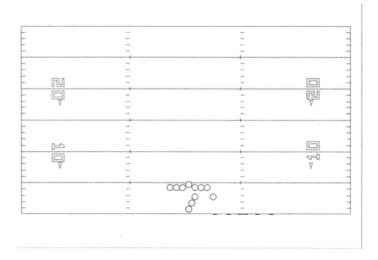

Figure III-A.

Power Hour Drill

Purpose: To teach the offense that the power, power sweep, and power pass (most importantly, the power play - WB/TB SEAL) is the heart and soul of this offense. The offense needs to have the confidence and ability to run it anywhere on the field and be successful. At times you can literally run this drill for one hour to work on improving the level of execution and confidence in your offense with these plays and prove your point that these three plays are really all you need to be successful moving the ball.

Set up: Place your offense on the ten yard line facing the goal line against a defense (Figure III-B). Initially the defense will start with eleven players or if you are short place what defenders you have on the play side (have a signal to the defensive coaches which side that is from play to play). The offensive coordinator will call the play and the offense will run the play. If they get the play into the end zone in four plays or less they get a point; if they don't or turnover the ball they lose a point. If the offense is moving the ball easily simply add more defenders (or coaches/parents with dummies) to add more resistance to the offense. There are times you will have the remaining lot of your team out on defense simply to prove a point. I have had 19 players aligned on the defensive side of the ball in one practice and our offense was still moving the ball running power, power sweep, power pass.

You can run this with any formation and edge tag, and you can also use audibles as the season progresses to further demonstrate to the offense that the use of the power plays in conjunction with audibles, forms a very strong punch that allows your offense to attack the defense. I typically run this drill for 20 minutes during team period and simply run power, power sweep, and power pass from our pass formation after we install the first three plays in our offense. This is supposed to be tough, so make it tough on them any way possible - if that means the coaches are adding additional emotional and mental barriers, e.g. noise (getting on them about proper stance, alignment, technique, etc.) and other, in an attempt to challenge their focus, then do it. Remember the intent is to build their individual and team confidence in our core plays. Anywhere on the field at any time!

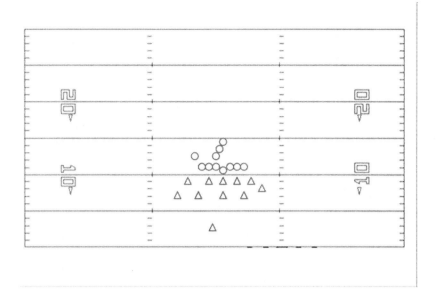

Figure III-B.

Half Line Drills Explanation

Half Line: Pull Side Puller Drills

Purpose: To isolate all of the pullers and backfield players and work on their specific techniques and execution under full speed conditions. This allows us to further develop the specific actions we are seeking in our players and to further enhance the concepts we want them to understand. The half line pull drills allow us to remove the wall side and focus solely on the backside pulling linemen and the backfield blockers so that we can work on timing, effort, and execution and properly critique this part of the unit as it is often very hard to address this portion of the offense under live eleven on eleven drills and running plays simply on air.

Set up: There are three edge play half line drills and three perimeter half line pull drill. Figure III-C is for our WB Seal play and can be altered for the QB Seal play by simply having the BSWB fake power sweep and the QB run the power. Figure III-D is the BB Kick Drill and Figure III-E is the WB Kick Drill (both of which can and should be run at the same time to add some confusion to the defensive side). Figure III-F is the WB Wide and Figure III-G is the WB MONSTER SWEEP while Figure III-H is WB WIDE REVERSE. All three of these drills can run at the same time as the set up is the same. There is always six defenders with shield (if you have them). The only drill where all six defenders are actually blocked is WB SEAL, WB WIDE, and WB MONSTER SWEEP. This leaves one defender free and this highlights the fact that often in our misdirection game that our runner must still battle through at least one defender at times. We have progression we use as we use these drills and the drills themselves are pretty much full speed once the progression is taught.

1)   Run it with the defenders static (with shield and no movement simply resistance upon contact)

2)   Run it with the defenders squeezing inward to close the tunnel.

3)   Run it live with the defenders ready to collapse and make a tackle.

4)   Great way to work on getting everyone pulling full speed and creating that tunnel for the runner and it is also a very good way to get the runner used to running in traffic and finding daylight.

You can work on all three of your EDGE plays at one time going in one direction or you can work on all three of your PERIMETER plays at one time going in one direction. The beauty of the half line pull drills is you can rotate in teams of pullers and backfield players and utilize your best defenders as well on the defensive side so that you are getting quality reps for your players as well as being able to correct stance, alignment, and technique issues.

Great way to make the play competitive: Give the pulling team 1 point for every time the runner makes it across the top cone and give one point to the defense for every time he doesn't or they cause a turnover. Bear in mind it will get very competitive so control the low tackling and cheap shots because they will happen.

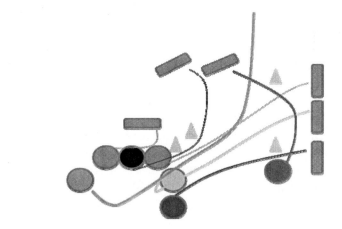

Figure III-C. WB SEAL PULL DRILL

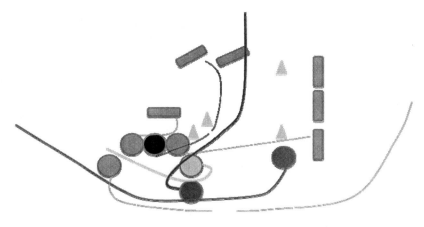

Figure III-D. BB Kick Pull Drill

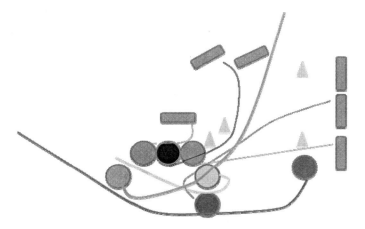

Figure III-E. WB KICK Pull Drill

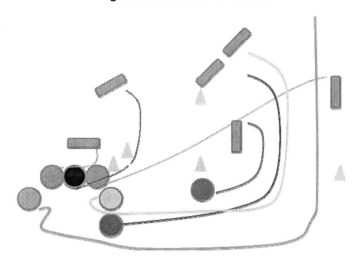

Figure III-F. WB WIDE Pull Drill

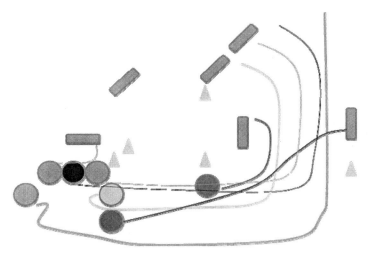

Figure III-G. WB Monster Sweep Pull Drill

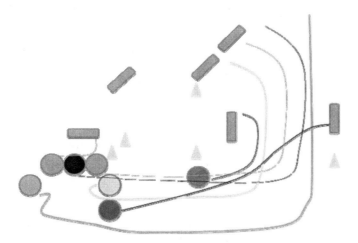

Figure III-H. WB WIDE REVERSE Pull Drill

Make these drills fast paced and work to get a maximum amount of quality reps. Typically, I'll take my starting pull side with starting backfield and work them against my best defenders; then we'll rotate in our wall side to get reps at pull side with our second backfield; from there we simply rotate in as groups (third pull side group and third backfield and so on). I try can get 3 to 5 reps for each play to one side. Often we only work one side and the next time we do the drill we work it to the other side.

Any formation can be used and we only use these drills with our compressed formations we never use expanded edge tags because the whole reason for the edge tags is to remove defenders away from the point of attack and the whole reason for the half line pull drills is to teach our team how to deal with an entire defense in a compressed area.

Appendix IV
Creating an Effective Practice Plan

I believe very strongly that a team's success is based completely on how well they practice on the field. If a coaching staff competently prepares for a season with a well developed practice plan that is structured and flexible, and they strive for the very best from their players they will have a successful season. Success is not always derived by having a winning season but on how well your players develop into a team of warriors committed to a common cause. Winning is simply the outcome of a well taught and well lead team. Bear in mind your practices should always be tougher than the games; i.e. your players should be challenged to the extent that the games should be easy by comparison.

What it takes to win

- Positive Attitude: Self, team, coaches, those around you.
- Great Effort: 100% effort towards anything you do on or off the field.
- Great Intensity: All out, full throttle, no holding back.
- Great Character: Honor, Courage, Commitment.
- Great Confidence: Believe in yourself, your team, and your coaches.
- Mentally Tough
- Emotionally Tough
- Physically Tough
- Care about those around you: your team mates, your family, your school, your coaches, your opponents.

Football is a Combat Sport

It is a sport that is based on precision execution and violent actions. The more precise your team's execution and the more violent your team's action the more successful you will be. Winning is based on a desire to hit the other team and their players on every play until one of you back down and quit.

If your team doesn't want to hit, you will not have a successful team; hitting comes from a sense of confidence and a desire to compete to be the best. Aggressiveness and violent actions come from both and in doing so you develop a winning attitude and a commitment to excel.

First, you have to teach them to be confident in themselves and in each other. That confidence has to do with their belief in their equipment to keep them safe and their belief in their fundamentals, techniques, and schemes they are taught by their coaching staff.

Second, we compete in everything we do except for warm-ups. If they do a drill, there will be a winner and a loser we build competition from within in everything we do. Kids must learn how to win and lose - and how to handle both. Kids need to learn how to compete and from that competitive spirit breeds the desire to be aggressive because the most aggressive often win the games that count. Third, every drill we do whether it is on bags or on a live body we go 100%, we might wrap up/tackle above the waist but we go 100%. Every time we make contact we do it violently so that in the game the habit is to make contact violently and with the proper instincts.

We constantly stress that football is a combat sport we hit and we hit as hard as possible every time. If you don't preach that and stress it in practice you will never see it on the game field. We always want our players making contact first. We have an attitude of hit first and try not to get hit, i.e. be the one delivering rather than receiving the blow.

Seven Key Attributes to a Winning Team

- Confidence
- Competitiveness
- Aggressiveness
- Violence
- Winning Attitude
- Commitment (to team and self)
- Ownership

Four C's of Confidence

- Confidence in Coaching Staff and their leadership.
- Confidence in Equipment and their protective gear.
- Confidence in Themselves
- Confidence in their Teammates

How do you develop Confidence

1)   Build a strong base of fundamentals (tackling, blocking, pursuit, ball handling skills, and most importantly hitting).
2)   Use a progression format when you teach new fundamentals and skills: bags to live bodies, slow to fast, and limit the live contact and scrimmages until you see that the majority of your players are confident in what they are doing.
3)   Use a hard but positive reinforcement approach. There is no room for quitting; if they fail in a drill, they learn why and they correct it.
4)   They must trust their coaching staff and know they are all on one page. Have a plan, develop your system, and work your plan. Changing for the sake of change is a fast way of losing your team's confidence and their ability to compete.
5)   Put players into leadership positions that are natural leaders and positive influences on the team. Correct negative influences and remove cancers quickly!
6)   Give the players ownership of their team. It is not the coaching staff's team. We are on the sidelines the players must own the team!

Confidences Breeds Competitiveness

- When a player is confident he is sure of himself and his team mates and staff.
- This builds a desire in the player to succeed and to push himself and in doing so brings out a natural desire to compete.

• You must develop that desire to compete by making every drill you do on the practice field competitive. It is YOU AGAINST HIM, IT IS US AGAINST THEM in every drill. They must learn how to win, how to lose, and how to handle both, so they can be emotionally and mentally prepared for it on the field.

Four Strengths Every Player Must Have!

- Physically Conditioned
  – Being able to cope with physical fatigue, pain, and exhaustion while executing your responsibilities as perfectly as possible each play throughout the entire game
- Emotionally Conditioned
  – Being able to cope with internal and external stress and control it and respond to it in a positive manner with maximum intensity and effort
  – Ignoring the noise around you so that you can execute!
- Mentally Conditioned
  – Being able to concentrate and focus on being successful for those few moments prior to and during a play with clarity to execute your technique flawlessly. (STANCE/ ALIGNMENT/TECHNIQUE = SAT)
- Ethically Conditioned
  – Being able to understand and comply to their commitments and responsibilities to their family, academics, team, and value systems at all times even in the face of peer pressure or when no one is looking. (DO IT RIGHT FOR THE RIGHT REASONS!)

Practice Development:

1) Don't waste time on anything not related to improving your player's and team's ability to be successful.
   a. Don't waste time having conservations with parents, administrators, or other coaches during practice.
   b. Don't discipline players with drills that are intended to make them better.
   c. Correct mistakes on the fly. Don't go into long explanations about scheme, philosophy, and technique; simply chalk it, walk it, run it. Reps improve muscle memory and reduce thinking making players more instinctive.
2) If it doesn't pertain to stance, alignment, technique, scheme, athletic development, execution, aggression, or conditioning it is not worth practicing.
3) Have objectives and a plan built around the objectives for the pre-season, season, and each week of practice and develop your practice plan around that.
4) Stick to your plan but make it flexible enough to adapt to needed changes each week and day of practice.
5) As a youth coach I believe one of my main responsibilities is to make sure every kid I coach is a better athlete. That requires that I make sure I work on athletic development over the entire season.

Practice should incorporate:

1. Fundamental Development
2. Competition
3. New concepts installed
4. Old concepts reviewed
5. Team, group and individual periods
6. Conditioning
7. Team Building
8. Leadership Development

A system is like a cook book, and the plays are like recipes in that cook book. The drills are like the ingredients that are used to create those recipes. If the ingredients are not applied in the right order and used in the right amount the recipe will not taste good and a offensive play is the same way. If the drills are not applied in the right manner and used correctly the plays will never work cohesively and the execution will never be what you want it to be and in the end you will have created a poor play.

Drills are used to teach stance, alignments, techniques, plays, and schemes as well as develop timing and execution. They are the fundamental part of creating a successful offensive play and in turn a successful offense.

Progressions are a series of drills used to teach both the players and coaching staff how to execute the drill and the fundamentals of tackling. It allows the instructor to correct both technical problems and instructions problems. Each drill is done back to back as they each build off of each other.

Circuits are used to save both time and maximize reps for every player once the fundamentals of tackling are taught and the coaching staff understands how to teach the specific drills and techniques. These are five basic circuits we use but you can mix and match drills in groups of three using any of the tackling drills. The important point is to do tackling every day because it is the cornerstone of every good defense. A team that can tackle will defend well. If you only have ten minutes then simply reduce your circuit down to two drills of five minutes.

Two Hour Practice Plan

This is based on having preseason of four weeks, which is pretty common for most youth football teams, and four days a week until the start of school when it goes down to three days a week. If you have more than four days a week at the front end (some have five days a week), I will note some adjustments you can make to the practice schedule. This practice plan is geared to the YDW Gun install and the 63 defense install for obvious reasons so if you plan on running a different defense, you would have to alter the defensive portions to accommodate the difference.

This plan is broken into several parts:

Preseason –

Evaluation Week –

Install Week 1 (focused on installing offense) –

Install Week 2 (focused on installing offense & installing defense) –

Install Week 3 (focused on installing defense and special teams) –

Season –

In – Season Practice Week –

Bye- week Practice –

Youth Double Wing II: The Gun!

Evaluation Week – The most important week of your season!

Event – Day 1	Time	Notes
Dynamic Warm Up	6:00	
OFF STANCE/LEG Progression	6:15	*Stance* *Kneeling Load and Explode Drill* *3-Point Stance Load Drill*
TACKLING LEG Progression	6:25	*Hitting position* *Approach & load,* *Load & explode (wrap up),*
Defensive Shed Progression	6:35	*Kneeling punch,* *hitting position punch*
EVAL Session 1	6:45	10 yard Dash & 20 yard Dash Quickness & Speed (2 sets for time take the best time)
Installation of Offense.	7:00	Positions, basic play calling, base formation, basic edge tags.
EVAL Session 2	7:15	40 yard Dash Breakaway Speed (2 sets for time)
DEFENSIVE INDIES DLINE LB/DE CB	7:30	EDD's for all sections. See 63 Defense EDD's for positions. Teaching of drills period – Why & How
Conditioning (Enduro)	7:45	Enduro Drill for 15 minutes
Team Circle	8:00	

Youth Double Wing II: The Gun!

Event – Day 2	Time	Notes
Dynamic Warm Up	6:00	
OFF STANCE/LEG Progression	6:15	*Stance* *Kneeling Load and Explode Drill* *3-Point Stance Load Drill*
TACKLING LEG Progression	6:25	*Hitting position* *Approach & load,* *Load & explode (wrap up),*
Defensive Shed Progression	6:35	*Kneeling punch,* *hitting position punch* *punch and rip (L&R)*
EVAL Session 3	6:45	Pro-Agility 5x10x5 (2 sets for time take the best time)
Installation of Offense	7:00	Review, Chalk and Walk Rip 26 Seal, Liz 45 Seal, Rip 28 Wide, and Liz 47 Wide.
EVAL Session 4	7:15	Six Cone Zig Zag (2 sets for time take the best time)
DEFENSIVE INDIES DLINE LB/DE CB	7:30	EDD's for all sections. Stance, Alignment, Technique Get off!!!
Conditioning (Tire Drill – three to four stations)	7:45	4 cones – 1 tire – 4 players each station. Player must pull that tire so they can touch their cone and win.
Team Circle	8:00	

Youth Double Wing II: The Gun!

Event – Day 3	Time	Notes
Dynamic Warm Up	6:00	
OFF STANCE/LEG Progression	6:15	*Stance* *Kneeling Load and Explode Drill* *3-Point Stance Load Drill* *3-Point Stance Load & Explode Drill*
TACKLING LEG Progression	6:25	*Hitting position* *Approach & load,* *Load & explode (wrap up),* *LEG Tackling ½ Speed*
Defensive Shed Progression	6:35	*Punch & Rip*
EVAL Session 5	6:45	20 Yard Bear Crawl Drill (2 sets for time take the best time)
OFFENSIVE INDIES QB/RB/WR OLINE	7:00	*Backs –* *RB Fundamental drills* *WB SEAL on air* *OLINE –* *Snapping Drill* *Wall Drill* *Pull & Seal* *Step Through Drill*
EVAL Session 6	7:15	20 Yard Dummy/Tire Flip Drill (2 sets for time take the best time)
DEFENSIVE INDIES DLINE LB/DE CB	7:30	EDD's for all sections.
Conditioning (Sprints)	7:45	All 30 yards (15 and back) 10, 8, 6, 4, 4, 4 reps. Rest 1 minute between each.

Youth Double Wing II: The Gun!

Team Circle	8:00	
Event – Day 4	**Time**	**Notes**
Dynamic Warm Up	6:00	
OFF STANCE/LEG Progression	6:15	*Stance* *Kneeling Load and Explode Drill* *3-Point Stance Load Drill* *3-Point Stance Load & Explode Drill*
TACKLING LEG Progression	6:25	*Hitting position* *Approach & load,* *Load & explode (wrap up),* *LEG Tackling ½ Speed*
Defensive Shed Progression	6:35	*Punch & Rip* *Speed Rip*
OFFENSIVE INDIES Backs Oline	6:45	Back – RB fundamental drills WB SEAL on air WB WIDE on air QB SEAL on air Line – WALL Drill Pull & Seal Drill Cut Off Drill
OFFENSIVE TEAM	7:00	SHIFT (review OVER/LOOSE) Rip 26 SEAL RIGHT Liz 45 SEAL LEFT 5 reps on air to develop timing WB SEAL Pull Drill (Group)

		WB WIDE Pull Drill
DEFENSIVE GROUP	7:15	Front Six – Stack drill 1 thru 3 Back Five – Hourglass drill 1 thru 3
DEFENSIVE INDIES DLINE LB/DE CB	7:30	EDD's for all sections.
Conditioning (push up progression)	7:45	Standard Push Ups 1 minute 30 yard sprint (15 and back) 6 reps Staggered Push Ups 1 minute 6 more sprints Walking Push Ups 1 minute 6 more sprints Sphinx Push Ups 1 minute 6 more sprints Dog Push Ups 1 minute 6 more sprints
Team Circle	8:00	

Youth Double Wing II: The Gun!

Install Week 1

We are concentrating on the offensive installation and defensive fundamentals this week. Once completed our power plays in our power series will be installed out of our base formation and we will have further developed our fundamentals and techniques for defense.

Event – Day 1	Time	Notes
Dynamic Warm Up	6:00	
OFF STANCE/LEG Progression	6:10	*Stance* *3-Point Stance Load Drill* *3-Point Stance Load & Explode Drill* *Paired Live LEG Drill (full speed)*
TACKLING LEG Progression	6:15	*Load & explode (wrap up),* *LEG Tackling ½ Speed* *LEG Tackling Full Speed – Ball Carrier resist.*
Defensive Shed Progression	6:20	*Punch & Rip* *Speed Rip* *Bull Rush install*
Blocking Progression (Chutes)	6:25	Live LEG blocking against a player holding a dummy. Drive back for 5 yards. Good stance, good get off, good LEG.
Tackling Progression (Chutes)	6:35	Live LEG tackling against a player holding a dummy (w/ resistance). On the ball moving.
Tackling Circuit (3 stations 5 minutes each)	6:45	Tackling Progression I
Offensive INDIES	7:00	Backs – RB Fundamental Drills WB SEAL, QB SEAL, WB WIDE, POWER PASS on air. Left and Right Station at the same time. Switch every 3 reps.

		LINE –
		WALL Drill
		Pulling Drills
		Wedge Progression
		Snapping Drill
Offensive Group	7:20	Half Line – Pull – WB SEAL
		Half Line – Pull – QB SEAL
		Half Line – Pull – WB WIDE
Offensive Team	7:40	Perfection Drill
		WB SEAL, QB SEAL, WB WIDE from SHIFT (LOOSE/OVER)
		Work on basic no huddle
Team Circle	8:00	Recap and Review

NOTE: all QB and Receivers show up 15 minutes early in pads to run
Two-sided Uncovered Pass: On Static Defenders.   All centers will execute ten direct and ten indirect snaps to each other prior to practice.

Event – Day 2	Time	Notes
Dynamic Warm Up	6:00	
OFF STANCE/LEG Progression	6:10	*Stance*
		3-Point Stance Load Drill
		3-Point Stance Load & Explode Drill
		Paired Live LEG Drill (full speed)
TACKLING LEG Progression	6:15	*Load & explode (wrap up),*
		LEG Tackling ½ Speed
		LEG Tackling Full Speed – Ball Carrier resist.
Defensive Shed Progression	6:20	*Punch & Rip*
		Speed Rip

		Bull Rush
Blocking Progression (Chutes)	6:25	Live LEG blocking against a player holding a dummy. Drive back for 5 yards. Good stance, good get off, and good LEG
Tackling Progression (Chutes)	6:35	Live LEG tackling against a player holding a dummy (w/ resistance). On the ball moving.
Tackling Circuit (3 stations 5 minutes each)	6:45	Tackling Progression II
Offensive Indys	7:00	Backs – WB SEAL, QB SEAL, WB WIDE, POWER PASS on air. Left and Right Station at the same time. Switch every 3 reps. Install BB/QB WEDGE Line – Wall Drill against static ODD/EVEN front Wedge Progression Sprint Pass Pro install Snapping Drill
Offensive Group	7:20	Half Line WIDE SWEEP DRILL Half Line POWER PASS DRILL
Offensive Team	7:40	Power Hour Drill WB/QB SEAL, WB WIDE, QB/BB WEDGE, POWER PASS SHIFT (LOOSE, OVER) RIP/LIZ
Team Circle	8:00	Recap and Review

NOTE: all QB and Receivers show up 15 minutes early in pads to run *Two-sided Uncovered Pass: On Static Defenders.* All centers will execute ten direct and ten indirect snaps to each other prior to practice.

Youth Double Wing II: The Gun!

Event – Day 3	Time	Notes
Dynamic Warm Up	6:00	
OFF STANCE/LEG Progression	6:10	*3-Point Stance Load & Explode Drill* *Paired Live LEG Drill (full speed)*
TACKLING LEG Progression	6:15	*LEG Tackling ½ Speed* *LEG Tackling Full Speed – Ball Carrier resist.*
Defensive Shed Progression	6:20	*Punch & Rip* *Speed Rip* *Bull Rush* *Install Wrist/Elbow/Shoulder Club & Rip*
Blocking Progression (Chutes)	6:25	Live LEG blocking against a defender offering resistance.
Tackling Progression (Chutes)	6:35	Live LEG tackling against a ball carrier offering resistance
Defensive Pursuit	6:45	Defensive Pursuit Circuit I
Offensive INDIES	7:00	Backs – WB SEAL, QB SEAL, WB WIDE, POWER PASS, QB/BB WEDGE on air. Left and Right Station at the same time. Switch every 3 reps. Line – Wall Drill against live ODD/EVEN Wedge Progression Pulling Competition Snapping Drill
Offensive Group	7:20	Half Line Pull Side – WB/QB SEAL Half Line Pull Side – WB WIDE QB/BB WEDGE against interior pressure (5 man defensive line)
Defensive INDIES	7:40	EDD's for all sections

| Team Circle | 8:00 | Recap and Review |

NOTE: all QB and Receivers show up 15 minutes early in pads to run *Two-sided Uncovered Pass: On Defender.* All centers will execute ten direct and ten indirect snaps to each other prior to practice.

Event – Day 4	Time	Notes
Dynamic Warm Up	6:00	
OFF STANCE/LEG Progression	6:10	*3-Point Stance Load & Explode Drill* *Paired Live LEG Drill (full speed)*
TACKLING LEG Progression	6:15	*LEG Tackling ½ Speed* *LEG Tackling Full Speed – Ball Carrier resist.*
Defensive Shed Progression	6:20	*Punch & Rip* *Speed Rip* *Bull Rush* *Wrist/Elbow/Shoulder Club & Rip*
Blocking Progression (Chutes)	6:25	Live LEG blocking against a defender offering resistance.
Tackling Progression (Chutes)	6:35	Live LEG tackling against a ball carrier offering resistance
Defensive Turnovers	6:45	Defensive Turnover Circuit I
Offensive INDIES	7:00	Backs – RB Fundamental Drills WB SEAL, QB SEAL, WB WIDE, POWER PASS, QB/BB WEDGE on air. Left and Right Station at the same time. Switch every 3 reps. Line – Pulling Drills Wedge Progression

		Sprint Pass Pro
Defensive Group	7:20	Stack Drills 1 thru 4
		Hourglass Drills 1 thru 4
Defensive INDIES	7:40	EDD's for all sections
Team Circle	8:00	Recap and Review

NOTE: all QB and Receivers show up 15 minutes early in pads to run *Two-sided Uncovered Pass: On Defender. All centers will execute ten direct and ten indirect snaps to each other prior to practice.*

Install Week 2

We are concentrating on the offensive installation and defensive installation. Once completed our entire base power series will be installed out of our base formation and we will have installed our basic defense.

Event – Day 1	Time	Notes
Dynamic Warm Up	6:00	
OFF STANCE/LEG Progression	6:10	*Paired Live LEG Drill (full speed)*
TACKLING LEG Progression	6:15	*LEG Tackling ½ Speed* *LEG Tackling Full Speed – Ball Carrier resist.*
Defensive Shed Progression	6:20	*Punch & Rip* *Speed Rip* *Bull Rush install* *Wrist/Elbow/Shoulder Club & Punch*
Blocking Progression (Chutes)	6:25	Live LEG blocking against a defender offering resistance.
Tackling Progression (Chutes)	6:30	Live LEG tackling against a ball carrier offering resistance
Tackling Circuit	6:35	Tackling Progression II

Offensive INDIES	6:50	Backs –
		RB Fundamental Drills
		Rep WB/QB SEAL, WB WIDE, QB/BB WEDGE, POWER PASS
		Install BB KICK and WB KICK
		LINE –
		WALL Drill w/ Live defenders
		Pulling Drills
		Wedge Progression
		Sprint Protection
		Snapping Drill
Offensive Group	7:20	Half Line – Pull – WB/QB SEAL
		Half Line – Pull – BB/WB KICK
		Half Line – Pull – WB WIDE
Offensive Team	7:40	Install Nasty OVER edge tag to SHIFT
		Explain Uncovered pass concept to team (SE and SLOT uncovered)
		Perfection Drill w/ Uncovered Audibles from sideline mixed in.
		WB/QB SEAL, BB/QB WEDGE, WB WIDE, BB/WB KICK, POWER PASS
		SHIFT/SHIFT LOOSE/SHIFT LOOSE OVER/ SHIFT NASTY OVER
		Work on basic no huddle
Team Circle	8:00	Recap and Review

NOTE: all QB and Receivers show up 15 minutes early in pads to run
Two-sided Uncovered Pass: On Defenders. All centers will execute ten direct and ten indirect snaps to each other prior to practice.

Youth Double Wing II: The Gun!

Event – Day 2	Time	Notes
Dynamic Warm Up	6:00	
OFF STANCE/LEG Progression	6:10	*Paired Live LEG Drill (full speed)*
TACKLING LEG Progression	6:15	*Load & explode (wrap up),* *LEG Tackling ½ Speed* *LEG Tackling Full Speed – Ball Carrier resist.*
Defensive Shed Progression	6:20	*Punch & Rip* *Speed Rip* *Bull Rush* *Wrist/Elbow/Shoulder Club & Punch*
Blocking Progression (Chutes)	6:25	Live LEG blocking against a defender offering resistance.
Tackling Progression (Chutes)	6:30	Live LEG tackling against a ball carrier offering resistance
Defensive Pursuit	6:35	Pursuit Ckt II
Defensive INDIES	6:50	EDD Progression for all positions CB LB/DE Defensive Line
Defensive Group	7:05	STACK DRILLS 1 thru 4 HOUR GLASS DRILLS 1 thru 4 Install STACK/RED/SKY CALL
Defensive Team	7:20	DEFENSE HALF LINE DRILL DIVE/ISO/TOSS SWEEP/PAP TE-FL and I/Split back formation SE side as well

Offensive Team	7:40	Perfection Drill Work for 5 plays a minute (50 play) WB/QB SEAL, BB/QB WEDGE, WB WIDE, BB/WB KICK, POWER PASS. Uncovered audibles. SHIFT (LOOSE/NASTY/OVER)
Conditioning	7:50	Push them to failure
Team Circle	8:00	

NOTE: all QB and Receivers show up 15 minutes early in pads to run
Two-sided Uncovered Pass: On Defenders. All centers will execute ten direct and ten indirect snaps to each other prior to practice.

Event – Day 3	Time	Notes
Dynamic Warm Up	6:00	
OFF STANCE/LEG Progression	6:10	*Paired Live LEG Drill (full speed)*
TACKLING LEG Progression	6:15	*LEG Tackling ½ Speed* *LEG Tackling Full Speed – Ball Carrier resist.*
Defensive Shed Progression	6:20	*Punch & Rip* *Speed Rip* *Bull Rush* *Wrist/Elbow/Shoulder Club & Punch*
Blocking Progression (Chutes)	6:25	Live LEG blocking against a defender offering resistance.
Tackling Progression (Chutes)	6:30	Live LEG tackling against a ball carrier offering resistance
Defensive Turnover	6:35	Turnover Ckt II
Defensive INDIES	6:50	EDD Progression for all positions

		CB
		LB/DE
		Defensive Line
Offensive INDIES	7:05	Backs –
		RB Fundamentals
		Rep – WB/QB SEAL, BB/QB WEDGE, WB WIDE, BB/WB KICK, POWER PASS
		Install WB REVERSE & RAZZLE AUDIBLE
		Introduce STAR formation
		Install BB SEAL, BB WIDE
		LINE –
		Snapping Drill
		SEAL Scheme on air
		WIDE Scheme on air
		KICK scheme on air
		Sprint PASS pro on air
		(bird dog/first step then ½ speed, then full speed)
Defensive Team	7:25	DEFENSE HALF LINE DRILL
		POWER/COUNTER/TRAP/PAP
		TE-FL and I/Split back formation
		SE side as well
Offensive Team	7:40	Perfection Drill
		Work for 5 plays a minute (50 play)
		WB/QB SEAL, BB/QB WEDGE, WB WIDE, BB/WB KICK, POWER PASS. Uncovered audibles.
		SHIFT (LOOSE/NASTY/OVER)
		STAR (BB POWER/BB

		WIDE/POWER PASS)
Conditioning	7:50	4 on a TIRE Drill
Team Circle	8:00	

NOTE: all QB and Receivers show up 15 minutes early in pads to run *Two-sided Uncovered Pass: On Defenders. All centers will execute ten direct and ten indirect snaps to each other prior to practice.*

Event – Day 4 (skip if scrimmage planned)	Time	Notes
Dynamic Warm Up	6:00	
OFF STANCE/LEG Progression	6:10	*3-Point Stance Load & Explode Drill* *Paired Live LEG Drill (full speed)*
TACKLING LEG Progression	6:15	*LEG Tackling ½ Speed* *LEG Tackling Full Speed – Ball Carrier resist.*
Defensive Shed Progression	6:20	*Punch & Rip* *Speed Rip* *Bull Rush* *Wrist/Elbow/Shoulder Club & Rip*
Blocking Progression (Chutes)	6:25	Live LEG blocking against a defender offering resistance.
Tackling Progression (Chutes)	6:35	Live LEG tackling against a ball carrier offering resistance
Offensive Team	6:45	Power Hour Work POWER/POWER SWEEP/POWER PASS from SHIFT and STAR.
Offensive INDIES	7:00	Backs – POWER PASS BOOT or WAGGLE AUDIBLE

		AWAY AUDIBLE
		Line –
		King of the Board
		Pulling Competition
		Pull and Go
Offensive Group	7:20	Half Line Pull Side – WB/QB/BB SEAL
		Half Line Pull Side – WB/BB WIDE
		Half Line Wall Side – Power Pass
Defensive Team	7:40	Review Defensive Structure
		CAP/SHOOT/FORCE/CONTAIN/ALLEY
		BCR
		PASS COVERAGE – STACK/RED/discuss RED SPREAD
Team Circle	8:00	Recap and Review

NOTE: all QB and Receivers show up 15 minutes early in pads to run *Two-sided Uncovered Pass: On Defender.   Also teach ALL STOP (HITCH concept first and IN/OUT read). All centers will execute ten direct and ten indirect snaps to each other prior to practice.*

Install Week 3

We are concentrating on the improving execution of base offense, installing additional elements and improving execution level of defense. Installing special teams elements as well. Work on conditioning, intensity, and situational awareness.

Event – Day 1	Time	Notes
Dynamic Warm Up	6:00	
OFF STANCE/LEG Progression	6:10	*Paired Live LEG Drill (full speed)*
TACKLING LEG Progression	6:15	*LEG Tackling Full Speed – Ball Carrier resist.*
Defensive Shed Progression	6:20	*Punch & Rip*

		Speed Rip
		Bull Rush
		Wrist/Elbow/Shoulder Club & Rip
Offensive INDIES	6:25	Backs
		RB Fundamentals
		Rep all SHIFT power series plays on air to the right
Offensive INDIES (continued)		Rep all STAR power series plays to the right
		Call a few audibles (RAZZLE. BOOT/WAGGLE, AWAY)
		Line –
		3-Point Stance Load Drill
		3-Point Stance Load and Explode Drill
		3-Point Stance Load, Explode and Go Drill
		Foot Fire Drill
		SEAL scheme
		WIDE scheme
		KICK scheme
		All against static defenders (bird dog – full speed)
Defensive INDIES	6:50	EDD for all positions and install the below:
		CB –press/sky call
		MIKE – ROVER/ROBBER call
		DE – FIRE/SPY call
Offensive Group	7:10	*Half Line Wide Sweep Drill (static/live)*
		Half Line Wide Reverse Drill (static/live)
		Half Line Pull – QB/WB Seal
		Half Line Pull – WB Wide
Defensive Team	7:30	Half Line Drill
		Flood pass, Bubble screen, speed option, quick pitch, lead

Conditioning	7:50	Push to failure – make leaders step up and push their team mates positively.
Team Circle	8:00	

NOTE: all QB and Receivers show up 15 minutes early in pads to run *Two-sided Uncovered Pass: On Defender. Work on ALL STOP and DUMP route combination. All centers will execute ten direct and ten indirect snaps to each other prior to practice.*

Event – Day 2	Time	Notes
Dynamic Warm Up	6:00	
OFF STANCE/LEG Progression	6:10	*Paired Live LEG Drill (full speed)* *Review STANCE/.LEG progression*
TACKLING LEG Progression	6:15	*LEG Tackling Full Speed – Ball Carrier resist.*
Defensive Shed Progression	6:20	*Punch & Rip* *Speed Rip* *Bull Rush* *Wrist/Elbow/Shoulder Club & Rip* *Install Punch & Swim (situational)*
Tackling & Turnovers	6:25	*Tackling Ckt III* *Turnover Ckt I (two station)*
Defensive INDIES	6:50	EDD for all position (review calls):
Defensive Group	7:05	Stack Drills 1 through 4 Hourglass Drills 1 through 5
Offensive INDIES	7:30	Backs – RB Fundamentals Rep all SHIFT and STAR Power Series plays on air to the left. Call in audibles Line –

		King of the Boards
		Foot Fire Drill
		SEAL/WIDE/KICK live pressure
Conditioning	7:50	Push to failure – make leaders step up and push their team mates positively.
Team Circle	8:00	

NOTE: all QB and Receivers show up 15 minutes early in pads to run
Two-sided Uncovered Pass: On Defender. Work on ALL STOP and DUMP route combination. All centers will execute ten direct and ten indirect snaps to each other prior to practice.

Event – Day 3	Time	Notes
Dynamic Warm Up	6:00	
OFF STANCE/LEG Progression	6:10	*Paired Live LEG Drill (full speed)* *Review STANCE/.LEG progression*
TACKLING LEG Progression	6:15	*LEG Tackling Full Speed – Ball Carrier resist.*
Defensive Shed Progression	6:20	*Punch & Rip* *Speed Rip* *Bull Rush* *Wrist/Elbow/Shoulder Club & Rip* *Punch & Swim (situational)*
Offensive INDIES	6:25	Backs Eagle Tank Read review Sting install Eagle Lead Draw/Draw install Line – *Seal/Wide/Kick/Sprint scheme on air* *Tank/Sting scheme* *Deuce Pass pro install*

Defensive INDIES	6:50	EDD for all positions and install the below: MIKE – MICKEY/MOUSE call
Offensive Group	7:10	Half Line Pull WB/QB SEAL Half Line Pull WB WIDE Half line Pull WB REVERSE
Offensive Team	7:30	Power Hour SHIFT/STAR Power/Power Sweep/Power Pass/Wedge on the goal line.
Conditioning	7:50	Push to failure – make leaders step up and push their team mates positively.
Team Circle	8:00	

NOTE: all QB and Receivers show up 15 minutes early in pads to run
Two-sided Uncovered Pass: On Defender. Work on ALL STOP, DUMP and OUT route combination. All centers will execute ten direct and ten indirect snaps to each other prior to practice.

Event – Day 4 **Ignore if Scrimmage Day**	Time	Notes
Dynamic Warm Up	6:00	
OFF STANCE/LEG Progression	6:10	*Paired Live LEG Drill (full speed)* *Review STANCE/.LEG progression*
TACKLING LEG Progression	6:15	*LEG Tackling Full Speed – Ball Carrier resist.*
Defensive Shed Progression	6:20	*Punch & Rip* *Speed Rip* *Bull Rush*

		Wrist/Elbow/Shoulder Club & Rip Punch & Swim (situational)
Offensive INDIES	6:25	Backs RB Fundamentals Line – Seal/Wide/Kick/Sprint scheme on air Tank/Sting/Deuce scheme on air
Defensive INDIES	6:45	EDD for all positions and install the below:
Offensive Group	7:00	Half Line Pull WB/QB SEAL Half Line Pull WB WIDE Half line Pull WB REVERSE Half line Pull Power Pass
Special Teams	7:20	Kick Off
Special Teams	7:30	Kick Off Return
Special Teams	7:40	PAT/FG
Special Teams	7:50	PAT/FG Block
Team Circle	8:00	

NOTE: all QB and Receivers show up 15 minutes early in pads to run
Two-sided Uncovered Pass: On Defender. Work on ALL STOP, DUMP, OUT and WHEEL route combination. All centers will execute ten direct and ten indirect snaps to each other prior to practice.

Install Week 4

We are concentrating on the improving execution of base offense, installing additional elements and improving execution level of defense. Improving execution of special teams elements as well. Work on conditioning, intensity, and situational awareness.

Event – Day 1	Time	Notes
Dynamic Warm Up	6:00	
OFF STANCE/LEG Progression	6:10	*Paired Live LEG Drill (full speed)*
TACKLING LEG Progression	6:15	*LEG Tackling Full Speed – Ball Carrier resist.*
Defensive Shed Progression	6:20	*Punch & Rip* *Speed Rip* *Bull Rush* *Wrist/Elbow/Shoulder Club & Rip*
Offensive INDIES	6:25	Backs RB Fundamentals Rep all SHIFT power series plays on air to the right Rep all STAR power series plays to the right
Offensive INDIES (continued)		Call a few audibles (RAZZLE. BOOT/WAGGLE, AWAY) Line – *Seal,Wide, Kick, Sprint against STATIC & LIVE pressure* *Wedge Progression* *Deuce pass protection Tank/Sting run scheme*
Defensive INDIES	6:50	EDD for all positions
Offensive Team	7:05	Perfection Drill 5 plays per minute – 125 plays Stress base plays – QB/BB WEDGE, WB/QB SEAL, WB

		WIDE, POWER PASS, WB REVERSE, WB/BB KICK Get 15 to 20 eagle plays into the list. (50/50 pass/run)
Defensive Group	7:30	STACK Drills HOURGLASS Drills
Conditioning	7:50	Push to failure – make leaders step up and push their team mates positively.
Team Circle	8:00	

NOTE: all QB and Receivers show up 15 minutes early in pads to run
Two-sided Uncovered Pass: On Defender. Work on ALL STOP, DUMP and WHEEL route combination. All centers will execute ten direct and ten indirect snaps to each other prior to practice.

Event – Day 2	Time	Notes
Dynamic Warm Up	6:00	
OFF STANCE/LEG Progression	6:10	*Paired Live LEG Drill (full speed)*
TACKLING LEG Progression	6:15	*LEG Tackling Full Speed – Ball Carrier resist.*
Defensive Shed Progression	6:20	*Review four basic defensive shed.* *Install WHEEL technique*
Offensive INDIES	6:25	Backs Rep all SHIFT power series plays on air to the left All plays two times. All groups Rep all STAR power series plays to the left. All plays two times. All groups EAGLE RUN GAME TANK/STING

		Line – *Pulling Drills* *Wedge Progression* *SEAL, KICK, WIDE live*
Defensive INDIES	6:50	EDD for all positions
Offensive Group	7:05	Half Line Pull – WB/QB SEAL WB/BB KICK WB REVERSE POWER PASS
Defensive Team	7:30	Passing Defense RED/RED SPREAD
Conditioning	7:50	Push to failure – make leaders step up and push their team mates positively.
Team Circle	8:00	

NOTE: all QB and Receivers show up 15 minutes early in pads to run
Two-sided Uncovered Pass: On Defender. Work on ALL STOP, DUMP, WHEEL, and OUT route combination. All centers will execute ten direct and ten indirect snaps to each other prior to practice.

Event – Day 3	Time	Notes
Dynamic Warm Up	6:00	
OFF STANCE/LEG Progression	6:10	*Paired Live LEG Drill (full speed), install LEG & TURN*
TACKLING LEG Progression	6:15	*LEG Tackling Full Speed – Ball Carrier resist.*
Defensive Shed Progression	6:20	*Review four basic defensive shed.* *Install WHEEL technique*
Offensive INDIES	6:25	Backs Rep all SHIFT power series plays on air to the right All plays two times. All groups

Youth Double Wing II: The Gun!

		Rep all STAR power series plays to the right. All plays two times. All groups EAGLE RUN GAME TANK/STING/LEAD DRAW/DRAW Line – *Blocking Chute (LEG live, LEG & TURN)*
Defensive INDIES	6:50	EDD for all positions
Offensive Team	7:05	Perfection Drill 100 plays Hurry Up – behind by 16 x2 (mid field and our own goal line)
Special Teams	7:25	KOR/KO/PAT
Conditioning	7:50	Push to failure – make leaders step up and push their team mates positively.
Team Circle	8:00	

NOTE: all QB and Receivers show up 15 minutes early in pads to run
Two-sided Uncovered Pass: On Defender. Work on ALL STOP, DUMP, WHEEL, and OUT route combination. All centers will execute ten direct and ten indirect snaps to each other prior to practice.

Event – Day 4 Ignore if scrimmage that week.	Time	Notes
Dynamic Warm Up	6:00	
OFF STANCE/LEG Progression	6:10	*Paired Live LEG Drill (full speed), LEG & TURN(1/2 and full speed)*
TACKLING LEG Progression	6:15	*LEG Tackling Full Speed – Ball Carrier resist and ball carrier spin.*
Defensive Shed Progression	6:20	*Review four basic defensive shed. WHEEL technique*
Offensive INDIES	6:25	Backs

		Rep all SHIFT power series plays on air to the left
		All plays two times. All groups
		Rep all STAR power series plays to the left
		All plays two times. All groups
		EAGLE RUN GAME
		TANK/STING/LEAD DRAW/DRAW
		Line –
		SEAL,WIDE, KICK, SPRINT (bird dog, live) TANK, STING, DRAW, DEUCE (bird dog, live)
Defensive INDIES	6:50	EDD for all positions
Tackling Ckt & Pursuit Ckt	7:05	TACKLING CKT III (2 stations)
		PURSUIT CKT II (2 stations)
		Hurry Up – behind by 16 x2 (mid field and our own goal line)
Offensive Team	7:25	Half Line Pull
		WB/QB SEAL (BB SEAL)
		WB WIDE (BB WIDE)
		WB REVERSE
		WB/BB KICK
		POWER PASS
Conditioning	7:50	Push to failure – make leaders step up and push their team mates positively.
Team Circle	8:00	

NOTE: all QB and Receivers show up 15 minutes early in pads to run *Two-sided Uncovered Pass: On Defender. Work on ALL STOP, DUMP, WHEEL, and OUT route combination. All centers will execute ten direct and ten indirect snaps to each other prior to practice.*

Youth Double Wing II: The Gun!

Normal Game Week Practice Schedule

Event – Day 1	Time	Notes
Dynamic Warm Up	6:00	
OFF STANCE/LEG Progression	6:10	*Paired Live LEG Drill (full speed), LEG & TURN(1/2 and full speed)* *Review LEG progression if needed*
TACKLING LEG Progression	6:15	*LEG Tackling Full Speed – Ball Carrier resist, ball carrier spin, cut in confined space.*
Defensive Shed Progression	6:20	*Review five basic defensive sheds* *Install a specific shed for individual player strengths.*
Offensive INDIES	6:25	Backs *Basics – ball carrying, gauntlet, blocking* *Reps on Air – Power Game and/or Eagle Run Game* *Install new concepts* Line *Blocking Fundamentals Pulling Drills or Wall Drills Blocking Schemes on air,(½ speed, live)* *Install new concepts*
Defensive INDIES	6:50	EDD for all positions
Defensive Group	7:05	STACK Drills 1 thru 4 HOURGLASS Drills 1 thru 5 Work on specific areas of need based on offensive scout report of opponent
Offensive Group	7:25	Power - Half Line Pull drills or Half Line Wall Drills Or Passing Game –

		QB/WR/Backs (if power game make sure TE's are involved) LINE (pass pro schemes either power or eagle series)
Offensive Team	7:50	Power Hour Drill 10 yards from goal line. Or Perfection Drill Situational sets, hurry up, penalties, injuries. Either case 50 plays in 10 minutes
Team Circle	8:00	

NOTE: all QB and Receivers show up 15 minutes early in pads to run
Two-sided Uncovered Pass: On Defender. Work on passing concepts (review and install). All centers will execute ten direct and ten indirect snaps to each other prior to practice.

Event – Day 2	Time	Notes
Dynamic Warm Up	6:00	
OFF STANCE/LEG Progression	6:10	*Paired Live LEG Drill (full speed), LEG & TURN(1/2 and full speed)* *Review LEG progression if needed*
TACKLING LEG Progression	6:15	*LEG Tackling Full Speed – Ball Carrier resist, ball carrier spin, cut in confined space.*
Defensive Shed Progression	6:20	*Review five basic defensive sheds* *Install a specific shed for individual player strengths.*
Offensive INDIES	6:25	Backs *Basics – ball carrying, gauntlet, blocking* *Reps on Air –*

		Power Game and/or Eagle Run Game
		Install new concepts
		Line Blocking Fundamentals Pulling Drills or Wall Drills Blocking Schemes on air,(½ speed, live)
		Install new concepts
Defensive INDIES	6:50	EDD for all positions
Defensive Fundamentals	7:05	Tackling Ckt Or Pursuit Ckt Or Turnover Ckt
Offensive Group	7:20	Power - Half Line Pull drills or Half Line Wall Drills Or Passing Game – QB/WR/Backs (if power game make sure TE's are involved) LINE (pass pro schemes either power or eagle series)
Offensive Team Offensive Team (continued)	7:50	Power Hour Drill 10 yards from goal line. Or Perfection Drill Situational sets, hurry up, penalties, injuries. Either case 50 plays in 10 minutes
Team Circle	8:00	

NOTE: all QB and Receivers show up 15 minutes early in pads to run
Two-sided Uncovered Pass: On Defender. Work on passing concepts (review and install). All centers will execute ten direct and ten indirect snaps to each other prior to practice.

Event – Day 3 (Helmet and Shorts) Special Teams and Review	Time	Notes
Dynamic Warm Up	6:00	
Kick Off Return	6:10	
Kick Off	6:20	
PAT/FG	6:30	
PAT/FG/Punt Block	6:40	
Punt Return	6:50	
Defensive Scout Report Review	7:00	
Offensive Scout Report Review or Perfection Drill (75 plays)	7:15	
Team Circle	7:30	Go home

NOTE: all QB and Receivers show up 15 minutes early in pads to run
Two-sided Uncovered Pass: On Defender. Work on passing concepts (review and install).
All centers will execute ten direct and ten indirect snaps to each other prior to practice.

Game Day Pre-Game Warm Up

We use the same structure that we use at the front of our practices to get the kids mentally, emotionally, and physically ready to play the game. I have found that using the same structure gives the kids a consistent set of drills and warm ups that get them ready for the game as well as practice. The warm ups get them out of "wake up mode" and into "game mode". The blocking warm up, tackling warm up, and defensive shed warm up are done at half speed the first two reps and full speed as violently as they can the remaining three to five reps. The effect we want for our kids is to turn on the competitive juices and flip the 'hitting' switch, so they are ready to play. By doing this we have consistently come out and not had our team "asleep on the field" the first series or first half of a game. They are alert, they know their jobs, and they know their gear and their teammates are ready.

Pre-Warm Up	Time	Notes
Dynamic Warm Up	0000	
OFF STANCE/LEG Progression Blocking Warm Up	0010	*Paired Live LEG Drill (1/2 speed & full speed), (2 reps each)* *LEG & TURN(1/2 and full speed) (2 reps each)*
TACKLING LEG Progression Tackling Warm Up	0015	*LEG Tackling Full Speed – Ball Carrier resist, ball carrier spin, cut in confined space.(2 reps each)*
Defensive Shed Progression	0020	*Rep Sheds that you will use in the game.*
PAT/FG	0025	*Starting Offense*
Review KOR	0035	Review Set up/Alignment/Who goes where/backups
Review KO	0040	Review Set up/Alignment/Who goes where/backups
Defensive EDD	0045	Review fundamentals
Defensive Review	0055	Defensive Review
Offensive Team Reps Until Start of Game	0060	Rep plays/Grab water/Go to the bathroom.
Team Captains to Officials		Always take Tails. Defer if we know the other team is outmanned so we can managed the game in the later half. Always shake your opponents hand and wish them good luck.

Appendix V
Order of Install

One of the questions asked most often by new coaches is "what plays should be installed first?" My first response is "what age group are you coaching, what level of experience do you have coaching, and what level of experience do your kids have playing organized football?"

I think there are really three levels of installs and they are totally dependent on the kids you are coaching and the coaching staff's base of knowledge of football and the double wing offense.

Categories

1)   None or very little knowledge of football coaching and the double wing offense. Kids are eight years are younger with little to no football experience.
2)   None or very little knowledge of football coaching and the double wing offense. Kids are older than eight years and have limited football experience.
3)   Experience coaching football and very little knowledge of the double wing offense. Kids are older than eight years and have a small amount of football experience.

Most coaches that ask me this question fall in one of these categories. Otherwise, they would probably know what plays to install based on the information provided, their knowledge of what the coaching staff can handle, and what the capabilities of the kids based on athletic ability and maturity (biological and age wise).

Below are three orders of installation based on the aforementioned categories.

Category 1

1)   Buck Wedge Series should be installed first (pre-season)
- Shift Rip 30 Wedge Right Buck
- Shift Rip 28 Wedge Right Arc Buck
- Shift Rip 17 Wall Right Drag Pass Buck
- Shift Rip 47 Wall Right Drag Pass Buck
- Flip and teach in the opposite direction
2)   Power Series Power Plays (prior to first game if ready otherwise delay)
- Shift Rip 26 Seal Right
- Shift Liz 45 Seal Left
- Shift Rip 28 Wide Right
- Shift Liz 47 Wide Right
- Shift Rip 30 Wedge Right
- Shift Liz 30 Wedge Right
3)   Additional Power Series Power Plays (when ready and if needed)

- Shift Rip 10 Wedge Right
- Shift Liz 10 Wedge Right
- Shift Rip 16 Seal Right
- Shift Liz 15 Seal Left
- Shift Rip Power Pass Right
- Shift Liz Power Pass Left

4)   Misdirection Power Series Plays (when ready and if needed)
- Shift Rip 47 Wide Reverse Left (Razzle audible as well)
- Shift Liz 28 Wide Reverse Right (Razzle audible as well)
- Shift Rip 33 Kick Left
- Shift Liz 34 Kick Right
- Boot or Waggle Audible

5)   Anything else you feel they will need or execute well.

6)   Twelve plays total plus two audibles (twenty four if you count both ways – I don't because we flip our line and I don't feel the backs have very hard responsibilities).

Category 2

1)   Power Series Power Plays (prior to first game if ready otherwise delay)
- Shift Rip 26 Seal Right
- Shift Liz 45 Seal Left
- Shift Rip 16 Seal Right
- Shift Liz 15 Seal Left
- Shift Rip 28 Wide Right
- Shift Liz 47 Wide Right
- Shift Rip Power Pass Right
- Shift Liz Power Pass Left
- Shift Rip 30 Wedge
- Shift Liz 30 Wedge
- Shift Rip 10 Wedge
- Shift Liz 10 Wedge

2)   Misdirection Power Series Plays (when ready and if needed)
- Shift Rip 47 Wide Reverse Left (Razzle audible as well)
- Shift Liz 28 Wide Reverse Right (Razzle audible as well)
- Shift Rip 33 Kick Left
- Shift Liz 34 Kick Right
- Shift Rip 45 Kick Left
- Shift Liz 26 Kick Right
- Boot/Waggle Audible

3)   Anything else you feel they will need or execute well.

Category 3

1)   Power Series Power Plays (prior to first game if ready otherwise delay)
- Shift Rip 26 Seal Right
- Shift Liz 45 Seal Left

- Shift Rip 16 Seal Right
- Shift Liz 15 Seal Left
- Shift Rip 28 Wide Right
- Shift Liz 47 Wide Right
- Shift Rip Power Pass Right
- Shift Liz Power Pass Left
- Shift Rip 30 Wedge
- Shift Liz 30 Wedge
- Shift Rip 10 Wedge
- Shift Liz 10 Wedge
- Uncovered Pass concepts/audible

2) Misdirection Power Series Plays (when ready and if needed)
- Shift Rip 47 Wide Reverse Left (Razzle audible as well)
- Shift Liz 28 Wide Reverse Right (Razzle audible as well)
- Shift Rip 33 Kick Left
- Shift Liz 34 Kick Right
- Shift Rip 45 Kick Left
- Shift Liz 26 Kick Right
- Boot/Waggle Audible
- Shift Rip 28 Monster Sweep Right
- Shift Liz 47 Monster Sweep Left

3) Anything else you feel they will need or execute well.

This is a simple installation based on the experience of the staff and the team. Obviously you can add and take away from it based on what you see with your specific team. It should not be something you set in stone based simply on the fact that I have put it on paper. Every year my basic installation stays the same but I vary the installation of the other plays (outside of power, power sweep, power pass) based on the speed my team is learning them, executing them, and if there is a need for them.

Appendix VI
Play List Charts

Tight/Shift/Nova Power Series Play List	Tight/Shift/Nova Lead Series Play List	Edge Tags
Rip 26 Seal Right Liz 45 Seal Left	Rip 28 Pin Right Liz 47 Pin Left	Shift: • On • Over • Loose (Loose Over) • Nasty (Nasty Over)
Rip 28 Wide Right Liz 47 Wide Left	Rip 37 Pin Right Liz 38 Pin Left	Star: • Over • Bunch (Bunch Over) • Trips (Trips Over)
Rip 28 Monster Sweep Right Liz 28 Monster Sweep Left	Rip 13 ISO Right Liz 14 ISO Left	Comet: • Over
Rip Power Pass Right Liz Power Pass Left	Rip 23 ISO Right Liz 24 ISO Left	Nova: • On • Offset • Over • Loose (Loose Over) • Nasty (Nasty Over)
Rip 30 Wedge Right Liz 30 Wedge Right	Rip 14 Double Right Liz 13 Double Left	**Uncovered Audibles**
Rip 10 Wedge Right Liz 10 Wedge Right	Rip 31 Dive Right Liz 32 Dive Left	Right Split End - Rookie Left Split End - Look
Rip 33 Kick Left Liz 34 Kick Right	Rip 14 Dive Right Liz 13 Dive Left	Right Slot - Broken Left Slot - Blender
Rip 45 Kick Left Liz 26 Kick Right	Rip Drag Pass Right Liz Drag Pass Left	**Key Breaker/Influence Audibles**
Rip 47 Wide Reverse Left Liz 28 Wide Reverse Right	Rip Reverse Pass Left Liz Reverse Pass Right	Away from Power Audibles: • Razzle (WB Reverse) • Boot • Fly • Jump •
		Away from Misdirection Audibles:

		• Away • Pitch
Additional Power Plays		
Shift Rip 34 Kick Right Trap Shift Liz 33 Kick Left Trap		
Shift Rip 25 Kick Left Cutback Shift Liz 46 Kick Right Cutback		
Shift Rip Fan Pass Right Shift Liz Fan Pass Left		
Tornado Series		
Shift Rip 30 Wedge Right Tornado Shift Liz 30 Wedge Right Tornado		
Shift Rip 33 Kick Left Tornado Shift Liz 34 Kick Right Tornado		
Shift Rip 16 Kick Right Tornado Shift Liz 15 Kick Left Tornado		
Shift Rip 28 Wide Right Tornado Shift Liz 47 Wide Left Tornado		
Shift Rip 47 Wide Reverse Tornado Shift Liz 28 Wide Reverse Tornado		
Buck Wedge Series		
Shift Rip 30 Wedge Right Buck Shift Liz 30 Wedge Right Buck		
Shift Rip 17 Wall Right Drag Pass Buck Shift Liz 18 Wall Right Drag Pass Buck		
Shift Rip 28 Wedge Arc Buck Shift Liz 47 Wedge Arc Buck		
Shift Rip 47 Wall Drag Pass Buck Shift Liz 28 Wall Drag Pass Buck		

Comet **Power Series Play List**	Comet Lead Series **Play List**	
Rip16 Seal Right Liz 15 Seal Left	Rip 18 Pin Right Liz 17 Pin Left	
Rip18 Wide Right Liz 17 Wide Left	Rip13 ISO Right Liz 14 ISO Left	
Rip18 Monster Sweep Right Liz 17 Monster Sweep Left	Rip 14 Double Right Liz 13 Double Left	
Rip Power Pass Right Liz Power Pass Left	Rip Drag Pass Right Liz Drag Pass Left	
Rip 30 Wedge Right Liz 30 Wedge Right	Rip Reverse Pass Left Liz Reverse Pass Right	
Rip 20 Wedge Right Liz 20 Wedge Right		
Rip 23 Kick Left Liz 44 Kick Right		
Rip 45 Kick Left Liz 26 Kick Right		
Rip 47 Wide Reverse Left Liz 28 Wide Reverse Right		
Additional Power Plays		
Rip 34 Kick Right Trap Liz 33 Kick Left Trap		
Rip 15 Kick Left Cutback Liz 16 Kick Right Cutback		
Rip Fan Pass Right Liz Fan Pass Left		

Star Power Series Play List	Star Lead Series Play List	
Rip 36 Seal Right Liz 35 Seal Left	Rip 38 Pin Right Liz 37 Pin Left	
Rip 38 Wide Right Rip 37 Wide Left	Rip 13 ISO Right Liz 14 ISO Left	
Rip 38 Monster Sweep Right Liz 37 Monster Sweep Left	Rip 34 Double Right Liz 33 Double Left	
Rip Power Pass Right Liz Power Pass Left	Rip 31 Dive Right Liz 32 Dive Left	
Rip 30 Wedge Right Liz 30 Wedge Left	Rip 14 Dive Right Liz 13 Dive Left	
Rip 10 Wedge Right Liz 10 Wedge Left	Rip Drag Pass Right Liz Drag Pass Left	
Rip 23 Kick Left Liz 44 Kick Right	Rip Reverse Pass Left Liz Reverse Pass Right	
Rip 45 Kick Left Liz 26 Kick Right		
Rip 47 Wide Reverse Left Liz 28 Wide Reverse Right		
Rip 36 Seal Right Liz 35 Seal Left		
Additional Power Plays		
Rip 34 Kick Right Trap Liz 33 Kick Left Trap		
Rip 35 Kick Left Cutback Liz 36 Kick Right Cutback		
Rip Fan Pass Right Liz Fan Pass Left		

Appendix VII
Pass Protection

Pass protection schemes are probably not an often discussed topic in most Double Wing playbooks or documents, but they are just as important as run blocking schemes. There are some distinct differences in how I use pass protection in this offense. I think it is very important that elements that are taught are easily transferred to other concepts in your offense and your overall scheme. This is probably one area I have probably altered and tinkered with the most as I have run the Double Wing. Passing has always been a very big part of what I do because I started my coaching career in a very pass heavy Run & Shoot/West Coast hybrid offense that relied on very solid pass protection schemes. For a very long time I tried to stick with the Double Wing pass protection philosophy but in my opinion there are elements of the pass protection theory that are flawed. Especially when you consider it at the youth level where pass protection in a power running game offense is often not as developed. This is a very important consideration because practice time, especially individual and group drills are where games and seasons are really won. With only a small percentage of your practice time spent on pass protection techniques, fundamentals, and schemes, how you get these schemes installed is going to be very significant to the success of your passing offense. A comprehensive discussion of the details related to drills and progressions for pass protection is beyond the scope of this book*, nevertheless I would like to introduce some important concepts that should serve as a good foundation on which to build.

The basic techniques and teaching progressions need to mirror how you already teach and what the players already know to increase the mastery level of these schemes naturally. The schemes themselves need to be simple but very efficient in their purpose and obviously that purpose is to protect the passer and ensure there is a high rate of success when we do pass (high passing completion percentage and a low turnover/sack rate).

*A detailed discussion of pass protection schemes, drills, and progressions will be published in the upcoming book YDW: The Passing Game.

Elements of a Successful Passing Game

In order to have an effective passing game you have to have a good passer, good receivers, and good pass protection. When it comes to pass protection I am not concerned with my line faking run or pulling. I am concerned with the play being successful and a major portion of that is protecting the passer. I let my eligible players fake and misdirect as my line protects. I have found that even though my offensive line does not pull on passing plays very few defenses can, or even attempt to try and recognize that, because our backfield action always appears to be moving forward or towards the perimeter. This forces the defense to respect run, especially when you consider we run the ball 80% or more of the time.

Levels of Pass Protection

Pass protection is broken into two levels of protection. Basic pass protection which is built off our wedge run blocking scheme - we use it for drop back and roll out type plays against basic defenses that are young and inexperienced. I also have a more advanced set of protection schemes for older teams and more advanced defenses that are well coached.

Wall Schemes

Wall – (Figure VII-A) is simply a wedge scheme with the center firing out to create vertical movement so the rest of the line can mesh. This basic concept eliminates inside penetration and the backs are responsible for sealing/walling out the edge defenders. The reasoning behind this is pretty simple often the best rushers are often on the edge and offensively our best athletes are in the backfield so obviously the best match up is linemen protect the interior and athletes (backfield) protect the edges.

Dash – (Figure VII-B) is wall protection with the backs walling in the edge defenders on the play side so the passer can get outside.

These are very simple schemes used against simple defenses with little experience in passing rushing. I have used them for years and have had very good success with them; so much so that when I was building a brand new select club team of 5th and 6th graders our entire protection scheme was built around these two concepts the first year and we managed to get a very young and inexperienced team into the playoffs keeping to these basic pass protection schemes. I have used installed these schemes with second graders all the way up to 6th graders and have had success with them at every level so they are very consistent schemes when used in conjunction with our wedge run blocking scheme.

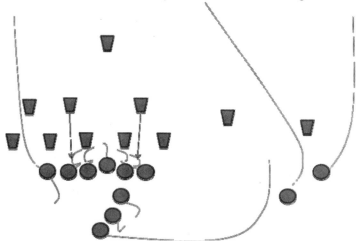

Figure VII-A. Wall protection out of Shift Loose Rip

In the wall scheme (Figure VII-A) if the center is covered he fires off and engages for three steps (LEG) and creates vertical movement. The guards and tackles mesh as if forming a wedge; so for the first three steps this is going to appear as if it is a wedge play. Once they mesh hips with the center they simply stay hip-to-hip. They allow no defender to their inside and force to the next blocker outside. The idea is to force every defender to go around the wall. If uncovered, he takes three steps and all three are short power steps. He then sets up and lets the rest of the line mesh.

BB or TB (depending on the pass pattern will cross over step and wall out the first defender to show past the wall tackle's outside hip.

In the power game this is really a 6 or 7 man pass pro because the back side TE can stay. If he is not involved in the pass pattern, he will simply HHM (HINGE HINGE MIRROR).

The use of the OVER tag will move the pull tackle to the play side and extend the wall on the wall side for additional protection so use over in the pass game to add additional protection on either side.

RB call – if we have a one on one situation and are facing a very aggressive pass rushing DE we can call CUT and the RB will cut the DE has he comes into the pocket. The RB will move to meet him as he normally does but just as contact is made he will take his outside shoulder and cross body cut the DE from outside in (NCAA Rules only).
You can also keep both the BB and the BSWB (TB) in and both block the play side with the BB taking first defender to show on the wall tackles outside hip and the BSWB (TB) taking the first defender to show past the BB. This is an easy way to account for the overloads on the wall side.

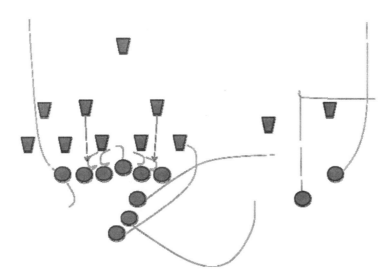

Figure VII-B. Dash Protection out of Shift Loose Rip

In the Dash scheme (Figure VII-B) the center, if covered, fires off and engages for three steps (LEG) and creates vertical movement. The guards and tackles mesh as if forming a wedge. Meshing hips with the center and so on. They allow no defender to their inside and force to the next blocker outside. The idea is to force every defender to go around the wall. If uncovered he takes three steps and all three are short power steps and he sets up and lets the rest of the line mesh.

BB or TB (depending on the pass pattern will cross over step gain depth and log (wall in) the first defender to show past the wall tackle's outside hip so the passer can bootleg/roll out side.

In the power game this is really a 6 or 7 man pass pro because the back side TE can stay. If he is not involved in the pass pattern, he will simply HHM (HINGE HINGE MIRROR).

The nice thing about this pass protection is that at the younger age the wedge is often run a lot; when the defense sees wedge the perimeter defenders attack the LOS aggressively and this allows us to wall them inside relatively easily. Even if the OLB gets penetration on the edge, the passer is often around him as his angle is inside to stop the wedge.

Advanced Pass Protection Schemes

Deuce – (Figure VII-C) is a drop back six/seven man pass protection scheme for the power schemes. In our power series if the backside tight end (pull tight end) is not involved in the pass pattern he simply mimics the rule of the pull tackle (back side tackle) and it becomes a six man pass protection scheme vice seven man. The RB blocks to the side on which he is aligned.

Joker – (Figure VII-D) is a drop back five man pass protection scheme we use when we want to release five receivers into the route. It is not often used in the power series, but if I do want to release all five eligible I want to have the pass protection in place to handle it. This scheme is often used in the eagle series when we want get the RB involved in the passing game.

Slide – (Figure VII-E) is a drop back seven/eight man pass protection scheme that uses slide protection pass concepts with the RB blocking to the side that is opposite to that on which he is aligned. This concept is a nice scheme designed to mimic the running game due to the crossing action of the backs.

Sprint – (Figure VII-F) is a roll out six/seven man pass protection scheme that employs slide protection pass concepts with the RB blocking the perimeter defender on the play side. It follows the same format as the Deuce protection as far as the back side tight end is concerned.

In the YDW you can use WALL or DUECE/JOKER/SLIDE for drop back passing and you can use DASH or SPRINT for rollout/bootleg plays depending on the experience of the coaching staff, the teams, and the opposing defense.

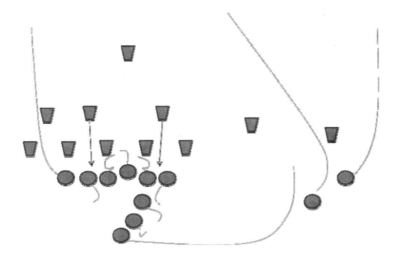

Figure VII-C. Deuce Protection in Shift Loose Rip

In the Deuce scheme (Figure VII-C), if the center is uncovered and no backer is over, he will double (SSM) with an OG that needs help. If neither OG needs help, he will drop down and work to the backside OT that needs help inside (KKM). This can be pre-determined or called via code word from offensive line. If covered, he will LEM (load explode mirror) the defender in front of him.

Guards will LEM if covered; if uncovered they will KKM with butt facing the passer. They should take short kick steps. Look for any defender coming inside/out mirror and LEM when he comes; if no one shows they can help to the center first and tackle second (SSM).

Tackles will LEM if covered; if uncovered they will KKM with butt facing the passer. They need to get depth quickly on their first step if they KKM. Look for any defender coming inside/out mirror and LEM when he comes. If no one shows they can help inside to the guard.

BB or BSWB (TB) will double the near side edge rusher (OT's man) on the outside or in the case of a overload/hanger (extra defender) will pick up the first defender to show on the outside hip of the near tackle.

In the power game this is really a 6 or 7 man pass pro because the back side TE can stay and mirror the backside tackle. If he is not involved in the pass pattern he will simply mimic the rule of the backside tackle.

You can also keep both the BB and the BSWB (TB) in and both block the play side with the BB taking first defender to show on the wall tackles outside hip and the BSWB (TB) taking the first defender to show past the BB. This is an easy way to account for the overloads on the wall side. This actually converts it to an eight man protection scheme if needed.

RB call – if we have a one-on-one situation and are facing a very aggressive pass rushing defender we can call CUT and the RB will cut the defender has he comes into the pocket.

The RB will move to meet him as he normally does but just as contact is made he will take his outside shoulder and cross body cut the defender from outside in. (NCAA Rules only)

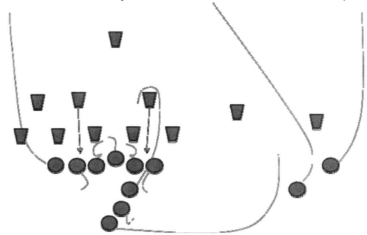

Figure VII-D. Joker Pass Protection out of Shift Loose Rip

In the Joker scheme (Figure VII-D), if the center is uncovered and no backer is over, he will double (SSM) with an OG that needs help. If neither OG needs help, he will drop down and work to the backside OT that needs help inside (KKM). This can be pre-determined or called via code word from offensive line. If covered, he will LEM (load explode mirror) the defender in front of him.

Guards will LEM if covered; if uncovered they will KKM with butt facing the passer. They should take short kick steps. Look for any defender coming inside/out mirror and LEM when he comes. If no one shows, he can help toward the center first and tackle second (SSM).

Tackles will LEM if covered; if uncovered they will KKM with butt facing the passer. They need to get depth quickly on their first step if they KKM. Look for any defender coming inside/out mirror and LEM when he comes. If no one shows they can help inside to the guard.

Both the BB and the TB are involved in the pass routes and will release to their respective sides (in tight he would motion and release to the motion side).

You can tag this with DELAY to tell them to first check and then release if blitz pressure is a concern. In that case the BB will check inside from the center's far side hip to the inside hip of the near side tackle. The TB (BSWB) will check from the outside hip of the near side tackle to the inside hip of the near side guard. If a defender does come they will block their defender and not release (this is an optional teach) and if the RB is in a primary route they don't check.

In the power game this is really a 5 or 6 man pass pro because the back side TE can stay and mirror the backside tackle. If he is not involved in the pass pattern he will simply mimic the rule of the backside tackle.

This pass protection allows us to get our backs into a route to exploit a defense that is not covering all of our backs or the space they attack.

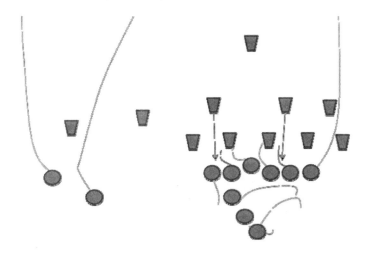

Figure VII-E. Slide Protection from Shift Loose Liz

In the Slide scheme (Figure VII-E), if the center is uncovered and no backer is over, he will double (SSM) with the wall OG. If covered or the backer over is a threat to blitz, he will LEM.

Wall guard will LEM if covered; if uncovered they will SSM towards the wall tackle and double with wall tackle if no other defender shows.

Wall tackle will LEM if covered; if uncovered he will KKM and gain depth with butt facing the passer. If no one shows he will work inside and help the wall guard from outside.

Pull guard will LEM if covered; if uncovered he will SSM towards the center and double with the center if no other defender shows.

Pull tackle will LEM if covered; if uncovered he will SSM towards the pull guard and double with the guard if no other defender shows.

If the Pull Tight end is not involved in the pass pattern he will mirror the tackles rule. No defender shows he will double with the pull tackle.

BB has the first defender to show on the outside hip of the pull tackle (pull tight end if he stays in) and wall out the first defender to cross his face.

BSWB (TB) can double a tough edge defender with the BB on the outside using the same rule as the BB or in the case of an overload he will take the first defender to cross his face as he sets under the BB.

As you cross the QB's face flash fake the hand off to hold the LB's in place so the receivers have more space to operate and slow the initial pass rush this makes everyone's job easier.

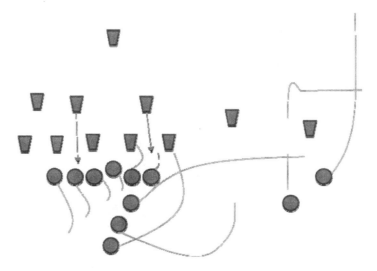

Figure VII-F. Sprint Protection in Shift Loose Rip

In the Sprint scheme (Figure VII-F), if the center is uncovered and no backer is over, he will hinge (HHM) with butt facing the passer. Block from play side hip to away hip helping the wall guard first if needed. If covered or the backer over is a threat to blitz, he will LEM.

Wall guard will LEM if covered; if uncovered they will SSM towards the wall tackle and double with wall tackle if no other defender shows.

Wall tackle will LEM if covered; if uncovered he will SSM to the next defender outside (this often means he will double the defender that the RB is logging (walling inside).

Pull guard he will hinge (HHM) with butt facing the passer; block with inside out priority. He will stay glued to the near hip of the center and bit deeper.

Pull tackle he will hinge (HHM) with butt facing the passer; block with inside out priority. He will stay glued to the near hip of the pull guard and a bit deeper.

Pull tight end he will hinge (HHM) with butt facing the passer; block with inside out priority. He will stay glued to the near hip of the pull tackle and a bit deeper. The pull tight end might not be involved in the pass protection if he is involved in the pass pattern.
RB (either BB or BSWB [TB]) will cross over and log (wall in) the first defender on the outside hip of the wall tackle.

As you cross the QB's face, flash fake the hand off to hold the LB's in place so the receivers have more space to operate and slow the initial pass rush. This makes everyone's job easier.

Pass Protection Progression

First, when we teach pass protection, we explain we will always be in zero splits so we should never see inside penetration because you will always have help.

Remember blockers on the edge have the toughest job as they often face the most athletic defenders. This is one of the reasons why I advocate having your better athletes from the outside in on the line. In EAGLE with five men on the line, our PULL GUARD moves to the left side tackle spot and the PULL TACKLE moves to right tackle while our WALL GUARD moves to the right guard and WALL TACKLE moves to left guard. This puts our best athletes on the edge and in a position to block those edge rushers.

Second we use a mirror drill with two cones and a defender and a blocker to teach blockers how to properly mirror whether it is LEM, HHM, SSM.

Modified LEG rules for pass pro:

LEM: LOAD, EXPLODE, MIRROR: Used when covered and it simulates our LEG but after making contact we mirror the defender as we give ground in very small chunks so we can stay in front of the defender. NUMBERS IN FRONT OF NUMBERS - NEVER LET EITHER OF HIS FEET GET BY YOU.

SLIDE, SLIDE, MIRROR (SSM): Used when uncovered and it basically has the blocker slide with near foot, far foot (explode into defender's chest), and mirror defender as above. This allows us to double up on a covered defender. If a line backer blitzes as the blocker slides he looks to backer over and if he comes he LEM to block that backer coming.

KICK, KICK, MIRROR (KKM): Used for an uncovered edge blocker in JOKER/DEUCE protection. KICKSLIDE with outside foot, KICKSLIDE with inside foot (explode into defender), mirror defender as above. Getting depth and width with the first step is important, as well as keeping the hips square on the first step to make sure the rusher doesn't make an inside move. On the second step, snap hips and on the third step, mirror the defender.

HINGE, HINGE, MIRROR (HHM): Used on the backside of SPRINT and SLIDE. The HINGE is much like the KICKSLIDE except the outside foot moves inside and back at a 45 degree angle and follows (HINGE-HINGE). On HINGE the outside foot will go back instead of out as he collapses inside. The outside foot always moves first because we assume contact is made on the second step and we want the inside foot down and planted.

Modified LEG (LEM progression)

1) LOAD/EXPLODE (we can already do this but we remind them of the progression because we want it to look like LEG). The key here is to make a violent hit on the EXPLODE that stands the defender up and negates his momentum and slows his rush.

2) After EXPLODE on the third step and every step there after the blocker gets good Z in the body and mirrors the defender (knees and hips). We yell RESET right as he takes his second step to remind him on his third step his body must be bent at the hips and knees.

The coach will line up all the blockers with about 1 yard of space in between them and go through the LEM...moving his hands/ball to simulate a rusher trying to get around the blocker so that on MIRROR they move their feet and body. LOAD and EXPLODE steps are 6 inches (small steps) but the MIRROR phase they can open up a little to make sure their body stays in front of the defender. Their steps should never be so wide that they lose their bend or balance.

Modified LEG (SSM progression)

1) SLIDE - SLIDE(EXPLODE): The first step is a slide step lateral staying in front of the defender he is sliding to the call side he can give up ground on both the near and far slide step so that he stays in front of the defender and keeps between the defender and passer. On the second step (far foot taking the second follow on slide step) he explodes into the defender to negate his rush and stand him up.

2) Every step thereafter is a mirror step as above.

The coach will use the same single file line as above and repeat the SSM to the left and right using the same method as above.

Modified LEG (KKM progression)

1) KICKSLIDE: The first step is the outside foot taking a quick big step back to get his body in between the defender and the QB. He should maintain BEND and BALANCE. Get numbers and feet pointed at the defender as he steps on his second step. First KICK is square to the line.

2) KICKSLIDE: follow on second step with inside foot. Another short quick step as he explodes into the defender to negate his rush and stand him up. Second KICK is numbers pointed at the defender as this ensures if the defender fakes and outside move and cuts inside the blocker is in position to engage him.

3) MIRROR - as above but maintain inside leverage by swinging hips inside as the need arises.

NOTE - On hinge we simply teach the blocker to take the foot straight back as he pivots, and on the second step he steps inside as the body turns to hinge off. We don't separate the two because the method is very simple, but we do teach the HINGE HINGE MIRROR first as we always install the POWER PASS first. The transition from HHM to KKM is very easy to teach as the basics are already taught, only differences in the footwork need to be addressed.

We teach this as the line progression when we do pass protection:

1) LEM (3 to 6 times)

2) SSM (L&R) 2 to 4 times each

3) HHM (L&R) 2 to 4 times each...once we install EAGLE, we do 2 to 4 HHM, and 2 to 4 KKM

Appendix VIII
Running Back Development

In order for your backs to be effective they must be aggressive blockers and good fakers, as well as runners. This offense requires that everyone not carrying the ball either block or fake. Executing these critical actions correctly makes this offense very deadly. The fewer defenders chasing the actual runner means more opportunities for him to have a breakaway play (Fewer Defenders to ball = Bigger chance of a TD!). Stress the little things at all times like proper stance, location, footwork, ball handling, and path to daylight. It is the little things that make each back and your offense successful.

Offensive Back Priorities:

1) Be an aggressive and fundamentally sound blocker.
2) Protect the ball at all times.
3) Hit the proper lane.
4) Get up field when you see daylight.
5) Never let a defender hit you. Make contact first.
6) Never let a single defender bring you down.
7) Never ever take negative yardage to get away from a defender.
8) Fake as if you have the ball and are really running with it (rock the cradle).

The Devil is in the Details

Although this offense is heavily geared to the offensive line, the reality is that every player on this offense must contribute in a positive and meaningful way for it to work. Because this offense is not an "athlete based" offense, i.e. it doesn't require a superstar at one or more of the skill positions to be effective, it does require that the level of execution be high at every position. One small mistake at any position can compromise the effectiveness of the offense. Since we deliberately play in a very compressed space, the margin for error is very small, and the consequence of the errors more detrimental as compared to an expanded front (specifically with wider splits). The blocking and faking of the backs is essential to the offense being successful. For example, the Power Play requires the blocking back and the quarterback to kick out the first defender to cross their respective faces; if either fails to accomplish this action, the play will likely fail, regardless of whether or not the line is doing their job. If the XX wingback doesn't carry out a good fake and the backside wing back doesn't fake his sweep the blocking back running wedge will be less effective as the perimeter defenders immediately collapse from the outside in, as they perceive no threat on their edge. Hold your backs accountable for being perfect in their execution. Stance, alignment, and technique are just as important to the backs as they are to the line.

Mentality of Contact (Tim Murphy – Head Coach Clovis East High School)

"We Break Tackles"

"First and Foremost you are a power runner who takes pride in breaking tackles! Breaking tackles has more to do with will and effort than anything else. I don't care if the entire defense hits you, jumps on you, or trips you. You will not go down!"

Note: Tim Murphy developed a great DVD on Running Back Development and I strongly recommend getting it for your team. It is one of the best Coaching DVD's you will get on developing the attitude and skills of your running back. You can find it at http://www.coachtimmurphy.com/Videos/videos.html

Training the Backs

Key elements:

1. Ball Security and Ball Handling (Protect the ball)
2. Good Stance and Position (QB/BB/WB)
3. Blocking
4. Faking
5. Footwork
6. Schemes
7. Power Running (make contact first! Better to be the hammer than the anvil!)

Running Back Escape Moves

These are moves that allow the running back or receiver to escape a defender prior to or during an attempt to make a tackle.

Ball Leverage

The running back must always keep the ball on the opposite side of the defenders who are approaching him. If he is near the sideline the ball will always go on the side near the boundary. This allows the runner to use the free arm, and it ensures that if the ball is stripped (it never should be) there is a good chance it will fall safely out of bounds.

Boundary and the Ball Carrier

A ball carrier should never ever go out of bounds willingly. He should always turn and attack the defender prior to the defender being ready to strike the ball carrier. Defenders are not used to the ball carriers attacking them and we have to make the ball carriers understand that they must become the aggressor and attack the defenders, hitting them first.

Using the Free Arm (based on Tim Murphy's presentation on RB Development given at the 5th Annual Double Wing Symposium in 2008)

Stiff Arm – This is a move with the free arm attacking the defender to push him away. The ball-carrier can fully extend his other arm, the elbow should not be locked but slightly bent, and outstretching his palm with thumb down. Then, the ball-carrier pushes directly outwards with the palm of his hand onto the chest, far shoulder, or the crown of the head of the would-be tackler. The stiff arm is a pushing action, rather than a striking action. A stiff-arm should cause the tackler to be driven to the ground, taking him out of the play. Even if the tackler keeps his feet, it becomes impossible for him to complete a tackle, as he cannot come close enough to get his body on the ball carrier or wrap his arms around the ball-carrier. It is executed on a defender coming from the side or at an angle.

Rip – This is a violent upward action coming from the hip with the open arm ripping through the defenders front arm and/or shoulder. The forearm, elbow, and bicep are used to strike the defender's arm and lift it out of the way as the ball carrier goes by. Where the stiff arm is used against a defender that is closing ground from an arm's length away or greater, the rip is used against defenders that are closer than an arm's length. It is executed on a defender coming from the side or at an angle and at a distance shorter than an arm's length.

Lift – This is a violent upward action with the free arm on a defender coming from the front. As the defender approaches the ball carrier loads his body and unloads his body and free arm into the defender's breast plate to lift him up and out of the way so that he cannot wrap up or tackle him. The use of the body, open shoulder, and open forearm are very important to the success of this action.

Escape Moves

Jump Cut (Figure VIII-A): an explosive move that has the ball carrier load or sink his body just as the defender approaches and he jumps by explosively unloading off his offside foot (1) and to the side that the defender his most vulnerable, landing on his near foot then his opposite foot, and then immediately accelerating forward and away from the defender. The feet should be slightly staggered as they land to assist in acceleration (it doesn't really matter how they are staggered).

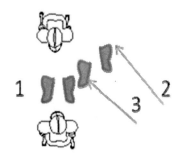

Figure VIII-A. Jump Cut Escape Move

Speed Cut (Figure VIII-B): this is a basic non-contact single juke move as the defender approaches. The ball carrier takes a juke step to the opposite side of the defender. It should be a big lateral step (not enough to remove the runner's center of gravity or balance) and he immediately shifts and steps to the other side and accelerates past the defender.

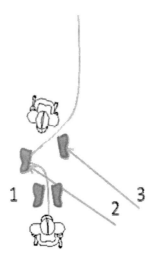

Figure VIII-B. Speed Cut Escape Move

Power Cut (Figure VIII-C): this is the same as a speed cut but contact is involved. On the cutback as the ball carrier takes his juke step he initiates contact through the opposite shoulder and executes a rip or a stiff arm as he goes by. This is a violent and very physical move to attack a defender so that the ball carrier can impose his will on the defender.

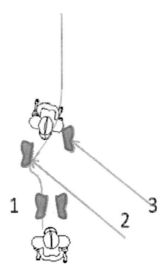

Figure VIII-C. Power Cut Escape Move

Bull Rush (Figure VIII-D): this is a simple head on attack by the ball carrier before the defender is ready to tackle the ball carrier. The use of the lift technique is used on a head on defender as the ball carrier will turn into the defender and attack him before he loads his body.

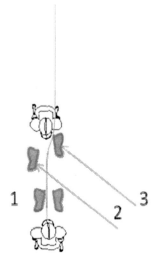

Figure VIII-D. Bull Rush Escape Move

Speed Spin (Figure VIII-E): a move that has the ball carrier take a short juke step with the opposite side foot and then an additional step with the spin side to the opposite side as he rotates his body 360 degrees and goes around the defender without making contact.

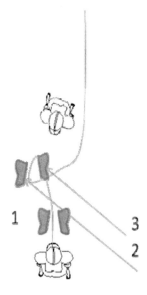

Figure VIII-E. Speed Spin Escape Move

Power Spin (Figure VIII-F): is the same as a speed spin except that contact is made and the ball carrier spins off the defender. Typically made while executing a rip or lift technique so that the defender will aggressively attack the ball carrier to the initial side he is moving.

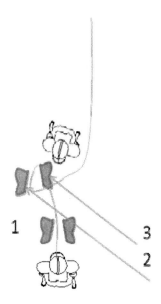

Figure VIII-F. Power Spin Escape Move

Drills used to Teach the Backs

When we start teaching backs, we stress stance, ball security, and ball handling first and foremost. Once we feel that all the backs understand the emphasis we place on them and they should place on protecting the ball, we move to blocking. Every back on this offense is required to know how to effectively execute the blocks for his position. Once these are established we start working on running schemes and within this process we start to emphasize faking and proper footwork. AT ALL TIMES, WE STRESS BALL SECURITY. We stress these areas specifically when teaching our backs the running game.

- Stay low and protect the ball
- Explosiveness
- Attack the hole
- Know the blocking scheme
- First daylight you see get up field immediately
- We never get tackled by one defender - period
- We hit them before they hit us

Stances

QB – balanced pigeon-toed two point stance. Low stance with bending at the hips and knees so that he is under center.

- Feet back as far as possible with arms fully extended to avoid colliding with pulling linemen (guards). Elbows should be slightly bent.
- Narrow stance with toes pointed in (pigeon toes) to make pivoting easier.
- Feet are shoulder width a part and knees are slightly bent.

BB – balanced three point stance. Head up.

WB – balanced two point stance tilted so that he is aiming right at the outside hip of the EMLOS and within arms distance with his inside toe in line with the BB's toes in GUN and in TIGHT (under center) formations the inside toe should be lined up with the heels of the QB.

TB – balanced two point stance six seven yards behind the QB. Eyes are looking right at the QB's back. Hands are resting on his thighs (this is the same stance the QB uses if in GUN).

Stance Drill

Purpose: to teach all backs the proper position stances.

Set up: The coach lines up all the backs and calls out a position and then calls DOWN and every back gets in that position. Use a cone to simulate their markers. So the marker is the QB when you call out BB, The center for the QB, EMLOS for the WB, and the QB for the TB. Simulate depth and proper positioning.

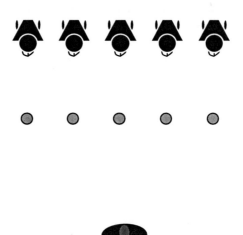

Figure VIII-G. Stance Drill

Ball Security and Handling

Holding the Ball

1)   One arm – Open Field Running - ball rests on the forearm with the rear point in the cup of the inner elbow and the top point is covered by the middle finger and cupped by the remaining fingers. The ball should be tight and resting against the chest.   The ball should always be on the opposite side of the tackler or pursuit if possible. Four points of contact (cup of elbow, forearm, cup of hand, and chest) and keep it tight against the chest and squeeze the top of the ball on contact.

2)   Two arms – Contact and passing the LOS – ball in the one arm method but the ball is moved to right below the chest plate and the opposite arm covers the top of the ball with the forearms resting on top of the ball as the ball is pressed into the body with the ball arm. The opposite arm's hand should rest over the cup of the ball arm's elbow. Whenever the runner is near the boundary line the ball should go to the near boundary arm.

3)   Switching the ball – the ball carrier moves the ball from one hand to the other by moving the ball across the lower chest line with forearm and palm of hand over the top of the ball facing inward. The opposite hand goes on top of the ball with the middle fingers now cupping the point in the carrying arm's elbow. He rolls the old arm down and out and rolls the new arm down and gets the near point into the cup of the elbow and down the side.

Make sure the runner moves the forearm and elbow of the arm holding the ball, but he must keep the ball on his chest and cupped. This will slow the runner a bit but the security of the ball is more important.

Hold and Switch Drill

Coach lines up all the backs in a line each with a ball (Figure VIII-H). He explains how to hold the ball in one arm and then in two arms and how to switch the ball when needed. He then has them all start with the ball in the left arm, checks it, then calls out switch and the ball carries switch to the right hand quickly and correctly. Coach watches each ball carrier and checks that the switch is correct. Walk around and tug on the ball on each ball carrier as well to check that they are holding the ball correctly.

Figure VIII-H. Hold and Switch Drill

Pairs and Tug Drill

Coach pairs up two runners facing each other (Figure VIII-I). One has a ball and the other is facing him an arm's length away. The coach calls the side the ball carrier places it and the defender swaps it. The ball carrier then switches the ball to the other side as fast as possible and the defender attempts to slap it. They keep doing this until the coach blows a whistle. This develops the switch that is needed for the back to move the ball to one side and the other when he is protecting the ball. The next set have the runner close his eyes and listen to the coach this will help the runner concentrate on the ball being secure and not the defender (which is exactly what happens in a game).

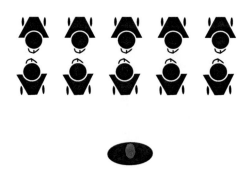

Figure VIII-I. Pairs and Tug Drill

Step and Go Drill

Purpose: Teaches the very basic juke or avoidance move.

Set up: 5 cones in a straight line 5 yards apart from each other and 5 yards from the runner (Figure VIII-J). At first tell the runners to start with a jog and concentrate on footwork. The footwork is key and as they gain confidence and skill in it they can increase the speed. The key to a good juke is the first step and where it goes. The cone represents a tackler and we tell the runner to run right at the cone and then (if juking to the right) lower your hips slightly (to lower center of gravity) to maintain control and speed while taking a hard step to the left. Aim for the outside of the left shoulder to force the defender to turn his hips and shoulders to the left and immediately step hard to the right with the right foot and get up field (vertical); one step and one step only. The wider and more controlled the step to the left is the more effective the juke will be on the defender. Make sure the runner doesn't step in front or short step that first step. He must lower his hips and step to the outside of the shoulder. We have the runners do it the right side going out and to the left side on the way back. We have them jog it until we see they have mastered the first step and hip drop. Then we have them go a little faster, and then we have them do it at full speed. Usually it takes a few weeks to get them going to full speed. Typically by the third or fourth week your runners should have a really nice juke move to counter open field tacklers and the infamous last defender on the edge.

Note: We always emphasize the importance of getting up field to daylight (get vertical to daylight!).

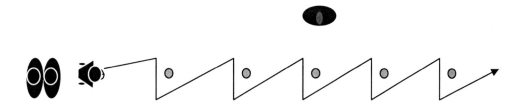

Figure VIII-J. Step and Go Drill

Step and Go with a Defender

Same drill but we add a player with a bag that the runner immediately lowers his non-ball shoulder and delivers a vertical blow (Figure VIII-K). He loads, explodes, and goes through the defender's shoulder on the rise. Running through and lifting the shoulder as contact is made is essential to breaking a tackle (bull rush).

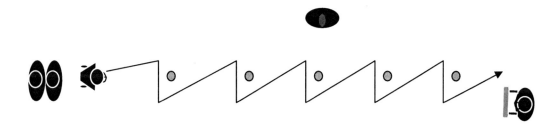

Figure VIII-K. Step and Go with a Defender

Singe-Cone and Two-Cone Weave

Purpose: The cone weave is used to develop quick feet and fast cutting ability that is need for a running back. The runner should first start the drill doing it slowly or jogging so that he can develop the proper movement patterns. What is important is to lower the hips and bend the knees as he moves laterally. It is important to keep the hips square as possible and not the cross the feet but take small fast steps that allow you to apply force from the ground.

1)   **Single Cone Weave** – the cones are spaced in a straight line with two feet between each cone (Figure VIII-L). Use eight cones and a ninth cone that is ten yards away. When the runner slides out from the last cone he steps and sprints to the ninth cone and jogs back to the end of the line.

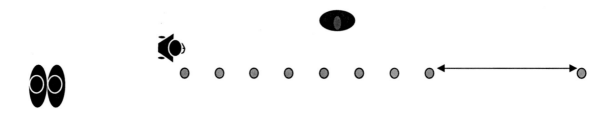

Figure VIII-L. Single Cone Weave

2)   **Two Cone Weave** – two cones are placed together and each set is offset by one cone so that it increases the weave and cutting of the runner (Figure VIII-M). Again eight sets are used with a ninth cone for a ten yard sprint.

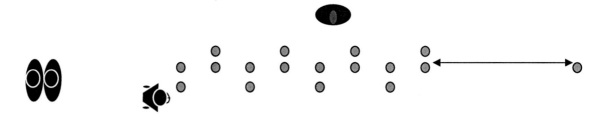

Figure VIII-M. Two Cone Weave

Note: You can have a RB at the end of the last cone with a shield or bag who aggressively attacks the runner to force him to make a move to get past the cone as the season progresses (jump cut, power cut, speed cut, bull rush, power spin, speed spin). This drill can used to teach the jump cut.

Mule Pull Drill

Need a piece of rope ½ inch wide 10 feet long with a piece of 2 foot water hose on it and knots at both ends to keep it from falling off and a speed harness (Figure VIII-N). Surgical tubing or resistance line can be used as well. At least two to four helps this go faster. A ball carrier starts in a two-point stance with ball in hand. The rope is around the chest plate and a resistance man is behind him with the line taunt (he is not putting his weight into it). On GO the runner explodes down the path for 10 yards (cones are used to mark off distance) and when the resistance man sees him pass it he releases the rope and lets him sprint for 10 more yards. They then switch and repeat the drill going the other way. The resistance man must keep the line tight but not pull on the rope at all. He should just relax and let the ball carrier pull him along. The runner must explode and increase speed and then burst into the next 10 yards. You can add a defender at the end of the drill with a shield to aggressively attack him and force him to make a move to get past him (jump cut, speed cut, power cut, bull rush, speed spin, power spin). Runner must stay low – this helps to improve his explosiveness coming out of his stance and into the hole. The distance that the runner goes under resistance should be no more than 10 yards.

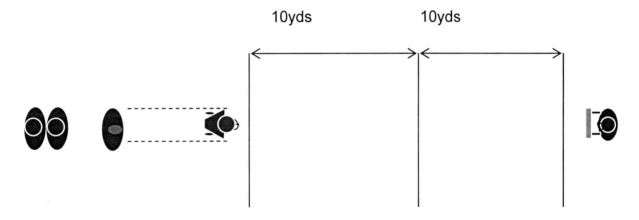

10yds   10yds

Figure VIII-N. Mule Pull Drill

Stiff Arm Progression Drill –

Purpose: Teaches a back how to properly execute a stiff arm (Kevin Thurman's drill).

Set up: SET 1 (Figure VIII-O) - Two cones ten yards apart with a coach over the inside cone and a runner 5 yards away from the inside cone. On GO, the runner (holding the ball with the outside arm) runs straight for the far cone. As he does, the Coach tosses the bag at the runner. He must vary the height from Knee to Shoulder height as well as varying the angle of the bag. The runner must use his inside hand (with thumb down) as the "lever" and use the bag's momentum to push himself away from the bag. If any part of the bag touches the runner he is tackled. Do not lock the elbow out; it should be slightly bent. This is also used to teach the rip technique as well using the same teaching method.

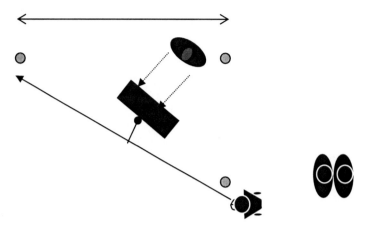

Figure VIII-O. Stiff Arm Progression Drill (SET 1)

Set 2 (Figure VIII-P) – Once the backs have mastered the technique involved in a stiff arm we then move to a live drill using a tackler. The tackle lines up over inside cone. On "GO" the tackler attempts to cut off the runner and tackle him. The runner must execute a correct stiff arm. We teach the tacklers they must hit the tackler where he exposes himself. The ideal points to use the stiff arm are: top of the helmet (not the facemask), top of the far shoulder pad plate, chest plate (try to get to the far shoulder plate to turn him away from you). This is also used to teach the rip technique using the same teaching method.

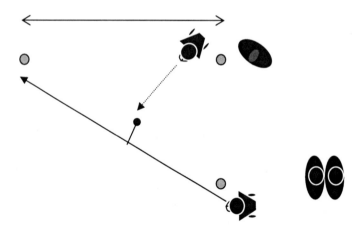

Figure VIII-P. Stiff Arm Progression Drill (SET 2)

Cut Back Drill

Purpose: Teaches how to make a proper cut back (Jump Cut, Speed Cut, Power Cut) and when to use it (Kevin Thurman's Drill).

Set up: Two traffic cones are placed 20 yards apart (Figure VIII-Q). A triangle of cones is set in the direct middle with the tip of the triangle at the center (10 yards) of the two traffic cones. The triangle is formed with three cones and it is 3 yards from top to bottom. The runner starts 5 yards from the bottom of the triangle. On GO he runs straight at the coach (holding a shield and inside the tip the triangle). When the coach slides to one side he must immediately cut to the opposite side into the triangle and bend his path back up field when he passes the traffic cone line. This can either be a jump cut, power cut, or speed cut. Repeat this several times to the left and right for each back. This develops his ability to make a cutback and reinforces the need to cut it vertically back up field as fast as possible.

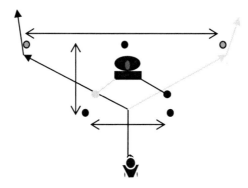

Figure VIII-Q. Cut Back Drill

Jump Cut Progression

Purpose – to teach the ball carrier to make multiple jump cuts followed up by a finish move when operating in space with multiple defenders coming at him.

Set up – one starting cone with a pair of cones three to five yards down the field and off set from the starting cone followed by two additional pairs in the same pattern (Figure VIII-R). The coach will call the snap count and the runner will attack the first pair make an immediate jump cut and accelerate to the next pair executing another jump cut and accelerating to the next pair. Step 1 he will simply execute a third jump cut and accelerate to the finish. Step 2 he will execute a speed spin on the final one and Step 3 he will execute a rip or stiff arm on a live defender to finish the drill.

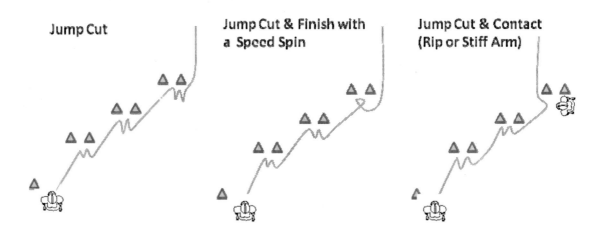

Jump Cut

Jump Cut & Finish with a Speed Spin

Jump Cut & Contact (Rip or Stiff Arm)

Figure VIII-R. Jump Cut Progression

Side Line Drill

Purpose – to teach the ball carrier how to secure the ball to the sideline arm and fight off a defender trying to drive him out of bounds.

Set up – The ball carriers will align behind a starting cone and there will be a pair of cones three to six yards away (Figure VIII-S). A defender will be the same distance from the pair of cones and when the ball carrier takes off he will take off and attack the ball carrier's near shoulder. All ball carriers will start with the ball on their field side arm and as they approach the pair of cones they will switch the ball and secure it. A set of boundary cones (4 to 6) will be set up four to six yards wide of the cone pair. The defender will attempt to drive the ball carrier out of bound and the ball carrier will do everything possible to stay in bounds and keep going vertical (rip, stiff arm, lift, set him up with an escape move). His job is to get by the defender are stay vertical for as long as possible. The defender will not go low or take any cheap shots (watch out for this because the drill can get competitive in a hurry).

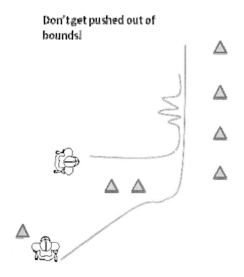

Don't get pushed out of bounds!

Figure VIII-S. Side Line Drill

Gauntlet Progression

Purpose - used to teach runners and blockers how to block and run with the ball explosively and violently in tight quarter.

Set up – this can be done using a gauntlet machine with a blocking dummy on a return track, a gauntlet machine with a defender holding a dummy at the end, or six defenders shoulder width apart attacking the ball carriers arms by swiping, grabbing, pulling, or punching at the ball with a defender at the end with a dummy (Figure VIII-T).

The first progression is simple; the ball carrier will be two to three yards back with the ball on the ground. On 'GO' he will pick up the ball, secure it, and explode into the gauntlet. He'll attempt to get through the gauntlet as fast and violently as possible. Once he gets through, he must immediately execute an escape move (we teach the lift with the bull rush in the gauntlet, but after a few weeks we let them execute the move they are accomplished executing.

In the second progression we add a lead blocker that will move through the gauntlet and explode into the dummy execute a wall/lead block. The ball carrier will cut based on the butt of the blocker.

The third progression is repping the kick out/FBI block. In the case of the BB, he will simply cross over and get into the gauntlet and execute a proper kick out block with good technique. The QB will align slightly deeper and either execute the under center spin and then his kick out or he will simulate the direct snap and simply cross over and execute the kick out. The WB will align at proper depth, execute an escape move to get up field and then violently execute the wall in block.

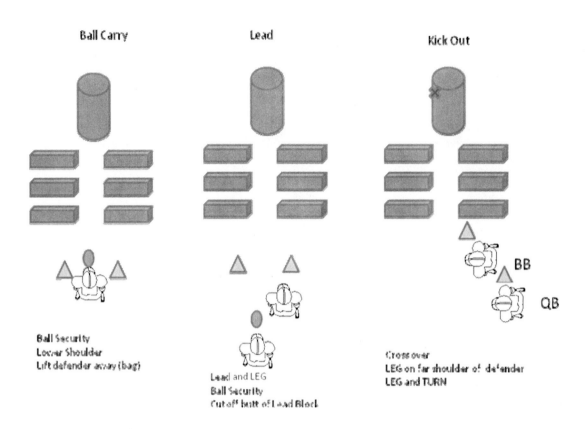

Figure VIII-T. Gauntlet Progression

LaVergne, TN USA
17 December 2010
209187LV00001B/14/P